College Accounting

College Accounting

FOURTH EDITION 1–15

Douglas J. McQuaig
Wenatchee Valley College

HOUGHTON MIFFLIN COMPANY   Boston

Dallas   Geneva, Illinois   Palo Alto   Princeton, New Jersey

This text and its related materials
are dedicated to the students who
will use them. My dream is to give
them a tool that is both practical
and understandable.

Cover image by Slide Graphics of New England, Inc.

Printed in the U.S.A.

Library of Congress Catalog Card No.: 88-81345

ISBN: 0-395-36918-5

DEFGHIJ-VH-954321

Contents

6 Closing Entries and the Post-Closing Trial Balance

Closing Entries / The Post-Closing Trial Balance / Interim Statements

Review of T Account Placement and Representative Transactions: Chapters 1 Through 6

Accounting Cycle Review Problem

C● Computer Practice Set: Sounds Abound

7 Accounting for Professional Enterprises: The Combined Journal (Optional)

The Accrual Basis / Cash-Receipts-and-Disbursements Basis / Modified Cash Basis / Example: Records of a Dentist / The Combined Journal / Accounting for Other Professional Enterprises / Designing a Combined Journal / Computers at Work: Pegboards—Manual and Computerized

Pegboard Practice Set: Plaza Fitness Center

8 Bank Accounts and Cash Funds

Using a Checking Account / Writing Checks / Bank Statements / The Petty Cash Fund / The Change Fund / Cash Short and Over

Appendix B: Bad Debts

9 Payroll Accounting: Employee Earnings and Deductions

Objectives of Payroll Records and Accounting / Employer/Employee Relationships / Laws Affecting Employees' Pay / Laws Affecting Employers' Payroll Taxes (Payroll Tax Expense) / How Employees Get Paid / Deductions from Total Earnings / Payroll Register / The Payroll Entry / Paycheck / Computers at Work: The Payroll Application

Payroll Practice Set: Island Floral

Preface

The goals for the fourth edition of *College Accounting* are the same as they have been for the previous editions: To provide students with a sound basic knowledge of accounting terms, concepts, and procedures, always taking into consideration students' widely varying objectives:

- Preparation for students entering the job market in accounting
- A practical background in accounting for students embarking on other careers, such as clerical, secretarial, technical, sales, and management positions.
- Preparation and background for students planning more advanced studies in accounting.

Based on more than 30 years teaching experience, the author has developed a method of presentation that reflects the need for an understandable and teachable basic accounting text that is logically organized, liberally illustrated, and paced in such a manner that it is easy for students to read and understand. This same approach has made previous editions successful with many teachers and students. At the same time, however, based on extensive reviews, campus visits, and conversations with many accounting teachers, the author has updated, revised, and improved both the text and the ancillary materials.

The accounting principles described are those endorsed by the Financial Accounting Standards Board and its predecessor, the Accounting Principles Board. Pertinent areas of the Tax Reform Act are included in the appropriate chapters.

CHARACTERISTICS OF COLLEGE ACCOUNTING

Accent on the Fundamentals

College Accounting, Fourth Edition presents the fundamentals of accounting in a practical, easy-to-understand manner that students can understand. Appropriate repetition enables students to develop confidence in themselves and to make progress in easy stages. This repetition is accomplished through extensive use of examples and illustrations.

Since an understanding of accounting fundamentals is based on understanding accounting transactions, great stress is devoted to analysis of transactions. Each newly introduced transaction is fully illustrated and supported with T account examples. Comprehensive reviews of T accounts, organized in relation to the fundamental accounting equation, appear after Chapters 6 and 10 to assist students as they review material during their course of study.

Reading Comprehension

College Accounting, Fourth Edition is a very readable text. Capitalizing on a direct approach, the author writes in short sentences that are supported by many illustrations that help students to understand the discussion. Each chapter is limited to the presentation of one major concept, which is well illustrated with business documents and report forms. As terms are introduced, they are defined thoroughly and are used in subsequent examples. Comprehension is also enhanced through the use of unique "Remembers." These short, marginal notes present a learning hint or a capsule summary of a major point made in preceding paragraphs. New end-of-chapter summaries also enhance comprehension.

Terminology

The author firmly believes that accounting is the language of business and that learning new terminology is an important part of a first course. Each key term is printed in red and is explained when it is first introduced. The end-of-chapter glossary repeats the definitions of the terms presented in the chapter.

Questions, Exercises, and Problems

College Accounting, Fourth Edition provides a wealth of exercise and problem material that is fully supported by the Working Papers, offering instructors a wide choice for classroom illustrations and assignments. Each chapter ends with comprehensive review and study material consisting of a chapter summary, a glossary, eight discussion questions, eight exercises, and two sets of comparable A and B problems. Exercises and problems have been rewritten for this edition.

- **Questions**   Eight questions, based on the main points in the text, are included at the end of each chapter.
- **Classroom Exercises**   For practice in applying concepts, eight exercises are provided with each chapter.
- **Problems**   Each chapter contains four A problems and four B problems. The A and B problems are parallel in content and level of difficulty. They are arranged in order of difficulty, with Problems 1A and 1B in each chapter being the simplest and the last problem in each series being the most comprehensive.

NEW FOUR-COLOR PEDAGOGY

The author, in conjunction with Houghton Mifflin Company, has developed a color-coded pedagogy that is designed to help students recognize and remember key points, understand the flow of accounting data, recognize different types of documents and reports used in accounting,

The Use of Color in McQuaig

Red	Green	Blue
Inputs $\longrightarrow$	**Process** $\longrightarrow$	**Outputs**
Source Documents Bank Statements and 　Reconciliations Tax Forms	Trial Balances Journals Ledgers Work Sheets Schedules Registers Inventory, Plant, 　and Equipment 　Records	**Financial** **Statements** 　Income Statements 　Statements of 　　Owner's Equity 　Balance Sheets 　Statements of 　　Retained Earnings 　Statements of Cash 　　Flows
Also 　Learning Objectives 　Tables 　Key Terms 　Emphasis		_Also_ 　Chapter Heads 　Remembers 　Computers at Work

identify the learning objectives for each chapter, see how each exercise and problem relates to the learning objectives for the chapter, and review material efficiently and effectively.

- **Learning objectives** are set in red throughout the text. They are listed at the beginning of each chapter and restated alongside the narrative related text discussion. They are referenced by learning objective number in the chapter summary and in the exercises and problems.
- **Key terms** are highlighted in red. They are defined in the text and repeated in a glossary at the end of the chapter.
- **Remembers,** which are printed in blue, are learning hints or summaries placed in the margin of the text. These marginal notes often alert students to common pitfalls and help them complete their work successfully.
- **Tables** are highlighted with a red screen, helping students quickly identify material that must be examined as a unit and is not part of running text.

The fourth edition's innovative use of color extends to the treatment of accounting forms, financial statements, and documents in the text and end-of-chapter assignments.

- **Working papers, journals, ledgers, trial balances, and other forms and schedules** used as part of the internal accounting process are shown in green.
- **Financial statements,** including balance sheets, income statements, statements of owners equity, and statements of cash flows, are shown in blue.

- **Source documents,** such as invoices, bank statements, facsimiles, and other material that originates with outside sources, are shown in red.

This distinctive treatment differentiates these elements and helps students to see where each element belongs in the accounting cycle. Seeing these relationships helps students understand how accountants transform data into useful information.

CHAPTER COVERAGE

College Accounting, Fourth Edition is designed primarily for use in a course extending two or three quarters or two semesters. The text may be divided into modules: Chapters 1–6 cover the full accounting cycle for a sole proprietorship service business. Chapters 7–10 cover bank accounts and payroll accounting. Chapters 11–15 cover the full accounting cycle for a merchandising firm.

Three appendixes expand content coverage and increase the instructor's options for structuring the course.

- **Appendix A: Methods of Depreciation** (after Chapter 5) Briefly describes methods of depreciation, including the Modified Accelerated Cost Recovery System.
- **Appendix B: Bad Debts** (after Chapter 8) Briefly describes the allowance and specific charge-off methods.
- **Appendix C: Financial Statement Analysis** (after Chapter 15) Briefly describes percentages and ratios used to interpret information in financial statements.

SPECIAL FEATURES

- **Extended Example** Paul's Auto Body, a fictional company, is used throughout Chapters 1–6 to illustrate accounting concepts
- **Accounting Cycle Review Problem** This mini-practice set, following Chapter 6, involves the full accounting cycle for a fictional company called Parkland Bumper Boats.
- **Representative T Accounts and Transactions** Simple charts organize this information for Chapters 1–6, 7–10, and 11–15.
- **Chapter 7: Accounting for Professional Enterprises** This optional chapter emphasizes the combined journal. (An alternative set of achievement tests that omits the combined journal is available for those instructors who do not use this chapter.)

COMPUTERS AT WORK

Microcomputers have brought major changes to the work environment in which today's graduates will be expected to function. The new *Com-*

puters at Work boxes, highlighted in blue, offer instructors a springboard for explaining the impact of these changes to students. Topics have been selected for their relevance to accounting and include:

- Types of Computers
- Parts of a Computer
- Computerized Accounting
- Pegboards—Manual and Computerized
- Payroll
- Sales and Inventory
- Integrated Accounting Software

CONTENT CHANGES IN THE FOURTH EDITION

The author has carefully revised and updated the entire text and the end-of chapter materials. Changes include an increased emphasis on explaining transactions and a step-by-step approach to transaction analysis and error correction. The learning objectives have been analyzed and improved by adding new learning objectives and breaking down complex learning objectives to increase student comprehension and understanding. In addition, a three-column purchases journal is introduced in Chapter 12.

Much care has been taken to make sure that *College Accounting*, Fourth Edition is as current as possible. The text discussion and examples that involve such topics as depreciation schedules, bad debt write-offs, and tax rates have been revised in light of the Tax Reform Act of 1986. The payroll chapters have been brought up to date and expanded in light of new tax laws. Appendixes have been replaced or updated. Appendix B, Bad Debts, which follows Chapter 8, illustrates write-offs of uncollectible accounts using the allowance and specific charge-off methods. Practice sets have been completely revised to reflect business situations with inherent appeal to today's students.

QUALITY CONTROL

Successful use of an accounting text depends on more than the interesting and memorable presentation of material by the instructor and the text. The overall quality of the examples, illustrations, end-of-chapter questions, exercises and problems, and ancillary materials are critical to learning and retention of the facts and concepts covered in the course. Instructors and students must be assured that these materials are complete, consistent, and accurate.

The author and the publisher of *College Accounting*, Fourth Edition have taken a multistep approach to ensure quality materials for classroom use. The quality control system begins with in-depth reviews of the original manuscript and concludes with accuracy reviews of page proof provided by academics teaching the course and by the international accounting firm of Arthur Young & Company.

SUPPLEMENTARY LEARNING AIDS FOR STUDENTS

For the fourth edition we have assembled the most comprehensive package of student and instructor aids to complement a wide variety of teaching styles and course emphases.

Working Papers

The Working Papers now include the learning objectives for each chapter, chapter summaries, lists of key terms, self-study review questions, an extended demonstrations problem and solution for each chapter (which is reproduced in the Instructor's Manual), forms for A and B problems and for the Accounting Cycle Review Problem, and answers to the self-study review questions, a list of check figures, and additional blank working paper forms. Working Papers 1–15 also includes a Review of Business Mathematics.

Manual Practice Sets

College Accounting, Fourth Edition is accompanied by the largest selection of manual practice sets available. These practice sets offer many different choices depending on student needs.

After Chapter 4   *Sailsports* is a unique exercise that requires students to work through seven months of business activity for a sole proprietorship sailboard rental company. Each month brings home to students the reality of paper handling, as they annotate, manage, file and retrieve source documents.

After Chapter 7   *Plaza Fitness Center* (new), a pegboard practice set, introduces the student to one-write accounting systems.

With Chapters 9 and 10   *Island Floral* (new) requires students to complete four payrolls—two months, semimonthly. The payrolls include the last month of one quarter and the first month of the next, giving students the opportunity not only to complete the current payroll month, but also to prepare the end-of-quarter tax work.

After Chapter 10 Three practice sets are available. Each covers the basic accounting cycle, cash management, and payroll for one month in the life of a sole proprietorship service business. All three are published in a business-papers format for the sake of realism.

- *Here's Video* (new) permits instructors to choose either a combined journal or a general journal.
- *C. W. Hale, M.D.,* has medical forms and business papers. A combined journal is used.
- *M. T. Chandler, Attorney at Law,* has legal forms and business papers. A combined journal is used.

After Chapter 15

- *Lakeside Water Scooters* (new) features business papers and special journals. It covers a one-month accounting cycle for a merchandising firm.
- *The Oak Shoppe: An Audit Problem with Business Papers.* This unique exercise requires students to detect and correct errors in one month's worth of financial records and to generate a set of corrected financial statements for a retail furniture merchandising business.
- *The Book Loft: A Cumulative Shoebox Practice Set with Business Papers.* In this realistic exercise the student/bookkeeper is "hired" by a sole proprietorship retail bookstore to organize a disordered set of source documents representing one month's financial activity, bring order to the company's books, and complete all year-end accounting tasks including formulating and recording adjusting and closing entries and preparing financial statements.

Computer-Assisted Practice Sets and Simulations

After Chapter 6 *Sounds Abound,* a computer practice set for one month in the life of a sole proprietorship service business, requires only two hours of computer time.

After Chapter 10 A computer job simulation for Payroll Clerk at Lawson's Supply Center.

After Chapter 11 A computer job simulation for Accounts Receivable Clerk at Lawson's Supply Center.

After Chapter 12 A computer job simulation for Accounts Payable Clerk at Lawson's Supply Center.

After Chapter 13 A computer job simulation for Cash Clerk at Lawson's Supply Center.

After Chapter 15   Two practice sets are available in addition to a computer job simulation for a General Ledger Clerk at Lawson's Supply Center.

- *Denton Appliance and Air Conditioning,* a computer practice set for a merchandising firm. Students begin the set by hand, using a general journal; they then key the entries into the computer.
- *Cook's Solar Energy Systems,* a computer practice set for one month in the life of a sole proprietorship merchandising firm.

Computer Applications for College Accounting: A General Ledger Package

This easy-to-use general ledger package offers complete coverage of accounting concepts and procedures, including graduated problems, exercises, and tutorials. Selected problems from *College Accounting,* Fourth Edition can be completed with this package. The icon in the margin identifies these problems in the text. A template disk is available to adopters.

Computerized Demonstration Problems: A Tutorial Approach

This exciting new program enables students to test their knowledge of accounting procedures by examining the demonstration problems from the Working Papers that accompany the McQuaig text. Unlike practice sets that require students to enter problem data and then print out the results, this tutorial prompts students to answer true-false or multiple-choice questions on a series of accounting procedures. As students respond to these questions, the program dynamically demonstrates—through moving displays of ledgers and journals—how transaction data flow through an accounting system and impact accounts.

Lotus Problems for Accounting: A Working Papers Approach

This innovative accounting software allows students to solve end-of-chapter problems using the Lotus 1-2-3 spreadsheet software. Students can select from 20 prepared templates and use them to solve most end-of-chapter problems. A template guide is included in the Instructor's Manual and Working Papers.

SOFTWARE SOLUTIONS SERIES

The Software Solutions Series offers a choice from seven popular application software packages. These inexpensive tutorial manuals and educational versions of popular software provide hands-on experience for your students. The seven manuals include:

Using PageMaker®
Using Lotus 1-2-3® Version 2.0
Using dBASE III Plus™
Using SuperCalc® 4
Using WordStar® 4.0
Using WordPerfect™ 4.2
Using Microsoft® Works

SUPPLEMENTARY TEACHING AIDS FOR INSTRUCTORS

Instructor's Manual with Solutions

This instructor's manual includes teaching suggestions for each chapter as well as complete solutions to all questions and exercises. Solutions to all A and B problems are shown on the same forms used in the Working Papers.

New to this edition are lecture outlines, key terms, learning objectives, chapter summaries, and a duplicate of the demonstration problems that appear in the Working Papers, as well as a cross-reference for each problem to the corresponding page of the Working Papers. Also new is a template guide for *Lotus Problems for Accounting: A Working Papers Approach*.

Teaching and Solutions Transparencies

Two sets of mylar transparencies are available to adopters. The improved two-color, typeset solutions cover every exercise and problem. Approximately 50 teaching and supplemental blank transparencies are also provided in this improved format.

Test Bank

For this edition, the number of questions has increased, and they are presented on a chapter-by-chapter basis. True-false, multiple-choice, and matching questions, as well as short problems are offered for each chapter. Final examinations with answers are presented in two versions.

The test problems, including the forms, and final examinations are presented in a format suitable for copying and distributing to classes. Also included are achievement test facsimiles. A microcomputer-based version of the main test bank and a call-in testing service are available. Final examinations covering Chapters 1–10, Chapters 1–15, and Chapters 16–29 are provided in ready-to-reproduce format.

Instructor's Resource Kit 1–15

The Instructor's Manual with Solutions (1–15), Teaching and Solutions Transparencies (1–15), and Test Bank are available in an attractive, durable case, which may be used to organize and store classroom support materials.

Achievement Tests

Preprinted tests are ready for class use. Each test covers two to three chapters in the text. Series A, which covers Chapters 1–15 and Chapters 16–29, provides 32 copies of each test. Series B is an alternative set of tests covering the same material.

The Video Workshop

New to this edition, a professionally prepared VHS video tape is available. Video Workshop presents key accounting topics and survival skills for students. A Video Guide with teaching tips is included.

Grade Performance Analyzer

Provided free to instructors, this computerized gradebook program for IBM PC and Apple II microcomputers facilitates orderly recordkeeping, calculation, and posting of student grades.

ACKNOWLEDGMENTS

Again, I would sincerely like to thank the editorial staff of Houghton Mifflin for their continuous support. I am still deeply appreciative of the assistance given to me during the preparation of the first edition of this text by Professors Hobart Adams, University of Akron, and Joseph Goodman, Chicago State University. The cooperation of my colleagues, Professors Audrey Chan-Nui, Geneva Knutson, and John Wisen, has been most helpful. Also, I want to thank my many students at Wenatchee Valley College for their observations and evaluations. Especially, I want to thank Donna L. Randall Lacey, Bunker Hill Community College, and Suzanne M. Williamson, C.P.A., for their diligent and comprehensive reviews. Patricia A. Bille, Highline Community College, provided invaluable help in her role as consulting editor. Her work in developing the Computers at Work boxed inserts is particularly appreciated.

During the writing of the fourth edition, I visited many users of the text throughout the country. Their constructive suggestions are reflected in the changes that have been made. Unfortunately, space does not permit mention of all those who have contributed to this volume. Some of those, however, who have been supportive and have influenced my efforts are:

Joseph F. Adamo, Cazenovia College
Stanley Augustine, Santa Rosa Junior College
Catherine Berg, Nassau Community College
Linda J. Block, Embry-Riddle Aeronautical University
Kenneth W. Brown, College of Technology, University of Houston—
   University Park
Anita Brownstein, Drake Business School
Howard Bryan, Santa Rosa Junior College
Theresa Capretta, North Harris County College
Clairmont P. Carter, University of Lowell
Michael S. Chaks, Riverside Community College
John Chestnutt, Allan Hancock College
Trudy Chiaravalli, Lansing Community College
Dana Crismond, Mt. Empire Community College
Martha J. Curry, Huston-Tillotson College
Leonard Delury, Portland Community College—Sylvania Campus
Irving Denton, Northern Virginia Community College
Allan Doyle, Pima Community College
Jerry Sue Dyess, San Jacinto College—Central Campus
William Evans, Cerritos College
Mary Foster, Illinois Central College
Walter A. Franklin, Palm Beach Junior College
Alan Fraser, Rio Hondo College
William French, Albuquerque Technical-Vocational Institute
Stuart M. Fukushige, Leeward Community College

Helen Gerrard, Miami University—Hamilton and Middletown Regional Campuses
Steven R. Graham, Vincennes University
Charles Grant, Skyline College
Marie Gressel, Santa Barbara City College
Robert E. Hartzell, Colorado Mountain College—Timberlane Campus
C. Robert Hellmer, Milwaukee Area Technical College
Joyce Henzel, Rogers State College
Carol Holcomb, Spokane Falls Community College
Donald L. Holloway, Long Beach City College
Janis Hutchins, Lamar University—Port Arthur
George Ihorn, El Paso Community College
Thomas Jackson, Cerritos College
Eugene Janner, Blinn College
Edward H. Julius, California Lutheran University
Andre E. Kelton, American Business Institute, New York
Jimmy King, McLennan Community College
Lydia C. K. Kinoshita, Cannon's Business College
Bobbie Krapels, Branell College
Frances Kubicek, Kalamazoo Valley Community College
Ronald Kulhanek, Great Lakes Junior College
Nathan R. Larsen, Ricks College
Elliott S. Levy, Bentley College
Loren Long, Elgin Community College
Joyce Loudder, Houston Community College
Donald MacGilvra, Shoreline Community College
Paul C. Maziarz, Bryant & Stratton Business Institute, Buffalo
Robert Mills, Texarkana Community College
Elizabeth Barnard Miller, Columbus Technical Institute
V. Eva Molnar, Riverside Community College District
Donald Morehead, Henry Ford Community College
Robert Nash, Henry Ford Community College
M. Salah Negm, Prince George's Community College
Dolores Osborn, Central Washington University
Vincent Pelletier, College of DuPage
Paul T. Ryan, Jackson State Community College
John T. Saleh, Tyler Junior College
H. Lee Schlorff, Bentley College
Steven Schmidt, Butte College
Nelda Shelton, Tarrant County Junior College
Eliot H. Sherman, Northeastern University
Elaine Simpson, St. Louis Community College at Florissant Valley
Sharon Smith, Texas Southmost College
Gary Stanton, Erie Community College—City
Mary E. Retterer, San Bernardino Valley College
Harold Steinhauser, Rock Valley Community College
Rahmat Tavallali, Wooster Business College

Alan Tucker, Everett Community College
Catherine P. Varca, Bryant & Stratton Business Institute, Buffalo
William G. Vendemia, Youngstown State University
Russell Vermillion, Prince George's Community College
Florence G. Waldman, Kilgore College
Emma Watts, Westark Community College
Robert Weaver, Malcolm X College
Penny Westerfeld, North Harris County College
Maxine Wilson, Los Angeles City College

A special note of thanks to the individuals who contributed greatly by reviewing and checking the end-of-chapter questions, exercises, and problems.

Carmela C. Caputo, Empire State College
Janet Cassagio, Nassau Community College
Carl Dauber, Southern Ohio College
Vicky C. Dominguez, Clark County Community College
Marlin Gerber, Kalamazoo Valley Community College
Ann King, Branell College, Riverdale Campus
Jan Mardon, Green River Community College
Bernard Piwkiewicz, Laney College
Joseph Stoffel, Waubonsee Community College
Ron Summers, Oklahoma City Community College
Stan Weikert, College of the Canyons

As always, I would like to thank my family for their understanding and cooperation. Without their support, this text would never have been written. My heartfelt appreciation is extended to my wife, Beverlie, for her detailed proofreading and for her willingness to put up with me. Pertinent suggestions for updating the material were given by my daughter, Judith Britton, C.P.A., of Bunday, Britton, and Horikawa; my son, John McQuaig, C.P.A., of McQuaig and Welk; and my son-in-law, Christopher Britton, C.P.A., of Touche Ross.

Douglas J. McQuaig

College Accounting

1

Analyzing Business Transactions: Asset, Liability, and Owner's Equity Accounts

LEARNING OBJECTIVES

After you have completed this chapter, you will be able to do the following:

1. Define accounting.
2. Define and identify asset, liability, and owner's equity accounts.
3. Record a group of business transactions, in column form, involving changes in assets, liabilities, and owner's equity.
4. Prepare a balance sheet.

Accounting is often called the language of business because when confronted with events of a business nature, all people in society—owners, managers, creditors, employees, attorneys, engineers, and so forth—must use accounting terms and concepts in order to describe these events. Examples of accounting terms are *net, gross, yield, valuation, accrued, deferred*—the list could go on and on. So it is logical that anyone entering the business world should know enough of the "language" to communicate with others and to understand their communications.

The meanings of some terms used in accounting differ from the meanings of the same words used in a nonbusiness situation. If you have studied a foreign language, you undoubtedly found that as you became more familiar with the language, you also became better acquainted with the country in which it is spoken as well as with the customs of the people. Similarly, as you acquire a knowledge of accounting, you will gain an understanding of the way businesses operate and the reasoning involved in the making of business decisions. Even if you are not involved directly in accounting activities, most assuredly you will need to be sufficiently acquainted with the "language" to be able to understand the meaning of accounting information, how it is compiled, how it can be used, and what its limitations are.

DEFINITION OF ACCOUNTING

Objective 1

Define accounting.

Accounting is the process of analyzing, classifying, recording, summarizing, and interpreting business transactions in financial or monetary terms. A business **transaction** is an event that has a direct effect on the operation of the economic unit and can be expressed in terms of money. Examples of business transactions are buying or selling goods, renting a building, paying employees, buying insurance, or any other activity of a business nature.

The accountant is the person who keeps the financial history of an economic unit in written form. The term **economic unit** includes not only business enterprises but also nonprofit entities, such as government bodies, churches, clubs, and fraternal organizations. All these entities require some type of accounting records. The primary purpose of accounting is to provide the financial information needed for the efficient operation of the economic unit and to make the information available in usable forms to the interested parties, such as owners, members, taxpayers, creditors, and so on.

Because it is important that all those who receive accounting reports be able to interpret them, a set of rules or guidelines has been developed. These guidelines, which describe how the accounting process should be done, are known as **generally accepted accounting principles (GAAP)**.

Bookkeeping and Accounting

There is considerable confusion over the distinction between bookkeeping and accounting. Actually the two processes are closely related, and there is no universally accepted line of separation. Generally, bookkeeping involves the systematic recording of business transactions in financial terms. Accounting is carried on at a higher level or degree than bookkeeping is. An accountant sets up the system that a bookkeeper will use to record business transactions. An accountant may supervise the work of the bookkeeper and prepare financial statements and tax reports. Although the work of the bookkeeper is more routine, it is hard to draw a line where the bookkeeper's work ends and the accountant's begins. The bookkeeper must understand the entire accounting system, exercise judgment in recording financial details, and organize and report the appropriate information.

CAREER OPPORTUNITIES IN ACCOUNTING

To find job opportunities in accounting, all you need to do is read the newspapers' classified advertisements. Although the jobs listed in these ads require varying amounts of education and experience, most of the jobs are for positions as accounting clerks, general bookkeepers, or accountants. Let's take a look at the requirements and duties of these positions.

Accounting Clerk

An accounting clerk does routine recording of financial information manually (by hand) or by machine. The duties of accounting clerks vary with the size of the company. In small businesses, accounting clerks handle most of the recordkeeping functions. In large companies, clerks specialize in one part of the accounting system, such as payroll, accounts receivable, accounts payable, cash, inventory, and purchases. The minimum requirement for most accounting clerk positions is one year of accounting courses.

General Bookkeeper

Many small- and medium-sized companies employ one person to oversee their bookkeeping operations. This person is called a general or full-charge bookkeeper. The general bookkeeper supervises the work of accounting clerks. Requirements for this job vary with the size of the company and the complexity of the accounting system. The minimum requirement for most general bookkeeper jobs is one or two years of accounting as well as experience as an accounting clerk.

Accountant

The term *accountant* describes a fairly broad range of jobs. The accountant may design and manage the entire accounting system for a business. The accountant may also prepare the financial statements and tax returns. Many accountants enter the field with a college degree in accounting. However, it is not unusual for accountants to start at entry-level positions and then work their way up to management positions. Although accountants are employed in every kind of economic unit, their work is divided into three categories: public accounting, managerial or private accounting, and not-for-profit accounting. We'll briefly look at these categories.

Public Accounting   Certified public accountants (CPAs) are independent professionals who provide services to clients for a fee. To become a CPA, a person must pass a rigorous examination and fulfill an experience requirement. Public accountants design accounting systems, prepare tax returns, and give management and financial advice about business operations.

Managerial or Private Accounting   Most people who are accountants work for private business firms. These accountants manage the accounting system, prepare budgets, determine costs of products, and provide financial information for managers. Because of the importance of accounting, there are many opportunities for accountants to advance into top management positions.

Not-for-Profit Accounting   Not-for-profit accounting is used for government agencies, hospitals, churches, and schools. Accountants for these organizations prepare budgets and maintain records of expenses. It should be noted that some not-for-profit organizations do in fact make a profit; however, the profit is kept in the organization and not distributed. For example, a hospital makes a profit and then reinvests the profit in modern equipment. Local, state, and federal government bodies employ vast numbers of people in accounting positions.

People's Need for Accounting

Anyone who aspires to a position of leadership in business or government needs a knowledge of accounting. A study of accounting gives a person the necessary background as well as an understanding of an organization's scope, functions, and policies.

Users of Accounting Information

Owners   Owners have invested their money in a business organization. They desire information regarding the company's earnings, its prospects for future earnings, and its ability to pay its debts.

Managers   Managers and supervisors have to prepare financial reports, understand accounting data contained in reports and budgets, and express future plans in financial terms. People who have management jobs must know how accounting information can be developed in order to evaluate performance in meeting goals.

Creditors   Creditors loan money or extend credit to the company for the purchase of goods and services. The company's creditors include suppliers, banks, and other lending institutions, such as loan companies. Creditors are interested in the ability of the firm to pay its debts.

Government Agencies   Taxing authorities verify information submitted by companies concerning a variety of taxes, such as income taxes, sales taxes, employment taxes, and so on. Public utilities, such as electric, gas, and telephone companies, must provide financial information to regulatory agencies.

Accounting and the Computer

Before the invention of calculators and computers, all business transactions were recorded by hand. Now computers perform routine record-keeping operations and prepare financial reports. Computers are used today in all types of businesses, both large and small.

Regardless of how or whether a business uses a computer, the nature of accounting is the same. Information must be recorded or entered into the system. The rules and principles presented in this text apply to both manual and computerized accounting systems. You must formulate or develop the correct information to feed into the system; otherwise, as the saying goes, it's "garbage in and garbage out."

ASSETS, LIABILITIES, AND OWNER'S EQUITY

Objective 2

Define and identify asset, liability, and owner's equity accounts.

Assets are properties or things of value, such as cash, equipment, buildings, and land, owned by an economic unit or business entity. Always remember that a **business entity** is considered to be separate and distinct from the persons who supply the assets it uses. Property acquired by the business is an asset of the business. The owner is separate from the business and, in fact, has claims upon it. If the business owes nothing against the assets, then the owner's right would be equal to the value of the assets. The owner's right or claim is expressed by the word **equity,** or *investment*. You often see these terms in the classified advertising section of a newspaper, in which a person wants to sell the ownership right to a property, such as a car or a house. Other terms that may be used include **capital,** *net worth*, or *proprietorship*.

Assets	= Owner's Equity
Properties or things of value owned by the business	Owner's right or investment in the business

Suppose that the total value of the assets is $10,000 and the business entity does not owe any amount against the assets. Then,

Assets	= Owner's Equity
$10,000 =	$10,000

Or suppose that the assets consist of a truck that costs $8,000; the owner has invested $2,000 for the truck, and the business entity has borrowed the remainder from the bank, which is the **creditor** (one to whom money is owed). This can be shown as follows:

Assets	=	Liabilities	+	Owner's Equity
Items owned		Amounts owed to creditors		Owner's investment
$8,000	=	$6,000	+	$2,000

We have now introduced a new classification, **liabilities,** which represents debts and includes the amounts that the business entity owes its creditors, or the amount by which it is liable to its creditors. The debts may originate because the business bought goods or services on a credit basis, borrowed money, or otherwise created an obligation to pay. The creditors' claims to the assets have priority over the claims of the owner.

An equation expressing the relationship of assets, liabilities, and owner's equity is called the **fundamental accounting equation.** We'll be dealing with this equation constantly from now on. If we know two parts of this equation, we can determine the third. Let's look at some examples.

Determine Assets   Ms. Smith has $9,000 invested in her advertising agency, and the agency owes creditors $3,000; that is, the agency has liabilities of $3,000. Then,

Assets	=	Liabilities	+	Owner's Equity
?	=	$3,000	+	$9,000

We can find the amount of the business's assets by adding the liabilities and the owner's equity:

```
   $ 3,000 Liabilities
 +   9,000 Owner's Equity
   $12,000 Assets
```

The completed equation now reads

Assets	=	Liabilities	+	Owner's Equity
$12,000	=	$3,000	+	$9,000

Determine Owner's Equity   Take Mr. Jones, who raises mushrooms to sell to canners. His business has assets of $20,000, and it owes creditors $4,000; that is, it has liabilities of $4,000. Then,

Assets	=	Liabilities	+	Owner's Equity
$20,000	=	$4,000	+	?

We find the owner's equity by subtracting the liabilities from the assets:

$20,000 Assets
−   4,000 Liabilities
$16,000 Owner's Equity

The completed equation now reads

Assets = Liabilities + Owner's Equity
$20,000 = $4,000   + $16,000

Determine Liabilities   Mr. Anderson's insurance agency has assets of $18,000; his investment (his equity) amounts to $12,000. Then,

Assets = Liabilities + Owner's Equity
$18,000 =   ?   + $12,000

To find the firm's total liabilities, we subtract the equity from the assets:

$18,000 Assets
−   12,000 Owner's Equity
$ 6,000 Liabilities

The completed equation reads

Assets = Liabilities + Owner's Equity
$18,000 = $6,000   + $12,000

Recording Business Transactions

Objective 3

Record a group of business transactions, in column form, involving changes in assets, liabilities, and owner's equity.

To repeat: Business transactions are events that have a direct effect on the operations of an economic unit or enterprise and are expressed in terms of money. Each business transaction must be recorded in the accounting records. As one records business transactions, one has to change the amounts listed under the headings Assets, Liabilities, and Owner's Equity. However, **the total of one side of the fundamental accounting equation should always equal the total of the other side.** The categories under these three main headings, as we shall see, are called **accounts.**

Let us now look at a group of business transactions. Although these transactions illustrate a service type of business, they would pertain to a professional enterprise as well. In these transactions, let's assume that Paul Greenwalt establishes his own business and calls it Paul's Auto

Body. Paul's Auto Body is a **sole proprietorship,** or one-owner business. Sole proprietorship is one of the three primary forms of business ownership. The other major forms of ownership are partnerships and corporations.

Transaction (a) Greenwalt invests $32,000 cash in his new business. This means that he deposits $32,000 in the bank in a new separate account entitled Paul's Auto Body. This separate bank account will help Greenwalt keep his business investment separate from his personal funds. The Cash account consists of bank deposits and money on hand. The business now has $32,000 more in cash than before, and Greenwalt's investment has also increased by $32,000. The account, denoted by the owner's name followed by the word *Capital,* records the amount of the owner's investment, or equity, in the business. The effect of this transaction on the fundamental accounting equation is as follows:

Assets	=	Liabilities	+	Owner's Equity
Items owned		Amounts owed to creditors		Owner's investment
Cash	=			Paul Greenwalt, Capital
(a) +32,000	=			+32,000

Transaction (b) Paul Greenwalt's first task is to get his repair shop ready for business, and to do that he will need the proper equipment. Accordingly, Paul's Auto Body buys $18,000 worth of equipment for cash. It is important to note that at this point Greenwalt has not invested any new money; he simply exchanged part of the business's cash for equipment. Because equipment is a new type of property for the firm, a new account, called Equipment, is created. Equipment is included under assets. As a result of this transaction, the accounting equation is changed as follows:

	Assets		=	Liabilities	+	Owner's Equity
	Items owned			Amounts owed to creditors		Owner's investment
	Cash + Equipment		=			Paul Greenwalt, Capital
Initial investment	32,000		=			32,000
(b)	−18,000 +	18,000				
New balances	14,000 +	18,000	=			32,000
	32,000				32,000	

Transaction (c) Paul's Auto Body buys $4,000 worth of equipment on credit from Osborne Equipment Company.

The Equipment account shows an increase because the business owns

$4,000 more in equipment. There is also an increase in liabilities because the business now owes $4,000. The liability account called **Accounts Payable** is used for short-term liabilities or charge accounts, usually due within thirty days. There is now a total of $36,000 on each side of the equals sign. Because Paul's Auto Body owes money to Osborne Equipment Company, Osborne Equipment is called a creditor of Paul's Auto Body.

	Assets	=	Liabilities	+	Owner's Equity
	Items owned		Amounts owed to creditors		Owner's investment
	Cash + Equipment	=	Accounts Payable	+	Paul Greenwalt, Capital
Previous balances	14,000 + 18,000	=			32,000
(c)	+4,000		+4,000		
New balances	14,000 + 22,000	=	4,000	+	32,000
	36,000			36,000	

Observe that the recording of each transaction must yield an equation that is in balance. For example, transaction **(c)** resulted in a $4,000 increase to both sides of the equation, and transaction **(b)** resulted in a minus $18,000 and a plus $18,000 *on the same side,* with nothing recorded on the other side. It does not matter whether you change one side or both sides. *The important point is that whenever a transaction is properly recorded, the accounting equation remains in balance.*

Transaction (d) Paul's Auto Body pays $1,000 to Osborne Equipment Company, to be applied against the firm's liability of $4,000.

In analyzing this payment, we recognize that cash is being reduced. At the same time, the firm *owes* less than before, so the transaction should be recorded as a reduction in liabilities.

	Assets	=	Liabilities	+	Owner's Equity
	Items owned		Amounts owed to creditors		Owner's investment
	Cash + Equipment	=	Accounts Payable	+	Paul Greenwalt, Capital
Previous balances	14,000 + 22,000	=	4,000	+	32,000
(d)	−1,000		−1,000		
New balances	13,000 + 22,000	=	3,000	+	32,000
	35,000			35,000	

Think of the accounting equation as a teeter-totter that you are trying to keep level. If you add to or subtract from one side, you have to do the same thing to the other side to keep the teeter-totter level (balanced).

Transaction (e) Paul's Auto Body buys paint, rubbing compounds, and other supplies on account from Todd Supply Company for $400. Paint and rubbing compounds are listed under Supplies instead of Equipment because an auto body repair shop uses up these items in a relatively short period of time—as a matter of fact, in one or a few repair jobs. Equipment, on the other hand, normally lasts a number of years.

	Assets		=	Liabilities	+	Owner's Equity
	Items owned			Amounts owed to creditors	+	Owner's investment
	Cash + Equip. + Supp.		=	Accounts Payable	+	Paul Greenwalt, Capital
Previous balances	13,000 + 22,000		=	3,000	+	32,000
(e)		+ 400		+400		
New balances	13,000 + 22,000 + 400		=	3,400	+	32,000
	35,400				35,400	

Accounting, as we said before, is the process of analyzing, classifying, recording, summarizing, and interpreting business transactions in terms of money. In relating these elements to the recording of the transactions for Paul's Auto Body that we have covered so far, see if you recognize that we have gone through certain steps (in the form of questions). These steps may be illustrated by transaction **(e),** buying paint and rubbing compounds on credit.

1. What accounts are involved? For example, Supplies and Accounts Payable are involved.
2. What are the classifications of the accounts involved? For example, Supplies is an asset, and Accounts Payable is a liability.
3. Are the accounts increased or decreased? For example, Supplies is increased because Paul's Auto Body has more supplies than before. Accounts Payable is also increased because Paul's Auto Body owes more than before.

Next, we record the transaction. We will be stressing this step-by-step process throughout the text. This example serves as an introduction to **double-entry accounting. The "double" element is demonstrated by the fact that each transaction must be recorded in at least two accounts, and the accounting equation must be kept in balance.**

Summary of Transactions

Let us now summarize the business transactions of Paul's Auto Body in column form, identifying each transaction by a letter of the alphabet. To test your understanding of the recording procedure, describe the nature of the transactions that have taken place.

	Assets			= Liabilities +	Owner's Equity
	Cash	+ Equip.	+ Supp.	Accounts Payable	Paul Greenwalt, Capital
Transaction (a)	+32,000			=	+32,000
Transaction (b)	−18,000	+ 18,000			
Balance	14,000	+ 18,000		=	32,000
Transaction (c)			+ 4,000	+4,000	
Balance	14,000	+ 22,000		= 4,000 +	32,000
Transaction (d)	−1,000			−1,000	
Balance	13,000	+ 22,000		= 3,000 +	32,000
Transaction (e)			+ 400	+400	
Balance	13,000	+ 22,000	+ 400	= 3,400 +	32,000
		35,400			35,400

The following observations apply to all types of business transactions:

1. Every transaction is recorded in terms of increases and/or decreases in two or more accounts.
2. One side of the equation is always equal to the other side of the equation.

As you have seen, in this chapter we used a column arrangement as a practical device to show how transactions are recorded. This arrangement is useful for showing increases and decreases in various accounts as a result of the transactions. We also showed new balances after recording each transaction.

We will continue with this column arrangement in Chapter 2. Then, in Chapter 3, we will record the same transactions in formal account form.

Chart of Accounts

Before recording transactions for a new business, the accountant must first think of all the possible types of transactions that the company will carry out. Based on this variety of possible transactions, the accountant makes a list of account titles to be used to record these transactions. This official list of account titles is called a **chart of accounts**

Regarding Paul's Auto Body, up to this point we have recorded only transactions involving asset, liability, and owner's equity accounts. As a means of getting started, we introduced new account titles as they came along. Now we can make a partial chart of accounts from the account titles we have introduced so far.

Assets	**Liabilities**
Cash	Accounts Payable
Supplies	
Equipment	**Owner's Equity**
	Paul Greenwalt, Capital

In Chapter 2 we will bring in additional classifications to come up with the complete chart of accounts for Paul's Auto Body.

THE BALANCE SHEET

Earlier we listed *summarizing* as one of the five basic tasks of the accounting process. To accomplish this task, accountants use financial statements. One of these financial statements, the **balance sheet,** summarizes the balances of the assets, liabilities, and owner's equity accounts on a given date (usually at the end of a month or year). The date shown on the balance sheet is like a snapshot—a picture of the business at that point in time. And the picture will change with the next transaction.

Actually, the balance sheet is a listing of the balances of the assets, liabilities, and owner's equity of a business enterprise as of a specified date. Two forms of the balance sheet are commonly used: the account form and the report form.

The Account Form

In the **account form** of the balance sheet, the elements in the accounting equation are presented side by side, as

Assets = Liabilities
+
Owner's Equity

After Paul's Auto Body records its initial transactions, a balance sheet prepared on June 15 in the account form would look like Figure 1-1.

FIGURE 1-1

Paul's Auto Body
Balance Sheet
June 15, 19–

Assets						Liabilities					
Cash	$13	0	0	0	00	Accounts Payable	$ 3	4	0	0	00
Supplies		4	0	0	00						
Equipment	22	0	0	0	00	Owner's Equity					
						Paul Greenwalt, Capital	32	0	0	0	00
						Total Liabilities and Owner's					
Total Assets	$35	4	0	0	00	Equity	$35	4	0	0	00

The Report Form

In the **report form** of the balance sheet, the elements in the accounting equation are presented one on top of the other, as

Assets
=
Liabilities
+
Owner's Equity

A balance sheet prepared on June 15 for Paul's Auto Body in report form would look like Figure 1-2.

FIGURE 1-2

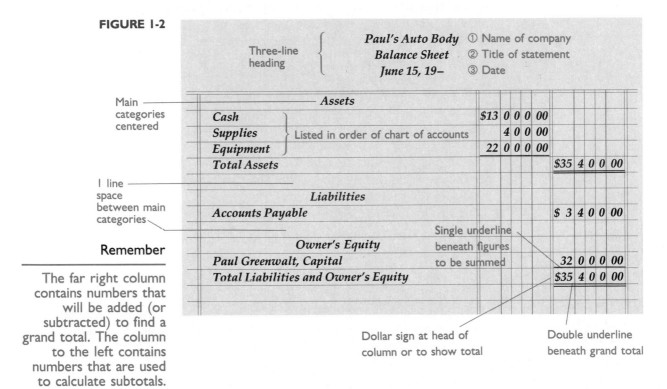

The report form of the balance sheet will be used throughout this text.
Let's note some details about the balance sheet:

1. The three-line heading consists of: the name of the company, the title of the financial statement, and the date of the financial statement. The heading is centered at the top of the page.
2. The headings for the major classifications of accounts (Assets, Liabilities, Owner's Equity) are all centered. The classifications are separated by the space of one line.
3. Dollar signs are placed only at the head of each column and with each total.

4. Single lines (drawn with a ruler) are used to show that figures above are being added or subtracted. Lines should be drawn across the entire column.
5. Double lines are used under the grand totals in a column.

Totals for the major classifications are shown in the right-hand money column. All other numbers are listed to the left.

The balance sheet shows the financial position of the company and is sometimes referred to as a *statement of financial position.* Financial position is shown by a list of balances of the assets or property, offset by the liabilities or amounts owed to creditors, and the owner's equity or financial interest. **Financial position,** as used in this accounting concept, means the same thing we would mean if we were to speak of the financial position of a person. A statement of financial position is a listing of what a business owns, as well as a listing of the claims of its creditors. The difference between the total amount owned and total amount owed is the owner's equity, that is, the value of the investment or the business's net worth.

Perhaps you noticed the balance sheets of commercial banks and savings and loan associations in the back pages of a newspaper. The law requires these institutions to publish their balance sheets in daily newspapers at certain times of the year. The purpose of these financial statements is to show the financial positions of these institutions; the total of the assets listed must equal the total claims of the depositors and creditors plus the owners' equity.

In the next chapter the fundamental accounting equation will be expanded to include additional items.

SUMMARY

L.O. 1   Accounting is often called the *language of business* because recordkeeping and financial reports use the terms and concepts of accounting. This chapter presented the definitions of accounting and business transactions.

L.O. 2   The fundamental accounting equation, consisting of three elements, is

$$\text{Assets} = \text{Liabilities} + \text{Owner's Equity}$$

Assets are cash, properties, and other things of value owned by the business. Liabilities are debts or amounts owed to creditors. Owner's equity accounts are used to record the owner's investment in the business; that is, his or her right to the assets of the business.

L.O. 3   An accountant analyzes business transactions to determine which accounts are involved and then records the transactions as increases or decreases in the appropriate accounts. After each transaction is recorded, the equation must always remain in balance.

L.O. 4   The **balance sheet**—which is a statement showing the balances of asset, liability, and owner's equity accounts—shows the financial position of an enterprise **as of a specific date.**

GLOSSARY

Account form   The form of the balance sheet in which assets, liabilities, and owner's equity are placed side by side, with assets on the left side and liabilities and owner's equity on the right side.

Accounting   The process of analyzing, classifying, recording, summarizing, and interpreting business transactions in financial or monetary terms.

Accounts   The categories under the main headings of Assets, Liabilities, and Owner's Equity.

Accounts Payable   A liability account used for short-term liabilities or charge accounts, usually due within thirty days.

Assets   Cash, properties, and other things of value owned by an economic unit or business entity.

Balance sheet   A financial statement showing the financial position of a firm or other economic unit on a given date, such as June 30 or December 31. The balance sheet lists the balances of the assets, liabilities, and owner's equity accounts.

Business entity   A business enterprise, separate and distinct from the persons who supply the assets it uses. Property acquired by a business is an asset of the business. The owner is separate from the business and occupies the status of a claimant of the business.

Capital   The owner's investment, or equity, in an enterprise.

Certified Public Accountant (CPA)   An independent licensed professional who provides services to clients for a fee.

Chart of accounts   The official list of account titles to be used to record the transactions of a business.

Creditor   One to whom money is owed.

Double-entry accounting   The system by which each business transaction is recorded in at least two accounts and the accounting equation is kept in balance.

Economic unit   Includes business enterprises and also nonprofit entities, such as government bodies, churches, clubs, and fraternal organizations.

Equity   The value of a right or claim to or financial interest in an asset or group of assets.

Financial position   The resources or assets owned by an economic unit at a point in time, offset by the claims against those resources; shown by a balance sheet.

Fundamental accounting equation   An equation expressing the relationship of assets, liabilities, and owner's equity.

Generally accepted accounting principles (GAAP)   The rules or guidelines used for carrying out the accounting process.

Liabilities   Debts, or amounts, owed to creditors.

Report form   The form of the balance sheet in which assets are placed at the top and the liabilities and owner's equity are placed below.

Sole proprietorship   One of the three primary forms of business ownership; a one-owner business.

Transaction   An event affecting an economic entity that can be expressed in terms of money and that must be recorded in the accounting records.

QUESTIONS, EXERCISES, AND PROBLEMS
Discussion Questions

1. How do you determine whether the fundamental accounting equation is in balance?
2. Give five examples of assets.
3. What do we mean by owner's equity?
4. What is a business transaction? Give three examples of business transactions.
5. What steps should you follow in analyzing a business transaction?
6. What effect will the purchase of equipment on account have on the fundamental accounting equation?
7. Why are at least two accounts affected by each business transaction?
8. What does a double ruling under column totals indicate?

Exercises

L.O. 2   **Exercise 1-1**   Complete the following equations.

    a. Assets of $21,000 = Liabilities of $4,200 + Owner's Equity of $ _16,800_
    b. Assets of $ _45,000_ = Liabilities of $16,000 + Owner's Equity of $29,000
    c. Assets of $31,000 − Owner's Equity of $15,000 = Liabilities of $ _16,000_

L.O. 2   **Exercise 1-2**   Determine the following amounts:

    a. The amount of the liabilities of a business having $54,761 of assets and in which the owner has a $33,900 equity. _$20,861_
    b. The equity of the owner of an automobile that cost $9,600 who owes $3,900 on an installment loan payable to the bank.
    c. The amount of the assets of a business having $8,430 in liabilities, in which the owner has a $21,000 equity.

L.O. 2   **Exercise 1-3**   Ruth Benson's Insurance Agency owns office equipment amounting to $9,600; a car, which is used for business purposes only, listed at $8,150; and other property that is used in her business amounting to $4,800. She owes business creditors a total of $1,720. What is the value of Benson's equity?

L.O. 2   **Exercise 1-4**   Dr. M. R. Hobbs is a veterinarian. As of April 30, Hobbs Veterinary Clinic owned the following property that related to his professional practice: Cash, $890; Supplies, $350; Professional Equipment, $19,500; Office Equipment, $4,260. On the same date, he owed the following business creditors: Berger Supply Company, $1,740; Barton Equipment Sales, $950. Compute the following amounts in the accounting equation:

    Assets _____ = Liabilities _____ + Owner's Equity _____

L.O. 3   **Exercise 1-5**   Describe the transactions recorded in the following equation:

		Assets		=	Liabilities	+	Owner's Equity
		Cash	+ Equipment		Accounts Payable		N. Taylor, Capital
(a)		+9,450		=			+9,450
(b)			+2,400		+2,400		
Bal.		9,450 +	2,400	=	2,400	+	9,450
(c)		−1,700	+1,700				
Bal.		7,750 +	4,100	=	2,400	+	9,450
(d)		−800	+3,300		+2,500		
Bal.		6,950 +	7,400	=	4,900	+	9,450

L.O. 2,3   **Exercise 1-6**   Describe a business transaction that will do the following:

a. Increase an asset and increase a liability.
b. Increase an asset and decrease an asset.
c. Decrease an asset and decrease a liability.
d. Increase an asset and increase owner's equity.

L.O. 3   **Exercise 1-7**   Dr. R. N. Scott is a dentist. Describe the transactions recorded below involving the asset, liability, and owner's equity accounts.

		Assets					=	Liabilities	+	Owner's Equity
	Cash +	Prepaid Insurance	+	Dental Equipment	+	Office Furniture and Equipment	=	Accounts Payable	+	R. N. Scott, Capital
Bal.	1,964 +	280	+	19,628	+	4,620	=	8,016	+	18,476
(a)	+1,200									+1,200
Bal.	3,164 +	280	+	19,628	+	4,620	=	8,016	+	19,676
(b)	−742							−742		
Bal.	2,422 +	280	+	19,628	+	4,620	=	7,274	+	19,676
(c)				+326				+326		
Bal.	2,422 +	280	+	19,954	+	4,620	=	7,600	+	19,676
(d)	−750			+1,850				+1,100		
Bal.	1,672 +	280	+	21,804	+	4,620	=	8,700	+	19,676

L.O. 4   **Exercise 1-8**   Using the ending balances from Exercise 1-7, prepare a balance sheet, dated as of December 31 of this year. Use notebook paper.

Problem Set A

L.O. 3   **Problem 1-1A**   Fagan Pest Control has just been established by the owner, C. B. Fagan, and engages in the following transactions:

a. Fagan deposited $16,500 in the Turner State Bank in the name of the business.
b. Bought equipment for use in the business with cash, $4,200.
c. Paid cash for supplies to use in the business, $840.
d. Bought additional equipment for the business on account from Harman Company, $7,640.
e. Invested an additional $1,900 in cash.
f. Paid Harman Company as part payment on account, $1,528.

Instructions

1. In the equation, record the owner's name beside the term *Capital*.
2. Record the transactions in column form, using plus and minus signs, and show the balance after each transaction.
3. Prove that the total on one side of the equation equals the total on the other side of the equation.

L.O. 4   **Problem 1-2A**   C. L. Lehman owns Lehman Advertising Agency. The company's books show the following account balances for assets, liabilities, and owner's equity as of August 31:

Cash	$ 2,880	Office Equipment	$ 14,040
Supplies	930	Office Furniture	12,600
Land	24,000	Accounts Payable	6,510
Building	84,000	C. L. Lehman, Capital	131,940

Instructions

Prepare a balance sheet using the report form as of August 31 of this year.

L.O. 3   **Problem 1-3A**   The Shelton Bookkeeping Service has just been established by the owner, R. C. Shelton. The following transactions affect the asset, liability, and owner's equity accounts:

a. Shelton deposited $16,420 in cash in the Texas State Bank in the name of the business.
b. Bought equipment for use in the business with cash, $6,466.
c. Bought office supplies consisting of stationery and business forms on account from Maxim Printers, $520.
d. Shelton invested in the business her own personal equipment, having a value of $3,740. (Add to Equipment, and add to R. C. Shelton, Capital.)
e. Paid cash for additional office supplies for use in the business, $126.
f. Paid Maxim Printers (creditor) $200 as part payment on account.
g. Bought additional equipment for use in the business on account from Burroughs Company, $3,648, paying $600 as a down payment. The remainder is due in 30 days.

Instructions

1. In the equation, record the owner's name beside the term *Capital*.
2. Record the transactions in column form, using plus and minus signs, and show the balances after each transaction.
3. Prove that the total on one side of the equation equals the total on the other side of the equation.

L.O. 4   **Problem I-4A**   Trevino Optical is owned by C. B. Trevino. Trevino Optical's accounts with their August 31 balances are listed in random order below.

Professional Equipment	$37,520	Supplies	$1,442
Cash	4,712	Office Equipment	4,848
C. B. Trevino, Capital	46,672	Accounts Payable	1,850

Instructions

Using a chart of accounts similar to the one on page 11, prepare a balance sheet using the report form as of August 31 of this year.

Problem Set B

L.O. 3   **Problem I-1B**   City Cleaners has just been established by the owner, L. R. Howell. It engages in the following transactions:

a. Howell deposited $19,200 in the Missouri State Bank in the name of the business.
b. Bought cleaning supplies for cash, $840.
c. Bought equipment for the business on account from Brighton Company, $10,800.
d. Howell invested an additional $4,800 in cash.
e. Paid Brighton Company $2,400 as part payment on account.
f. Bought additional equipment for the business for cash, $2,130.

Instructions

1. In the equation, record the owner's name beside the term *Capital*.
2. Record the transactions in column form, using plus and minus signs, and show the balances after each transaction.
3. Prove that the total on one side of the equation equals the total on the other side of the equation.

L.O. 4   **Problem I-2B**   N. R. Russo owns the Russo Insurance Agency. On September 30, the company's books show the following account balances for assets, liabilities, and owner's equity accounts:

Cash	$ 1,800	Office Equipment	$ 5,280
Supplies	1,035	Office Furniture	6,000
Land	9,600	Accounts Payable	9,270
Building	36,600	N. R. Russo, Capital	51,045

Instructions

Prepare a balance sheet using the report form as of September 30 of this year.

L.O. 3   **Problem 1-3B**   Allen's Janitorial Service has just been established by the owner, M. L. Allen. The following transactions affect the asset, liability, and owner's equity accounts.

a. Allen deposited $27,300 in cash in the Florida State Bank in the name of the business.
b. Bought equipment for use in the business with cash, $18,930.
c. Bought cleaning supplies on account from Welch Company, $1,027.
d. Paid cash for additional cleaning supplies for use in the business, $144.
e. Allen invested in the business his personal equipment having a value of $1,080. (Add to Equipment, and add to M. L. Allen, Capital.)
f. Paid Welch Company as part payment on account, $180.
g. Bought additional equipment for use in the business on account from Jasper Company, $2,100, paying $300 as a downpayment. The remainder is due in 30 days.

Instructions

1. In the equation, record the owner's name beside the term *Capital*.
2. Record the transactions in column form, using plus and minus signs, and show the balances after each transaction.
3. Prove that the total on one side of the equation equals the total on the other side of the equation.

L.O. 4   **Problem 1-4B**   Superb Aerobics is owned by B. C. Landers. The accounts of Superb Aerobics with their October 31 balances are listed below in random order.

Supplies	$1,566	Professional Equipment	$13,698
Cash	922	B. C. Landers, Capital	20,262
Accounts Payable	254	Furniture and Fixtures	4,330

Instructions

Using a chart of accounts similar to the one on page 11, prepare a balance sheet using the report form as of October 31 of this year.

2

Analyzing Business Transactions: Revenue and Expense Accounts

LEARNING OBJECTIVES

After you have completed this chapter, you will be able to do the following:

1. Record a group of business transactions in column form, involving all five elements of the fundamental accounting equation.
2. Prepare an income statement.
3. Prepare a statement of owner's equity.
4. Prepare a statement of owner's equity when there is an additional investment and a net loss.

In Chapter 1, we analyzed and recorded a number of transactions in asset, liability, and owner's equity accounts and did so in a way that was consistent with the definition of accounting. In this chapter we shall introduce the remaining two classifications of accounts: revenues and expenses. We shall record business transactions involving revenue and expense accounts in the same type of column arrangement we used in Chapter 1. Again let us stress that, after each transaction has been recorded, the total of the balances of the accounts on one side of the equals sign should equal the total of the balances of the accounts on the other side of the equals sign. We shall continue to use transactions of Paul's Auto Body as examples.

REVENUE AND EXPENSE ACCOUNTS

Revenues are the amounts earned by a business. Examples of revenues are fees earned for performing services, sales involving the exchange of merchandise, rental income for providing the use of property, and interest income for lending money. Revenues may be in the form of cash and credit card receipts like those from VISA and MasterCard. Revenue may also result from credit sales to charge customers, in which case cash will be received at a later time.

Expenses are the costs that relate to the earning of revenue (or the costs of doing business). Examples of expenses are wages expense for labor performed, rent expense for the use of property, interest expense for the use of money, and advertising expense for the use of newspaper space. Expenses may be paid in cash when incurred (that is, immediately) or at a later time. Expenses to be paid at a later time involve Accounts Payable.

Revenues and expenses directly affect owner's equity. If a business earns revenue, there is an increase in owner's equity. If a business incurs or pays expenses, there is a decrease in owner's equity. For the present, let us think of it this way: if the company makes money, the owner's equity is increased. On the other hand, if the company has to pay out money for the costs of doing business, then the owner's equity is decreased. So we place revenue and expenses under the "umbrella" of owner's equity: revenue increases owner's equity; expenses decrease owner's equity.

Chart of Accounts

In Chapter 1, we briefly introduced a partial chart of accounts. We stated that the chart of accounts is the official list of accounts tailor-made for the business. Also, all the company's transactions must be recorded using the official account titles.

We now present the full chart of accounts for Paul's Auto Body. Some of the accounts are new to you, but they will be explained as we move along.

Chart of Accounts

Assets

Cash
Accounts Receivable
Supplies
Prepaid Insurance
Equipment

Liabilities

Accounts Payable

Owner's Equity

Paul Greenwalt, Capital
Paul Greenwalt, Drawing

Revenue

Income from Services

Expenses

Wages Expense
Rent Expense
Advertising Expense
Utilities Expense

Recording Business Transactions

Objective 1

Record a group of business transactions in column form, involving all five elements of the fundamental accounting equation.

Soon after the opening of Paul's Auto Body, the first customers arrive, beginning a flow of revenue for the business. Let us now examine further transactions of Paul's Auto Body for the first month of operations.

Transaction (f)   Paul's Auto Body receives cash revenue in return for services performed for customers for the week, $600. In other words, the company earned $600 for services performed for cash customers. As we said, revenue has the effect of increasing owner's equity. However, it is better to keep the revenue separate from the capital account until you have prepared financial statements. We will call the revenue account for Paul's Auto Body Income from Services. As a result of this transaction, the accounting equation is affected as follows (PB stands for previous balance, and NB stands for new balance):

	Assets			= Liabilities +	Owner's Equity	
	Cash +	Equipment +	Supplies	Accounts Payable	Paul Greenwalt, Capital	+ Revenue
PB	13,000 +	22,000 +	400	= 3,400 +	32,000	
(f)	+600					+600
						(Income from Services)
NB	13,600 +	22,000 +	400	= 3,400 +	32,000 +	600
		36,000			36,000	

Transaction (g)   Shortly after opening the business, Paul's Auto Body pays the month's rent of $400. Rent is payment for the privilege of occupying a building.

It seems logical that if revenue is added to owner's equity, then expenses (the opposite of revenue) must be subtracted from owner's equity. **We want to have a running total of the amount of expenses to be subtracted from owner's equity. To keep up this running total, as each new expense is incurred (or comes into being), it must be added to the previous total.** Later we will consider revenues and expenses as separate elements in the fundamental accounting equation. At that time, through the medium of the financial statements, they will be connected with owner's equity. For now, however, we will list them under the heading Owner's Equity.

	Assets			= Liabilities +	Owner's Equity		
	Cash +	Equipment +	Supplies	Accounts Payable	Paul Greenwalt, Capital	+ Revenue	− Expenses
PB	13,600 +	22,000 +	400 =	3,400 +	32,000 +	600	
(g)	−400						+400
							(Rent Expense)
NB	13,200 +	22,000 +	400 =	3,400 +	32,000 +	600 −	400
		35,600				35,600	

Because the time period represented by the rent payment is one month or less, we record the $400 as an expense. If the payment covered a period longer than one month, we would record the amount under Prepaid Rent, which is an asset account.

Again, let us stress the mental process for formulating the entry with these questions:

1. What are the accounts involved? In this transaction they are Cash and Rent Expense.
2. What are the classifications of the accounts involved? Cash is an asset and Rent Expense is an expense.
3. Are the accounts increased or decreased? Cash is decreased because after the payment we have less cash than before. Rent Expense is increased. We are trying to keep track of the total rent paid, and now there is an additional $400.

Transaction (h)   Paul's Auto Body pays $240 in wages for a part-time employee for June 1 through June 10. This additional expense of $240 is added to the previous balance of $400, resulting in a new running total of $640. Now the equation looks like this:

	Assets			= Liabilities +	Owner's Equity		
	Cash +	Equipment +	Supplies	Accounts Payable	Paul Greenwalt, Capital	+ Revenue	− Expenses
PB	13,200 +	22,000 +	400 =	3,400 +	32,000 +	600 −	400
(h)	−240						+240
							(Wages Expense)
NB	12,960 +	22,000 +	400 =	3,400 +	32,000 +	600 −	640
		35,360				35,360	

Transaction (i)   Paul's Auto Body pays $320 for a two-year liability insurance policy. As it expires, the insurance will become an expense. **However, because it is paid in advance for a period longer than one month, it has value and is therefore recorded as an asset.**

	Assets				= Liabilities +		Owner's Equity		
	Cash	+ Equip.	+ Supp.	+ Ppd. Ins.	Accounts Payable	+	Paul Greenwalt, Capital	+ Revenue	− Expenses
PB	12,960	+ 22,000	+ 400		= 3,400	+	32,000	+ 600	− 640
(i)	−320			+320					
NB	12,640	+ 22,000	+ 400	+ 320 =	3,400	+	32,000	+ 600	− 640
		35,360					35,360		

At the end of the year or accounting period, an adjustment will have to be made, taking out the expired portion (that is, the coverage or months that have been used up) and recording it as an expense. We will discuss this adjustment in Chapter 5.

Transaction (j)   Paul's Auto Body receives cash revenue for the second week, $760.

	Assets				= Liabilities +		Owner's Equity		
	Cash	+ Equip.	+ Supp.	+ Ppd. Ins.	Accounts Payable	+	Paul Greenwalt, Capital	+ Revenue	− Expenses
PB	12,640	+ 22,000	+ 400	+ 320 =	3,400	+	32,000	+ 600	− 640
(j)	+760							+760	
								(Income from Services)	
NB	13,400	+ 22,000	+ 400	+ 320 =	3,400	+	32,000	+ 1,360	− 640
		36,120					36,120		

Remember

In recording revenue, part of the entry is always an increase in a revenue account.

Observe that each time a transaction is recorded, the total amount on one side of the equation *remains equal* to the total amount on the other side. As proof of this equality, look at the following computation:

	Total		Total
		Accounts Payable	$ 3,400
Cash	$13,400	Paul Greenwalt, Capital	32,000
Equipment	22,000	Revenue	1,360
Supplies	400		$36,760
Prepaid Insurance	320	Expenses	−640
	$36,120		$36,120

Let us now continue with the transactions.

Transaction (k)　Paul's Auto Body receives a bill from the Daily News for newspaper advertising, $180. Paul's Auto Body has simply received the bill for advertising; it has not paid any cash. Previously, we described an expense as money to be paid for the cost of doing business. An expense of $180 has now been incurred and should be recorded as an increase in expenses (Advertising Expense). Also, since the company owes $180 more than before, this amount should be recorded as an increase in Accounts Payable.

Remember

In recording an expense, part of the entry is always an increase in an expense account.

	Assets				=	Liabilities +		Owner's Equity			
	Cash	+ Equip.	+ Supp.	+ Ppd. Ins.	=	Accounts Payable	+	Paul Greenwalt, Capital	+ Revenue	−	Expenses
PB (k)	13,400	+ 22,000	+ 400	+ 320	=	3,400 +180	+	32,000	+ 1,360	−	640 +180 (Advertising Expense)
NB	13,400	+ 22,000	+ 400	+ 320	=	3,580	+	32,000	+ 1,360	−	820
		36,120						36,120			

Transaction (l)　Paul's Auto Body pays $1,800 to Osborne Equipment Company, its creditor (the party to whom it owes money), as part payment on account.

	Assets				=	Liabilities +		Owner's Equity			
	Cash	+ Equip.	+ Supp.	+ Ppd. Ins.	=	Accounts Payable	+	Paul Greenwalt, Capital	+ Revenue	−	Expenses
PB (l)	13,400 −1,800	+ 22,000	+ 400	+ 320	=	3,580 −1,800	+	32,000	+ 1,360	−	820
NB	11,600	+ 22,000	+ 400	+ 320	=	1,780	+	32,000	+ 1,360	−	820
		34,320						34,320			

Transaction (m)　Paul's Auto Body receives a bill for heat, power, and lights, showing that $220 of electricity has been used. Because the bill had not been previously recorded as a liability, and it is to be paid now, the accounting equation is affected as follows:

	Assets				= Liabilities +	Owner's Equity		
	Cash +	Equip. +	Supp. +	Ppd. Ins.	Accounts Payable	Paul Greenwalt, Capital	+ Revenue	− Expenses
PB (m)	11,600 + −220	22,000 +	400 +	320 =	1,780 +	32,000	+ 1,360	− 820 +220 (Utilities Expense)
NB	11,380 +	22,000 +	400 +	320 =	1,780 +	32,000	+ 1,360	− 1,040
		34,100				34,100		

Transaction (n) Now Paul's Auto Body pays $180 to the Daily News for advertising. Recall that this bill had previously been recorded as a liability. The equation is as follows:

	Assets				= Liabilities +	Owner's Equity		
	Cash +	Equip. +	Supp. +	Ppd. Ins.	Accounts Payable	Paul Greenwalt, Capital	+ Revenue	− Expenses
PB (n)	11,380 + −180	22,000 +	400 +	320 =	1,780 + −180	32,000	+ 1,360	− 1,040
NB	11,200 +	22,000 +	400 +	320 =	1,600 +	32,000	+ 1,360	− 1,040
		33,920				33,920		

Transaction (o) Paul's Auto Body receives cash revenue for the third week, $830.

	Assets				= Liabilities +	Owner's Equity		
	Cash +	Equip. +	Supp. +	Ppd. Ins.	Accounts Payable	Paul Greenwalt, Capital	+ Revenue	− Expenses
PB (o)	11,200 + +830	22,000 +	400 +	320 =	1,600 +	32,000	+ 1,360 +830 (Income from Services)	− 1,040
NB	12,030 +	22,000 +	400 +	320 =	1,600 +	32,000	+ 2,190	− 1,040
		34,750				34,750		

Transaction (p) Paul's Auto Body signs a contract with Hughes Taxi to paint or repair damages to their vehicles on a credit basis. Paul's Auto Body completes a minor paint job and bills Hughes Taxi $80 for services performed.

A company uses the **Accounts Receivable** account to record the amounts owed by charge customers. These receivable accounts represent credit, usually extended for thirty days. Since Hughes Taxi owes Paul's Auto Body $80 more than before the transaction took place, it seems logical to add $80 to Accounts Receivable. Revenue is earned or counted when the service is performed, so there is an increase in revenue. Keep in mind that Accounts Receivable is an asset. An asset is something that is owned, and Paul's Auto Body owns a claim of $80 against Hughes Taxi.

	Assets				= Liabilities +		Owner's Equity		
	Cash + Equip. + Supp. +		Ppd. Ins. +	Accts. Rec.	Accounts Payable	Paul Greenwalt, Capital	+ Revenue − Expenses		
PB (p)	12,030 + 22,000 + 400 +		320	+80	= 1,600 +	32,000	+ 2,190 − 1,040 +80 (Income from Services)		
NB	12,030 + 22,000 + 400 +		320 +	80	= 1,600 +	32,000	+ 2,270 − 1,040		
	34,830					34,830			

When Hughes Taxi pays the $80 bill in cash, Paul's Auto Body will record this transaction as an increase in Cash and a decrease in Accounts Receivable. Paul's Auto Body does not have to make an entry for the revenue account because the revenue was earned and recorded when the service was performed.

Transaction (q)   Paul's Auto Body pays wages of a part-time employee, $390, for June 11 through June 24.

	Assets				= Liabilities +		Owner's Equity		
	Cash + Equip. + Supp. +		Ppd. Ins. +	Accts. Rec.	Accounts Payable	Paul Greenwalt, Capital	+ Revenue − Expenses		
PB (q)	12,030 + 22,000 + 400 + −390		320 +	80	= 1,600 +	32,000	+ 2,270 − 1,040 +390 (Wages Expense)		
NB	11,640 + 22,000 + 400 +		320 +	80	= 1,600 +	32,000	+ 2,270 − 1,430		
	34,440					34,440			

Transaction (r)   Paul's Auto Body buys additional equipment for $940 from Osborne Equipment Company, paying $140 down, with the remaining $800 on account. Because buying an item on account is the same as buying it on credit, both expressions, *on account* and *on credit*, are used to describe such transactions.

	Assets					=	Liabilities +		Owner's Equity		
	Cash	+ Equip.	+ Supp.	+ Ppd. Ins.	+ Accts. Rec.	=	Accounts Payable	+	Paul Greenwalt, Capital	+ Revenue	− Expenses
PB (r)	11,640 −140	+ 22,000 +940	+ 400	+ 320	+ 80	=	1,600 +800	+	32,000	+ 2,270	− 1,430
NB	11,500	+ 22,940	+ 400	+ 320	+ 80	=	2,400	+	32,000	+ 2,270	− 1,430
		35,240							35,240		

Again, because the equipment will last a long time, Paul's Auto Body lists this $940 as an increase in the assets. Note that there are three accounts involved in this transaction: Cash, because cash was paid out; Equipment, because the company has more equipment than before; and Accounts Payable, because the company owes more than before.

Transaction (s) Paul's Auto Body receives revenue from cash customers for the rest of the month, $960.

	Assets					=	Liabilities +		Owner's Equity		
	Cash	+ Equip.	+ Supp.	+ Ppd. Ins.	+ Accts. Rec.	=	Accounts Payable	+	Paul Greenwalt, Capital	+ Revenue	− Expenses
PB (s)	11,500 +960	+ 22,940	+ 400	+ 320	+ 80	=	2,400	+	32,000	+ 2,270 +960 (Income from Services)	− 1,430
NB	12,460	+ 22,940	+ 400	+ 320	+ 80	=	2,400	+	32,000	+ 3,230	− 1,430
		36,200							36,200		

Transaction (t) Paul's Auto Body receives $60 from Hughes Taxi to apply against the amount billed previously in transaction **(p)**. Hughes Taxi now owes Paul's Auto Body less than before, so Paul's Auto Body deducts the $60 from Accounts Receivable. The equation now looks like the one shown below:

	Assets					=	Liabilities +		Owner's Equity		
	Cash	+ Equip.	+ Supp.	+ Ppd. Ins.	+ Accts. Rec.	=	Accounts Payable	+	Paul Greenwalt, Capital	+ Revenue	− Expenses
PB (t)	12,460 +60	+ 22,940	+ 400	+ 320	+ 80 −60	=	2,400	+	32,000	+ 3,230	− 1,430
NB	12,520	+ 22,940	+ 400	+ 320	+ 20	=	2,400	+	32,000	+ 3,230	− 1,430
		36,200							36,200		

Since Paul's Auto Body previously listed the amount as revenue, it should definitely not be recorded as revenue again. Think of paying income tax on the $60—once is enough.

Transaction (u)   At the end of the month, Greenwalt withdraws $1,000 in cash from the business for his personal living costs. A **withdrawal** may be considered the opposite of an investment in cash by the owner.

		Assets			= Liabilities +		Owner's Equity	
Cash	+ Equip.	+ Supp.	+ Ppd. Ins.	+ Accts. Rec.	Accounts Payable	Paul Greenwalt, Capital	+ Revenue	− Expenses
PB 12,520	+ 22,940	+ 400	+ 320	+ 20	= 2,400	+ 32,000	+ 3,230	− 1,430
(u) −1,000						−1,000 (Drawing)		
NB 11,520	+ 22,940	+ 400	+ 320	+ 20	= 2,400	+ 31,000	+ 3,230	− 1,430
		35,200					35,200	

Because the owner is taking cash out of the business, there is a decrease of $1,000 in Cash. The withdrawal also decreases Capital, because Greenwalt has now reduced his equity. We record $1,000 as a minus under Capital and label it as Drawing.

Think of how this transaction affects the accounting equation. As a result of the transaction, the firm has less cash (decrease in assets). On the other side of the equals sign, liabilities are not involved because the company does not owe any more or any less money. Revenue is not involved, because the firm has not earned any more money. Expenses are not involved, because an amount was not paid to anyone outside the business for services performed or materials received that would benefit the business. Therefore, owner's equity is the logical classification to decrease, since Paul Greenwalt's interest or investment in the company is now less than before he took the money out of the business.

Summary of Transactions

Figure 2-1 on the next page summarizes the business transactions of Paul's Auto Body, with the transactions identified by letter. To test your understanding of the recording procedure, describe the nature of the transactions that have taken place. The computation at the top of page 32 shows that the fundamental accounting equation holds true. On both the balance line of Figure 2.1 and the computation on page 32, assets are shown in green, liabilities are shown in red, and owner's equity amounts are shown in blue.

FIGURE 2-1

31

	Assets					=	Liabilities +		Owner's Equity		
	Cash	+ Equip.	+ Supp.	+ Ppd. Ins.	+ Accts. Rec.	=	Accounts Payable	+	Paul Greenwalt, Capital	+ Revenue	− Expenses
Bal.	13,000	+ 22,000	+ 400			=	3,400	+	32,000		
(f)	+600									+600	
										(Income from Services)	
Bal.	13,600	+ 22,000	+ 400			=	3,400	+	32,000	+ 600	
(g)	−400										+400
											(Rent Expense)
Bal.	13,200	+ 22,000	+ 400			=	3,400	+	32,000	+ 600	− 400
(h)	−240										+240
											(Wages Expense)
Bal.	12,960	+ 22,000	+ 400			=	3,400	+	32,000	+ 600	− 640
(i)	−320			+320							
Bal.	12,640	+ 22,000	+ 400	+ 320		=	3,400	+	32,000	+ 600	− 640
(j)	+760									+760	
										(Income from Services)	
Bal.	13,400	+ 22,000	+ 400	+ 320		=	3,400	+	32,000	+ 1,360	− 640
(k)							+180				+180
											(Advertising Expense)
Bal.	13,400	+ 22,000	+ 400	+ 320		=	3,580	+	32,000	+ 1,360	− 820
(l)	−1,800						−1,800				
Bal.	11,600	+ 22,000	+ 400	+ 320		=	1,780	+	32,000	+ 1,360	− 820
(m)	−220										+220
											(Utilities Expense)
Bal.	11,380	+ 22,000	+ 400	+ 320		=	1,780	+	32,000	+ 1,360	− 1,040
(n)	−180						−180				
Bal.	11,200	+ 22,000	+ 400	+ 320		=	1,600	+	32,000	+ 1,360	− 1,040
(o)	+830									+830	
										(Income from Services)	
Bal.	12,030	+ 22,000	+ 400	+ 320		=	1,600	+	32,000	+ 2,190	− 1,040
(p)					+ 80					+80	
										(Income from Services)	
Bal.	12,030	+ 22,000	+ 400	+ 320 +	80	=	1,600	+	32,000	+ 2,270	− 1,040
(q)	−390										+390
											(Wages Expense)
Bal.	11,640	+ 22,000	+ 400	+ 320 +	80	=	1,600	+	32,000	+ 2,270	− 1,430
(r)	−140	+940					+800				
Bal.	11,500	+ 22,940	+ 400	+ 320 +	80	=	2,400	+	32,000	+ 2,270	− 1,430
(s)	+960									+960	
										(Income from Services)	
Bal.	12,460	+ 22,940	+ 400	+ 320 +	80	=	2,400	+	32,000	+ 3,230	− 1,430
(t)	+60				−60						
Bal.	12,520	+ 22,940	+ 400	+ 320 +	20	=	2,400	+	32,000	+ 3,230	− 1,430
(u)	−1,000								−1,000		
									(Drawing)		
Bal.	11,520	+ 22,940	+ 400	+ 320 +	20	=	2,400	+	31,000	+ 3,230	− 1,430

	Total		**Total**
Cash	$11,520	Accounts Payable	$ 2,400
Equipment	22,940	Paul Greenwalt, Capital	31,000
Supplies	400	Revenue	3,230
Prepaid Insurance	320		$36,630
Accounts Receivable	20	Expenses	−1,430
	$35,200		$35,200

MAJOR FINANCIAL STATEMENTS

A financial statement is a report prepared by accountants for managers and others both inside and outside the business. In Chapter 1, we discussed the balance sheet. We will now consider the income statement and the statement of owner's equity.

The Income Statement

Objective 2

Prepare an income statement.

The income statement shows total revenue minus total expenses, which yields the net income or net loss. **The income statement pictures the results of the business transactions involving revenue and expense accounts over a period of time.** In other words, the income statement shows how the business has performed or fared over a period of time, usually a month or year. When total revenue exceeds total expenses over the period, the result is **net income,** or profit. Other terms that are identical with the name *income statement* are *statement of income and expenses* or *profit and loss statement*. If the total revenue is less than the total expenses, the result is a **net loss.**

The income statement in Figure 2-2 shows the results of the first month of operations for Paul's Auto Body. (Note that the net income figure presented here represents net income before adjustments. We shall discuss adjustments in Chapter 5.)

Note that as **in all financial statements, the heading requires three lines:**

1. Name of company (or owner, if there is no company name).
2. Title of the financial statement (in this case, income statement).
3. Period of time covered by the financial statement or its date.

For convenience, the individual expense amounts are recorded in the first amount column. In this way, the total expenses ($1,430) may be subtracted directly from the total revenue ($3,230).

The income statement covers a period of time, whereas the balance sheet has only one date: the end of the financial period. Look at the third line of the heading of the income statement shown in Figure 2-2 on page 33. Then compare it with the third line of the balance sheet shown

FIGURE 2-2

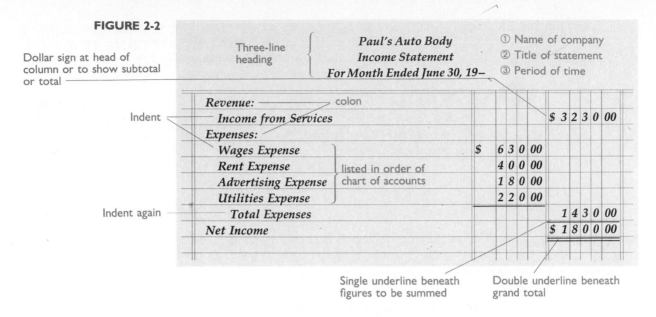

Dollar sign at head of column or to show subtotal or total

Three-line heading

Paul's Auto Body
Income Statement
For Month Ended June 30, 19—

① Name of company
② Title of statement
③ Period of time

Indent

Revenue:	colon		
Income from Services			$ 3 2 3 0 00
Expenses:			
Wages Expense	$ 6 3 0 00		
Rent Expense	4 0 0 00		
Advertising Expense	1 8 0 00		
Utilities Expense	2 2 0 00		
Total Expenses		1 4 3 0 00	
Net Income		$ 1 8 0 0 00	

listed in order of chart of accounts

Indent again

Single underline beneath figures to be summed

Double underline beneath grand total

in Figure 2-4 on page 34. On the income statement the revenue for June, less the expenses for June, shows the results of operations—a net income of $1,800. To the accountant, the term *net income* means "clear" income, or profit after all expenses have been deducted. Expenses are usually listed in the same order as in the chart of accounts, which is the official list of all the accounts in which transactions are recorded.

The Statement of Owner's Equity

Objective 3

Prepare a statement of owner's equity.

We said that revenue and expenses are connected with owner's equity through the medium of the financial statements. Let us now demonstrate this by a **statement of owner's equity,** shown in Figure 2-3 on page 34, which the accountant prepares after he or she has determined the net income or net loss in the income statement. The statement of owner's equity shows how—and why—the owner's equity, or capital, account has changed over a stated period of time (in this case, the month of June). Notice the third line in the heading of Figure 2-3. It shows that the statement of owner's equity covers the same period of time as the income statement.

Now look at the body of the statement. The first line shows the balance in the capital account at the beginning of the month. Two items have affected owner's equity during the month. A net income of $1,800 was earned, and the owner withdrew $1,000. To perform the calculations smoothly, move to the left one column and then list the two items, subtracting the withdrawals from the net income. The difference, representing an increase in capital, is placed in the right-hand column to be added directly to the beginning capital. The final figure is the ending amount in the owner's capital account.

FIGURE 2-3

Dollar sign at head of column or to show subtotal or total

Three-line heading {

Paul's Auto Body
Statement of Owner's Equity
For Month Ended June 30, 19–

① Name of company
② Title of statement
③ Period of time

Paul Greenwalt, Capital, June 1, 19–					$32 0 0 0 00
Net Income for June	$1 8 0 0 00				
Less Withdrawals for June	1 0 0 0 00				
Increase in Capital					8 0 0 00
Paul Greenwalt, Capital, June 30, 19–					$32 8 0 0 00

Single underline beneath figures to be summed

Double underline beneath grand total

The Balance Sheet

After preparing the statement of owner's equity, we prepare a balance sheet (shown in Figure 2-4). In the balance sheet, we record the ending capital balance, which is taken from the statement of owner's equity. Note that the accounts appear in the same order as they are listed in the chart of accounts.

FIGURE 2-4

Paul's Auto Body
Balance Sheet
June 30, 19–

Assets		
Cash	$11 5 2 0 00	
Accounts Receivable	2 0 00	
Supplies	4 0 0 00	
Prepaid Insurance	3 2 0 00	
Equipment	22 9 4 0 00	
Total Assets		$35 2 0 0 00
Liabilities		
Accounts Payable		$ 2 4 0 0 00
Owner's Equity		
Paul Greenwalt, Capital		32 8 0 0 00
Total Liabilities and Owner's Equity		$35 2 0 0 00

Income Statement Involving More Than One Revenue Account

When a business firm or other economic unit has more than one distinct source of revenue, separate revenue accounts are set up for each source. See, for example, the income statement of The Ninth Avenue Theater presented in Figure 2-5.

FIGURE 2-5

The Ninth Avenue Theater
Income Statement
For Month Ended September 30, 19–

Revenue:		
Admissions Income	$6 9 6 8 00	
Concessions Income	1 7 4 3 00	
Total Revenue		$8 7 1 1 00
Expenses:		
Film Rental Expense	$3 3 2 5 00	
Wages Expense	1 3 5 3 00	
Advertising Expense	9 2 5 00	
Utilities Expense	3 1 6 00	
Cleaning Expense	2 2 1 00	
Miscellaneous Expense	1 4 5 00	
Total Expenses		6 2 8 5 00
Net Income		$2 4 2 6 00

Statement of Owner's Equity Involving an Additional Investment and a Net Loss

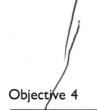

Objective 4

Prepare a statement of owner's equity when there is an additional investment and a net loss.

Any additional investment by the owner during the period covered by the financial statements should be shown in the statement of owner's equity, since such a statement should show what has affected the Capital account from the *beginning* until the *end* of the period covered by the financial statements. For example, assume the following for the L. V. Smith Company, which has a net income:

Balance of L. V. Smith, Capital, on April 1	$86,000
Additional investment by L. V. Smith on April 12	9,000
Net income for the month (from income statement)	1,500
Total withdrawals for the month	1,200

The statement of owner's equity in Figure 2-6 shows this information.

FIGURE 2-6

L. V. Smith Company
Statement of Owner's Equity
For Month Ended April 30, 19–

L. V. Smith, Capital, April 1, 19–							$86	0	0	0	00
Additional Investment, April 12, 19–							9	0	0	0	00
Total Investment							$95	0	0	0	00
Net Income for April	$1	5	0	0	00						
Less Withdrawals for April	1	2	0	0	00						
Increase in Capital								3	0	0	00
L. V. Smith, Capital, April 30, 19–							$95	3	0	0	00

The additional investment may be in the form of cash. Or, the investment may be in the form of other assets, such as tools, equipment, or similar items. In the case of investments in assets other than cash, the assets should be recorded at their fair market value. **Fair market value** is the present worth of an asset, or the amount that would be received if the asset were sold to an outsider on the open market. Fair market value may differ greatly from the amount the owner paid for the asset originally.

As another example, assume the following for the C. P. Thompson Company, which has a net loss:

C. P. Thompson, Capital, on Oct. 1	$70,000
Additional investment by C. P. Thompson on Oct. 25	6,000
Net loss for the month (from income statement)	250
Total withdrawals for the month	420

Again, the statement of owner's equity in Figure 2-7 shows this information.

FIGURE 2-7

C. P. Thompson Company
Statement of Owner's Equity
For Month Ended October 31, 19–

C. P. Thompson, Capital, October 1, 19–							$70	0	0	0	00
Additional Investment, October 25, 19–							6	0	0	0	00
Total Investment							$76	0	0	0	00
Less: Net Loss for October	$	2	5	0	00						
Withdrawals for October		4	2	0	00						
Decrease in Capital								6	7	0	00
C. P. Thompson, Capital, October 31, 19–							$75	3	3	0	00

CMPUTERS AT WORK

Types of Computers: Mainframes, Minis, and Micros

Computers may be divided into three categories by size: mainframe computers (large), minicomputers (medium), and microcomputers (small). Microcomputers are also called personal computers and have become very popular over the last ten years, both for business use and for the home. While a small business may have only a single microcomputer, many large organizations have computers in all three categories. A mainframe may maintain the accounting records, handle payroll, and turn out regular reports. Minicomputers may help individual engineers and scientists carry out research and design responsibilities. And microcomputers may put high-tech efficiency within the grasp of the ordinary employee. Today the boundaries between the categories are blurring. A modern microcomputer has more power than the earliest mainframe computers, and the cost of computing power has plummeted. Even though it is not as easy as it once was to define each of these categories, it still helps to have a general idea of the difference between them.

Mainframes are most likely to be used by large economic units, such as petroleum and airline companies, research laboratories, banks, stock exchanges, universities, defense installations, the Internal Revenue Service, and other government agencies. A mainframe and the software needed to run it may call for an investment of several million dollars. Because these machines can process 100 million or more operations per second, their cost per calculation can actually be lower than that of a much smaller machine. The question an organization must ask is how much computing power does it really need.

Minicomputers are compact, powerful computers used in business, education, and government. The cost of these machines begins at under $10,000, and they are frequently used by individual scientists or engineers. When they are connected to remote terminals or keyboards, minicomputers can link branch offices to an organization's main office. They may be used in libraries and insurance agencies and to monitor patients in health-care facilities, handle the recordkeeping of large car rental agencies, and manage hotel reservation systems.

Microcomputers have changed both business and personal information management. As their cost has fallen to well below $3,000, they have become increasingly popular. Low-cost software packages allow people who are not computer experts to perform many useful tasks quickly and easily. Small businesses use these computers for accounting applications, data management, text editing, list management, and maintenance of tax files. Major accounting firms and individual tax preparers also rely on microcomputers.

SUMMARY

L.O. 1   We have now defined the final two elements of the fundamental accounting equation: revenues and expenses. Business transactions involving the earning of revenue are recorded as increases in revenue; those involving the incurring of expenses are recorded as increases in expenses. Withdrawals by the owner are labeled as Drawing and recorded as decreases under the capital heading. The fundamental accounting equation always remains in balance.

L.O. 2   The owners or managers of a business look on their financial statements as a coach looks on the scoreboard and team statistics: as showing the results of the present game as well as the team's standing. The income statement shows the results of operations for the current month or year. It condenses the results of operations into one figure, either net income or net loss. The income statement is prepared first so that the net income can be

L.O. 3,4   recorded in the statement of owner's equity, which comes next. The statement of owner's equity shows why—and how—the owner's investment has changed during the period. The ending capital balance from the statement of owner's equity is used on the balance sheet, which shows the present standing or financial position of the business. All these relationships are shown in Figure 2-8.

FIGURE 2-8

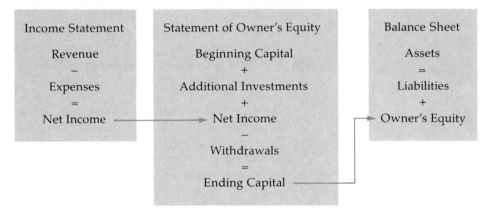

Income Statement	Statement of Owner's Equity	Balance Sheet
Revenue	Beginning Capital	Assets
−	+	=
Expenses	Additional Investments	Liabilities
=	+	+
Net Income ⟶	Net Income	Owner's Equity
	−	
	Withdrawals	
	=	
	Ending Capital	

GLOSSARY

Accounts Receivable   Accounts used to record the amounts owed by charge customers. These accounts represent credit, usually extended for thirty-day periods.

Expenses   The costs that relate to the earning of revenue (the cost of doing business); examples are wages, rent expense, interest expense, advertising expense; may be paid in cash or at a later time (Accounts Payable).

Fair market value   The present worth of an asset, or the amount that would be received if the asset were sold to an outsider on the open market.

Income statement   A financial statement showing the results of business transactions involving revenue and expense accounts over a period of time: total revenue minus total expenses.

Net income   The result when total revenue exceeds total expenses over a period of time.

Net loss   The result when total expenses exceed total revenue over a period of time.

Revenues   The amounts a business earns; examples are fees earned for performing services, sales, rent income, and interest income; may be in the form of cash, credit card receipts, or accounts receivable (charge accounts).

Statement of owner's equity   A financial statement showing how—and why—the owner's equity, or capital, account has changed over the financial period.

Withdrawal   The taking of cash or goods out of a business by the owner for his or her own personal use. (This is also referred to as a *drawing*.) A withdrawal is treated as a temporary decrease in the owner's equity, since it is anticipated that it will be offset by net income.

QUESTIONS, EXERCISES, AND PROBLEMS
Discussion Questions

1. How does an income statement differ from a balance sheet?
2. Explain the difference between accounts receivable and accounts payable.
3. Name two ways to increase owner's equity and two ways to decrease owner's equity.
4. What is the difference between the headings required for statements of owner's equity and the headings required for balance sheets?
5. Define the term *expense*. Does every payment of cash by a business indicate that an expense has been incurred?
6. What titles might you select to describe the kinds of expenses a shoe repair shop would incur in its operations?
7. Why is a withdrawal not considered an expense of the business?
8. Suggest some groups other than the owner or owners of a business who would be interested in data contained in the firm's financial statements. What is the specific interest of each group?

Exercises

L.O. 1   **Exercise 2-1**   Describe a transaction that will do the following:

a. Decrease an asset and increase an expense.
b. Increase an asset and increase a liability.
c. Decrease an asset and decrease a liability.
d. Increase an asset and increase owner's equity.
e. Decrease an asset and increase another asset.

L.O. 1   **Exercise 2-2**   Describe a transaction that caused the following for Jones Cycle Repair:

a. Accounts Payable is decreased by $620, and Cash is decreased by $620.
b. Rent Expense is increased by $740, and Cash is decreased by $740.
c. Repair Parts is increased by $92, and Accounts Payable is increased by $92.

d. Accounts Receivable is increased by $127, and Service Income is increased by $127.

e. Cash is decreased by $310, and C. Jones, Drawing is increased by $310.

f. Advertising Expense is increased by $84, and Accounts Payable is increased by $84.

g. Cash is increased by $121, and Accounts Receivable is decreased by $121.

h. Equipment is increased by $242, Cash is decreased by $100, and Accounts Payable is increased by $142.

L.O. I   **Exercise 2-3**   Label the following accounts as asset (A), liability (L), owner's equity (OE), revenue (R), or expense (E):

a. Prepaid Insurance   f. Utilities Expense
b. Professional Fees   g. Accounts Receivable
c. Rent Expense   h. Supplies
d. J. Rule, Capital   i. Service Income
e. Accounts Payable   j. J. Rule, Drawing

L.O. I   **Exercise 2-4**   Describe the transactions recorded in the following equation:

		Assets		= Liabilities +		Owner's Equity		
	Cash	+ Accounts Receivable	+ Equipment	Accounts Payable	L. Reyes, Capital	+ Revenue	− Expenses
(a)	+16,000		+ 5,000 =		+ 21,000		
(b)	−900						+900
Bal.	15,100		+ 5,000 =		+ 21,000		− 900
(c)		+2,700				+2,700	
Bal.	15,100 +	2,700	+ 5,000 =		+ 21,000 +	2,700 −	900
(d)	−3,000		+12,000	+9,000			
Bal.	12,100 +	2,700	+ 17,000 =	9,000	+ 21,000 +	2,700 −	900
(e)	−1,800				−1,800 (Drawing)		
Bal.	10,300 +	2,700	+ 17,000 =	9,000	+ 19,200 +	2,700 −	900

L.O. I   **Exercise 2-5**   From the following balances, in the elements of the fundamental accounting equation, determine the amount of the ending capital.

Assets	$71,000
Liabilities	12,000
Capital (beginning)	36,000
Revenue	57,000
Expenses	34,000

L.O. I   **Exercise 2-6**   H. L. Finch is a printer. Describe the transactions that have been completed for Finch Printing.

	Assets				= Liabilities +		Owner's Equity		
	Cash +	Accts. Rec. +	Supp. +	Equip.	Accounts Payable	+	H. L. Finch, Capital	+ Revenue	− Expenses
Bal.	1,620 +	810 +	819 +	7,493 =	2,416	+	8,326		
(a)	+360	−360							
Bal.	1,980 +	450 +	819 +	7,493 =	2,416	+	8,326		
(b)	−418								+418 (Rent Expense)
Bal.	1,562 +	450 +	819 +	7,493 =	2,416	+	8,326		− 418
(c)	+2,730							+2,730 (Income from Services)	
Bal.	4,292 +	450 +	819 +	7,493 =	2,416	+	8,326	+ 2,730	− 418
(d)	−300				−300				
Bal.	3,992 +	450 +	819 +	7,493 =	2,116	+	8,326	+ 2,730	− 418
(e)	−410								+410 (Wages Expense)
Bal.	3,582 +	450 +	819 +	7,493 =	2,116	+	8,326	+ 2,730	− 828
(f)	−1,200						−1,200 (Drawing)		
Bal.	2,382 +	450 +	819 +	7,493 =	2,116	+	7,126	+ 2,730	− 828
(g)	−875				−875				
Bal.	1,507 +	450 +	819 +	7,493 =	1,241	+	7,126	+ 2,730	− 828

L.O. 2,3 **Exercise 2-7**   From Exercise 2-6, present an income statement, a statement of owner's equity, and a balance sheet for the month ended September 30 of this year. List the expenses in the order that they appear in the Expenses column. Rent Expense is first.

L.O. 4 **Exercise 2-8**   On January 1, N. J. Hart's equity in his business, Hart's Electric, was $56,000. On May 22, Hart made an additional investment of $4,000. The firm's net income for the year was $23,500. Hart's total withdrawals amounted to $18,000. Prepare a statement of owner's equity for the year ended December 31.

Problem Set A

L.O. 1,2,3 **Problem 2-1A**   On April 1 of this year, A. R. Ball, Optometrist, established an office for the practice of optometry. The account headings are presented below. Transactions completed during the month follow.

	Assets			= Liabilities +	Owner's Equity		
Cash +	Supp. +	Prof. Equip. +	Office Equip.	Accounts Payable	A. R. Ball, Capital	+ Revenue	− Expenses

a. Deposited $10,500 in a bank account entitled A. R. Ball, Optometrist.
b. Paid office rent for the month, $640.

c. Bought supplies for cash, $1,216.

d. Bought professional equipment on account from Vision Equipment Supply, $15,290.

e. Bought a computer from Ryan Office Outfitters, $3,840, paying $800 in cash and putting the remainder on account.

f. Received cash for professional fees earned, $1,421 (Professional Fees).

g. Paid Ryan Office Outfitters $800 as part payment on amount owed on office equipment, recorded previously in transaction (e).

h. Received and paid bill for utilities, $153.

i. Paid salary of assistant, $950 (Salary Expense).

j. Earned professional fees, receiving $2,414 cash.

k. Ball withdrew cash for personal use, $1,250.

Instructions

1. In the equation, complete the asset section and list the owner's name beside the term *Capital*.

2. Record the transactions and the balance after each transaction. Identify the account affected when the transaction involves revenue, expenses, or a drawing.

3. Prepare an income statement and a statement of owner's equity for April and a balance sheet as of April 30. List the expenses in the order they appear in the Expenses column. List Rent Expense first.

L.O. 1,2,3,4 **Problem 2-2A**   M. A. Pitts, a photographer, opened a studio for her professional practice on July 1. The account headings are presented below. Transactions completed during the month follow.

Assets					= Liabilities +	Owner's Equity		
Cash +	Supplies +	Ppd. Ins. +	Photo. Equip. +	Office Equip.	Accounts Payable	M. A. Pitts, Capital	+ Revenue	− Expenses

a. Deposited $14,620 in a bank account in the name of the business, Pitts Photographic Studio.

b. Bought photographic equipment on account from Superior Equipment, $7,121.

c. Invested personal office equipment, $5,162. (Increase the account for Office Equipment, and include in the statement of owner's equity as Additional Investment as shown on page 36.)

d. Paid office rent for the month, $550.

e. Bought photographic supplies for cash, $796.

f. Paid premium for a two-year insurance policy on photographic equipment, $124.

g. Received $896 as professional fees for services rendered (Professional Fees).

h. Paid salary of part-time assistant, $600 (Salary Expense).

i. Received and paid bill for telephone service, $64 (Telephone Expense).

j. Paid Superior Equipment part of the amount owed on the purchase of photographic equipment, $420.

k. Received $1,548 as professional fees for services rendered.

l.   Paid for minor repairs to photographic equipment (Repair Expense), $76.
m. Pitts withdrew cash for personal use, $960.

Instructions

1. In the equation, complete the asset section and list the owner's name beside the term *Capital*.
2. Record the transactions and the balances after each transaction. Identify the account affected when the transaction involves revenue, expenses, or a drawing.
3. Prepare an income statement and a statement of owner's equity for July and a balance sheet as of July 31. List expenses in the order that they appear in the Expenses column. List Rent Expense first.

L.O. 2,3   **Problem 2-3A**   An accountant determines the following balances, which are listed in random order, for Alpha Dental Clinic as of October 31 of this year:

Cash	$4,394	Rent Expense	$1,170
Advertising Expense	945	Supplies	1,842
Income from Services	15,048	L. O. Sammons, Capital, Oct. 1	56,457
Wages Expense	9,621	Miscellaneous Expense	462
Accounts Receivable	8,619	Equipment	45,492
Accounts Payable	4,040	L. O. Sammon, Drawing	3,000

Instructions

Prepare an income statement and a statement of owner's equity for October and a balance sheet as of October 31. List expenses in the order that they appear above.

L.O. 1,2,3   **Problem 2-4A**   On September 1 of this year, D. L. Porter established Porter Catering Service. The account headings are presented below. During September, Porter completed these transactions.

Assets						= Liabilities +	Owner's Equity		
Cash +	Acct. Rec. +	Supp. +	Ppd. Ins. +	Truck +	Equip.	Accounts Payable	D. L. Porter, Capital	+ Revenue	− Expenses

a. Invested cash in the business, $14,500.
b. Bought a truck for use in the business from Compton Motors for $12,490, paying $3,500 in cash, with the balance due in thirty days.
c. Bought catering equipment on account from Gallo Company, $2,236.
d. Paid rent for the month, $520.
e. Cash receipts for the first half of the month from cash customers, $1,920 (Income from Services).
f. Paid cash for property and liability insurance on truck for the year, $454.
g. Bought catering supplies for cash, $172.
h. Received and paid heating bill, $54 (Utilities Expense).

  i. Received bill for gas and oil used for the truck during the current month from Clark Company, $93 (Gas and Oil Expense).

  j. Billed customers for services performed on account, $416.

  k. Receipts for the remainder of the month from cash customers, $2,412.

  l. Paid salary of assistant, $1,240 (Salary Expense).

  m. Porter withdrew cash for personal use, $1,950.

Instructions

1. List the owner's name beside the term *Capital* in the equation.
2. Record the transactions and the balances after each transaction. Identify the account affected when the transaction involves revenue, expenses, or a drawing.
3. Prepare an income statement and a statement of owner's equity for September and a balance sheet as of September 30. List expenses in the order that they appear in the Expenses column. Begin with Rent Expense.

Problem Set B

L.O. 1,2,3   **Problem 2-1B**   In June of this year, R. P. Bryan established a business under the name of Bryan Realty. The account headings are presented below. Transactions completed during the month follow.

Assets	= Liabilities +	Owner's Equity
Cash + Supplies + Equipment	Accounts Payable	R. P. Bryan, + Revenue − Expenses Capital

  a. Deposited $12,000 in a bank account entitled Bryan Realty.

  b. Paid office rent for the month, $700.

  c. Bought supplies consisting of stationery, folders, and stamps for cash, $364.

  d. Bought office equipment consisting of a calculator, typewriter, and a check writer on account from Baxter Company, $6,200.

  e. Received bill from the Daily Times for advertising, $382.

  f. Paid $900 to Baxter Company as part payment on purchase of office equipment recorded previously.

  g. Earned sales commissions, receiving cash, $3,160 (Sales Commissions).

  h. Received and paid bill for utilities, $148.

  i. Paid bill for advertising recorded previously, $382.

  j. Paid automobile expenses, $256 (Automobile Expense).

  k. Bryan withdrew cash for personal use, $1,030.

Instructions

1. In the equation, complete the asset section and list the owner's name beside the term *Capital*.
2. Record the transactions and the balance after each transaction. Identify the account affected when the transaction involves revenue, expenses, or a drawing.
3. Prepare an income statement and a statement of owner's equity for June and a balance sheet as of June 30. List expenses in the order that they appear in the Expenses column. List Rent Expense first.

L.O. 1,2,3,4 **Problem 2-2B** A. P. Karas, Attorney at Law, opened her office on September 1. The account headings are presented below. Transactions completed during the month follow.

Assets	= Liabilities +	Owner's Equity
Cash + Supp. + Ppd. + Office + Library Ins. Equip.	Accounts Payable	A. P. Karas, + Revenue − Expenses Capital

a. Deposited $21,000 in a bank account in the name of the business, A. P. Karas, Attorney at Law.
b. Bought office equipment on account from Morgan Company, $14,700.
c. Invested in a professional library costing $5,700. (Increase the account for Library and the account of A. P. Karas, Capital, and include in the statement of owner's equity as Additional Investment, as shown on page 36.)
d. Paid office rent for the month, $760.
e. Bought office supplies for cash, $885.
f. Paid the premium for a two-year insurance policy on the equipment and the library, $186.
g. Received professional fees for services rendered, $2,460 (Professional Fees).
h. Received and paid bill for telephone service, $228 (Telephone Expense).
i. Paid salary of part-time receptionist, $960.
j. Paid automobile expense, $288 (Automobile Expense).
k. Received professional fees for services rendered, $2,120.
l. Paid Morgan Company part payment on amount owed for the purchase of office equipment recorded earlier, $1,500.
m. Karas withdrew cash for personal use, $2,075.

Instructions

1. In the equation, complete the asset section and list the owner's name beside the term *Capital*.
2. Record the transactions and the balances after each transaction. Identify the account affected when the transaction involves revenue, expenses, or a drawing.
3. Prepare an income statement and a statement of owner's equity for September and a balance sheet as of September 30. List expenses in the order that they appear in the Expenses column. List Rent Expense first.

L.O. 2,3 **Problem 2-3B** Nash and Associates hires an accountant, who determines the following account balances, listed in random order, as of October 31 of this year:

Cash	$ 5,292	Supplies	$ 348
Wages Expense	6,200	Advertising Expense	345
Professional Fees	11,750	Accounts Payable	4,272
Accounts Receivable	2,163	B. R. Nash, Drawing	3,400
Rent Expense	1,650	Equipment	10,748
B. R. Nash, Capital, Oct. 1	14,460	Miscellaneous Expense	336

Instructions

Prepare an income statement and a statement of owner's equity for October and a balance sheet as of October 31. List expenses in the order that they appear above.

L.O. 1,2,3   **Problem 2-4B**   N. R. Cooke started Cooke's Spray Service on April 1 of this year. The account headings are presented below. During April, Cooke completed the transactions that follow.

Assets						= Liabilities +	Owner's Equity		
Cash +	Accts. Rec.	+ Supp.	+ Ppd. Ins.	+ Truck	+ Equip.	Accounts Payable	N. R. Cooke, Capital	+ Revenue	− Expenses

a. Invested cash in the business, $6,000.
b. Bought a truck from Domke Motors for $11,250, paying $1,200 in cash, with the remainder due in thirty days.
c. Bought equipment on account from Fancher Company, $1,800.
d. Paid rent for the month, $260.
e. Paid cash for insurance on truck for the year, $576.
f. Cash receipts for the first half of the month from cash customers, $2,175 (Income from Services).
g. Bought supplies for cash, $573.
h. Billed customers on account for services performed, $444.
i. Paid cash for utilities, $96.
j. Received bill for gas and oil used for the truck during the current month, $327 (Gas and Oil Expense).
k. Receipts for remainder of the month from cash customers, $1,642.
l. Cooke withdrew cash for personal use, $1,050.
m. Paid wages to employees, $2,040.

Instructions

1. List the owner's name beside the term *Capital* in the equation.
2. Record the transactions and the balances after each transaction. Identify the account affected when the transaction involves revenue, expenses, or a drawing.
3. Prepare an income statement and a statement of owner's equity for April and a balance sheet as of April 30. List expenses in the order that they appear in the Expenses column. Begin with Rent Expense.

3

Recording Business Transactions in T Account Form; The Trial Balance

LEARNING OBJECTIVES

After you have completed this chapter, you will be able to do the following:

1. Determine balances of T accounts having entries recorded on both sides of the accounts.

2. Record a group of business transactions for a service business directly in T accounts involving changes in assets, liabilities, owner's equity, revenue, and expense accounts.

3. Present the fundamental accounting equation with the T account forms, the plus and minus signs, and the debit and credit sides labeled.

4. Prepare a trial balance.

Up to now we have discussed the fundamental accounting equation in two places. In Chapter 1 we described it as *Assets = Liabilities + Owner's Equity*. In Chapter 2 we introduced the recording of transactions involving two new classifications of accounts: *Revenue* and *Expenses*. With the addition of Revenue and Expenses, the fundamental accounting equation was brought up to its full size of five account classifications. There are only five; so, as far as you go in accounting—whether you are dealing with a small one-owner business or a large corporation—there will be only these five major classifications of accounts.

In this chapter we shall record in T account form the same transactions we used in Chapters 1 and 2, and we shall prove the equality of both sides of the fundamental accounting equation. We will do this by means of a trial balance, which we will discuss later in this chapter.

THE T ACCOUNT FORM

In Chapters 1 and 2, we recorded business transactions in a column arrangement. For example, the Cash account column in the books of Paul's

Auto Body is shown below.

Cash Account Column

Transaction	**(a)**	+32,000
Transaction	**(b)**	−18,000
Balance		14,000
Transaction	**(d)**	−1,000
Balance		13,000
Transaction	**(f)**	+600
Balance		13,600
Transaction	**(g)**	−400
Balance		13,200
Transaction	**(h)**	−240
Balance		12,960
Transaction	**(i)**	−320
Balance		12,640
Transaction	**(j)**	+760
Balance		13,400
Transaction	**(l)**	−1,800
Balance		11,600
Transaction	**(m)**	−220
Balance		11,380
Transaction	**(n)**	−180
Balance		11,200
Transaction	**(o)**	+830
Balance		12,030
Transaction	**(q)**	−390
Balance		11,640
Transaction	**(r)**	−140
Balance		11,500
Transaction	**(s)**	+960
Balance		12,460
Transaction	**(t)**	+60
Balance		12,520
Transaction	**(u)**	−1,000
Balance		11,520

Cash

+		−	
(a)	32,000	**(b)**	18,000
(f)	600	**(d)**	1,000
(j)	760	**(g)**	400
(o)	830	**(h)**	240
(s)	960	**(i)**	320
(t)	60	**(l)**	1,800
	35,210	**(m)**	220
		(n)	180
		(q)	390
		(r)	140
		(u)	1,000

Footings ———————————→ 23,690

Balance → 11,520

As an introduction to the recording of transactions, the column arrangement has the following advantages:

1. In the process of analyzing the transaction, you
   a. Recognize the need to determine which accounts are involved.

b. Determine the classification of the accounts involved.

c. Decide whether the transaction results in an increase or a decrease in each of these accounts.

2. You further realize that after each transaction has been recorded, the balance of each account, when combined with the balances of other accounts, proves the equality of the two sides of the fundamental accounting equation. In other words, the total of one side of the accounting equation equals the total of the other side.

Now, instead of recording transactions in a column for each account, we will use a **T account form** for each account. *The T account form has the advantage of providing two sides for each account; one side is used to record increases in the account, while the other side is used to record decreases.* The T account form also takes up less space.

Compare the transactions of Paul's Auto Body involving cash as they were recorded in Chapters 1 and 2 in one column with the same transactions recorded in T account form. (See pages 11 and 31 for a summary of the transactions.)

Objective 1

Determine balances of T accounts having entries recorded on both sides of the accounts.

After we record a group of transactions in an account, we add both sides and record the totals in small pencil-written figures called **footings**. (We use pencil because these footings are temporary.) Next, we subtract one footing from the other to determine the balance of the account. For the account shown above, the balance is $11,520 ($35,210 − $23,690).

We now record the balance on the side of the account having the larger footing, which, with a few minor exceptions, is the plus (+) side. The plus side of a T account is the side that represents the **normal balance** of the account. The normal balance may, however, fall on either the left or the right side of an account. For example, we presented the T account for Cash. Cash is classified as an asset, and all *assets* are

+	−
Left	Right

However, as we will show in the development of the fundamental accounting equation, **not all classifications of accounts have the increase side on the left.** Let us proceed.

Each classification of accounts uses a consistent placement of the plus and minus signs. For example, the T accounts for *all* assets are

Assets

+	−
Left	Right

In Chapter 2 we placed revenue and expenses under the "umbrella" of owner's equity. Revenue increases owner's equity, and expenses decrease owner's equity. The T accounts are shown at the top of the next page.

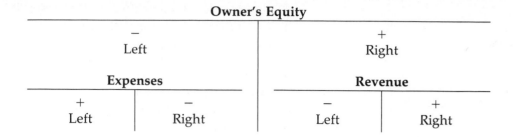

Increases in owner's equity are recorded on the right side. Since revenue increases owner's equity, additional revenue is recorded on the right side of the account.

Decreases in owner's equity are recorded on the left side. Since expenses decrease owner's equity, additional expenses are recorded on the left side of the account.

In Chapter 2, using the five classifications of accounts, we stated the fundamental accounting equation like this:

Assets = Liabilities +   Owner's Equity
                        Capital + Revenue − Expenses

Because revenue and expenses appear separately in the income statement, we will stretch out the equation to include them as separate headings, like this:

Assets = Liabilities + Owner's Equity + Revenue − Expenses

We can now restate the equation with the T forms and plus and minus signs for each account classification:

Assets		=	Liabilities		+	Owner's Equity		+	Revenue		−	Expenses	
+	−		−	+		−	+		−	+		+	−
Left	Right		Left	Right		Left	Right		Left	Right		Left	Right

Before we go on, let us stress and point out the increase or plus sides of each account classification. You can recognize these in the accounting equation having T accounts.

Assets   The *left* side is the *increase* side.
Liabilities   The *right* side is the *increase* side.
Owner's Equity (Capital)   The *right* side is the *increase* side.
Revenue   The *right* side is the *increase* side.
Expenses   The *left* side is the *increase* side.

Since revenue is an addition to owner's equity, the placement of the plus and minus signs is the same as in owner's equity. On the other hand, since expenses are treated as deductions from owner's equity, the placement of the plus and minus signs is reversed. We shall use this form of the fundamental accounting equation throughout the remainder of the text.

Your accounting background up to this point has taught you to analyze business transactions in order to determine which accounts are involved and to recognize that the amounts should be recorded as either an increase or a decrease in the accounts. Now, the recording process becomes a simple matter of knowing which side of the T accounts should be used to record increases and which side to record decreases. **Generally, you will not be using the minus side of the revenue and expense accounts, since transactions involving revenue and expense accounts usually result in increases in these accounts.**

Objective 2

Record a group of business transactions for a service business directly in T accounts involving changes in assets, liabilities, owner's equity, revenue, and expense accounts.

RECORDING TRANSACTIONS IN T ACCOUNT FORM

Our task now is to learn how to record business transactions in the T account form. To bring about this transition, let's use the transactions of Paul's Auto Body again; we are familiar with them and can readily recognize the increases or decreases in the accounts involved.

There are only five classifications of accounts. These classifications are contained in the fundamental accounting equation:

Assets		=	Liabilities		+	Owner's Equity		+	Revenue		−	Expenses	
+	−		−	+		−	+		−	+		+	−
Left	Right		Left	Right		Left	Right		Left	Right		Left	Right

The fundamental accounting equation with T accounts for Paul's Auto Body is presented at the top of page 52. We have given specific account titles for revenue and expense accounts as stated in the company's chart of accounts. This is necessary because we will need to list each account separately in the income statement. Also, the order of presentation of the asset accounts has been changed, so that their sequence is now consistent with the chart of accounts shown on page 22.

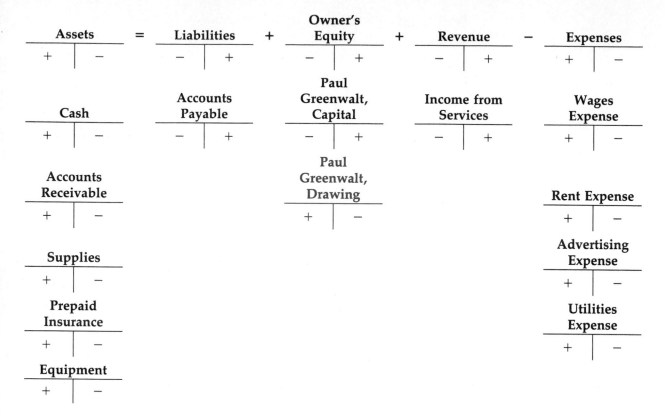

To stress the Drawing account, which can cause some confusion, we have printed it in color. One might think of the relationship between Drawing and Capital like this: Amounts put into the business are recorded as increases, and amounts taken out of the business are recorded as decreases:

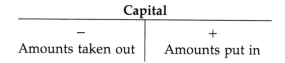

Capital	
−	+
Amounts taken out	Amounts put in

We would like to reserve the minus side of the Capital account for permanent withdrawals, either because the owner intends to reduce the size of the business permanently or because a net loss forces this reduction. However, as we said earlier, amounts taken out for the owner's personal use may be considered to be temporary. Because the owner plans to replace these withdrawals with the net income earned by the firm, it is much more convenient to use a separate account to record these withdrawals. Therefore, withdrawals by the owner will be listed on the plus side of Drawing. This concept can be illustrated by showing the Drawing T account under the umbrella or wing of the Capital account on the top of the next page.

Capital

−	+

Drawing

+	−

Decreases in Capital are recorded on the left side. Since Drawing decreases Capital, additional Drawing is recorded on the left side of the account.

Drawing is placed under the heading of owner's equity because it appears in the statement of owner's equity. As you will recall, in the statement of owner's equity, we list beginning capital, plus net income, minus withdrawals. When we want to treat one account as a deduction from another, we reverse the plus and minus signs.

Transaction (a) Paul Greenwalt invests $32,000 cash in his new business. This transaction results in an increase in Cash and an increase in the Capital account, affecting the T accounts shown below:

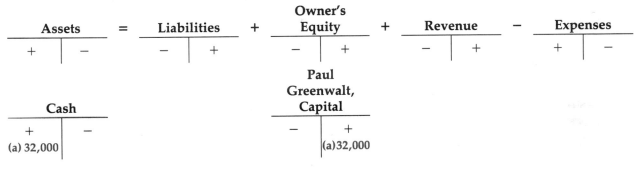

Transaction (b) Paul's Auto Body buys $18,000 worth of equipment, paying cash. This transaction results in an increase in Equipment and a decrease in Cash.

Assets	=	Liabilities	+	Owner's Equity	+	Revenue	−	Expenses
+ −		− +		− +		− +		+ −

Cash

+	−
	(b)18,000

Equipment

+	−
(b)18,000	

Assets =

Assets

+	−

Cash

+	−
(f) 600	

Assets =

Assets

+	−

Cash

+	−
	(g) 400

LE

In r
one
side
emp
Pau

Tra
(lef

(a)

Tr
pay

(b)

Tr
Os
sic

(c)

ou
in
of
ri

T
th
of

(a
(f
(j
(o
(s
(t

Bal.

(p
Bal.

(e)

(i)

(b)
(c)
(r)
Bal.

Obj

Pre

Account Titles	Trial Balance	
	Left or Debit Balances	Right or Credit Balances
	Assets	
		Liabilities
		Capital
	Drawing	
		Revenue
	Expenses	
Totals	XXXX XX	XXXX XX

Errors Exposed by the Trial Balance

If the debit and credit columns are not equal, then it is evident that we have made an error. Possible causes of errors include the following:

- Making errors in arithmetic, such as errors in adding the trial balance columns or in finding the balances of the accounts.
- Recording only half an entry, such as a debit without a corresponding credit, or vice versa.
- Recording both halves of the entry on the same side, such as two debits, rather than a debit and a credit.
- Recording one or more amounts incorrectly.

Procedure for Locating Errors

Suppose that you are in a business situation in which you have recorded transactions for a month in the account books, and the accounts do not balance. To save yourself time, you need to have a definite procedure for tracking down the errors. The best method is to do everything in reverse, as follows:

- Re-add the trial balance columns.
- Check the transferring of the figures from the accounts to the trial balance.
- Verify the footings and balances of the accounts.

As an added precaution, form the habit of verifying all addition and subtraction as you go along. You can thus correct many mistakes *before* the time comes to make up a trial balance.

When the trial balance totals do not balance, the difference might indicate you forgot to record half of an entry in the accounts. For example, if the difference in the trial balance totals is $20, you may have recorded $20 on the debit side of one account without recording $20 on the credit side of another account. Another possibility is to divide the difference by 2; this may provide a clue that you accidentally recorded half an entry twice. For example, if the difference in the trial balance is $600, you may have recorded $300 on the debit side of one account and an additional $300 on the debit side of another account. Look for a transaction that involved $300 and then see if you have recorded both a debit and a credit. By knowing which transactions to check, you can save a lot of time.

Transpositions and Slides

If the difference is evenly divisible by 9, the discrepancy may be either a **transposition** or a **slide.** A transposition means that the digits have been transposed, or switched around. For example, one transposition of digits in 916 can be written as 619:

$$
\begin{array}{r}
916 \\
- \ 619 \\
\hline
297
\end{array}
\qquad
\begin{array}{r}
33 \\
\hline
9\overline{)297}
\end{array}
$$

A slide is an error in placing the decimal point, in other words, a slide in the decimal point. For example, $163 could be inadvertently written as $1.63:

$$
\begin{array}{r}
\$163.00 \\
- \quad 1.63 \\
\hline
\$161.37
\end{array}
\qquad
\begin{array}{r}
17.93 \\
\hline
9\overline{)161.37}
\end{array}
$$

Or the error may be a combination of transposition and slide, such as when $216 is written as $6.21:

$$
\begin{array}{r}
\$216.00 \\
- \quad 6.21 \\
\hline
\$209.79
\end{array}
\qquad
\begin{array}{r}
23.31 \\
\hline
9\overline{)209.79}
\end{array}
$$

Again, the difference is evenly divisible by 9.

SUMMARY

L.O. 1,2,3   There are only five classifications of accounts. These classifications are embodied in the fundamental accounting equation:

Assets		=	Liabilities		+	Owner's Equity		+	Revenue		−	Expenses	
+	−		−	+		−	+		−	+		+	−
Left	Right		Left	Right		Left	Right		Left	Right		Left	Right
Debit	Credit		Debit	Credit		Debit	Credit		Debit	Credit		Debit	Credit

CMPUTERS AT WORK

Parts of a Computer

Computer systems are made up of software, hardware, and people. Software consists of the programs that provide a set of instructions for the computer to follow. Hardware is the physical equipment in the system. Hardware and software work together to provide useful information to people and organizations.

Computer hardware cannot work without **software,** which provides instructions to the hardware and to the operator. A wide variety of programs are available for such applications as general ledger, accounts payable, accounts receivable, inventory, and payroll as well as for word processing, manufacturing, and design applications. Well-designed software helps prevent operator mistakes, provides useful information at a reasonable cost, and can even help prevent fraud.

Hardware consists of input devices, the central processing unit (CPU), and output devices. *Input devices* give instructions and data to the computer system. *Input media* include disks, card and tape readers, magnetic tapes, optical scanners, magnetic ink readers, audio units, numeric pads, light pens, mice, and keyboards.

The second hardware element is the *CPU.* The *control unit* interprets instructions from a program, an *arithmetic-logic unit* performs calculations and executes instructions, and a *memory section* stores data. Read Only Memory (ROM) stores programs built into the computer by the manufacturer. Random Access Memory (RAM) allows the computer to receive information and store it efficiently. Memory is measured in kilobytes. One kilobyte stores 1,024 characters.

Output devices provide permanent or temporary storage of data and display results to people or to other machines. External storage is much less expensive than memory. Hard or floppy disks, printers, card punches, and monitors are all output devices. A disk system is very flexible. Floppy disks are easily stored and moved from one machine to another; hard disks store more information and provide faster access but are usually installed in the machine itself. A floppy disk looks like a small phonograph record with a cover. Computers can quickly access data from anywhere on the disk. A tape must run in sequence, and it may take several minutes to locate specific data on a tape. Tape storage is often used for records that are infrequently accessed, records that are always run in order, or for backup.

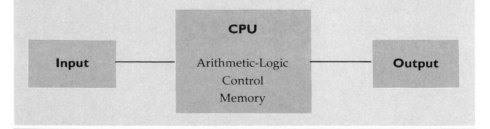

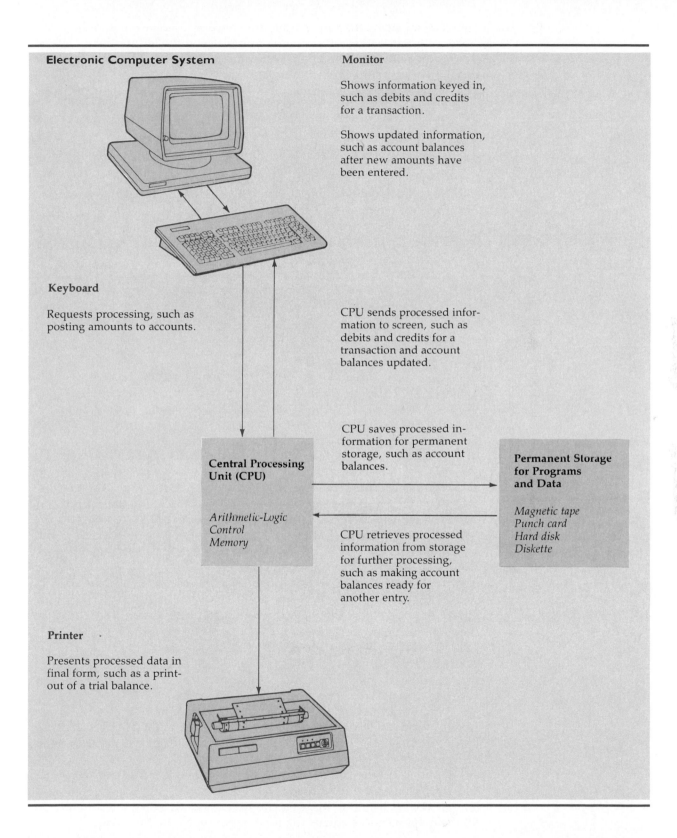

Electronic Computer System

Monitor

Shows information keyed in, such as debits and credits for a transaction.

Shows updated information, such as account balances after new amounts have been entered.

Keyboard

Requests processing, such as posting amounts to accounts.

CPU sends processed information to screen, such as debits and credits for a transaction and account balances updated.

CPU saves processed information for permanent storage, such as account balances.

Central Processing Unit (CPU)

Arithmetic-Logic
Control
Memory

Permanent Storage for Programs and Data

Magnetic tape
Punch card
Hard disk
Diskette

CPU retrieves processed information from storage for further processing, such as making account balances ready for another entry.

Printer

Presents processed data in final form, such as a printout of a trial balance.

Let us again stress the most important concept in accounting. When you are recording transactions, the amount you place on the left, or debit, side of an account (or accounts) must equal the amount you place on the right, or credit, side of another account (or accounts).

The process of analyzing a business transaction can be boiled down to these questions:

1. What accounts are affected?
2. Where do the accounts belong in the fundamental accounting equation?
3. Are the accounts increased or decreased?
4. Which account is debited and which account is credited?
5. Do total debits equal total credits?

L.O. 4   At the end of the month, to prove the equality of debit and credit balances, prepare a trial balance.

Accounting may be considered as a game of accounts and balances. If you know the rules and make the right moves, you can win the game. The rules are the fundamentals, and they are based on logical assumptions. The consequences of a move follow you throughout the game. Take it as a challenge! As a starter, concentrate on mastering the fundamentals.

GLOSSARY

Compound entry   A transaction that requires more than one debit or more than one credit to be recorded.

Credit   The right side of a T account; to credit is to record an amount on the right side of a T account. Credits represent increases in liability, capital, and revenue accounts and decreases in asset, drawing, and expense accounts.

Debit   The left side of a T account; to debit is to record an amount on the left side of a T account. Debits represent increases in asset, drawing, and expense accounts and decreases in liability, capital, and revenue accounts.

Footings   The totals of each side of a T account, recorded in small pencil-written figures.

Ledger   A book, a loose-leaf binder, or a whole filing system containing all the accounts of an enterprise.

Normal balance   The plus side of a T account.

Separate entity concept   A business is treated as being a separate economic or accounting entity. The business is independent or stands by itself; it is separate from its owners, creditors, and customers.

Slide   An error in placing the decimal point of a number.

T account form   A form of account shaped like the letter T; one side is for entries on the debit, or left, side, and one side is for entries on the credit, or right, side.

Transposition   An error that involves interchanging, or switching around, the digits during the recording of a number.

Trial balance   A list of all ledger account balances to prove that the total of all the debit balances equals the total of all the credit balances.

QUESTIONS, EXERCISES, AND PROBLEMS
Discussion Questions

1. What is meant by the separate entity concept?
2. What is the purpose of a trial balance?
3. Does the term *debit* always mean increase? Does the term *credit* always mean decrease? Explain.
4. Give an example of (a) a transposition and (b) a slide.
5. Regarding the five classifications of accounts, indicate the normal balance (whether debit or credit) of each account classification.
6. What is the reason for using a separate owner's drawing account?
7. What is a compound entry?
8. C. Sturgis runs a painting contracting business and keeps his own books. Upon taking a trial balance, Sturgis finds that total debits amount to $106,800 and total credits amount to $107,600. What are some possible reasons for the $800 difference between debit and credit totals?

Exercises

L.O. 3 **Exercise 3-1**   Answer by adding the word *debit* or the word *credit*.

a. The Professional Fees account is increased by entering a _credit_.
b. The Wages Expense account is increased by entering a _debit_.
c. The Accounts Payable account is decreased by entering a _credit_.
d. The Capital account is increased by entering a _credit_.
e. The Accounts Receivable account is decreased by entering a _debit_.
f. The Supplies account is decreased by entering a _debit_.
g. The Drawing account is increased by entering a _debit_.

L.O. 1,3 **Exercise 3-2**   On a sheet of paper set up the fundamental accounting equation with T accounts under each of the five account classifications, noting plus and minus signs on the appropriate sides of each account. Under each of the five classifications, set up T accounts—again with the correct plus and minus signs—for each of the following accounts of the Super Car Wash: Cash; Accounts Receivable; Supplies; Truck; Equipment; Accounts Payable; C. Rice, Capital; C. Rice, Drawing; Cleaning Income; Rent Expense; Gas and Oil Expense; Wages Expense; Utilities Expense; Miscellaneous Expense. In addition, use the abbreviations DR and CR to identify the debit and credit sides of each T account.

L.O. 1 **Exercise 3-3**   N. R. Robins operates Robins Carpet Cleaners. The company has the following chart of accounts:

Assets
Cash
Accounts Receivable
Supplies
Prepaid Insurance
Cleaning Equipment
Truck
Office Equipment

Liabilities
Accounts Payable

Owner's Equity
N. R. Robins, Capital
N. R. Robins, Drawing

Revenue
Income from Services

Expenses
Wages Expense
Truck Expense
Utilities Expense
Advertising Expense

On a sheet of ordinary notebook paper, record the following transactions directly in pairs of T accounts, presenting the T account with the debit on the left. Show plus and minus signs. (*Example:* Received and paid telephone bill, $18.)

Utilities Expense		Cash	
+	−	+	−
18			18

a. Received premium bill and paid liability insurance premium, $440.
b. Received and paid bill for advertising, $72.
c. Robins withdrew cash for personal use, $192.
d. Paid creditors on account, $570.
e. Received $882 from charge customers to apply on account.
f. Received and paid electric bill, $38.
g. Received and paid gasoline bill for truck, $216.
h. Bought supplies on account, $93.
i. Charged customers for services rendered, $216.
j. Returned defective supplies previously bought on account, $27.

L.O. 1   **Exercise 3-4**   During the first month of operation, Dillard's Welding recorded the following transactions. Describe transactions **a** through **k.**

Cash				Accounts Payable		F. M. Dillard, Capital		Income from Services		Rent Expense	
(a)	2,600	(c)	63	(b)	290	(a)	2,600	(h)	795	(e)	320
(k)	840	(e)	320	(g)	900	(d)	3,800	(k)	840		
		(f)	70								
		(g)	1,000							Utilities Expense	
		(i)	200			F. M. Dillard, Drawing				(j)	71
		(j)	71			(i)	200				

Accounts Receivable		Advertising Expense	
(h)	795	(c)	63

Welding Supplies		Miscellaneous Expense	
(b)	290	(f)	70

Welding Equipment	
(d)	3,800
(g)	1,900

L.O. 4   **Exercise 3-5**   From the accounts in Exercise 3-4, prepare a trial balance for Dillard's Welding, dated September 30 of this year.

L.O. 4 **Exercise 3-6** Which of the following errors would cause a trial balance to have unequal totals? Explain your answers.

a. A payment of $75 to a creditor was recorded as a debit to Accounts Payable for $75 and a credit to Cash for $57.
b. A payment of $100 to a creditor was debited to Accounts Receivable and credited to Cash for $100 each.
c. A purchase of office supplies for $280 was recorded as a debit to Office Supplies for $28 and a credit to Cash for $28.
d. A purchase of equipment for $300 was recorded as a debit to Supplies for $300 and a credit to Cash for $300.

L.O. 4 **Exercise 3-7** Perfect Hair Design hired a new bookkeeper who is not entirely familiar with the process for preparing a trial balance. All the accounts have normal balances. Find the errors and prepare a corrected trial balance for September 30 of this year.

Perfect Hair Design
Trial Balance
September 30, 19–

ACCOUNT NAME	DEBIT	CREDIT
Accounts Payable	11 4 0 0 00	
Accounts Receivable	16 2 0 0 00	
Cash	2 2 0 0 00	
R. Davis, Capital		42 2 0 0 00
R. Davis, Drawing		1 2 0 0 00
Equipment	40 0 0 0 00	
Income from Services	44 0 0 0 00	
Prepaid Insurance		6 0 0 00
Rent Expense		4 2 0 0 00
Supplies	6 4 0 0 00	
Utilities Expense	2 2 0 0 00	
Wages Expense	24 6 0 0 00	
	147 0 0 0 00	48 2 0 0 00

L.O. 4 **Exercise 3-8** Assume that a trial balance has been prepared and that the total of the debit balances is not equal to the total of the credit balances. On a sheet of paper, set up like the example on the next page, note the amount by which the two totals would differ. Identify which column is understated or overstated.

Error	Amount of Difference	Debit or Credit Column Understated or Overstated
Example: A $142 debit to Prepaid Insurance was not recorded.	$142	Debit column understated
a. A $47 credit to Cash was not recorded.		
b. A $420 debit to Supplies was recorded twice.		
c. A $34 debit to Equipment was recorded as $340.		
d. A $36 debit to Supplies was recorded as a $36 debit to Miscellaneous Expense.		
e. A $91 debit to Accounts Payable was recorded twice.		
f. A $48 debit to Accounts Receivable was recorded as $84.		

Problem Set A

L.O. 3   **Problem 3-1A**   During November of this year, D. A. Pomeroy established Pomeroy's Bakery. The following asset, liability, and owner's equity accounts are included in the chart of accounts: Cash; Bakery Supplies; Baking Equipment; Office Equipment; Truck; Accounts Payable; D. A. Pomeroy, Capital. During November, the following transactions occurred:

a. Pomeroy invested $24,200 in the business.
b. Bought used ovens for $5,264, paying cash.
c. Bought pans and other supplies for cash, $521.
d. Bought sugar, flour, and other supplies from Culinary Supply Company, with payment due in thirty days, $943.
e. Bought a typewriter, desk, and filing cabinet for cash, $612.
f. Bought a delivery truck for $9,200 from Ronson Automotive, paying $950 down; the balance is due in thirty days.
g. Paid $240 on account to Culinary Supply Company.

Instructions

1. Label the account titles under the appropriate headings in the fundamental accounting equation.
2. Correctly place the plus and minus signs under each T account, and label the debit and credit sides of the T account.
3. Record the amounts in the proper positions in the T accounts. Key each entry to the alphabetical symbol identifying each transaction.

L.O. 1,2,3,4   **Problem 3-2A**   R. C. Pryor established Pryor's Secretarial Service during October of this year. The accountant prepared the following chart of accounts.

Assets
Cash
Supplies
Computer Programs
Office Equipment
Neon Sign

Liabilities
Accounts Payable

Owner's Equity
R. C. Pryor, Capital
R. C. Pryor, Drawing

Revenue
Income from Services

Expenses
Rent Expense
Utilities Expense
Wages Expense
Advertising Expense
Miscellaneous Expense

The following transactions occurred during the month:

a. Pryor invested $12,900 cash to establish the business.
b. Paid rent for the month, $545.
c. Bought office desks and filing cabinets for cash, $1,262.
d. Bought a computer and printer for use in the business from Pollard Computer Center for $12,400; paid $2,500 down, with the balance due in thirty days (Office Equipment).
e. Bought a neon sign for $625; paid $300 down, with the balance due in thirty days.
f. Pryor invested in the business her personal computer programs with a fair market value of $1,410.
g. Received bill for advertising from *City News and Views*, $89.
h. Received cash for services rendered, $614.
i. Received and paid electric bill, $147.
j. Paid bill for advertising, recorded previously in transaction **g.**
k. Received cash for services rendered, $1,092.
l. Paid wages to employees, $610.
m. Received and paid for city business license, $32.
n. Pryor withdrew cash for personal use, $450.
o. Bought print-out paper and stationery from Lowery, Inc., with payment due in thirty days, $114.

Instructions

1. Record the owner's name in the Capital and Drawing T accounts.
2. Record the plus and minus signs under each T account, and label the debit and credit sides of the T accounts.
3. Record the transactions in the T accounts. Key each entry to the alphabetical symbol identifying each transaction.
4. Foot the T accounts and show balances.
5. Prepare a trial balance with a three-line heading, dated October 31.

L.O. 1,2,3,4   **Problem 3-3A**   A. C. Kent, an optometrist, opens an office for the practice of optometry, A. C. Kent, O.D. Her accountant recommends the chart of accounts shown at the top of the next page.

Assets
Cash
Accounts Receivable
Office Equipment
Office Furniture
Professional Equipment

Liabilities
Accounts Payable

Owner's Equity
A. C. Kent, Capital
A. C. Kent, Drawing

Revenue
Professional Fees

Expenses
Salary Expense
Rent Expense
Utilities Expense
Miscellaneous Expense

The following transactions occurred during May of this year:

a. Kent invested $12,000 cash in her professional enterprise.
b. Bought a typewriter for $495 from Mid-City Office Machines, paying $250 down; the balance is due in thirty days.
c. Kent invested in the enterprise her personal professional equipment with a fair market value of $8,200 (additional investment).
d. Bought waiting room chairs and carpets (Office Furniture), paying cash, $1,516.
e. Bought an intercom system on account from Roark Office Supply (Office Equipment), $318.
f. Received and paid telephone bill, $92.
g. Billed patients for professional services performed, $1,314.
h. Received and paid electric bill for heat and lights, $87.
i. Paid expenses for trip to State Optometric Convention, $172.
j. Bought a copy machine on account from Roark Office Supply, $547.
k. Billed patients for additional professional services, $1,963.
l. Paid office rent for the month, $520.
m. Paid salary of receptionist, $750.
n. Kent withdrew cash for her personal use, $900.
o. Received $119 on account from patients who were billed previously.

Instructions

1. Record the owner's name in the Capital and Drawing T accounts.
2. Correctly place plus and minus signs under each T account, and label the debit and credit sides of the T accounts.
3. Record the transactions in the T accounts. Key each entry to the alphabetical symbol identifying each transaction.
4. Foot the T accounts and show balances.
5. Prepare a trial balance as of May 31, 19–.
6. Prepare an income statement for May.
7. Prepare a statement of owner's equity for May.
8. Prepare a balance sheet as of May 31, 19–.

L.O. 1,2,4   **Problem 3-4A**   On April 1, B. P. Greer opened a coin-operated laundry under the name Greer's Self-Service Laundry. Greer's accountant listed the following account titles for the chart of accounts: Cash; Supplies; Prepaid Insurance; Equipment; Furniture and Fixtures; Accounts Payable; B. P. Greer,

Capital; B. P. Greer, Drawing; Laundry Revenue; Wages Expense; Rent Expense; Power Expense; Miscellaneous Expense. During April the following transactions were completed:

a. Greer deposited $16,420 in a bank account in the name of the business.
b. Bought chairs and tables for cash, $324.
c. Bought laundry detergent on account from Evenson Supply Company, $311.
d. Paid rent for the month, $770.
e. Bought washing machines and dryers from Eakin Equipment Company, $15,500; paid $2,700 down, with the remainder due in thirty days.
f. Received $1,340 from cash customers for the first half of the month.
g. Paid $240 cash for a liability insurance policy for twelve months.
h. Paid $260 as a part payment on account for the equipment purchased from Eakin Equipment Company.
i. Received and paid electric bill, $163.
j. Received $516 from cash customers for the second half of the month.
k. Paid wages to employees, $1,020.
l. Greer withdrew cash for his personal use, $850.
m. Paid $245 on account for the washing supplies acquired in transaction **c**.
n. Received bill for advertising in *The Neighborhood News*, $66.

Instructions

1. Record the owner's name in the Capital and Drawing T accounts.
2. Correctly place the plus and minus signs under each T account, and label the debit and credit sides of the T accounts.
3. Record the transactions in the T accounts. Key each entry to the alphabetical symbol identifying each transaction.
4. Foot the T accounts and show balances.
5. Prepare a trial balance as of April 30, 19–.
6. Prepare an income statement for April.
7. Prepare a statement of owner's equity for April.
8. Prepare a balance sheet as of April 30, 19–.

Problem Set B

L.O. 3 **Problem 3-1B**   During January of this year, C. P. Lincoln established the Lincoln Shoe Repair. The following asset, liability, and owner's equity accounts are included in the chart of accounts: Cash; Supplies; Shop Equipment; Store Equipment; Office Equipment; Accounts Payable; C. P. Lincoln, Capital. The following transactions occurred during the month of January:

a. Lincoln invested $19,000 cash in the business.
b. Bought shop equipment for cash, $1,621.
c. Bought leather, heels, glue, and incidental supplies from Lester and Company, $524; payment is due in thirty days.
d. Bought store fixtures for $917 from Jordan Hardware; payment is due in thirty days.
e. Bought a typewriter and calculator for $526 from Regal Office Supply, paying $300 down; the balance is due in thirty days.

   f.   Paid $350 on account for the store fixtures in transaction **d.**

   g. Lincoln invested in the business his personal tools with a fair market value of $256.

Instructions

1. Label the account titles under the appropriate headings in the fundamental accounting equation.
2. Correctly place the plus and minus signs under each T account, and label the debit and credit sides of the T account.
3. Record the amounts in the proper positions in the T accounts. Key each entry to the alphabetical symbol identifying each transaction.

L.O. 1,2,3,4   **Problem 3-2B**   K. T. Pittman established the Pittman Secretarial Service during May of this year. The accountant prepared the following chart of accounts:

Assets
Cash
Supplies
Computer Programs
Office Equipment
Neon Sign

Liabilities
Accounts Payable

Owner's Equity
K. T. Pittman, Capital
K. T. Pittman, Drawing

Revenue
Income from Services

Expenses
Rent Expense
Utilities Expense
Wages Expense
Advertising Expense
Miscellaneous Expense

The following transactions occurred during the month:

a. Pittman invested $12,700 cash to establish the business.
b. Bought an office desk and filing cabinet for cash, $515.
c. Bought computer programs for use in the business from Temco Computer Center for $8,900, paying $1,500 down; the balance is due in thirty days.
d. Paid rent for the month, $530.
e. Received cash for services rendered, $516.
f. Bought a neon sign for $914 from Lang Sign Company, with $200 as a down payment; the balance is due in thirty days.
g. Received bill for advertising, $323, from *The Daily Chronicle*.
h. Bought print-out paper and stationery from Hanson and Bacon, $229, with payment due in thirty days.
i. Received and paid electric bill, $124.
j. Paid bill for advertising recorded previously in transaction **g.**
k. Received cash for services rendered, $1,090.
l. Paid wages to employee, $540.
m. Pittman invested in the business his personal computer programs with a fair market value of $762.
n. Pittman withdrew cash for personal use, $450.
o. Received and paid for city business license, $36.

Instructions

1. Record the owner's name in the Capital and Drawing T accounts.
2. Correctly place the plus and minus signs under each T account, and label the debit and credit sides of the accounts.
3. Record the transactions in the T accounts. Key each entry to the alphabetical symbol identifying each transaction.
4. Foot the T accounts and show balances.
5. Prepare a trial balance, with a three-line heading, dated May 31.

L.O. 1,2,3,4   **Problem 3-3B**   S. C. Long, a chiropractor, opens Long's Chiropractic Clinic. Her accountant recommends the following chart of accounts:

Assets	**Revenue**
Cash	Professional Fees
Accounts Receivable	**Expenses**
Office Equipment	Salary Expense
Office Furniture	Rent Expense
Professional Equipment	Utilities Expense
Liabilities	Miscellaneous Expense
Accounts Payable	

Owner's Equity
S. C. Long, Capital
S. C. Long, Drawing

The following transactions occurred during June of this year:

a. Long invested $14,000 cash in her professional practice.
b. Bought telephone equipment on account from Ladd Office Supply (Office Equipment), $326.
c. Paid cash for chairs and carpets (Office Furniture) for the waiting room, $462.
d. Bought an electronic typewriter for $540 from Jones Office Machines, paying $140 down; the balance is due in thirty days.
e. Received and paid telephone bill, $99.
f. Billed patients for professional services performed, $1,612.
g. Long invested in the firm her professional equipment with a fair market value of $7,200 (additional investment).
h. Paid $164 in expenses for trip to state chiropractic convention.
i. Received and paid electric bill, $91.
j. Received $690 from patients previously billed in transaction **f.**
k. Paid $160 as part payment on account for the filing cabinets purchased from Ladd Office Supply.
l. Paid office rent for the month, $500.
m. Received $242 from cash patients (not recorded previously).
n. Paid salary of receptionist, $825.
o. Long withdrew cash for personal use, $1,150.

Instructions

1. Record the owner's name in the Capital and Drawing T accounts.
2. Correctly place plus and minus signs under each T account and label the debit and credit sides of the T accounts.

3. Record the transactions in the T accounts. Key each entry to the alphabetical symbol identifying each transaction.
4. Foot the T accounts and show balances.
5. Prepare a trial balance as of June 30, 19–.
6. Prepare an income statement for June.
7. Prepare a statement of owner's equity for June.
8. Prepare a balance sheet as of June 30, 19–.

L.O. 1,2,3,4   **Problem 3-4B**   On October 1, M. A. Dore opened a coin-operated laundry called City Self-Service Laundry. Dore's accountant listed the following accounts in the chart of accounts: Cash; Supplies; Prepaid Insurance; Equipment; Furniture and Fixtures; Accounts Payable; M. A. Dore, Capital; M. A. Dore, Drawing; Laundry Revenue; Wages Expense; Rent Expense; Power Expense; Miscellaneous Expense. During October the following transactions were completed:

a. Dore deposited $19,200 in a bank account in the name of the business.
b. Bought tables and chairs for cash, $296.
c. Paid rent for the month, $695.
d. Bought washers and dryers for $16,300, giving $3,100 cash as a down payment, with the remainder due in thirty days.
e. Bought washing supplies on account from Aiken Distributing Company, $519.
f. Received $796 from cash customers for the first half of the month.
g. Paid $214 for a one-year liability insurance policy.
h. Paid $350 as a partial payment on the equipment purchased in transaction **d.**
i. Received and paid electric bill, $194.
j. Paid $123 on account for the washing supplies acquired in transaction **e.**
k. Received $792 from cash customers for the second half of the month.
l. Paid $42 for license and other miscellaneous expenses.
m. Paid wages to employees, $1,035.
n. Dore withdrew cash for personal use, $950.

Instructions

1. Record the owner's name beside the Capital and Drawing T accounts.
2. Correctly place the plus and minus signs under each T account, and label the debit and credit sides of the T accounts.
3. Record the transactions in the T accounts. Key each entry to the alphabetical symbol identifying each transaction.
4. Foot the T accounts and show balances.
5. Prepare a trial balance as of October 31, 19–.
6. Prepare an income statement for October.
7. Prepare a statement of owner's equity for October.
8. Prepare a balance sheet as of October 31, 19–.

4

The General Journal and the General Ledger

LEARNING OBJECTIVES

After you have completed this chapter, you will be able to do the following:

1. Record a group of transactions pertaining to a service-type enterprise in a two-column general journal.
2. Post entries from a two-column general journal to general ledger accounts.
3. Correct entries using the ruling method.
4. Correct entries using the correcting entry method.

In Chapter 3 we recorded business transactions as debits and credits to T accounts. We introduced T accounts because, in the process of formulating debits and credits for business transactions, it's easiest to visualize the T accounts involved with their plus and minus sides. **Without a doubt, formulating the appropriate transaction debits and credits is the most important element in the accounting process.** It represents the very basic foundation of accounting, and all the superstructure represented by financial statements and other reports is entirely dependent upon it.

Now we need to backtrack slightly to introduce journal entries. Journal entries are our way of formally recording the debits and credits of business transactions.

The initial steps in the accounting process are

1. Record business transactions in a journal.
2. Post entries to accounts in the ledger.
3. Prepare a trial balance.

In this chapter we shall present the general journal and the posting procedure.

THE GENERAL JOURNAL

We have seen that an accountant must keep a written record of each transaction. One could record the transactions directly in T accounts;

however, only part of the transaction would be listed in each T account. A **journal** is a book for recording business transactions as they happen. The journal serves the function of recording both the debits and credits of the entire transaction. This journal is like a diary for the business, in which one records in day-by-day order all the events involving financial affairs. A journal is called a **book of original entry.** In other words, a transaction is always recorded in the journal first and then recorded in the ledger accounts. The process of recording a business transaction in the journal is called **journalizing.** The information about transactions comes from business papers, such as checks, invoices, receipts, letters, and memos. These **source documents** furnish proof that a transaction has taken place, so they should be identified in the journal entry whenever possible. Later we shall introduce a variety of special journals. However, the basic form of journal is the **two-column general journal.** The term *two-column* refers to the two money columns used for debit and credit amounts.

As an example of journalizing business transactions, let's use the transactions for Paul's Auto Body listed in Chapter 3. Each page of the journal is numbered in consecutive order. This is the first page, so we write a 1 in the space for the page number. Also, we must write the date of transaction. Now let's get on with the first entry.

Objective 1

Record a group of transactions pertaining to a service-type enterprise in a two-column general journal.

Transaction (a)   June 1: Paul Greenwalt deposited $32,000 in a bank account in the name of Paul's Auto Body.

We write the year and month in the left part of the Date column. Traditionally, bookkeepers would squeeze the year in small figures just above the month. Today, most businesses keep their journals and ledgers in binders that hold the records for just one year or they keep their records on computers, so there is no need to write the year on the actual accounts. For clarity—and to remind you how important it is to record the exact date of every transaction—we show the year on a separate line in our illustrations of journals and ledgers. We don't have to repeat the year and month until we start a new page, or until the year or month changes. (Our illustrations, however, may repeat the month simply to eliminate confusion.) We write the day of the month in the right part of the date column, and we repeat the day for each journal entry.

	DATE	DESCRIPTION	POST. REF.	DEBIT	CREDIT	
1	*19—*					1
2	*June* *1*					2
3						3

GENERAL JOURNAL   Page number   PAGE ___*1*___

Date {

Since we are familiar with the accounts, the next step is to decide which accounts should be debited and which credited. We do this by first figuring out which accounts are involved and whether they are increased or decreased. We then visualize the accounts mentally with their respective plus and minus sides.

Cash is involved in our example. Cash is considered to be an asset because it falls within the definition of "things owned." Cash is increased, so we debit Cash.

Paul Greenwalt, Capital is involved; this is an owner's equity account because it represents the owner's investment. Paul Greenwalt, Capital is increased, so we credit Paul Greenwalt, Capital. Let's show these entries by reverting back to our reliable fundamental accounting equation with the accompanying T accounts:

Assets	=	Liabilities	+	Owner's Equity	+	Revenue	−	Expenses
+ −		− +		− +		− +		+ −
Debit Credit		Debit Credit		Debit Credit		Debit Credit		Debit Credit

Cash	Paul Greenwalt, Capital
+ −	− +
32,000	32,000

As we said earlier, you perform this process mentally. If the transaction is more complicated, then use scratch paper, drawing the T accounts. Using T accounts is the accountant's way of drawing a picture of the transaction. This is why we stressed the fundamental accounting equation, with the T accounts and plus and minus signs, so heavily in Chapter 3. You are most definitely urged to get in the T account habit.

Always record the debit part of the entry first. Enter the account title—in this case, Cash—in the Description column. Record the amount—$32,000—in the Debit amount column.

GENERAL JOURNAL   PAGE ___1___

Account title

Debit amount

	DATE	DESCRIPTION	POST. REF.	DEBIT	CREDIT	
1	19–					1
2	June 1	Cash		32 0 0 0 00		2
3						3

Next, record the credit part of the entry. Enter the account title—in this case, Paul Greenwalt, Capital—on the line below the debit, in the Description column, indented about one-half inch. Do not let it extend into the Posting Reference column. On the same line, write the amount in the credit column. By custom, accountants don't generally abbreviate account titles.

Indent account title credited

GENERAL JOURNAL   PAGE _1_

	DATE		DESCRIPTION	POST. REF.	DEBIT	CREDIT	
1	19–						1
2	June	1	Cash		32 0 0 0 00		2
3			Paul Greenwalt, Capital			32 0 0 0 00	3
4							4

You should now give a brief explanation, in which you may refer to business papers, such as check numbers or invoice numbers; you may also list names of charge customers or creditors, or terms of payment. Enter the explanation below the credit entry, indented an additional one-half inch.

Indent again for explanation

GENERAL JOURNAL   PAGE _1_

	DATE		DESCRIPTION	POST. REF.	DEBIT	CREDIT	
1	19–						1
2	June	1	Cash		32 0 0 0 00		2
3			Paul Greenwalt, Capital			32 0 0 0 00	3
4			Original investment by				4
5			Greenwalt in Paul's Auto Body.				5
6							6

For an entry in the general journal to be complete, it must contain (1) the date, (2) a debit entry, (3) a credit entry, and (4) an explanation. To anyone thoroughly familiar with the accounts, the explanation may seem to be quite obvious or redundant. This will take care of itself later, but in the meantime, let us record the explanation as a required, integral part of the entry.

Transaction (b) June 2: Paul's Auto Body buys $18,000 worth of equipment, for cash.

Decide which accounts are involved. Next classify them under the five possible classifications. Visualize the plus and minus signs under the classifications. Now decide whether the accounts are increased or decreased. When you use T accounts to analyze the transaction, the results are as follows:

Equipment		Cash	
+	−	+	−
Debit	Credit	Debit	Credit
18,000			18,000

Now journalize this analysis below the first transaction. To make the journal entries easier to read, leave one blank line between each transaction. Record the day of the month in the Date column. Remember, you do not have to record the month and year again until the month or year changes or you use a new journal page.

GENERAL JOURNAL   PAGE ___1___

	DATE		DESCRIPTION	POST. REF.	DEBIT	CREDIT	
1	19–						1
2	June	1	Cash		32 0 0 0 00		2
3			Paul Greenwalt, Capital			32 0 0 0 00	3
4			Original investment by				4
5			Greenwalt in Paul's Auto Body.				5
6							6
7		2	Equipment		18 0 0 0 00		7
8			Cash			18 0 0 0 00	8
9			Bought equipment for cash.				9
10							10

Skip a line between entries

Transaction (c) On June 2 Paul's Auto Body buys $4,000 worth of equipment on account from Osborne Equipment Company. To get organized, think of the T accounts first.

Equipment		Accounts Payable	
+	−	−	+
Debit	Credit	Debit	Credit
4,000			4,000

Skip a line in the journal and record the day of the month and then the entry. In journalizing a transaction involving Accounts Payable, always state the name of the creditor. Similarly, in journalizing a transaction involving Accounts Receivable, always state the name of the charge customer.

		GENERAL JOURNAL								PAGE __1__		
	DATE	DESCRIPTION	POST. REF.		DEBIT				CREDIT			
10												10
11	2	Equipment		4	0	0	0	00				11
12		Accounts Payable							4	0	0 0 00	12
13		Bought equipment on account										13
14		from Osborne Equipment Co.										14
15												15

When a business buys an asset, the asset should be recorded at the actual cost. This is called the **cost principle**. For example, suppose that Paul's Auto Body bought the equipment from Osborne Company at a real bargain price of $4,000. Osborne Company had been asking $5,500 for the equipment. The day after Paul's Auto Body took possession of the equipment, it received an offer of $4,800 from another party, but the offer was declined. However, Paul's Auto Body *should record the equipment for the actual amount of the transaction that took place, which is $4,000.* This is true even though the fair market value may be $4,800.

Transaction (d)   On June 4, Paul's Auto Body pays $1,000 to be applied against the firm's liability of $4,000. Picture the T accounts like this:

Cash		Accounts Payable	
+	−	−	+
Debit	Credit	Debit	Credit
	1,000	1,000	

Cash is an easy account to recognize. So, in every transaction, ask yourself, "Is Cash involved?" If Cash is involved, determine whether it is coming in or going out. In this case we see that cash is going out, so we

16												16
17	4	Accounts Payable		1	0	0	0	00				17
18		Cash							1	0	0 0 00	18
19		Paid Osborne Equipment										19
20		Company on account.										20
21												21

record it on the minus side. We now have a credit to Cash and half of the entry. Next, we recognize that Accounts Payable is involved. We ask ourselves, "Do we owe more or less as a result of this transaction?" The answer is "less," so we record it on the minus, or debit, side of the account.

Now let's list the transactions for June for Paul's Auto Body with the date of each transaction. The journal entries are illustrated on the following pages in Figures 4-1, 4-2, and 4-3.

Remember

Six types of information must be entered in the general journal for each transaction: the date, the title of the account to be debited, the amount of the debit, the title of the account to be credited, the amount of the credit, and the explanation.

June	1	Greenwalt invests $32,000 cash in his new business.
	2	Buys $18,000 worth of equipment for cash.
	2	Buys $4,000 worth of equipment on credit from Osborne Equipment Company.
	4	Pays $1,000 to Osborne Equipment Company, to be applied against the firm's liability of $4,000.
	4	Buys paint and other supplies on credit from Todd Supply Company, $400.
	7	Cash revenue received for first week, $600.
	8	Pays rent for the month, $400.
	10	Pays wages to part-time employee, $240, June 1 through June 10.
	10	Pays for a two-year insurance policy, $320.
	14	Cash revenue received for second week, $760.
	14	Receives bill for newspaper advertising, from the Daily News, $180.
	15	Pays $1,800 to Osborne Equipment Company as part payment on account.
	15	Receives and pays bill for utilities, $220.
	15	Pays the Daily News for advertising, $180. (This bill has previously been recorded.)
	21	Cash revenue received for third week, $830.
	23	Paul's Auto Body signs a contract with Hughes Taxi to paint or repair damages to their vehicles on a credit basis. Paul's Auto Body completes a paint job and bills Hughes Taxi $80 for services performed.
	24	Pays wages of part-time employee, $390, June 11 through June 24.
	26	Buys additional equipment on account, $940 from Osborne Equipment Company, paying $140 down with the remaining $800 on account.
	30	Cash revenue received for the remainder of the month, $960.
	30	Receives $60 from Hughes Taxi to apply on amount previously billed.
	30	Greenwalt withdraws cash for personal use, $1,000.

FIGURE 4-1

GENERAL JOURNAL

PAGE _1_

	DATE		DESCRIPTION	POST. REF.	DEBIT	CREDIT	
1	19–						1
2	June	1	Cash		32 0 0 0 00		2
3			Paul Greenwalt, Capital			32 0 0 0 00	3
4			Original investment by				4
5			Greenwalt in Paul's Auto Body.				5
6							6
7		2	Equipment		18 0 0 0 00		7
8			Cash			18 0 0 0 00	8
9			Bought equipment for cash.				9
10							10
11		2	Equipment		4 0 0 0 00		11
12			Accounts Payable			4 0 0 0 00	12
13			Bought equipment on account				13
14			from Osborne Equipment				14
15			Company.				15
16							16
17		4	Accounts Payable		1 0 0 0 00		17
18			Cash			1 0 0 0 00	18
19			Paid Osborne Equipment				19
20			Company on account.				20
21							21
22		4	Supplies		4 0 0 00		22
23			Accounts Payable			4 0 0 00	23
24			Bought paint and other				24
25			supplies on account				25
26			from Todd Supply Company.				26
27							27
28		7	Cash		6 0 0 00		28
29			Income from Services			6 0 0 00	29
30			For week ended June 7.				30
31							31
32		8	Rent Expense		4 0 0 00		32
33			Cash			4 0 0 00	33
34			For month ended June 30.				34
35							35
36		10	Wages Expense		2 4 0 00		36
37			Cash			2 4 0 00	37
38			Paid wages, June 1 to June 10.				38
39							39

FIGURE 4-2

GENERAL JOURNAL

PAGE 2

	DATE		DESCRIPTION	POST. REF.	DEBIT	CREDIT	
1	19–						1
2	June	10	Prepaid Insurance		3 2 0 00		2
3			Cash			3 2 0 00	3
4			Premium for two-year				4
5			insurance policy.				5
6							6
7		14	Cash		7 6 0 00		7
8			Income from Services			7 6 0 00	8
9			For week ended June 14.				9
10							10
11		14	Advertising Expense		1 8 0 00		11
12			Accounts Payable			1 8 0 00	12
13			Received bill for advertising				13
14			from the Daily News.				14
15							15
16		15	Accounts Payable		1 8 0 0 00		16
17			Cash			1 8 0 0 00	17
18			Paid Osborne Equipment				18
19			Company on account.				19
20							20
21		15	Utilities Expense		2 2 0 00		21
22			Cash			2 2 0 00	22
23			Paid bill for utilities.				23
24							24
25		15	Accounts Payable		1 8 0 00		25
26			Cash			1 8 0 00	26
27			Paid Daily News for advertising.				27
28							28
29		21	Cash		8 3 0 00		29
30			Income from Services			8 3 0 00	30
31			For week ended June 21.				31
32							32
33		23	Accounts Receivable		8 0 00		33
34			Income from Services			8 0 00	34
35			Hughes Taxi, for services				35
36			rendered.				36
37							37
38							38
39							39

Remember

Every business transaction requires a debit and a credit entry. In a general journal, the debit part of the entry is recorded first. The credit part of the entry is recorded next and followed by a brief explanation of the transaction.

FIGURE 4-3

GENERAL JOURNAL   PAGE ___3___

	DATE		DESCRIPTION	POST. REF.	DEBIT	CREDIT	
1	19–						1
2	June	24	Wages Expense		3 9 0 00		2
3			Cash			3 9 0 00	3
4			Paid wages, June 11 to June 24.				4
5							5
6		26	Equipment		9 4 0 00		6
7			Cash			1 4 0 00	7
8			Accounts Payable			8 0 0 00	8
9			Bought equipment on account				9
10			from Osborne Equipment				10
11			Company.				11
12							12
13		30	Cash		9 6 0 00		13
14			Income from Services			9 6 0 00	14
15			For remainder of June, ended				15
16			June 30.				16
17							17
18		30	Cash		6 0 00		18
19			Accounts Receivable			6 0 00	19
20			Hughes Taxi, to apply on				20
21			account.				21
22							22
23		30	Paul Greenwalt, Drawing		1 0 0 0 00		23
24			Cash			1 0 0 0 00	24
25			Withdrawal for personal use.				25

POSTING TO THE GENERAL LEDGER

Objective 2

Post entries from a two-column general journal to general ledger accounts.

From this example, you can see that the journal is indeed the *book of original entry*. Each transaction must first be recorded in the journal in full. However, from the general journal entries, it is virtually impossible to determine readily the balance of any one account, such as Cash, for example. So the **ledger account** has been devised to give us a complete record of the transactions recorded in each individual account. **The general ledger is simply a book that contains all the accounts.** The book used for the ledger is usually a loose-leaf binder, so that one can add or remove leaves. The process of transferring figures from the journal to the ledger accounts is called **posting**.

The Chart of Accounts

One arranges the accounts in the ledger according to the chart of accounts. As we said previously, the **chart of accounts** is the official list of the ledger accounts in which transactions of a business are to be recorded. Assets are listed first, liabilities second, owner's equity third, revenue fourth, and expenses fifth. We will now insert account numbers. The chart of accounts for Paul's Auto Body is as follows:

Chart of Accounts

Assets (100–199)
111 Cash
112 Accounts Receivable
113 Supplies
114 Prepaid Insurance
121 Equipment

Liabilities (200–299)
211 Accounts Payable

Owner's Equity (300–399)
311 Paul Greenwalt, Capital
312 Paul Greenwalt, Drawing

Revenue (400–499)
411 Income from Services

Expenses (500–599)
511 Wages Expense
512 Rent Expense
513 Advertising Expense
514 Utilities Expense

Notice that the arrangement consists of the balance sheet accounts followed by the income statement accounts. The numbers preceding the account titles are the **account numbers.** Accounts in the ledger are kept by numbers rather than by pages because it is hard to tell in advance how many pages to reserve for a particular account. When you use the number system, you can add sheets quite readily. The digits in the account numbers also indicate *classifications* of accounts: For most companies, assets start with 1, liabilities with 2, owner's equity with 3, revenue with 4, and expenses with 5. The second and third digits indicate the positions of the individual accounts within their respective classifications.

Regarding the assets, notice the gap in the account numbers between 114 and 121. Generally the account numbers from 120 to 129 are reserved for assets that have a length of life of more than one year, such as equipment, buildings, and land.

The Ledger Account Form (Running Balance Format)

We have been looking at accounts in the simple T account form primarily because T accounts illustrate situations so well. The debit and credit sides are readily apparent. As we have said, accountants usually use the T account form to solve problems because it is such a good way to visualize accounts. However, the T account form is awkward when you are trying to determine the balance of an account. One must add both columns and subtract the smaller total from the larger. To overcome this disadvantage, accountants generally use the four-column account form with balance columns. Let's look at the Cash account of Paul's Auto Body in four-column form (Figure 4-4) compared with the T form. Temporarily, the

FIGURE 4-6

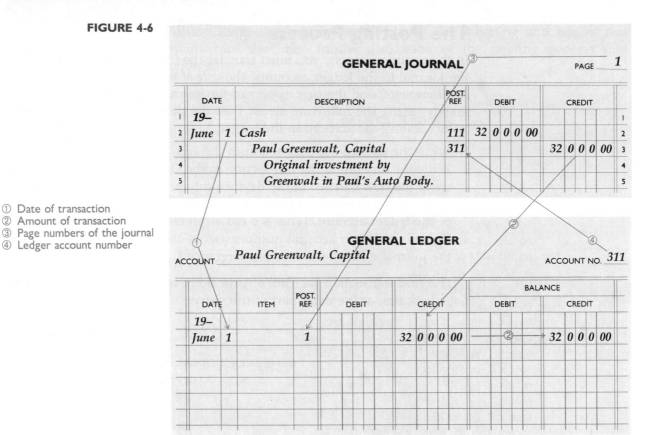

① Date of transaction
② Amount of transaction
③ Page numbers of the journal
④ Ledger account number

The accountant usually uses the Item column only at the end of a financial period. The words that may appear in this column are *balance*, *closing*, *adjusting*, and *reversing*. We will introduce these terms later.

Incidentally, some accountants use running balance type ledger account forms having only one balance column. However, we have used the two-balance-column arrangement to designate clearly the appropriate balance of an account. For example, in Figure 4-6, Cash has a $32,000 balance recorded in the Debit column (normal balance). In Figure 4-6, Paul Greenwalt, Capital has a $32,000 balance recorded in the Credit column (normal balance).

In the recording of the second transaction, shown in Figure 4-7, see if you can identify in order the four steps in the posting process.

FIGURE 4-7

GENERAL JOURNAL   PAGE ___1___

	DATE	DESCRIPTION	POST. REF.	DEBIT	CREDIT	
6						6
7	2	Equipment	121	18 0 0 0 00		7
8		Cash	111		18 0 0 0 00	8
9		Bought equipment for cash.				9
10						10

FIGURE 4-7
(continued)

GENERAL LEDGER

ACCOUNT _Equipment_   ACCOUNT NO. _121_

DATE		ITEM	POST. REF.	DEBIT	CREDIT	BALANCE DEBIT	BALANCE CREDIT
19–							
June	2		1	18 0 0 0 00		18 0 0 0 00	

ACCOUNT _Cash_   ACCOUNT NO. _111_

DATE		ITEM	POST. REF.	DEBIT	CREDIT	BALANCE DEBIT	BALANCE CREDIT
19–							
June	1		1	32 0 0 0 00		32 0 0 0 00	
	2		1		18 0 0 0 00	14 0 0 0 00	

Let us now look at the journal entries for the first month of operation for Paul's Auto Body. As you can see from the general journal and general ledger in Figure 4-8, the Posting Reference column has been filled in, since the posting has been completed.

FIGURE 4-8

GENERAL JOURNAL   PAGE _1_

	DATE		DESCRIPTION	POST. REF.	DEBIT	CREDIT	
1	19–						1
2	June	1	Cash	111	32 0 0 0 00		2
3			Paul Greenwalt, Capital	311		32 0 0 0 00	3
4			Original investment by				4
5			Greenwalt in Paul's Auto Body.				5
6							6
7		2	Equipment	121	18 0 0 0 00		7
8			Cash	111		18 0 0 0 00	8
9			Bought equipment for cash.				9
10							10
11		2	Equipment	121	4 0 0 0 00		11
12			Accounts Payable	211		4 0 0 0 00	12
13			Bought equipment on account				13
14			from Osborne Equipment				14
15			Company.				15
16							16
17		4	Accounts Payable	211	1 0 0 0 00		17
18			Cash	111		1 0 0 0 00	18
19			Paid Osborne Equipment				19
20			Company on account.				20

(continued)

FIGURE 4-8
(continued)

	DATE	DESCRIPTION	POST. REF.	DEBIT	CREDIT	
21						21
22	4	Supplies	113	4 0 0 00		22
23		Accounts Payable	211		4 0 0 00	23
24		Bought paint and other				24
25		supplies on account				25
26		from Todd Supply Company.				26
27						27
28	7	Cash	111	6 0 0 00		28
29		Income from Services	411		6 0 0 00	29
30		For week ended June 7.				30
31						31
32	8	Rent Expense	512	4 0 0 00		32
33		Cash	111		4 0 0 00	33
34		For month ended June 30.				34
35						35
36	10	Wages Expense	511	2 4 0 00		36
37		Cash	111		2 4 0 00	37
38		Paid wages, June 1 to June 10.				38
39						39

GENERAL JOURNAL   PAGE ___2___

	DATE		DESCRIPTION	POST. REF.	DEBIT	CREDIT	
1	19–						1
2	June	10	Prepaid Insurance	114	3 2 0 00		2
3			Cash	111		3 2 0 00	3
4			Premium for two-year				4
5			insurance policy.				5
6							6
7		14	Cash	111	7 6 0 00		7
8			Income from Services	411		7 6 0 00	8
9			For week ended June 14.				9
10							10
11		14	Advertising Expense	513	1 8 0 00		11
12			Accounts Payable	211		1 8 0 00	12
13			Received bill for advertising				13
14			from the Daily News.				14
15							15
16		15	Accounts Payable	211	1 8 0 0 00		16
17			Cash	111		1 8 0 0 00	17
18			Paid Osborne Equipment				18
19			Company on account.				19
20							20
21		15	Utilities Expense	514	2 2 0 00		21
22			Cash	111		2 2 0 00	22
23			Paid bill for utilities.				23

(continued)

FIGURE 4-8
(continued)

		DESCRIPTION	POST. REF.	DEBIT		CREDIT	
24							24
25	15	Accounts Payable	211	1 8 0 00			25
26		Cash	111		1 8 0 00		26
27		Paid Daily News for advertising.					27
28							28
29	21	Cash	111	8 3 0 00			29
30		Income from Services	411		8 3 0 00		30
31		For week ended June 21.					31
32							32
33	23	Accounts Receivable	112	8 0 00			33
34		Income from Services	411		8 0 00		34
35		Hughes Taxi, for services					35
36		rendered.					36
37							37
38							38

GENERAL JOURNAL
PAGE __3__

	DATE		DESCRIPTION	POST. REF.	DEBIT	CREDIT	
1	19–						1
2	June 24	Wages Expense		511	3 9 0 00		2
3			Cash	111		3 9 0 00	3
4			Paid wages, June 11 to June 24.				4
5							5
6	26	Equipment		121	9 4 0 00		6
7			Cash	111		1 4 0 00	7
8			Accounts Payable	211		8 0 0 00	8
9			Bought equipment on account				9
10			from Osborne Equipment				10
11			Company.				11
12							12
13	30	Cash		111	9 6 0 00		13
14			Income from Services	411		9 6 0 00	14
15			For remainder of June, ended				15
16			June 30.				16
17							17
18	30	Cash		111	6 0 00		18
19			Accounts Receivable	112		6 0 00	19
20			Hughes Taxi, to apply on				20
21			account.				21
22							22
23	30	Paul Greenwalt, Drawing		312	1 0 0 0 00		23
24			Cash	111		1 0 0 0 00	24
25			Withdrawal for personal use.				25
26							26

FIGURE 4-8
(continued)

GENERAL LEDGER

ACCOUNT _Cash_   ACCOUNT NO. _111_

DATE		ITEM	POST. REF.	DEBIT	CREDIT	BALANCE DEBIT	BALANCE CREDIT
19–							
June	1		1	32 000 00		32 000 00	
	2		1		18 000 00	14 000 00	
	4		1		1 000 00	13 000 00	
	7		1	600 00		13 600 00	
	8		1		400 00	13 200 00	
	10		1		240 00	12 960 00	
	10		2		320 00	12 640 00	
	14		2	760 00		13 400 00	
	15		2		1 800 00	11 600 00	
	15		2		220 00	11 380 00	
	15		2		180 00	11 200 00	
	21		2	830 00		12 030 00	
	24		3		390 00	11 640 00	
	26		3		140 00	11 500 00	
	30		3	960 00		12 460 00	
	30		3	60 00		12 520 00	
	30		3		1 000 00	11 520 00	

ACCOUNT _Accounts Receivable_   ACCOUNT NO. _112_

DATE		ITEM	POST. REF.	DEBIT	CREDIT	BALANCE DEBIT	BALANCE CREDIT
19–							
June	23		2	80 00		80 00	
	30		3		60 00	20 00	

ACCOUNT _Supplies_   ACCOUNT NO. _113_

DATE		ITEM	POST. REF.	DEBIT	CREDIT	BALANCE DEBIT	BALANCE CREDIT
19–							
June	4		1	400 00		400 00	

FIGURE 4-8
(continued)

ACCOUNT   *Prepaid Insurance*   ACCOUNT NO. **114**

DATE	ITEM	POST. REF.	DEBIT	CREDIT	BALANCE DEBIT	BALANCE CREDIT
19–						
June 10		2	3 2 0 00		3 2 0 00	

ACCOUNT   *Equipment*   ACCOUNT NO. **121**

DATE	ITEM	POST. REF.	DEBIT	CREDIT	BALANCE DEBIT	BALANCE CREDIT
19–						
June 2		1	18 0 0 0 00		18 0 0 0 00	
2		1	4 0 0 0 00		22 0 0 0 00	
26		3	9 4 0 00		22 9 4 0 00	

ACCOUNT   *Accounts Payable*   ACCOUNT NO. **211**

DATE	ITEM	POST. REF.	DEBIT	CREDIT	BALANCE DEBIT	BALANCE CREDIT
19–						
June 2		1		4 0 0 00		4 0 0 00
4		1	1 0 0 00			3 0 0 00
4		1		4 0 0 00		3 4 0 00
14		2		1 8 0 00		3 5 8 0 00
15		2	1 8 0 0 00			1 7 8 0 00
15		2	1 8 0 00			1 6 0 0 00
26		3		8 0 0 00		2 4 0 0 00

ACCOUNT   *Paul Greenwalt, Capital*   ACCOUNT NO. **311**

DATE	ITEM	POST. REF.	DEBIT	CREDIT	BALANCE DEBIT	BALANCE CREDIT
19–						
June 1		1		32 0 0 0 00		32 0 0 0 00

FIGURE 4-8
(continued)

ACCOUNT   *Paul Greenwalt, Drawing*   ACCOUNT NO. *312*

DATE	ITEM	POST. REF.	DEBIT	CREDIT	BALANCE DEBIT	BALANCE CREDIT
19–						
June 30		3	1 0 0 0 00		1 0 0 0 00	

ACCOUNT   *Income from Services*   ACCOUNT NO. *411*

DATE	ITEM	POST. REF.	DEBIT	CREDIT	BALANCE DEBIT	BALANCE CREDIT
19–						
June 7		1		6 0 0 00		6 0 0 00
14		2		7 6 0 00		1 3 6 0 00
21		2		8 3 0 00		2 1 9 0 00
23		2		8 0 00		2 2 7 0 00
30		3		9 6 0 00		3 2 3 0 00

ACCOUNT   *Wages Expense*   ACCOUNT NO. *511*

DATE	ITEM	POST. REF.	DEBIT	CREDIT	BALANCE DEBIT	BALANCE CREDIT
19–						
June 10		1	2 4 0 00		2 4 0 00	
24		3	3 9 0 00		6 3 0 00	

ACCOUNT   *Rent Expense*   ACCOUNT NO. *512*

DATE	ITEM	POST. REF.	DEBIT	CREDIT	BALANCE DEBIT	BALANCE CREDIT
19–						
June 8		1	4 0 0 00		4 0 0 00	

ACCOUNT   *Advertising Expense*   ACCOUNT NO. *513*

DATE	ITEM	POST. REF.	DEBIT	CREDIT	BALANCE DEBIT	BALANCE CREDIT
19–						
June 14		2	1 8 0 00		1 8 0 00	

FIGURE 4-8
(continued)

					BALANCE	
DATE	ITEM	POST. REF.	DEBIT	CREDIT	DEBIT	CREDIT
19–						
June 15		2	2 2 0 00		2 2 0 00	

ACCOUNT _Utilities Expense_   ACCOUNT NO. _514_

For the purpose of journal illustrations in this chapter, assume that a full journal page permits thirty-eight lines of entries. Remember that one blank line is left between complete entries.

In making a journal entry, you will probably face the situation in which you get to the bottom of a page and there are not enough lines to record the entire entry. In this case, do not split up the entry; instead, record the entire entry on the next journal page.

A trial balance is presented in Figure 4-9.

FIGURE 4-9

Paul's Auto Body
Trial Balance
June 30, 19–

ACCOUNT NAME	DEBIT	CREDIT
Cash	11 5 2 0 00	
Accounts Receivable	2 0 00	
Supplies	4 0 0 00	
Prepaid Insurance	3 2 0 00	
Equipment	22 9 4 0 00	
Accounts Payable		2 4 0 0 00
Paul Greenwalt, Capital		32 0 0 0 00
Paul Greenwalt, Drawing	1 0 0 0 00	
Income from Services		3 2 3 0 00
Wages Expense	6 3 0 00	
Rent Expense	4 0 0 00	
Advertising Expense	1 8 0 00	
Utilities Expense	2 2 0 00	
	37 6 3 0 00	37 6 3 0 00

If the temporary balance of an account happens to be zero, insert long dashes through both the Debit Balance and Credit Balance columns. We'll use another business, the Donegal Company, in this example. Its Accounts Receivable ledger account appears below.

ACCOUNT _Accounts Receivable_   ACCOUNT NO. _112_

DATE		ITEM	POST. REF.	DEBIT	CREDIT	BALANCE DEBIT	BALANCE CREDIT
19–							
Oct.	7		96	1 4 0 00		1 4 0 00	
	19		97	2 3 8 00		3 7 8 00	
	21		97		1 4 0 00	2 3 8 00	
	29		98		2 3 8 00	———	———
	31		98	1 6 2 00		1 6 2 00	

Steps in the Accounting Process

1. **Record the transactions of a business in a journal (book of original entry—the day-by-day record of the transactions of a firm).**

   Entry should be based on some source document or evidence that a transaction has occurred, such as an invoice, a receipt, or a check.

2. **Post entries to the accounts in the ledger.**

   Transfer the amounts from the journal to the Debit or Credit columns of the specified accounts in the ledger. Use a cross-reference system. Accounts are placed in the ledger according to the account numbers assigned to them in the chart of accounts.

3. **Prepare a trial balance.**

   Record the balances of the ledger accounts in the appropriate Debit or Credit column of the trial balance form. Prove that the total of the debit balances equals the total of the credit balances.

Source Document

We have been stressing source documents as being evidence for a journal entry. Figure 4-10 is an example of a source document followed by the journal entry and ledger accounts.

FIGURE 4-10

TODD SUPPLY COMPANY   No. 4-962
2430 East Second Street
Bartell, LA 70990

Sold By: ___203___   Date: _6/4/_____

Name: _Paul's Auto Body_____

Address: _1628 East Fifth Avenue_____

_Bartell, LA 70990_____

Terms: _Net 30 days_____

QUANTITY	DESCRIPTION	AMOUNT	
8 gal.	Lacquer L411C @ $19 per gal.	152	00
2 gal.	Lacquer thinner @ $8.35 per gal.	16	70
4 gal.	Lacquer primer @ $25.44 per gal.	101	76
5 tubes	Spot putty @ $7.43 per tube	37	15
3 sleeves	Wet or dry sandpaper @ $19.13 per sleeve	57	39
2 gal.	Liquid rubbing compound @ $17.50 per gal.	35	00
	Total	400	00

Record in the journal

21		4	Supplies	113	4 0 0	00					21
22			Accounts Payable	211			4 0 0	00			22
23			Bought paint and other								23
24			supplies on account from								24
25			Todd Supply Company,								25
			invoice no. 4-962.								

Post to the ledger

ACCOUNT   _Supplies_   ACCOUNT NO. _113_

DATE		ITEM	POST. REF.	DEBIT	CREDIT	BALANCE	
						DEBIT	CREDIT
19–							
June	4		1	4 0 0 00		4 0 0 00	

FIGURE 4-10
(continued)

	DATE	ITEM	POST. REF.	DEBIT	CREDIT	BALANCE DEBIT	BALANCE CREDIT	
	19–							
	June 2		1		4 0 0 0 00		4 0 0 0 00	previous postings
	4		1	1 0 0 0 00			3 0 0 0 00	
	4		1		4 0 0 00		3 4 0 0 00	

ACCOUNT *Accounts Payable*   ACCOUNT NO. *211*

Prepare a trial balance like the one in Figure 4-9 on page 103.

CORRECTION OF ERRORS

Without a doubt, errors will occasionally be made in recording journal entries and posting to the ledger accounts. Never erase them, because it might look as if you are trying to conceal something. The method for correcting errors depends on how and when the error was made. There are two approved methods for correcting errors: the ruling method and the correcting entry method.

Ruling Method

Objective 3

Correct entries using the ruling methods.

You can use the ruling method to correct errors before or after an entry has been posted.

Correcting Errors Before Posting Has Taken Place   When an error has been made in recording an account title in a journal entry, draw a line through the incorrect account title in the journal entry and write the correct account title immediately above. Include your initials with the correction. For example, an entry to record payment of $700 rent was incorrectly debited to Salary Expense.

	DATE	DESCRIPTION	POST. REF.	DEBIT	CREDIT	
1	19–					1
2	Mar. 1	~~Salary Expense~~ Rent Expense *DJM*		7 0 0 00		2
3		Cash			7 0 0 00	3
4		*Paid rent for the month.*				4

When an error has been made in recording an amount, draw a line through the incorrect amount in the journal entry and write the correct amount immediately above. For example, an entry for a $230 payment for office supplies was recorded as $320.

	DATE		DESCRIPTION	POST. REF.	DEBIT	CREDIT	
1	*19–*						1
2	*Apr.*	*6*	*Office Supplies*		~~2 3 0 00~~ ~~3 2 0 00~~		2
3			*Cash*			~~2 3 0 00~~ ~~3 2 0 00~~	3
4			*Bought office stationery.*				4
5							5

Correcting Errors After Posting Has Taken Place   When an entry was journalized correctly but one of the amounts was posted incorrectly, correct the error by ruling a single line through the amount, and record the correct amount above. For example, an entry to record cash received for professional fees was correctly journalized as $400. However, it was posted as a debit to Cash for $400 and a credit to Professional Fees for $4,000. In the Professional Fees account, draw a line through $4,000 and insert $400 above. Change the running balance of the account.

ACCOUNT   *Professional Fees*   ACCOUNT NO. *411*

						BALANCE	
DATE	ITEM	POST. REF.	DEBIT	CREDIT	DEBIT	CREDIT	
19–							
Feb. 6		94		*DJM* ~~4 0 0 00~~ ~~4 0 0 0 00~~	*DJM*	25 ~~6 0 0 00~~ 29 ~~2 0 0 00~~	

Correcting Entry Method

Objective 4

Correct entries using the correcting entry method.

You should use the correcting entry method when amounts have been posted to the wrong account. The correcting entry should *always* include an explanation. For example, a $620 payment for repairs was journalized and posted as a debit to Miscellaneous Expense for $620 and a credit to Cash for $620.

	DATE		DESCRIPTION	POST. REF.	DEBIT	CREDIT	
1	*19–*						1
2	*Jan.*	*9*	*Repair Expense*		6 2 0 00		2
3			*Miscellaneous Expense*			6 2 0 00	3
4			*To correct error of January 9*				4
5			*in which a payment for Repair*				5
6			*Expense was debited to*				6
7			*Miscellaneous Expense.*				7
8							8

COMPUTERS AT WORK

Computerized Accounting

Computers' quick and accurate manipulation of numbers makes them perfect tools for improving the efficiency of accounting systems. In many businesses, accounting software and computer disks have replaced handwritten journals and ledgers. With the proper accounting software, a computer can significantly reduce time spent on routine tasks. A general ledger package can speed up many of the processes involved:

- Journalizing
- Posting
- Producing trial balances and financial statements
- Printing reports and reprinting them after correcting an error

Of course, any company debating a move to computerized accounting must weigh these benefits against the costs involved. Companies that already use computers extensively can often purchase accounting software packages that will run on their existing computers. Companies that don't already own computers will face the prospect of buying both hardware and software.

In either case, switching to a computerized accounting system will mean spending money on a software package and possibly on a new printer and printout forms. The company must also be ready to invest time in training its employees to use the new system. While everyone is getting used to the new system, the company will have to keep two sets of accounts, one computerized and one manual, in order to avoid disaster if the new system breaks down. A company can give up the manual accounting system only when its accountants feel confident that all the bugs have been worked out of the computerized system.

Companies also have to invest time in choosing the right system. Each accounting software package provides the same basic features, but the packages vary in terms of how much computer power they need, how quickly they function, what special features they offer, how easy they are to learn and use, and how costly they are. The software should come with clear instruction manuals, and the software dealer should be willing to provide assistance during the long getting-acquainted period. Employees who will be using the system need to read reviews, observe demonstrations, talk to others in the industry, and actually try out various packages before they can select the best one. Only after they have decided on the software should they select the computer hardware to run it on.

Companies that expect a computer to solve all their accounting problems may be sorely disappointed. A computerized system may just amplify problems in the existing manual system. The secret to success in using even the most advanced automated accounting system is knowing accounting basics and entering debits and credits correctly, as a computer will only do what it is told.

After the correcting entry has been journalized, the accounts would be posted like any other entry. After posting, the account balances should be correct.

SUMMARY

L.O. 1   The journal is a day-by-day record of the business transactions of a firm. The first step in the accounting process is recording the transactions in the journal. Each journal entry should be based on a source document showing that a transaction has occurred, such as a sales invoice, a receipt, or a check. The **L.O. 2**   second step in the accounting process is posting entries to the accounts in the ledger. This step consists of transferring the amounts to the Debit or Credit columns of the specified accounts in the ledger, using a cross-reference system. The general ledger is the book in which all accounts are kept. Accounts are placed in the ledger according to the account numbers assigned to them in the chart of accounts. After a group of transactions for a period of time has been journalized and posted, a trial balance is prepared to prove that the totals of the debit balances and of the credit balances of the **L.O. 3,4**   ledger accounts are equal. If an error has been made in journalizing or posting an entry, it is necessary to correct the entry using either the ruling method or the correcting entry method. The ruling method is used if the error is discovered before the entry has been posted. The correcting entry method is used after an amount has been posted to the wrong account.

GLOSSARY

Account numbers The numbers assigned to accounts according to the chart of accounts.

Chart of accounts The official list of the ledger accounts in which transactions of a business are to be recorded.

Cost principle A purchased asset should be recorded at its actual cost (the agreed amount of a transaction).

Cross-reference The ledger account number in the Posting Reference column of the journal or the journal page number in the Posting Reference column of the ledger account.

Journal The book in which a person makes the original record of a business transaction; commonly referred to as a *book of original entry*.

Journalizing The process of recording a business transaction in a journal.

Ledger account A complete record of the transactions recorded in each individual account.

Posting The process of transferring figures from the journal to the ledger accounts.

Source documents Business papers such as checks, invoices, receipts, letters, and memos that furnish proof that a transaction has taken place.

Two-column general journal A general journal in which there are two money columns used for debit and credit amounts.

QUESTIONS, EXERCISES, AND PROBLEMS

Discussion Questions

1. What is the advantage of recording a transaction in a journal as opposed to recording a transaction directly in T accounts?
2. What is a journal entry based on? Why is the journal called the book of original entry?
3. Does double-entry accounting refer to entering a transaction in both the journal and the ledger? Explain.
4. What is a chart of accounts?
5. Is it necessary to add the columns of a two-column general journal?
6. In the process of recording transactions in a journal, which is recorded first—the title of the account debited or the title of the account credited?
7. Arrange the following steps in the posting process in proper order:
   a. Write the page number of the journal in the Posting Reference column of the ledger account.
   b. Write the amount of the transaction.
   c. Record the ledger account number in the Posting Reference column of the journal.
   d. Write the date of the transaction.
8. In recording a transaction, what does a cross-reference involve?

Exercises

L.O. 2   **Exercise 4-1**   The following T account shows the cash transactions for a month.

	Cash		No. 111
3/1	10,000	3/2	700
3/7	1,400	3/5	400
3/14	5,200	3/9	1,900
3/21	400	3/22	4,700
3/28	4,900		

Post the amounts to the ledger account for Cash. Assume that all transactions appear on page 5 of the journal.

ACCOUNT   *Cash*   ACCOUNT NO.   *111*

					BALANCE	
DATE	ITEM	POST. REF.	DEBIT	CREDIT	DEBIT	CREDIT

L.O. 1   **Exercise 4-2**   In the two-column general journal below, the capital letters represent parts of a journal entry. On notebook paper, write the numbers 1 through 8. Alongside each number, write the letter that indicates where in the journal the items are recorded.

	GENERAL JOURNAL			PAGE_____
DATE	DESCRIPTION	POST. REF.	DEBIT	CREDIT
G				
H *I* *J*		*O*	*M*	
	K	*P*		*N*
	L			

1. Ledger account number of account credited
2. Month
3. Explanation
4. Title of account debited
5. Year
6. Day of the month
7. Title of account credited
8. Amount of debit

L.O. 1   **Exercise 4-3**   The following transactions of Nordby Company occurred during this year. Journalize the transactions in general journal form, including brief explanations.

Nov.   7 Bought equipment for $6,200 from Norton Equipment Company, paying $1,500 down; balance due in 30 days.
       9 Paid wages for the period November 1 through 8, $1,250.
    12 Billed Mitchell Company for services performed, $192.

L.O. 2   **Exercise 4-4**   Arrange the following steps of the posting process in proper order.

a. The page number of the journal is recorded in the Posting Reference column of the ledger.
b. The amount of the transaction is recorded in the Debit or Credit column of the ledger account.
c. The ledger account number is recorded in the Posting Reference column of the journal.
d. The amount of the balance of the ledger account is recorded in the Debit or Credit column under the Balance heading.
e. The date of the transaction is recorded in the Date column of the ledger account.

L.O. 1   **Exercise 4-5**   McGee Construction completed the following selected transactions. Journalize the transactions in general journal form, including brief explanations.

Oct.   6 Collected $742 from L. Hedges, a charge customer.
    12 Issued a check in full payment of an Account Payable to Griffin Company, $116.
    18 C. L. McGee (the owner) withdrew cash for personal use, $1,400.

L.O. 1,2   **Exercise 4-6**   Which of the following errors would cause unequal totals in a trial balance? Explain why or why not.

a.   An accountant recorded a $67 payment for Travel Expense as a debit to Travel Expense of $76 and a credit to Cash of $67.

b.   An accountant recorded a withdrawal of $320 in cash by the owner as a debit to Miscellaneous Expense of $320 and a credit to Cash of $320.

c.   An accountant recorded a $96 payment to a creditor by a debit to Accounts Payable of $69 and a credit to Cash of $69.

L.O. 3   **Exercise 4-7**   The bookkeeper of Ramirez Company has prepared the following trial balance.

Ramirez Company
Trial Balance
June 30, 19–

ACCOUNT NAME	DEBIT	CREDIT
Cash		2 4 0 0 00
Accounts Receivable	8 4 0 0 00	
Supplies	3 0 0 00	
Prepaid Insurance	4 5 0 00	
Equipment	15 0 0 0 00	
Accounts Payable		3 3 0 0 00
L. Ramirez, Capital		12 0 0 0 00
L. Ramirez, Drawing	3 0 0 0 00	
Income from Services		18 4 5 0 00
Rent Expense	6 0 0 0 00	
Miscellaneous Expense	1 5 0 0 00	
	34 6 5 0 00	36 1 5 0 00

The bookkeeper is quite upset and has asked for your help. In examining the firm's journal and ledger, you discover the following:

a.   The debits to the Cash account total $6,000, and the credits total $3,600.

b.   A $300 payment to a creditor was entered in the journal but was not posted to the Accounts Payable account. Cash was properly posted.

c. The first two digits in the balance of the Accounts Receivable account were transposed in copying the balance from the ledger to the trial balance.

Prepare a corrected trial balance.

L.O. 3,4 **Exercise 4-8** In reviewing the work of the bookkeeper, the office manager discovered the following errors:

a. A typewriter was purchased for $620, and cash was paid and credited. The debit was posted twice in the asset account; the credit was posted correctly.
b. A debit to the Cash account of $1,510 was posted as $1,150; the credit was posted correctly.
c. Cash collections of $1,740 from customers in payment of their accounts were not posted to the Accounts Receivable account but were posted correctly to the Cash account.

For each error, indicate the effect of the error using the following form:

Error	Is the trial balance out of balance?	If yes, by how much?	Which would be incorrect?	
			Debit total	Credit total
a.				
b.				
c.				

Problem Set A

L.O. 1 **Problem 4-1A** The chart of accounts of the Fisher Dance Studio is given below, followed by the transactions that took place during October of this year:

Assets
111 Cash
112 Accounts Receivable
117 Supplies
118 Prepaid Insurance
121 Equipment
122 Furniture

Liabilities
211 Accounts Payable

Owner's Equity
311 M. O. Fisher, Capital
312 M. O. Fisher, Drawing

Revenue
411 Dance Revenue

Expenses
511 Wages Expense
512 Advertising Expense
513 Rent Expense
514 Utilities Expense
519 Miscellaneous Expense

Oct.   1 Bought a tape recorder and speaker system on account from C and H Electronics, $2,700. Paid $1,200 as a downpayment with the balance due in 30 days.

3 Bought chairs on account from Jarvis Furniture, $627, with the balance due in 30 days.

5 Paid $39 for business cards (Supplies).

6 Received cash for dance lessons, $357. (Students were not billed previously.)

7 Paid rent for the month, $420.

10 Received and paid electric bill, $74.

12 Billed students for dance lessons, $1,294.

15 Paid wages to part-time assistants, $650.

16 Paid cash for liability insurance premium (one year), $330.

19 Fisher invested in the business his personal typewriter having a fair market value of $416.

21 Received bill from Ross Advertising Agency to be paid in 30 days, $179.

23 Received cash for dance lessons, $426. (Students were not billed previously.)

24 Paid wages to part-time assistants, $460.

27 Received and paid telephone bill, $72.

30 Billed students for dance lessons, $942.

30 Paid wages to part-time assistants, $695.

31 Fisher withdrew cash for personal use, $1,000.

Instructions

Record the transactions in a general journal, including a brief explanation for each entry. Number the journal pages 24, 25, and 26.

L.O. 2   **Problem 4-2A**   The journal entries in the Working Papers relate to Paul's Auto Body for its second month of operation. The balances of the accounts as of July 1 have been entered in the accounts in the ledger.

Instructions

1. Post the journal entries to the ledger accounts.
2. Prepare a trial balance as of July 31.
3. Prepare an income statement for the two months ended July 31.
4. Prepare a statement of owner's equity for the two months ended July 31.
5. Prepare a balance sheet as of July 31.

L.O. 1,2   **Problem 4-3A**   The chart of accounts of A. L. Guest, M.D., is shown on the next page.

Assets
111 Cash
112 Accounts Receivable
113 Supplies
114 Prepaid Insurance
121 Equipment

Liabilities
211 Accounts Payable

Owner's Equity
311 A. L. Guest, Capital
312 A. L. Guest, Drawing

Revenue
411 Professional Fees

Expenses
511 Salary Expense
512 Laboratory Expense
513 Rent Expense
514 Utilities Expense

Dr. Guest completed the following transactions during November:

Nov.
1 Paid office rent for the month, $600.
2 Bought laboratory equipment from Guy Company on account, $930.
3 Bought bandages and other supplies on account from Dow Company, $82.72.
5 Received cash on account from patients, $2,900.
7 Paid cash to Hoyt Surgical Supply (a creditor) on account, $1,264.
9 Received and paid bill for laboratory analyses, $262.50.
10 Billed patients on account for professional services rendered, $2,130.
12 Paid cash for premium on a one-year property insurance policy, $137.
15 Part of the laboratory equipment purchased on November 2 was defective. Returned the equipment and received a reduction in the bill, $64.
16 Received cash for professional services, $390.
29 Paid monthly salary of part-time nurse, $1,050.
30 Received and paid telephone bill for the month, $72.
30 Billed patients on account for professional services rendered, $1,480.
30 Dr. Guest withdrew $1,520 in cash for personal use.

Instructions

1. Journalize the transactions for November beginning with page 21.
2. Post the entries to the ledger accounts. (Because the professional enterprise was in operation previously, the balances have been recorded in the ledger accounts. A check mark has been placed in the Posting Reference column to represent the various pages of the journal from which the entries were posted.)
3. Prepare a trial balance as of November 30.

L.O. 1,2 **Problem 4-4A** Leahy Building Security had the transactions shown on page 116 during April of this year. The chart of accounts is as follows:

Assets
111 Cash
112 Accounts Receivable
113 Supplies
114 Prepaid Insurance
121 Weapons and Communication
      Equipment
122 Patrol Cars

Liabilities
211 Accounts Payable

Owner's Equity
311 P. Leahy, Capital
312 P. Leahy, Drawing

Revenue
411 Security Service Revenue

Expenses
511 Salary Expense
512 Rent Expense
513 Gas and Oil Expense
514 Utilities Expense

Apr.   2 Leahy transferred cash from a personal bank account to an account to be used for the business, $18,600.

2 Paid rent for the month, $340.

5 Bought a used patrol car for $8,400 from the City of Pembrook, paying $6,000 down, with the balance due in 30 days.

6 Leahy invested personal weapons in the business; the weapons have fair market value of $942.

7 Bought communication equipment on account from Roget's Sound, $1,086.

12 Performed security services at a special rock concert. Billed Davis Enterprises for services rendered, $993.

16 Received bill from Landon Printing for office stationery, $181.74.

17 Purchased additional weapons for cash from Crawford and Son, $442.

18 Billed Fenton Property Management for services rendered, $2,430.

19 Paid Roget's Sound $300 to apply on account.

19 Performed security services at a jewelers' convention. Billed Coast Jewelers' Association for services rendered, $774.

22 Received and paid insurance premium to Earnest Fidelity for bonding employees, $479.

25 Received bill for gas and oil for patrol car from State-wide Services, $100.30.

26 Billed City Merchants Association for services rendered, $1,643.

27 Received $993 from Davis Enterprises in full payment of account.

30 Paid salaries to employees, $2,620.

30 P. Leahy withdrew $1,200 for personal use.

30 Received and paid telephone bill, $108.

Instructions

1. Record the transactions in the general journal, beginning with page 1. Give a brief explanation for each entry.
2. In the general ledger, record the account titles and numbers.
3. Post the entries to the ledger accounts.
4. Prepare a trial balance dated April 30, 19–.

Problem Set B

L.O. 1 **Problem 4-1B** The chart of accounts of the Findlay Flying School is given below, followed by the transactions that took place during November of this year:

Assets
111 Cash
112 Accounts Receivable
117 Prepaid Insurance
121 Airplane
123 Equipment

Liabilities
211 Accounts Payable

Owner's Equity
311 R. T. Findlay, Capital
312 R. T. Findlay, Drawing

Revenue
411 Flying Revenue

Expenses
511 Salary Expense
512 Rent Expense
513 Gas and Oil Expense
514 Advertising Expense
515 Repair Expense
516 Telephone Expense
529 Miscellaneous Expense

Nov. 1 Paid $1,640 for liability insurance for one year.
      2 Received bill for advertising from the City Gazette, $316.
      4 Paid hangar rent for the month, $425.
      6 Received bill for engine repair from Aero Mechanical Service, $284.
      8 Billed students for flying lessons, $929.
     11 Received and paid telephone bill, $67.
     14 Bought lockers and storage cabinet on account from Cresswell and Company, $356, payment due in 30 days.
     17 Paid bill for advertising, charged previously on November 2.
     19 R. T. Findlay withdrew $540 for personal use.
     22 Received bill from Duncan Oil Company for gas and oil used in the firm's operations, $202.
     24 Received cash from students, $369. (Students were not billed previously.)
     25 Paid salary of assistant, $1,400.
     26 Bought a desk and chair from Helm's Furniture, $229, with payment due in 30 days.
     28 Received $600 in cash from students previously billed.
     30 Billed students for flying lessons, $1,426.
     30 Paid $214 in expenses for travel to air safety show.
     30 R. T. Findlay withdrew $140 for personal use.

Instructions

Record the transactions in a general journal, including a brief explanation for each entry. Number the journal pages 31, 32, and 33.

L.O. 2 **Problem 4-2B** The journal entries in the Working Papers relate to Jean's Car Repair for its second month of operation. The balances of the accounts as of July 1 have been recorded in the accounts in the ledger.

Instructions

1. Post the journal entries to ledger accounts.
2. Prepare a trial balance as of July 31.
3. Prepare an income statement for the two months ended July 31.
4. Prepare a statement of owner's equity for the two months ended July 31.
5. Prepare a balance sheet as of July 31.

L.O. 1,2   **Problem 4-3B**   Following is the chart of accounts of A. L. Guest, M.D.:

Assets
111 Cash
112 Accounts Receivable
113 Supplies
114 Prepaid Insurance
121 Equipment

Liabilities
211 Accounts Payable

Owner's Equity
311 A. L. Guest, Capital
312 A. L. Guest, Drawing

Revenue
411 Professional Fees

Expenses
511 Salary Expense
512 Laboratory Expense
513 Rent Expense
514 Utilities Expense

Dr. Guest completed the following transactions during November:

Nov.   2 Bought laboratory equipment on account from Gorton Surgical Supply Company, $1,075.50.
         3 Paid office rent for the month, $700.
         3 Received cash on account from patients, $2,082.
         5 Bought bandages and other supplies on account from Wiley Company, $88.75.
         9 Received and paid bill for laboratory analyses, $274.50.
        12 Paid cash for a one-year property insurance policy, $129.
        13 Billed patients on account for professional services rendered, $2,367.
        16 Received cash for professional services, $281. (Patients were not billed previously.)
        17 Part of the laboratory equipment purchased on November 2 was defective; returned equipment and received a reduction in bill, $73.
        30 Paid monthly salary of part-time nurse, $980.
        30 Received and paid telephone bill for the month, $42.
        30 Billed patients on account for professional services rendered, $1,527.
        30 Dr. Guest withdrew cash for personal use, $1,012.

Instructions

1. Journalize the transactions for November beginning with page 21.
2. Post the entries to the ledger accounts. (Because the professional enterprise was in operation previously, the balances have been recorded in the

ledger accounts. A check mark has been placed in the Posting Reference column to represent the various pages of the journal from which the entries were posted.)

3. Prepare a trial balance as of November 30.

L.O. 1,2 **Problem 4-4B** Salazar Building Security uses the following chart of accounts:

Assets
111 Cash
112 Accounts Receivable
113 Supplies
114 Prepaid Insurance
121 Weapons and Communication
     Equipment
122 Patrol Cars

Liabilities
211 Accounts Payable

Owner's Equity
311 D. Salazar, Capital
312 D. Salazar, Drawing

Revenue
411 Security Service Revenue

Expenses
511 Salary Expense
512 Rent Expense
513 Gas and Oil Expense
514 Utilities Expense

The following transactions were completed during October:

Oct. 1 Salazar transferred cash from a personal bank account to an account to be used for the business, $24,300.
      3 Salazar invested in the business personal weapons having a fair market value of $1,113.
      4 Bought communication equipment on account from Kreiger Electronics, $1,374.
      5 Paid rent for the month, $365.
      6 Bought a used patrol car for $9,300 from the City of Brighton, paying $4,500 down, with the balance due in 30 days.
      9 Received and paid insurance premium to Sanders Fidelity Company for bonding employees, $771.
     12 Performed security services for Raymond Galleries. Billed Raymond for services rendered, $825.
     16 Received bill from Argo Printers for office stationery, $175.72.
     17 Billed Morrison Construction for services rendered, $1,479.
     22 Received and paid bill from Regal Service for gas and oil for patrol car, $72.
     24 Performed security services at rare gems convention. Billed Western Gem Association for services rendered, $711.
     27 Paid Kreiger Electronics $450 to apply on account.
     29 Received $825 from Raymond Galleries in full payment of account.
     30 Billed City Merchants Association for services rendered, $2,160.
     31 Received and paid telephone bill, $103.
     31 Paid salaries to employees, $3,150.
     31 Salazar withdrew cash for personal use, $1,800.

Instructions

1. Record the transactions in the general journal, beginning with page 1 and giving a brief explanation for each entry.
2. In the general ledger, record the account titles and numbers.
3. Post the entries to the ledger accounts.
4. Prepare a trial balance dated October 31, 19–.

5 Adjustments and the Work Sheet

LEARNING OBJECTIVES

After you have completed this chapter, you will be able to do the following:

1. Complete a work sheet for a service-type enterprise, involving adjustments for supplies used, expired insurance, depreciation, and accrued wages.

2. Prepare an income statement, a statement of owner's equity, and a balance sheet for a service-type business directly from the work sheet.

3. Journalize and post the adjusting entries.

4. Prepare an income statement, a statement of owner's equity, and a balance sheet for a business with more than one revenue account and more than one accumulated depreciation account.

Now that you have become familiar with the classifying and recording phase of accounting for a service-type enterprise, let's look at the remaining steps in the accounting process.

FISCAL PERIOD

A **fiscal period** is any period of time covering a complete accounting cycle. A **fiscal year** is a fiscal period consisting of twelve consecutive months. It does not have to coincide with the calendar year. If a business has seasonal peaks, it is a good idea to complete the accounting operations at the end of the most active season. At that time the management wants to know the results of the year and where the business stands financially. As an example, the fiscal period of a resort that is operated during the summer months may be from October 1 of one year to September 30 of the next year. Governments, at some levels, have a fiscal period from July 1 of one year to June 30 of the following year. Department stores often use a fiscal period extending from February 1 of one year to January 31 of the next year. For income tax purposes, any period of twelve consecutive months may be selected. However, you have to be consistent and use the same fiscal period from year to year.

THE ACCOUNTING CYCLE

The **accounting cycle** represents the steps in the accounting process that are completed during the fiscal period. Figure 5-1 shows how we introduce these steps on a chapter-by-chapter basis. This outline brings you up to date on what we have accomplished so far and how each chapter fits into the steps in the accounting cycle.

FIGURE 5-1

Chapter 1
> Analysis of Business Transactions
>
> Assets = Liabilities + Owner's Equity

Chapter 2
> Analysis of Business Transactions
>
> Assets = Liabilities + Capital + Revenue − Expenses

Chapter 3
> Analysis of Business Transactions
>
> Assets = Liabilities + Capital + Revenue − Expenses
>
> +|−   −|+   −|+   −|+   +|−

Chapter 4
> Journalize and Post Business Transactions.
>
> Prepare a Trial Balance.

Chapter 5
> Gather the Adjustment Data.
> Complete a Work Sheet.
> Prepare Financial Statements.
> Journalize and Post Adjusting Entries.

Chapter 6
> Journalize and Post Closing Entries.
> Prepare a Post-Closing Trial Balance.

THE WORK SHEET

At the moment we are concerned with the work sheet. The **work sheet** is a working paper used by accountants to record necessary adjustments

Objective 1

Complete a work sheet for a service-type enterprise, involving adjustments for supplies used, expired insurance, depreciation, and accrued wages.

and provide up-to-date balances needed to prepare the financial statements. The work sheet is simply a tool used to help accountants prepare the financial statements. As a tool, the work sheet serves as a medium or central place, where the information needed to record the adjustments is brought together. Once the accountant has up-to-date account balances, the accountant can prepare the financial statements. (As you may recall, we said the income statement and balance sheet that we looked at in Chapter 2 were tentative because adjustments had not been recorded at that time.)

First, we will present the work sheet form, so that you can see what you will be working with. Next, we will describe and show examples of adjustments. Finally, we will show how the adjustments are entered on the work sheet and how the work sheet is completed.

For our purposes, we will use a ten-column work sheet—so called because two amount columns are provided for each of the work sheet's five major sections. We will discuss the function of each of these sections, again basing our discussion on the accounting activities of Paul's Auto Body. But first, we need to fill in the heading, which consists of three lines: (1) the name of the company, (2) the title of the working paper, and (3) the period of time covered.

Paul's Auto Body
Work Sheet
For Month Ended June 30, 19–

ACCOUNT NAME	TRIAL BALANCE		ADJUSTMENTS		ADJUSTED TRIAL BALANCE		INCOME STATEMENT		BALANCE SHEET	
	DEBIT	CREDIT	DEBIT	CREDIT	DEBIT	CREDIT	DEBIT	CREDIT	DEBIT	CREDIT

Next, we want to point out the classification of accounts that are placed in each column.

The Columns of the Work Sheet

Trial Balance Columns   When you use a work sheet, you do not have to prepare a trial balance on a separate sheet of paper. Instead, you enter the account balances in the first two columns of the work sheet. List the accounts in the Account Name column in the same order that they appear in the chart of accounts. Assuming normal balances, the account classifications are listed in the Trial Balance columns below. We presented a trial balance in Chapter 3. The same classifications are recorded in the Debit and Credit columns on the work sheet.

Account Name	Trial Balance		Adjustments		Adjusted Trial Balance		Income Statement		Balance Sheet	
	Debit	Credit	Debit	Credit	Debit	Credit	Debit	Credit	Debit	Credit
	Assets				Assets					
		Liabilities				Liabilities				
		Capital				Capital				
	Drawing				Drawing					
		Revenue				Revenue				
	Expenses				Expenses					

As we move along in this chapter, we will discuss the adjustments. The Adjusted Trial Balance columns contain the same account classifications as the Trial Balance columns. **The Adjusted Trial Balance columns are merely extensions of the Trial Balance columns after the amounts of the adjustments have been included.** In other words, amounts are carried over from the Trial Balance columns through the Adjustments columns and into the Adjusted Trial Balance columns.

Income Statement Columns   An income statement simply contains the revenue minus the expenses. Revenue accounts have credit balances, so they are recorded in the Income Statement Credit column. Expense accounts, on the other hand, have debit balances, so they are recorded in the Income Statement Debit column.

Account Name	Trial Balance		Adjustments		Adjusted Trial Balance		Income Statement		Balance Sheet	
	Debit	Credit	Debit	Credit	Debit	Credit	Debit	Credit	Debit	Credit
	Assets				Assets					
		Liabilities				Liabilities				
		Capital				Capital				
	Drawing				Drawing					
		Revenue				Revenue		Revenue		
	Expenses				Expenses		Expenses			

Balance Sheet Columns   As you recall, the balance sheet is simply a statement showing assets, liabilities, and owner's equity. Asset accounts have debit balances, so they are recorded in the Balance Sheet Debit column. Liability accounts have credit balances, so they are recorded in the Balance Sheet Credit column. The Capital account has a credit balance, so it is recorded in the Balance Sheet Credit column. Because the Drawing account is a deduction from Capital, it has a debit balance and is recorded in the Balance Sheet Debit column (the opposite column from that in which Capital is recorded).

Account Name	Trial Balance		Adjustments		Adjusted Trial Balance		Income Statement		Balance Sheet	
	Debit	Credit	Debit	Credit	Debit	Credit	Debit	Credit	Debit	Credit
	Assets				Assets				Assets	
		Liabilities				Liabilities				Liabilities
		Capital				Capital				Capital
	Drawing				Drawing				Drawing	
		Revenue				Revenue		Revenue		
	Expenses				Expenses		Expenses			

ADJUSTMENTS

Adjustments may be considered *internal transactions*. They have not been recorded in the accounts up to this time because no outside party has been involved. Adjustments are determined after the trial balance has been prepared.

The accounts that require adjusting are few in number and, after one has a limited exposure to accounting, are easy to recognize. They are used by service, merchandising, and all other kinds of businesses. To describe the reasons for—and techniques of handling—adjustments, let's return to Paul's Auto Body. First, let's select the accounts that require adjustments. For the moment, we will show the adjusting entries by T accounts; later we will enter them on the work sheet and record them in the journal.

Supplies

In the trial balance, the Supplies account has a balance of $400. Each time Paul's Auto Body bought supplies, Greenwalt wrote the entry as a debit to Supplies and a credit to either Cash or Accounts Payable. Thus he recorded each purchase of supplies as an increase in the Supplies account.

But we have not taken into consideration the fact that any business is continually using up supplies in the process of carrying on business operations. For Paul's Auto Body, the items recorded under Supplies consist of paint and other supplies. At the end of the month, obviously some of these supplies have been used. It would be very time consuming to keep a continual record of the exact amount of supplies on hand, so at the end of the month, someone takes a physical count of the amount on hand.

When Greenwalt takes an inventory on June 30, he finds that there are $320 worth of supplies left. The situation looks like this:

Had	$400	(Recorded under Supplies)
− Have left	− 320	(Determined by taking an inventory)
Used	$ 80	(The amount used is an expense of doing business. This is Supplies Expense.)

To bring the books up to date, Greenwalt has to make an **adjusting entry,** which is an entry to help bring the books up to date at the end of the fiscal period. Let's look at this in the form of T accounts. We need to take the amount of supplies used ($80) out of the Supplies account and put it into the Supplies Expense account.

(a)

Supplies				Supplies Expense		
+		−		+		−
(Old) Balance	400	Adjusting	80	Adjusting	80	
(New) Balance	320					

Drawing T accounts on scratch paper is an excellent way of organizing the adjusting entry. By making this entry, Greenwalt has merely taken the amount used out of Supplies and put it into Supplies Expense. The new balance of Supplies, $320, represents the cost of supplies that are on hand and should therefore appear in the balance sheet. The $80 in Supplies Expense represents the cost of supplies that have been used and should therefore appear in the income statement.

When supplies are bought and originally recorded as an asset (as we have been doing), figure the amount of the adjusting entry like this:

Amount of adjusting entry = balance of Supplies account
                          − amount of supplies remaining

The amount should be debited to Supplies Expense and credited to Supplies.

Prepaid Insurance

The $320 balance in Prepaid Insurance stands for the premium paid in advance for a two-year liability insurance policy. One month of the twenty-four months of premium has now expired, which amounts to $13.33:

$$\frac{\$\ 13.33 \text{ per month}}{24 \text{ months})\$320.00}$$

In the adjustment, Greenwalt deducts the expired or used portion from Prepaid Insurance and transfers it to Insurance Expense.

(b)

Prepaid Insurance		Insurance Expense	
+	−	+	−
(Old) Balance 320.00	Adjusting 13.33	Adjusting 13.33	
(New) Balance 306.67			

The new balance of Prepaid Insurance, $306.67 ($320 − $13.33), represents the cost of insurance that is now paid in advance and should therefore appear in the balance sheet. The $13.33 figure in Insurance Expense represents the cost of insurance that has expired and should therefore appear in the income statement.

Depreciation of Equipment

We have followed the policy of recording durable items such as appliances and fixtures under Equipment because they will last longer than one year. The benefits derived from these assets will eventually be used up (they will either wear out or become obsolete). Therefore, we should systematically spread out their costs over the period of their useful lives. In other words, we write off the cost of the assets as an expense over the *estimated useful life of the equipment* and call it **depreciation** because such equipment loses its usefulness. In the case of Paul's Auto Body, the Equipment account has a balance of $22,940. Suppose we estimate that the equipment will have a useful life of six years, with a trade-in value of $2,294 at the end of that time. Then the total depreciation over the estimated useful life of the equipment is $20,646 ($22,940 − $2,294). The calculation of the depreciation for one month is given below.

$$\frac{\$\ 3,441 \text{ per year}}{6 \text{ years})\$20,646 \text{ full depreciation}}$$

$$\frac{\$\ 286.75 \text{ per month}}{12 \text{ months})\$3,441.00}$$

When depreciation is recorded, we do not take away or subtract directly from the asset account. In asset accounts, such as Equipment or Building, we must keep the original cost recorded in the account intact. Consequently, the amount of depreciation has to be recorded in another account; that account is Accumulated Depreciation.

One always records the adjusting entry for depreciation as a debit to Depreciation Expense (an income statement item) and a credit to Accumulated Depreciation (a balance sheet item) because both accounts are increased. The adjustment in T account form would appear as follows.

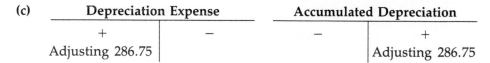

(c)

Depreciation Expense		Accumulated Depreciation	
+	−	−	+
Adjusting 286.75			Adjusting 286.75

On the balance sheet, the balance of Accumulated Depreciation is deducted from the balance of the related asset account as illustrated below on the partial balance sheet for Paul's Auto Body. The net figure shown, $22,653.25, is referred to as the **book value** of the asset. Thus, book value is the cost of an asset minus accumulated depreciation.

Paul's Auto Body
Balance Sheet
June 30, 19–

Assets		
Equipment	$22 9 4 0 00	
Less Accumulated Depreciation	2 8 6 75	$22 6 5 3 25

Accumulated Depreciation is contrary to, or a deduction from, Equipment, so we call it a **contra account**. To show the accounts under their proper headings, let's look at the fundamental accounting equation. (Brackets indicate that Accumulated Depreciation is a deduction from the Equipment account. Note that the plus and minus signs are switched around.)

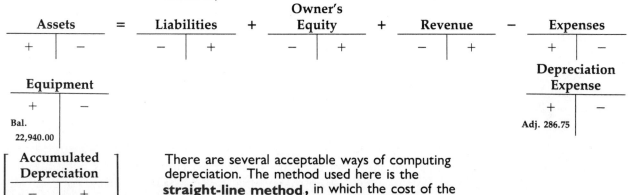

Assets	=	Liabilities	+	Owner's Equity	+	Revenue	−	Expenses
+ | −		− | +		− | +		− | +		+ | −

Equipment
+ | −
Bal.
22,940.00

Accumulated
Depreciation
− | +
Adj. 286.75

Depreciation
Expense
+ | −
Adj. 286.75

There are several acceptable ways of computing depreciation. The method used here is the **straight-line method,** in which the cost of the asset, less any trade-in value, is allocated on an average basis over the useful life of the asset.

Accumulated Depreciation, as the title implies, is the total depreciation that the company has taken since the original purchase of the asset. Rather than crediting the Equipment account, Paul's Auto Body keeps track of the total depreciation taken since it first acquired the asset in a separate account. The maximum depreciation it could take would be the cost of the equipment, $22,940, less trade-in value of $2,294. So, for the first year, Accumulated Depreciation will increase at the rate of $286.75 per month, assuming that no additional equipment has been purchased. For example, at the end of the second month, Accumulated Depreciation will amount to $573.50 ($286.75 + $286.75), and at the end of the second month, the book value will be $22,366.50 ($22,940.00 − $573.50).

Wages Expense

The end of the fiscal period and the end of the employee's payroll period rarely fall on the same day. A diagram of the situation looks like this:

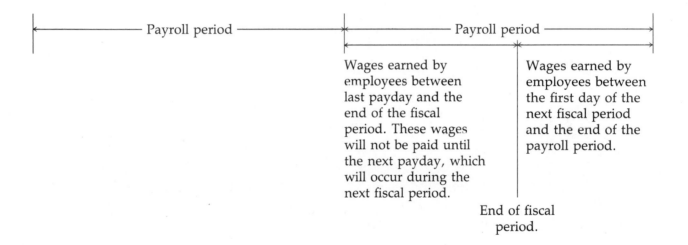

In brief, we are faced with a situation where the last day of the fiscal period falls in the middle of the payroll period. So, we have to split up the wages earned between the fiscal period just ending and the new fiscal period.

As an example, we will use another company. Assume that this firm pays its employees a total of $400 per day and that payday falls on Friday throughout the year. When the employees pick up their paychecks on Friday, at the end of the work day, the amount of the checks includes their wages for that day as well as for the preceding four days. The employees work a five-day week. And suppose that the last day of the fiscal period falls on Wednesday, December 31. We can diagram this as shown in the illustration at the top of the next page.

				Dec. 26	End of Fiscal Year				
					Dec. 29	Dec. 30	Dec. 31	Jan. 1	Jan. 2
Mon	Tue	Wed	Thur	Fri	Mon	Tue	Wed	Thur	Fri
$400	$400	$400	$400	$400	$400	$400	$400	$400	$400

← ——————— Payroll period ——————— → ← ——————— Payroll period ——————— →

Payday $2,000   Payday $2,000

$1,200 $800

December

S	M	T	W	T	F	S
	1	2	3	4	(5)	6
7	8	9	10	11	(12)	13
14	15	16	17	18	(19)	20
21	22	23	24	25	(26)	27
28	29	30	31			

— Paydays

To have the Wages Expense account reflect an accurate balance for the fiscal period, you need to add $1,200 for the cost of labor between the last payday, December 26, and the end of the year, December 31 ($400 for December 29; $400 for December 30; $400 for December 31). Because the $1,200 will not be paid at this time but is owed to the employees at December 31, you also need to add $1,200 to Wages Payable, a liability account.

Wages Expense			Wages Payable	
+	−		−	+
Balance 104,000				Adjusting 1,200
Adjusting 1,200				

Returning to our illustration of Paul's Auto Body: The last payday was June 24. Between June 24 and the end of the month, Paul's Auto Body owes an additional $100 in wages to its employee. Accountants refer to this extra amount that has not been recorded at the end of the month as **accrued wages.** In accounting terms, *to accrue* means to recognize an expense or a revenue that has been incurred or earned but has not yet been recorded. Here, we are concerned with an expense only, which in this case is Wages Expense.

Wages Expense		
+		–
(Old) Balance 630		
Adjusting 100		
(New) Balance 730		

Wages Payable	
–	+
	Adjusting 100

One always records the adjusting entry for accrued wages as a debit to Wages Expense and a credit to Wages Payable because both accounts are increased.

Placement of Accounts in the Work Sheet

First we have to enter the adjustments on the work sheet. But before doing so, let's digress briefly to discuss the Drawing and Accumulated Depreciation accounts, as well as net income, and their effect on the work sheet.

The Drawing Account

Paul Greenwalt, Drawing	
+	–
Debit	Credit
Balance	

Drawing is a deduction from capital and is shown in the column opposite the normal balance of the Capital account.

The Accumulated Depreciation Account

Accumulated Depreciation	
–	+
Debit	Credit
	Balance

Accumulated depreciation is a deduction from the respective asset, such as Equipment or Building. As a deduction, it is shown in the column opposite the normal balance of the asset account.

Net Income

Net income (or net loss) is the difference between revenue and expenses. It is used to balance off the Income Statement columns; and, since revenue is normally larger than expenses, the balancing-off amount must be added to the expense side. Net income (or net loss) is also used to balance off the Balance Sheet columns. As on the statement of owner's equity, one adds net income to the owner's beginning Capital balance. Since the Capital balance is located in the Balance Sheet Credit column, net income must also be added to that side. The following diagram shows these relationships:

Account Name	Trial Balance		Adjustments		Adjusted Trial Balance		Income Statement		Balance Sheet	
	Debit	Credit	Debit	Credit	Debit	Credit	Debit	Credit	Debit	Credit
	A + E + Draw.	L + Cap. + R + Accum. Depr.			A + E + Draw.	L + Cap. + R + Accum. Depr.	E	R	A + Draw.	L + Cap. + Accum. Depr.
Net Income							NI			NI

On the other hand, if expenses are larger than revenue, the result is a net loss. One must add net loss to the revenue side to balance off the Income Statement columns. Also, because one deducts a net loss from the owner's equity, one includes net loss in the debit side of the Balance Sheet columns, thereby balancing off these columns. To show this, let's look at the Income Statement and Balance Sheet columns diagrammed here.

	Income Statement		Balance Sheet	
	Debit	Credit	Debit	Credit
	E	R	A + Draw.	L + Cap. + Accum. Depr.
Net Loss		NL	NL	

Summary of Adjustments by T Accounts

To test your understanding, describe why the following adjustments are necessary. The answers are shown below the accounts.

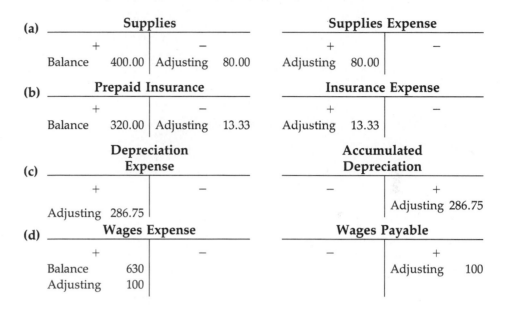

(a)

	Supplies		
	+		−
Balance	400.00	Adjusting	80.00

	Supplies Expense	
	+	−
Adjusting	80.00	

(b)

	Prepaid Insurance		
	+		−
Balance	320.00	Adjusting	13.33

	Insurance Expense	
	+	−
Adjusting	13.33	

(c)

	Depreciation Expense	
	+	−
Adjusting	286.75	

	Accumulated Depreciation	
−		+
		Adjusting 286.75

(d)

	Wages Expense	
	+	−
Balance	630	
Adjusting	100	

	Wages Payable	
−		+
		Adjusting 100

Remember

The amount of the adjusting entry for supplies used equals the balance of the Supplies account minus the amount of the supplies inventory (left over).

a. To record the cost of supplies used during June, $80.
b. To record the insurance expired during June, $13.33.
c. To record the depreciation for the month of June, $286.75.
d. To record accrued wages owed at the end of June, $100.

At this point, take particular notice of the fact that **each adjusting entry contains an income statement account (revenue or expense) and a balance sheet account (asset or liability).**

Recording the Adjustments on the Work Sheet

In the examples above, we used T accounts to explain how to handle adjustments. T accounts, as you are aware, represent a reliable method of organizing any type of accounting entry into debits and credits. Now it is time to record adjustments on the work sheet. To help you remember which classifications of accounts appear in each column of the work sheet, we will label the columns by letter, for example, *A* for assets and *L* for liabilities.

After completing the trial balance in the first two columns of the work sheet, enter the adjustments directly in the Adjustments columns. Note that this is the same trial balance for Paul's Auto Body presented in Chapter 3, page 67.

Adjustments Columns of the Work Sheet

When we enter the adjustments, we identify them as (*a*), (*b*), (*c*), and (*d*) to indicate the relationships between the debit and credit sides and the sequence of the individual adjusting entries, as shown in Figure 5-2.

FIGURE 5-2

Paul's Auto Body
Work Sheet
For Month Ended June 30, 19–

	ACCOUNT NAME	TRIAL BALANCE DEBIT A + E + Draw.	TRIAL BALANCE CREDIT L + C + R + Accum. Deprec.	ADJUSTMENTS DEBIT	ADJUSTMENTS CREDIT	
1	Cash	11 5 2 0 00				1
2	Accounts Receivable	2 0 00				2
3	Supplies	4 0 0 00			(a) 8 0 00	3
4	Prepaid Insurance	3 2 0 00			(b) 1 3 33	4
5	Equipment	22 9 4 0 00				5
6	Accounts Payable		2 4 0 0 00			6
7	Paul Greenwalt, Capital		32 0 0 0 00			7
8	Paul Greenwalt, Drawing	1 0 0 0 00				8
9	Income from Services		3 2 3 0 00			9
10	Wages Expense	6 3 0 00		(d) 1 0 0 00		10
11	Rent Expense	4 0 0 00				11
12	Advertising Expense	1 8 0 00				12
13	Utilities Expense	2 2 0 00				13
14		37 6 3 0 00	37 6 3 0 00			14
15	Supplies Expense			(a) 8 0 00		15
16	Insurance Expense			(b) 1 3 33		16
17	Depreciation Expense			(c) 2 8 6 75		17
18	Accumulated Depreciation				(c) 2 8 6 75	18
19	Wages Payable				(d) 1 0 0 00	19
20				4 8 0 08	4 8 0 08	20

Supplies Expense, Insurance Expense, Depreciation Expense, Accumulated Depreciation, and Wages Payable did not appear in the trial balance, as there were no balances in the accounts to record. We wrote them below the Trial Balance totals in order to complete the worksheet. Some people consider them new accounts because they were never used during the fiscal period. But observe that they all have one thing in common: *They are all increased.* In other words, you bring a new account into existence in order to increase it, definitely not to decrease it. This hint can help you formulate any adjusting entry correctly.

At this point, here is a brief review of the adjustments:

a. To record the $80 cost of supplies used during June.
b. To record the $13.33 cost of insurance expired during June.
c. To record $286.75 depreciation for the month of June.
d. To record $100 of accrued wages owed at the end of June.

Steps in the Completion of the Work Sheet

Before proceeding to the completion of the work sheet, let us list the recommended steps to follow.

Remember

Ruling columns correctly is very important. Always draw a single rule below a column to be added. Draw double rules below the totals.

1. Complete the Trial Balance columns, making sure both columns are equal, that is, balanced and ruled. In the Account Name column above the trial balance totals, we list only the accounts having balances, as in the trial balances in Chapters 3 and 4.
2. Complete the Adjustments columns, labeling each adjustment as (*a*), (*b*), (*c*), and so on. Make sure both columns are balanced and ruled.
3. Complete the Adjusted Trial Balance columns, carrying across any balance from the Trial Balance columns plus or minus any amounts appearing in the Adjustments columns. Make sure both columns are balanced and ruled.
4. Complete the Income Statement and Balance Sheet columns, distributing each amount from the Adjusted Trial Balance columns, according to the account classification, to either the Income Statement or the Balance Sheet columns, but **never to more than one column.** For example, Accounts Payable is a liability, and liabilities are recorded in the Balance Sheet Credit column only.
5. Add the Income Statement Debit and Credit columns and find the difference between the two columns. (The difference represents the net income or net loss.) Use the amount of the net income or net loss to balance off the two columns.
6. Add the Balance Sheet Debit and Credit columns and insert the amount of the net income or net loss to balance off the two columns.

Now we include the Adjusted Trial Balance columns, as shown in Figure 5-3 on the next page, bringing the balances of the accounts that were adjusted up to date.

After the Adjusted Trial Balance columns are completed, go through the mental process of classifying the accounts so that you know where to place the classifications in the various columns. Next

FIGURE 5-3

	ACCOUNT NAME	TRIAL BALANCE DEBIT A + E + Draw.					TRIAL BALANCE CREDIT L + C + R + Accum. Deprec.				
1	Cash	11	5	2	0	00					
2	Accounts Receivable			2	0	00					
3	Supplies		4	0	0	00					
4	Prepaid Insurance		3	2	0	00					
5	Equipment	22	9	4	0	00					
6	Accounts Payable							2	4	0	0	00
7	Paul Greenwalt, Capital						32	0	0	0	00
8	Paul Greenwalt, Drawing	1	0	0	0	00					
9	Income from Services							3	2	3	0	00
10	Wages Expense		6	3	0	00					
11	Rent Expense		4	0	0	00					
12	Advertising Expense		1	8	0	00					
13	Utilities Expense		2	2	0	00					
14		37	6	3	0	00	37	6	3	0	00
15	Supplies Expense										
16	Insurance Expense						Step 1				
17	Depreciation Expense										
18	Accumulated Depreciation										
19	Wages Payable										
20											
21											
22											
23											

Remember

After the first month, Accumulated Depreciation will have a balance, and so it will be listed immediately below the asset being depreciated (which in this example is Equipment). Consequently, Accumulated Depreciation will no longer appear at the bottom of the work sheet.

enter each account balance in the appropriate column. Now carry forward the amounts in the Adjusted Trial Balance columns to the remaining four columns, recording each amount in only one column. Net income or net loss is recorded in both the Income Statement column and the Balance Sheet column to balance off the columns. The completed work sheet is shown in Figure 5-4 on page 138.

Accountants refer to accounts like Supplies and Prepaid Insurance, as they appear in the trial balance, as **mixed accounts**—accounts with balances that are partly income statement amounts and partly balance sheet amounts. For example, Supplies is recorded as $400 in the Trial Balance, but after adjustment this amount is split up or apportioned as $80 in Supplies Expense in the Income Statement columns and $320

Paul's Auto Body
Work Sheet
For Month Ended June 30, 19–

	ADJUSTMENTS			ADJUSTED TRIAL BALANCE			INCOME STATEMENT		BALANCE SHEET		
	DEBIT	CREDIT		DEBIT A + E + Draw.	CREDIT L + C + R + Accum. Deprec.		DEBIT E	CREDIT R	DEBIT A + Draw.	CREDIT L + C + Accum. Deprec.	
				11 5 2 0 00							1
				2 0 00							2
		(a)	8 0 00	3 2 0 00							3
		(b)	1 3 33	3 0 6 67							4
				22 9 4 0 00							5
					2 4 0 0 00						6
					32 0 0 0 00						7
				1 0 0 0 00							8
					3 2 3 0 00						9
(d)	1 0 0 00			7 3 0 00							10
				4 0 0 00							11
				1 8 0 00							12
				2 2 0 00							13
											14
(a)	8 0 00			8 0 00							15
(b)	1 3 33			1 3 33							16
(c)	2 8 6 75			2 8 6 75							17
		(c)	2 8 6 75		2 8 6 75						18
		(d)	1 0 0 00		1 0 0 00						19
	4 8 0 08		4 8 0 08	38 0 1 6 75	38 0 1 6 75						20
											21
	Step 2			Step 3							22
											23

in Supplies in the Balance Sheet columns. Similarly, Prepaid Insurance is recorded as $320 in the Trial Balance columns but apportioned as $13.33 in Insurance Expense in the Income Statement columns and as $306.67 in Prepaid Insurance in the Balance Sheet columns. In other words, portions of these trial balance amounts are recorded in each section.

After the first fiscal period, Accumulated Depreciation will always have a balance until the related asset is sold or disposed of. Consequently, it will be listed in the Trial Balance columns immediately below the appropriate asset (Equipment, in this case). In the demonstration problem shown in your Working Papers, you can see an example of a work sheet for a company that was in business before the present fiscal year.

Paul's Auto Body
Work Sheet
For Month Ended June 30, 19–

	ACCOUNT NAME	TRIAL BALANCE DEBIT A + E + Draw.	TRIAL BALANCE CREDIT L + C + R + Accum. Deprec.	ADJUSTMENTS DEBIT	ADJUSTMENTS CREDIT
1	Cash	11 5 2 0 00			
2	Accounts Receivable	2 0 00			
3	Supplies	4 0 0 00			(a) 8 0 00
4	Prepaid Insurance	3 2 0 00			(b) 1 3 33
5	Equipment	22 9 4 0 00			
6	Accounts Payable		2 4 0 0 00		
7	Paul Greenwalt, Capital		32 0 0 0 00		
8	Paul Greenwalt, Drawing	1 0 0 0 00			
9	Income from Services		3 2 3 0 00		
10	Wages Expense	6 3 0 00		(d) 1 0 0 00	
11	Rent Expense	4 0 0 00			
12	Advertising Expense	1 8 0 00			
13	Utilities Expense	2 2 0 00			
14		37 6 3 0 00	37 6 3 0 00		
15	Supplies Expense			(a) 8 0 00	
16	Insurance Expense		Step 1	(b) 1 3 33	
17	Depreciation Expense			(c) 2 8 6 75	
18	Accumulated Depreciation				(c) 2 8 6 75
19	Wages Payable				(d) 1 0 0 00
20				4 8 0 08	4 8 0 08
21	Net Income				
22				Step 2	
23					
24					
25					
26					
27					
28					
29					
30					
31					
32					
33					

Regarding the work sheet, again, let us emphasize that it is strictly a working paper or tool that is used to gather together all the up-to-date information needed to prepare the financial statements. The adjustments are always recorded in the work sheet first.

FIGURE 5-4

ADJUSTED TRIAL BALANCE		INCOME STATEMENT		BALANCE SHEET		
DEBIT	CREDIT	DEBIT	CREDIT	DEBIT	CREDIT	
A + E + Draw.	L + C + R + Accum. Deprec.	E	R	A + Draw.	L + C + Accum. Deprec.	
11 5 2 0 00				11 5 2 0 00		1
2 0 00				2 0 00		2
3 2 0 00				3 2 0 00		3
3 0 6 67				3 0 6 67		4
22 9 4 0 00				22 9 4 0 00		5
	2 4 0 0 00				2 4 0 0 00	6
	32 0 0 0 00				32 0 0 0 00	7
1 0 0 0 00				1 0 0 0 00		8
	3 2 3 0 00		3 2 3 0 00			9
7 3 0 00		7 3 0 00				10
4 0 0 00		4 0 0 00				11
1 8 0 00		1 8 0 00				12
2 2 0 00		2 2 0 00				13
						14
8 0 00		8 0 00				15
1 3 33		1 3 33				16
2 8 6 75		2 8 6 75				17
	2 8 6 75				2 8 6 75	18
	1 0 0 00				1 0 0 00	19
38 0 1 6 75	38 0 1 6 75	1 9 1 0 08	3 2 3 0 00	36 1 0 6 67	34 7 8 6 75	20
		1 3 1 9 92			1 3 1 9 92	21
	Step 3	3 2 3 0 00	3 2 3 0 00	36 1 0 6 67	36 1 0 6 67	22
						23
		Steps 4, 5, 6				24
						25
						26
						27
						28
						29
						30
						31
						32
						33

Remember

A net income amount is recorded in the Income Statement Debit column and the Balance Sheet Credit column (same side as the increase side of Capital). A net loss is recorded in the Income Statement Credit column and the Balance Sheet Debit column (same side as the decrease side of Capital).

Work Sheet Requiring Two Pages

Sometimes it may be necessary to continue the work sheet on another page. An example is shown at the top of page 140.

(First Page)

Account Name	Trial Balance		Adjustments	
Wages Expense	3,240 00		(c) 220 50	
Totals carried forward	98,312 00	91,146 10	962 50	126 50

(Second Page)

Account Name	Trial Balance		Adjustments	
	Debit	Credit	Debit	Credit
Totals brought forward	98,312 00	91,146 10	962 50	126 50
Wages Payable				(c) 220 50

Note the totals at the bottom of the first page are labeled "Totals carried forward" in the Account Name column. At the top of the second page, the totals are repeated and labeled "Totals brought forward" in the Account Name column.

Finding Errors in the Income Statement and Balance Sheet Columns

As you have seen, the amount of the net income or net loss must be recorded in both an Income Statement column and a Balance Sheet column. After adding the net income to the Balance Sheet Credit column, let's say that the Balance Sheet columns are not equal. To find the error, follow this procedure:

1. Verify the addition of all the columns.
2. Check to see that the amount of the net income or loss is recorded in the correct columns. For example, net income is placed in the Income Statement Debit column and the Balance Sheet Credit column.
3. Look to see if the appropriate amounts have been recorded in the Income Statement and Balance Sheet columns. For example, asset amounts should be listed in the Balance Sheet Debit column, expense amounts should be listed in the Income Statement Debit column, and so forth.

4. Verify, by adding or subtracting across a line, that the amounts carried over from the Trial Balance columns through the Adjustments columns into the Adjusted Trial Balance columns and either the Income Statement or Balance Sheet Columns are correct.

Generally, one of these steps will expose the error.

Completion of the Financial Statements

Objective 2

Prepare an income statement, a statement of owner's equity, and a balance sheet for a service-type business directly from the work sheet.

As we stated, the purpose of the work sheet is to help the accountant prepare the financial statements. Since we have completed the work sheet for Paul's Auto Body, we can now prepare the income statement, the statement of owner's equity, and the balance sheet, by taking the figures directly from the work sheet. These statements are shown in Figure 5-5 on page 142.

Note that one records Accumulated Depreciation in the asset section of the balance sheet as a direct deduction from Equipment. As we have said, accountants refer to it as a **contra account,** because it is contrary to its companion account. The difference, $22,653.25, is called the **book value** because it represents the cost of the assets after Accumulated Depreciation has been deducted.

When preparing the statement of owner's equity, always remember to check the beginning balance of Capital with the balance shown in the Capital account in the general ledger. During the fiscal period, an additional investment may have been made, and you need to record this additional investment in the statement of owner's equity as shown on page 36 in Chapter 2.

JOURNALIZING ADJUSTING ENTRIES

Objective 3

Journalize and post the adjusting entries.

To change the balance of a ledger account, you need a journal entry as evidence of the change. So far, we have been listing adjustments only in the Adjustments columns of the work sheet. Since the work sheet does not constitute a journal, we must journalize the adjustments to bring the ledger accounts up to date. You take the information for these entries directly from the Adjustments columns of the work sheet, debiting and crediting exactly the same accounts and amounts in the journal entries.

In the Description column of the general journal, write "Adjusting Entries" before you begin making these entries. This eliminates the need to write explanations for each entry. The adjusting entries for Paul's Auto Body are shown in Figure 5-6 on page 143.

FIGURE 5-5

Paul's Auto Body
Income Statement
For Month Ended June 30, 19–

Revenue:		
Income from Services		$3 2 3 0 00
Expenses:		
Wages Expense	$ 7 3 0 00	
Rent Expense	4 0 0 00	
Advertising Expense	1 8 0 00	
Utilities Expense	2 2 0 00	
Supplies Expense	8 0 00	
Insurance Expense	1 3 33	
Depreciation Expense	2 8 6 75	
Total Expenses		1 9 1 0 08
Net Income		$1 3 1 9 92

Paul's Auto Body
Statement of Owner's Equity
For Month Ended June 30, 19–

Paul Greenwalt, Capital, June 1, 19–		$32 0 0 0 00
Net Income for June	$1 3 1 9 92	
Less Withdrawals for June	1 0 0 0 00	
Increase in Capital		3 1 9 92
Paul Greenwalt, Capital June 30, 19–		$32 3 1 9 92

Paul's Auto Body
Balance Sheet
June 30, 19–

Assets		
Cash		$11 5 2 0 00
Accounts Receivable		2 0 00
Supplies		3 2 0 00
Prepaid Insurance		3 0 6 67
Equipment	$22 9 4 0 00	
Less Accumulated Depreciation	2 8 6 75	22 6 5 3 25
Total Assets		$34 8 1 9 92
Liabilities		
Accounts Payable	$2 4 0 0 00	
Wages Payable	1 0 0 00	
Total Liabilities		$ 2 5 0 0 00
Owner's Equity		
Paul Greenwalt, Capital		32 3 1 9 92
Total Liabilities and Owner's Equity		$34 8 1 9 92

FIGURE 5-6

GENERAL JOURNAL   PAGE ___4___

DATE		DESCRIPTION	POST. REF.	DEBIT	CREDIT
19–		*Adjusting Entries*			
June	30	Supplies Expense	515	8 0 00	
		Supplies	113		8 0 00
	30	Insurance Expense	516	1 3 33	
		Prepaid Insurance	114		1 3 33
	30	Depreciation Expense	517	2 8 6 75	
		Accumulated Depreciation	122		2 8 6 75
	30	Wages Expense	511	1 0 0 00	
		Wages Payable	212		1 0 0 00

When you post the adjusting entries to the ledger accounts, write the word "Adjusting" in the Item column of the ledger account. For example, the adjusting entry for Supplies is posted as shown below:

GENERAL LEDGER

ACCOUNT *Supplies*   ACCOUNT NO. *113*

DATE		ITEM	POST. REF.	DEBIT	CREDIT	BALANCE DEBIT	BALANCE CREDIT
19–							
June	4		1	4 0 0 00		4 0 0 00	
	30	Adjusting	4		8 0 00	3 2 0 00	

ACCOUNT *Supplies Expense*   ACCOUNT NO. *515*

DATE		ITEM	POST. REF.	DEBIT	CREDIT	BALANCE DEBIT	BALANCE CREDIT
19–							
June	30	Adjusting	4	8 0 00		8 0 00	

In the above adjusted entries, notice that the intent is to make sure that the expenses are recorded to match up or compare with the revenue for the same period of time. In other words, for the month of June, we record all the revenue for June and all the expenses for June. Thus the revenue and expenses of the same time period are matched. This is called the **matching principle.**

Objective 4

Prepare an income statement, a statement of owner's equity, and a balance sheet for a business with more than one revenue account and more than one accumulated depreciation account.

Businesses with More Than One Revenue Account and More Than One Accumulated Depreciation Account

The only revenue account for Paul's Auto Body is Income from Services. However, a business may have several distinct sources of revenue. For example, City Veterinary Clinic has two revenue accounts, Professional Fees and Boarding Fees. Figure 5-7 illustrates the placement of these accounts in the income statement.

FIGURE 5-7

City Veterinary Clinic
Income Statement
For Year Ended December 31, 19–

Revenue:		
Professional Fees	$ 111 720 00	
Boarding Fees	22 080 00	
Total Revenue		$ 133 800 00
Expenses:		
Salaries Expense	$ 84 000 00	
Depreciation Expense, Building	6 480 00	
Depreciation Expense, Equipment	3 840 00	
Supplies Expense	3 720 00	
Insurance Expense	720 00	
Miscellaneous Expense	2 160 00	
Total Expenses		100 920 00
Net Income		$ 32 880 00

In the example of Paul's Auto Body, Equipment is the only type of asset that is subject to depreciation, so the related accounts can simply be titled Depreciation Expense and Accumulated Depreciation. On the other hand, if Paul's Auto Body buys a building that is also subject to depreciation, it would be necessary to separate the depreciation taken on the equipment from the depreciation taken on the building. As a result, separate related accounts would be set up for each type of asset: Depreciation Expense, Equipment and Accumulated Depreciation, Equipment; Depreciation Expense, Building and Accumulated Depreciation, Building.

To illustrate the placement of these accounts in a balance sheet, let's use another example. Standard Travel Agency has the balance sheet shown in Figure 5-8.

FIGURE 5-8

Standard Travel Agency
Balance Sheet
September 30, 19–

Assets				
Cash			$ 6 2 4 0 00	
Supplies			2 0 0 00	
Land			4 4 0 0 00	
Building	$26 7 0 0 00			
Less Accumulated Depreciation	1 4 0 0 00	25 3 0 0 00		
Office Equipment	$ 4 6 0 0 00			
Less Accumulated Depreciation	2 2 0 0 00	2 4 0 0 00		
Total Assets			$38 5 4 0 00	
Liabilities				
Accounts Payable			$ 2 8 0 0 00	
Owner's Equity				
Stanley C. Clay, Capital			35 7 4 0 00	
Total Liabilities and Owner's Equity			$38 5 4 0 00	

Land supposedly will last forever; consequently, land is not depreciated. Separate adjustments would already have been recorded in the work sheet for depreciation of office equipment and building.

SUMMARY

The steps in the accounting cycle that we have talked about up to this point are listed here:

1. Analyze source documents and record business transactions in a journal.
2. Post to the accounts in the ledger.
3. Record the trial balance in the first two columns of the work sheet.
4. Record any adjustments on the work sheet.
5. Complete the work sheet.
6. Prepare the financial statements.
7. Record adjusting entries in the journal and post to the ledger accounts.

L.O. 1   Adjustments are necessary to bring the accounts up to date. One first records adjustments on the work sheet, but to do so, one must know the classification of accounts that occupy the various columns of the work sheet.

Account Classification	Trial Balance		Adjustments		Adjusted Trial Balance		Income Statement		Balance Sheet	
	Debit	Credit	Debit	Credit	Debit	Credit	Debit	Credit	Debit	Credit
Assets	X				X				X	
Liabilities		X				X				X
Capital		X				X				X
Drawing	X				X				X	
Revenue		X				X		X		
Expenses	X				X		X			

L.O. 2,3   After the work sheet is completed, the financial statements are prepared from it. The adjusting entries must then be journalized. This is accomplished by taking the information in these entries directly from the Adjustments column of the work sheet and debiting and crediting exactly the same accounts.

L.O. 4   Businesses that have more than one source of revenue or more than one type of asset that is subject to depreciation must show a separate account for each one on the income statement and the balance sheet.

GLOSSARY

Accounting cycle   The steps in the accounting process that are completed during the fiscal period.

Accrued wages   The amount of unpaid wages owed to employees for the time between the last payday and the end of the fiscal period.

Adjusting entry   An entry to help bring the books up to date at the end of the fiscal period.

Adjustments   Internal transactions that bring ledger accounts up to date, as a planned part of the accounting procedure. They are first recorded in the Adjustments columns of the work sheet.

Book value   The cost of an asset minus the accumulated depreciation.

Contra account   An account that is contrary to, or a deduction from, another account; for example, Accumulated Depreciation entered as a deduction from Equipment.

Depreciation   An expense, based on the expectation that an asset will gradually decline in usefulness due to time, wear and tear, or obsolescence; the cost of the asset is therefore spread out over its estimated useful life. A part of depreciation expense is apportioned to each fiscal period.

Fiscal period or year   Any period of time covering a complete accounting cycle, generally consisting of twelve consecutive months.

Matching principle The revenue for one time period is matched up or compared with the expenses for the same time period.

Mixed accounts Certain accounts that appear in the trial balance that are partly income statement amounts and partly balance sheet amounts—for example, Prepaid Insurance and Supplies.

Straight-line method A means of calculating depreciation in which the cost of an asset, less any trade-in value, is allocated on an average basis over the useful life of the asset.

Work sheet A working paper used by accountants to record necessary adjustments and provide up-to-date account balances needed to prepare the financial statements.

QUESTIONS, EXERCISES, AND PROBLEMS
Discussion Questions

1. Why may adjusting entries be considered internal transactions?
2. In which section of a work sheet would the adjusted balances of the following accounts appear? Be specific as to the Debit or Credit column of the Income Statement or Balance Sheet sections.

   a. Rent Expense
   b. Prepaid Insurance
   c. Wages Payable
   d. Income from Services

   e. Depreciation Expense
   f. Supplies
   g. Accumulated Depreciation
   h. L. R. Smith, Drawing

3. At the end of the fiscal period, the usual adjusting entry to record insurance expired was unintentionally omitted. What is the effect of the omission on (a) the amount of net income for the period? (b) the balance sheet as of the end of the fiscal period?
4. Why is it necessary to journalize the adjusting entries?
5. If it is agreed that there is a need to make adjusting entries at the end of a fiscal period, does this mean that errors were made in the accounts during the period? Explain.
6. On a work sheet, if the Debit column total of the Income Statement section is larger than that of the Credit column total, does the business have a net income or a net loss? Why?
7. What is meant by a mixed account? Give an example.
8. What is a contra account? Give an example.

Exercises

L.O. 1 **Exercise 5-1** From the following list of accounts that appear in the Trial Balance columns of a work sheet, indicate the ones that will most likely require adjustment and explain your reasoning:

   a. Accounts Receivable
   b. Equipment
   c. L. Booker, Drawing
   d. Supplies
   e. Accounts Payable

   f. Accumulated Depreciation
   g. L. Booker, Capital
   h. Salary Expense
   i. Prepaid Insurance

L.O. 1   **Exercise 5-2**   Using a form similar to the one shown below, list the following classifications of accounts in all the columns in which they appear in the work sheet, with the exception of the Adjustments columns: Liabilities, Capital, Expenses, Accumulated Depreciation, Revenue, Net Income, Drawing. (*Example:* Assets)

Trial Balance		Adjustments		Adjusted Trial Balance		Income Statement		Balance Sheet	
Debit	Credit	Debit	Credit	Debit	Credit	Debit	Credit	Debit	Credit
Assets				Assets				Assets	

L.O. 1   **Exercise 5-3**   In transferring amounts from the Adjusted Trial Balance columns, indicate the specific Income Statement or Balance Sheet column in which the balance of each of the following accounts will be placed.

a. Commissions Income
b. Prepaid Insurance
c. Accumulated Depreciation
d. Advertising Expense
e. D. Finch, Drawing
f. Professional Fees
g. Depreciation Expense
h. Supplies

i. Equipment
j. Wages Payable
k. Insurance Expense
l. Accounts Receivable
m. Accounts Payable
n. D. Finch, Capital
o. Wages Expense

L.O. 3   **Exercise 5-4**   Journalize adjusting entries **(a)** through **(e)** from the following T accounts.

Supplies		Depreciation Expense		Accumulated Depreciation		Prepaid Insurance	
916	**(a)** 510	**(b)** 728			1,960	640	**(c)** 418
					(b) 728		

Wages Payable		Taxes Expense		Prepaid Taxes		Wages Expense	
	(d) 420	**(e)** 406		523	**(e)** 406	4,296	
						(d) 420	

Insurance Expense		Supplies Expense	
(c) 418		**(a)** 510	

L.O. 3   **Exercise 5-5**   Journalize the necessary adjusting entries at June 30, the close of the current fiscal year, based on the following data:

a. The Prepaid Insurance account before adjustments on June 30 has a balance of $1,260. You now figure out that $820 worth of the insurance has expired during the year.

b. The Supplies account before adjustments on June 30 has a balance of $872. By taking a physical inventory, you now determine that the amount of supplies on hand is worth $260.

c. The last payday was June 27. From June 28 to 30, there is $590 of accrued wages.

L.O. 3 **Exercise 5-6** Journalize the year-end adjusting entry for each of the following:

a. Equipment costing $19,300 has a useful life of five years with a $2,000 trade-in value at the end of five years. Record the depreciation for the year.

b. The payment of the $360 insurance premium for three years in advance was originally recorded as Prepaid Insurance. One year of the policy has now expired.

c. The Supplies account had a balance of $116 on January 1, the beginning of the year. $340 worth of supplies were bought during the year. A year-end inventory shows that $180 worth are still on hand.

d. Two employees earn a total of $200 per day for a five-day week beginning on Monday and ending on Friday. They were paid for the workweek ending December 28. They worked on Monday, December 31.

L.O. 1 **Exercise 5-7** If the required adjusting entries for Exercise 5-6 were not made at the end of the year, how would these omissions affect net income?

L.O. 3 **Exercise 5-8** Record the adjusting entry in each of the following situations:

a.

Supplies			**Supplies Expense**	
+		−	+	−
Bal. 260				
Purchases 490				

Ending inventory, $135.

b.

Supplies			**Supplies Expense**	
+		−	+	−
Bal. 400				
Purchases 920				

Supplies used, $840.

Problem Set A

L.O. 1 **Problem 5-1A** The trial balance of the Rowland Company as of September 30, after the company has completed the first month of operations, is shown at the top of the next page.

Rowland Company
Trial Balance
September 30, 19–

ACCOUNT NAME	DEBIT	CREDIT
Cash	3 8 2 7 00	
Accounts Receivable	6 2 1 4 00	
Office Equipment	4 8 2 0 00	
Accounts Payable		7 6 4 00
C. Rowland, Capital		12 1 3 8 00
C. Rowland, Drawing	1 4 0 0 00	
Commissions Earned		4 6 7 0 00
Salary Expense	9 0 0 00	
Rent Expense	2 5 0 00	
Advertising Expense	9 5 00	
Utilities Expense	4 0 00	
Miscellaneous Expenses	2 6 00	
	17 5 7 2 00	17 5 7 2 00

Instructions

1. Record the trial balance in the Trial Balance columns of the work sheet.
2. Record the letters or abbreviations standing for the account classifications (A, E, Draw., etc.) at the top of each column of the work sheet (as shown in Figure 5-4 on page 138).
3. Complete the work sheet by making the following adjustments: depreciation expense of office equipment, $114; accrued salaries, $122.

L.O. 2,3 **Problem 5-2A** The Working Papers present the completed work sheet for R. Bryan, Licensed Surveyor, for the month of October.

Instructions

1. Prepare an income statement.
2. Prepare a statement of owner's equity. Assume no additional investments were made during October.
3. Prepare a balance sheet.
4. Journalize the adjusting entries.

L.O. 1,3 **Problem 5-3A** The trial balance of Dan-Dee Cleaners at December 31, the end of the current year, is presented on the next page.
Data needed for year-end adjustments are as follows:

a. Inventory of cleaning supplies at December 31, $943.
b. Insurance expired during the year, $242.
c. Depreciation of furniture and equipment, $1,720.
d. Wages accrued at December 31, $126.

Dan-Dee Cleaners
Trial Balance
December 31, 19–

ACCOUNT NAME	DEBIT	CREDIT
Cash	2 4 6 2 00	
Cleaning Supplies	2 9 1 3 00	
Prepaid Insurance	4 6 8 00	
Furniture and Equipment	32 8 2 4 00	
Accumulated Depreciation		19 7 6 0 00
Accounts Payable		3 2 9 00
L. Manley, Capital		24 3 7 8 00
L. Manley, Drawing	9 2 6 0 00	
Income from Services		29 8 1 7 00
Wages Expense	20 4 0 0 00	
Rent Expense	3 6 0 0 00	
Utilities Expense	1 5 7 0 00	
Advertising Expense	4 2 9 00	
Miscellaneous Expense	3 5 8 00	
	74 2 8 4 00	74 2 8 4 00

Instructions

1. Complete the work sheet.
2. Journalize the adjusting entries.

L.O. 1,2,3,4   **Problem 5-4A**   The trial balance of Lakeland Leisure Lanes, a bowling alley, as of October 31, is shown on the next page.

Data for month-end adjustments are as follows:

a. Inventory of supplies at October 31, $318.
b. Insurance expired during the month, $420.
c. Depreciation of bowling equipment for the month, $15,200.
d. Depreciation of furniture and fixtures for the month, $1,560.
e. Depreciation of building for the month, $2,840.
f. Wages accrued at October 31, $364.

Instructions

1. Complete the work sheet for the month.
2. Prepare an income statement, a statement of owner's equity, and a balance sheet. Assume that no additional investments were made during October.
3. Journalize the adjusting entries.

Lakeland Leisure Lanes
Trial Balance
October 31, 19–

ACCOUNT NAME	DEBIT	CREDIT
Cash	2 854 00	
Supplies	896 00	
Prepaid Insurance	650 00	
Land	19 000 00	
Building	82 800 00	
Accumulated Depreciation, Building		24 000 00
Bowling Equipment	88 720 00	
Accumulated Depreciation, Bowling Equipment		58 700 00
Furniture and Fixtures	8 600 00	
Accumulated Depreciation, Furniture and Fixtures		4 280 00
Accounts Payable		4 180 00
Mortgage Payable		56 000 00
C. P. Cooke, Capital		35 668 00
C. P. Cooke, Drawing	4 000 00	
Bowling Fees Income		42 721 00
Concession Income		6 142 00
Wages Expense	15 800 00	
Advertising Expense	3 960 00	
Repair Expense	2 278 00	
Utilities Expense	1 640 00	
Miscellaneous Expense	493 00	
	231 691 00	231 691 00

Problem Set B

L.O. 1   **Problem 5-1B**   On the following page is the trial balance for the Hoyt Insurance Agency as of June 30, after the firm has completed its first month of operations.

Instructions

1. Record the trial balance in the Trial Balance columns of the work sheet.
2. Record the letters or abbreviations standing for the account classifications (A, E, Draw., etc.) at the top of each column of the work sheet (as shown in Figure 5-4 on page 138).
3. Complete the work sheet by making the following adjustments: depreciation expense of office equipment, $22; expired insurance, $26.

Hoyt Insurance Agency
Trial Balance
June 30, 19–

ACCOUNT NAME	DEBIT	CREDIT
Cash	2 5 1 6 00	
Accounts Receivable	1 2 0 8 00	
Prepaid Insurance	2 7 2 00	
Office Equipment	3 8 4 0 00	
Accounts Payable		9 6 2 00
P. Hoyt, Capital		6 6 2 8 00
P. Hoyt, Drawing	6 0 0 00	
Commissions Earned		1 4 9 0 00
Rent Expense	3 0 0 00	
Advertising Expense	1 5 6 00	
Travel Expense	1 1 4 00	
Utility Expense	6 0 00	
Miscellaneous Expense	1 4 00	
	9 0 8 0 00	9 0 8 0 00

L.O. 2,3　**Problem 5-2B**　The Working Papers present the completed work sheet for L. Bodwa, Licensed Surveyor, for the month of October.

Instructions

1. Prepare an income statement.
2. Prepare a statement of owner's equity. Assume that no additional investments were made during October.
3. Prepare a balance sheet.
4. Journalize the adjusting entries.

L.O. 1,3　**Problem 5-3B**　The trial balance of Casandra's Style Center as of December 31, the end of the current year, is presented on the next page.

Data for the year-end adjustments are as follows:

a. Inventory of beauty supplies at December 31, $728.
b. Insurance expired during the year, $142.
c. Depreciation of shop equipment for the year, $9,680.

Instructions

1. Complete the work sheet.
2. Journalize the adjusting entries.

Casandra's Style Center
Trial Balance
December 31, 19–

ACCOUNT NAME	DEBIT	CREDIT
Cash	1 3 2 0 00	
Beauty Supplies	3 1 6 2 00	
Prepaid Insurance	3 2 8 00	
Shop Equipment	38 7 9 0 00	
Accumulated Depreciation		17 6 4 0 00
Accounts Payable		5 2 6 00
C. Granger, Capital		25 1 4 4 00
C. Granger, Drawing	11 6 0 0 00	
Income from Services		24 7 1 4 00
Wages Expense	9 6 0 0 00	
Rent Expense	2 4 0 0 00	
Utilities Expense	5 1 8 00	
Telephone Expense	1 2 0 00	
Miscellaneous Expense	1 8 6 00	
	68 0 2 4 00	68 0 2 4 00

L.O. 1,2,3,4   **Problem 5-4B**   The trial balance for Conner's Miniature Golf at September 30 is shown on page 155.

C●   Data for month-end adjustments are as follows:

a. Inventory of supplies at September 30, $210.
b. Insurance expired during the month, $188.
c. Depreciation of field equipment for the month, $3,750.
d. Depreciation of lighting fixtures for the month, $410.
e. Wages accrued at September 30, $300.

Instructions

1. Complete the work sheet for the month.
2. Prepare an income statement, a statement of owner's equity, and a balance sheet. Assume that no additional investments were made during September.
3. Journalize the adjusting entries.

Conner's Miniature Golf
Trial Balance
September 30, 19–

ACCOUNT NAME	DEBIT	CREDIT
Cash	1 868 00	
Supplies	417 00	
Prepaid Insurance	540 00	
Golf Clubs	749 00	
Field Equipment	32 760 00	
Accumulated Depreciation, Field Equipment		7 120 00
Lighting Fixtures	1 916 00	
Accumulated Depreciation, Lighting Fixtures		418 00
Notes Payable		421 00
Accounts Payable		940 00
D. C. Conner, Capital		26 935 00
D. C. Conner, Drawing	1 680 00	
Golf Fees Income		22 728 00
Concession Income		961 00
Wages Expense	16 750 00	
Repair Expense	2 084 00	
Rent Expense	520 00	
Miscellaneous Expense	239 00	
	59 523 00	59 523 00

APPENDIX A
Methods of Depreciation

Three methods of depreciation will be illustrated using the example of a delivery truck. Assume the truck was bought at the beginning of Year 1 at a cost of $10,000. The truck is estimated to have a useful life of five years and a trade-in value of $2,500 at the end of the five-year period. The three methods to be described are straight-line, sum-of-the-years'-digits, and double-declining balance.

STRAIGHT-LINE METHOD

Incidentally, we showed this method in Chapter 5, providing for an equal amount of depreciation each year.

$$\text{Yearly depreciation} = \frac{\text{Cost of asset} - \text{Trade-in value}}{\text{Years of life}} = \frac{\$10,000 - \$2,500}{5 \text{ years}}$$

$$= \frac{\$7,500}{5 \text{ years}} = \$1,500 \text{ per year}$$

Year	Depreciation for the Year	Accumulated Depreciation	Book Value (Cost Less Accumulated Depreciation)
1	$7,500 ÷ 5 years = $1,500	$1,500	$10,000 − $1,500 = $8,500
2	$7,500 ÷ 5 years = $1,500	$1,500 + $1,500 = $3,000	$10,000 − $3,000 = $7,000
3	$7,500 ÷ 5 years = $1,500	$3,000 + $1,500 = $4,500	$10,000 − $4,500 = $5,500
4	$7,500 ÷ 5 years = $1,500	$4,500 + $1,500 = $6,000	$10,000 − $6,000 = $4,000
5	$7,500 ÷ 5 years = $1,500	$6,000 + $1,500 = $7,500	$10,000 − $7,500 = $2,500
	$7,500		

SUM-OF-THE-YEARS'-DIGITS METHOD

Add the number of years and use the sum as the denominator of the fractions. As numerators in the fractions, use the years in reverse order.

$$1 + 2 + 3 + 4 + 5 = 15$$

$$\frac{5}{15} + \frac{4}{15} + \frac{3}{15} + \frac{2}{15} + \frac{1}{15} = \frac{15}{15}$$

Year	Depreciation for the Year	Accumulated Depreciation	Book Value (Cost Less Accumulated Depreciation)
1	$7,500 × $5/15$ = $2,500	$2,500	$10,000 − $2,500 = $7,500
2	$7,500 × $4/15$ = $2,000	$2,500 + $2,000 = $4,500	$10,000 − $4,500 = $5,500
3	$7,500 × $3/15$ = $1,500	$4,500 + $1,500 = $6,000	$10,000 − $6,000 = $4,000
4	$7,500 × $2/15$ = $1,000	$6,000 + $1,000 = $7,000	$10,000 − $7,000 = $3,000
5	$7,500 × $1/15$ = $ 500	$7,000 + $ 500 = $7,500	$10,000 − $7,500 = $2,500
15	$15/15$ $7,500		

DOUBLE-DECLINING-BALANCE METHOD

The term *double* refers to double the straight-line rate. With a life of five years, the straight-line rate is $1/5$, or .2. Twice, or double, the straight-line rate is $2/5$ ($1/5$ × 2), or .4. **The trade-in value is not counted until the end of the schedule.** Multiply *book value* at beginning of year by twice the straight-line rate.

Year	Depreciation for the Year	Accumulated Depreciation	Book Value (Cost Less Accumulated Depreciation)
1	$10,000 × .4 = $4,000	$4,000	$10,000 − $4,000 = $6,000
2	$6,000 × .4 = $2,400	$4,000 + $2,400 = $6,400	$10,000 − $6,400 = $3,600
3	$3,600 − $2,500 = $1,100	$6,400 + $1,100 = $7,500	$10,000 − $7,500 = $2,500
4	0	$7,500	$10,000 − $7,500 = $2,500
5	0	$7,500	$10,000 − $7,500 = $2,500
	$7,500		

As long as the methods are used consistently, companies may choose any of the three methods for their own financial statements. However, for tax purposes, the Internal Revenue Service stipulates certain rates for specific classes of assets. The rates also vary depending on the time the assets were placed in service. We will show the most recent rates.

ASSETS PLACED IN SERVICE AFTER DECEMBER 31, 1986

Most businesses use the Modified Accelerated Cost Recovery System (MACRS) as defined by the Internal Revenue Service for federal income tax purposes. The Accelerated Cost Recovery System (ACRS) first took effect in 1981 and was later modified for assets placed in service after December 31, 1986 by the Tax Reform Act of 1986. The term *recovery* is used because

MACRS is a means of recovering or deducting the cost of an asset. According to MACRS, property is divided into eight classes, as follows:

3-year property—certain horses and tractor units for use over the road

5-year property—autos, trucks, computers, typewriters, and copiers

7-year property—office furniture and fixtures and any property that does not have a class life and that is not, by law, in any other class

10-year property—vessels, barges, tugs, and similar water transportation equipment

15-year property—wharves, roads, fences, and any municipal wastewater treatment plant

20-year property—certain farm buildings and municipal sewers

27.5-year residential rental property—rental houses and apartments

31.5-year real property—office buildings and warehouses

Under MACRS trade-in value is ignored.

Our light truck qualifies as five-year property. The approximate rates (rounded off for the sake of this illustration) are: first year, 20 percent; second year, 32 percent; third year, 19 percent; fourth year, 15 percent; fifth year, 14 percent. Congress may change the lives of property and/or the rates at which it is taxed.

Year	Depreciation for the Year	Accumulated Depreciation	Book Value (Cost Less Accumulated Depreciation)
1	$10,000 × .20 = $2,000	$2,000	$10,000 − $ 2,000 = $8,000
2	10,000 × .32 = 3,200	$2,000 + $3,200 = 5,200	10,000 − 5,200 = 4,800
3	10,000 × .19 = 1,900	5,200 + 1,900 = 7,100	10,000 − 7,100 = 2,900
4	10,000 × .15 = 1,500	7,100 + 1,500 = 8,600	10,000 − 8,600 = 1,400
5	10,000 × .14 = 1,400	8,600 + 1,400 = 10,000	10,000 − 10,000 = 0

In preparing financial reports for its own use, a company may calculate depreciation using any of the methods described in this appendix. However, for federal income tax purposes, a company must use the current MACRS for assets placed in service after December 31, 1986. The IRS also allows businesses to use an alternative straight-line depreciation, which differs slightly from the method presented in the text.

Problems

Problem A-1   A delivery van was bought for $14,400. The estimated life of the van is four years. The trade-in value at the end of four years is estimated to be $2,400. Prepare a depreciation schedule for the four-year period using the straight-line method.

Problem A-2   Using the information in Problem A-1, prepare a depreciation schedule using the sum-of-the-years'-digits method.

Problem A-3   Assume the van was purchased after January 1, 1987. Using the information in Problem A-1, prepare a schedule of depreciation under MACRS.

6 Closing Entries and the Post-Closing Trial Balance

LEARNING OBJECTIVES

After you have completed this chapter, you will be able to do the following:

1. Recall the steps in the accounting cycle.
2. Journalize and post closing entries for a service-type enterprise.
3. Prepare a post-closing trial balance for any type of enterprise.
4. Prepare interim statements.

Objective 1

Recall the steps in the accounting cycle.

So that you can see what we have covered so far, the steps in the accounting cycle for an entire fiscal period (generally twelve consecutive months) are now repeated:

1. Analyze source documents and record business transactions in a journal.
2. Post journal entries to the accounts in the ledger.
3. Prepare a trial balance.
4. Gather adjustment data and record the adjusting entries on a work sheet.
5. Complete the work sheet.
6. Prepare financial statements from the data on the work sheet.
7. Journalize and post the adjusting entries from the data on the work sheet.
8. Journalize and post the closing entries.
9. Prepare a post-closing trial balance.

This chapter explains the procedure for completing the final steps, closing entries and the post-closing trial balance.

Adjusting entries, closing entries, and the post-closing trial balance are usually prepared only at the end of a twelve-month fiscal period. However, to expose you to these final steps in the accounting cycle, we assumed here and in Chapter 5 that the fiscal period for Paul's Auto Body consists of only one month. We made this assumption so that we could

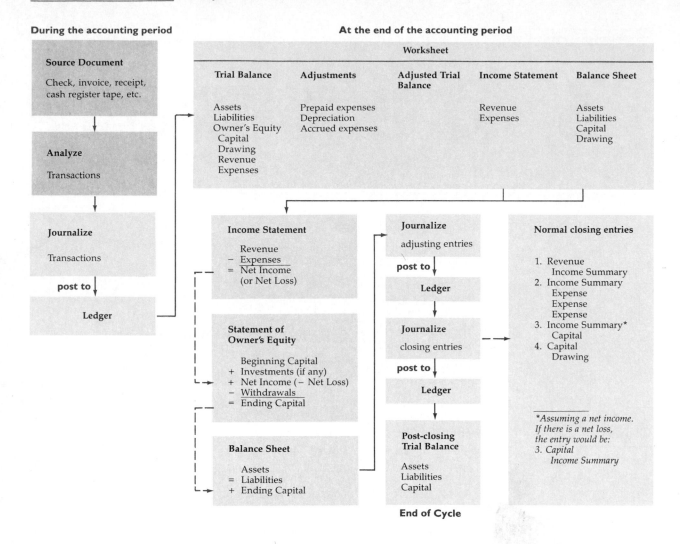

thoroughly cover the material and give you a chance to practice its application. The entire accounting cycle is outlined in Figure 6-1.

CLOSING ENTRIES

So that you will understand the reason for the closing entries, let us first repeat the fundamental accounting equation:

Assets = Liabilities + Owner's Equity + Revenue − Expenses

We know that the income statement, as stated in the third line of its heading, covers a definite period of time. The income statement consists of revenue minus expenses for this period of time only. So, when this period is over, we should start from zero for the next period. In other words, we wipe the slate clean, so that we can start all over again next period.

Purposes of Closing Entries

This brings us to the *purpose* of the **closing entries,** which is to close off the revenue and expense accounts. We do this because their balances apply to only one fiscal period. As stated before, with the coming of the next fiscal period, we want to start from scratch, recording brand-new revenue and expenses. Accountants also refer to this as *clearing the accounts.* For income tax purposes, this is certainly understandable. No one wants to pay income tax more than once on the same income, and the Internal Revenue Service doesn't allow you to count an expense more than once. So now we have this:

$$\text{Assets} = \text{Liabilities} + \underset{\text{(Capital)}}{\text{Owner's Equity}} + \overset{\text{(closed)}}{\cancel{\text{Revenue}}} - \overset{\text{(closed)}}{\cancel{\text{Expenses}}}$$

The assets, liabilities, and owner's capital accounts remain open. The balance sheet, with its one date in the heading, merely gives the present balances of these accounts. The accountant carries the asset, liability, and capital account balances over to the next fiscal period.

Procedure for Closing

Objective 2

Journalize and post closing entries for a service-type enterprise.

The procedure for closing is simply to balance off the account, in other words, to make the balance *equal to zero.* This meets our objective, which is to start from zero in the next fiscal period. Let's illustrate this first with T accounts. Suppose an account happens to have a debit balance of $960; then, to make the balance equal to zero, we *credit* the account for $960. We write "Closing" in the Item column of the ledger account.

Debit		Credit	
Balance	960	Closing	960

To take another example, suppose an account happens to have a credit balance of $1,200; then, to make the balance equal to zero, we *debit* the account for $1,200.

Debit		Credit	
Closing	1,200	Balance	1,200

Every entry must have both a debit and a credit. So, to record the other half of the closing entry, we bring into existence **Income Summary.** The Income Summary account does not have plus and minus signs. There are four steps in the closing procedure:

1. **Close the revenue accounts into Income Summary.**
2. **Close the expense accounts into Income Summary.**
3. **Close the Income Summary account into the Capital account.**
4. **Close the Drawing account into the Capital account.**

To illustrate by making the entries directly in T accounts, we return to Paul's Auto Body. For the purpose of the illustration, assume that Paul's Auto Body's fiscal period consists of one month. We have the following balances in the revenue and expense accounts after the adjustments have been posted.

Income from Services		Utilities Expense	
−	+	+	−
	Balance 3,230.00	Balance 220.00	

Wages Expense		Supplies Expense	
+	−	+	−
Balance 730.00		Balance 80.00	

Rent Expense		Insurance Expense	
+	−	+	−
Balance 400.00		Balance 13.33	

Advertising Expense		Depreciation Expense	
+	−	+	−
Balance 180.00		Balance 286.75	

Step 1   Close the revenue account, or accounts, into Income Summary. In order to make the balance of Income from Services equal to zero, we *balance it off,* or debit it, in the amount of $3,230. Because we need an offsetting credit, we credit Income Summary for the same amount.

Income from Services		Income Summary	
−	+		
Closing 3,230.00	Balance 3,230.00		3,230.00

In essence, the balance of Income from Services is transferred to Income Summary.

Now let's look at the journal entry for this step (Figure 6-2). Notice how writing *Closing Entries* in the Description column eliminates the need to write explanations for all the closing entries.

FIGURE 6-2

GENERAL JOURNAL   PAGE ___4___

DATE	DESCRIPTION	POST. REF.	DEBIT	CREDIT
	Closing Entries			
30	*Income from Services*		3 2 3 0 00	
	Income Summary			3 2 3 0 00

Step 2 Close the expense accounts into Income Summary. To make the balances of the expense accounts equal to zero, we need to balance them off, or credit them. Again the T accounts are useful for formulating this journal entry. In essence, the total of all the individual balances of each expense account is transferred to Income Summary, as shown in Figure 6-3 at the top of the next page.

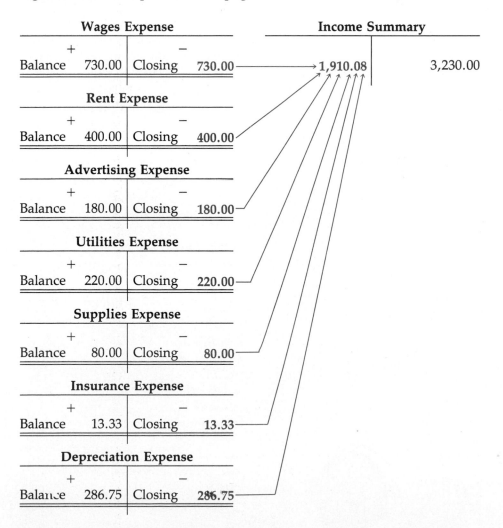

FIGURE 6-3

GENERAL JOURNAL   PAGE ___4___

DATE	DESCRIPTION	POST. REF.	DEBIT	CREDIT
	Closing Entries			
30	*Income from Services*		3 2 3 0 00	
	Income Summary			3 2 3 0 00
30	*Income Summary*		1 9 1 0 08	
	Wages Expense			7 3 0 00
	Rent Expense			4 0 0 00
	Advertising Expense			1 8 0 00
	Utilities Expense			2 2 0 00
	Supplies Expense			8 0 00
	Insurance Expense			1 3 33
	Depreciation Expense			2 8 6 75

Step 1 (bracket spans Income from Services / Income Summary)

Step 3 Recall that we created Income Summary so that we could have a debit and credit with each closing entry. Now that it has done its job, we close it out. We use the same procedure as before, in that we make the balance equal to zero, or balance off the account. We transfer, or close, the balance of the Income Summary account into the Capital account, as shown in the T accounts and in Figure 6-4.

FIGURE 6-4

GENERAL JOURNAL   PAGE ___4___

DATE	DESCRIPTION	POST. REF.	DEBIT	CREDIT
	Closing Entries			
30	*Income from Services*		3 2 3 0 00	
	Income Summary			3 2 3 0 00
30	*Income Summary*		1 9 1 0 08	
	Wages Expense			7 3 0 00
	Rent Expense			4 0 0 00
	Advertising Expense			1 8 0 00
	Utilities Expense			2 2 0 00
	Supplies Expense			8 0 00
	Insurance Expense			1 3 33
	Depreciation Expense			2 8 6 75
30	*Income Summary*		1 3 1 9 92	
	Paul Greenwalt, Capital			1 3 1 9 92

Step 1 (bracket spans Income from Services / Income Summary)
Step 2 (bracket spans Income Summary through Depreciation Expense)

Income Summary		Paul Greenwalt, Capital	
		−	+
1,910.08	3,230.00		Balance 32,000.00
Closing **1,319.92**			(Net Inc.) **1,319.92**

Income Summary is always closed into the Capital account by the amount of the net income or the net loss. Comparing net income or net loss with the closing entry for Income Summary can serve as a check point or verification for you.

Net income is added or credited to the Capital account because in the statement of owner's equity, as we have seen, net income is treated as an addition. Net loss, on the other hand, should be subtracted from or debited to the Capital account because net loss is treated as a deduction in the statement of owner's equity. Here's how one would close Income Summary for J. Doe Company, which had a net loss of $200.

Income Summary		J. Doe, Capital	
(Expenses) 900	(Revenue) 700	(Net Loss) 200	Balance 30,000
	Closing **200**		

The entry to close Income Summary into Doe's Capital account would look like this:

	GENERAL JOURNAL			PAGE __3__
DATE	DESCRIPTION	POST. REF.	DEBIT	CREDIT
	Closing Entries			
31	*J. Doe, Capital*		2 0 0 00	
	Income Summary			2 0 0 00

Step 4   Let us return to the example of Paul's Auto Body. The Drawing account applies to only one fiscal period, so it too must be closed. You may recall from Chapter 2 that Drawing is not an expense because no money is paid to anyone outside the business. And because Drawing is not an expense, it cannot affect net income or net loss. It appears in the statement of owner's equity as a deduction from the Capital account, and so it is closed directly into the Capital account. So we balance off the Drawing account, or make the balance of it equal to zero. The balance of Drawing is transferred to the Capital account.

Paul Greenwalt, Drawing		Paul Greenwalt, Capital	
+	−	−	+
Balance 1,000.00	Closing 1,000.00	1,000.00	Balance 32,000.00
			(Net Inc.) 1,319.92

The four journal entries in the closing procedure are illustrated in Figure 6-5.

FIGURE 6-5

GENERAL JOURNAL   PAGE ___4___

	DATE	DESCRIPTION	POST. REF.	DEBIT	CREDIT
		Closing Entries			
Step 1	30	Income from Services		3 2 3 0 00	
		Income Summary			3 2 3 0 00
	30	Income Summary		1 9 1 0 08	
		Wages Expense			7 3 0 00
		Rent Expense			4 0 0 00
Step 2		Advertising Expense			1 8 0 00
		Utilities Expense			2 2 0 00
		Supplies Expense			8 0 00
		Insurance Expense			1 3 33
		Depreciation Expense			2 8 6 75
Step 3	30	Income Summary		1 3 1 9 92	
		Paul Greenwalt, Capital			1 3 1 9 92
	30	Paul Greenwalt, Capital		1 0 0 0 00	
		Paul Greenwalt, Drawing			1 0 0 0 00

As a memory tool to learn the sequence of steps in the closing procedure, one can use the letters of the closing elements, **RESD: R**evenue, **E**xpenses, **S**ummary, **D**rawing.

These closing entries show that Paul's Auto Body has net income of $1,319.92, the owner has withdrawn $1,000 for personal expenses, and $319.92 has been retained or plowed back into the business, thereby increasing capital.

Closing Entries Taken Directly from the Work Sheet

One can gather the information for the closing entries either directly from the ledger accounts or from the work sheet. Since the Income Statement columns of the work sheet consist entirely of revenues and expenses, one can pick up the figures for three of the four closing entries from these columns. Figure 6-6 shows a partial work sheet for Paul's Auto Body.

You may formulate the closing entries by simply balancing off all the figures that appear in the Income Statement columns. For example, in the Income Statement column, there is a credit for $3,230, so we debit that account for $3,230 and credit Income Summary for $3,230.

There are debits for $730, $400, $180, $220, $80, $13.33, and $286.75. So now we *credit* these accounts for the same amounts, and we debit Income Summary for their total.

Next, as usual, we close Income Summary into Capital, by using the net income figure already shown on the work sheet.

FIGURE 6-6

	ACCOUNT NAME	TRIAL BALANCE DEBIT	TRIAL BALANCE CREDIT	ADJUSTED TRIAL BALANCE DEBIT	ADJUSTED TRIAL BALANCE CREDIT	INCOME STATEMENT DEBIT	INCOME STATEMENT CREDIT	
1	Cash	11 5 2 0 00						1
2	Accounts Receivable	2 0 00						2
3	Supplies	4 0 0 00			(a) 8 0 00			3
4	Prepaid Insurance	3 2 0 00			(b) 1 3 33			4
5	Equipment	22 9 4 0 00						5
6	Accounts Payable		2 4 0 0 00					6
7	Paul Greenwalt,							7
8	Capital		32 0 0 0 00					8
9	Paul Greenwalt,							9
10	Drawing	1 0 0 0 00						10
11	Income from Services		3 2 3 0 00				3 2 3 0 00	11
12	Wages Expense	6 3 0 00		(d) 1 0 0 00		7 3 0 00		12
13	Rent Expense	4 0 0 00				4 0 0 00		13
14	Advertising Expense	1 8 0 00				1 8 0 00		14
15	Utilities Expense	2 2 0 00				2 2 0 00		15
16		37 6 3 0 00	37 6 3 0 00					16
17	Supplies Expense			(a) 8 0 00		8 0 00		17
18	Insurance Expense			(b) 1 3 33		1 3 33		18
19	Depreciation Expense			(c) 2 8 6 75		2 8 6 75		19
20	Accumulated							20
21	Depreciation				(c) 2 8 6 75			21
22	Wages Payable				(d) 1 0 0 00			22
23				4 8 0 08	4 8 0 08	1 9 1 0 08	3 2 3 0 00	23
24						1 3 1 9 92		24
25	Net Income					3 2 3 0 00	3 2 3 0 00	25
26								26
27								27
28								28
29								29
30								30

Remember

The temporary-equity accounts (revenue, expenses, Drawing, and Income Summary) are closed out because they apply to only one fiscal period.

We would of course have to pick up the last entry from the Balance Sheet columns to close Drawing.

Incidentally, accountants call the accounts that are to be closed (such as revenue, expenses, Income Summary, and Drawing) **nominal** or **temporary-equity accounts**. These accounts are *temporary* in that their balances apply to one fiscal period only. The *equity* aspect pertains because these accounts all come under the umbrella of owner's equity, as we showed in Chapter 2.

On the other hand, accountants call the accounts that remain open (such as assets, liabilities, and Capital) **real** or **permanent accounts**. These accounts have balances that will be carried over to the next fiscal period. They are *permanent* in the sense that as long as the company exists there will be balances in these accounts.

We indicate that the accounts are closed by writing the word *Closing* in the Item column of the ledger and by extending a line through both the Debit Balance and Credit Balance columns.

Posting the Closing Entries

After we have posted the closing entries, the Capital, Drawing, Income Summary, revenue, and expense accounts of Paul's Auto Body appear as follows:

GENERAL LEDGER

ACCOUNT *Paul Greenwalt, Capital*   ACCOUNT NO. *311*

						BALANCE	
DATE	ITEM	POST. REF.	DEBIT	CREDIT		DEBIT	CREDIT
19–							
June 1		1		32 0 0 0 00			32 0 0 0 00
30		4		1 3 1 9 92			33 3 1 9 92
30		4	1 0 0 0 00				32 3 1 9 92

ACCOUNT *Paul Greenwalt, Drawing*   ACCOUNT NO. *312*

						BALANCE	
DATE	ITEM	POST. REF.	DEBIT	CREDIT		DEBIT	CREDIT
19–							
June 30		3	1 0 0 0 00			1 0 0 0 00	
30	*Closing*	4		1 0 0 0 00			

GENERAL LEDGER

ACCOUNT _Income Summary_   ACCOUNT NO. _313_

DATE		ITEM	POST. REF.	DEBIT	CREDIT	BALANCE DEBIT	BALANCE CREDIT
19–							
June	30		4		3 2 3 0 00		3 2 3 0 00
	30		4	1 9 1 0 08			1 3 1 9 92
	30	Closing	4	1 3 1 9 92			

ACCOUNT _Income from Services_   ACCOUNT NO. _411_

DATE		ITEM	POST. REF.	DEBIT	CREDIT	BALANCE DEBIT	BALANCE CREDIT
19–							
June	7		1		6 0 0 00		6 0 0 00
	14		2		7 6 0 00		1 3 6 0 00
	21		2		8 3 0 00		2 1 9 0 00
	23		2		8 0 00		2 2 7 0 00
	30		3		9 6 0 00		3 2 3 0 00
	30	Closing	4	3 2 3 0 00			

ACCOUNT _Wages Expense_   ACCOUNT NO. _511_

DATE		ITEM	POST. REF.	DEBIT	CREDIT	BALANCE DEBIT	BALANCE CREDIT
19–							
June	10		1	2 4 0 00		2 4 0 00	
	24		3	3 9 0 00		6 3 0 00	
	30	Adjusting	4	1 0 0 00		7 3 0 00	
	30	Closing	4		7 3 0 00		

ACCOUNT _Rent Expense_   ACCOUNT NO. _512_

DATE		ITEM	POST. REF.	DEBIT	CREDIT	BALANCE DEBIT	BALANCE CREDIT
19–							
June	8		1	4 0 0 00		4 0 0 00	
	30	Closing	4		4 0 0 00		

ACCOUNT _Advertising Expense_   ACCOUNT NO. _513_

DATE		ITEM	POST. REF.	DEBIT	CREDIT	BALANCE DEBIT	BALANCE CREDIT
19–							
June	14		2	1 8 0 00		1 8 0 00	
	30	Closing	4		1 8 0 00	—	—

ACCOUNT _Utilities Expense_   ACCOUNT NO. _514_

DATE		ITEM	POST. REF.	DEBIT	CREDIT	BALANCE DEBIT	BALANCE CREDIT
19–							
June	15		2	2 2 0 00		2 2 0 00	
	30	Closing	4		2 2 0 00	—	—

ACCOUNT _Supplies Expense_   ACCOUNT NO. _515_

DATE		ITEM	POST. REF.	DEBIT	CREDIT	BALANCE DEBIT	BALANCE CREDIT
19–							
June	30	Adjusting	4	8 0 00		8 0 00	
	30	Closing	4		8 0 00	—	—

ACCOUNT _Insurance Expense_   ACCOUNT NO. _516_

DATE		ITEM	POST. REF.	DEBIT	CREDIT	BALANCE DEBIT	BALANCE CREDIT
19–							
June	30	Adjusting	4	1 3 33		1 3 33	
	30	Closing	4		1 3 33	—	—

ACCOUNT _Depreciation Expense_   ACCOUNT NO. _517_

DATE		ITEM	POST. REF.	DEBIT	CREDIT	BALANCE DEBIT	BALANCE CREDIT
19–							
June	30	Adjusting	4	2 8 6 75		2 8 6 75	
	30	Closing	4		2 8 6 75	—	—

THE POST-CLOSING TRIAL BALANCE

Objective 3

Prepare a post-closing trial balance for any type of enterprise.

After posting the closing entries and before going on to the next fiscal period, one should verify the balances of the accounts that remain open. To do so, make up a **post-closing trial balance, using the final balance figures from the ledger accounts.** The purpose of the post-closing trial balance is to make absolutely sure that the debit balances equal the credit balances.

Note that the accounts listed in the post-closing trial balance (assets, liabilities, and Capital) are the *real or permanent accounts.* (See Figure 6–7.) The accountant carries forward the balances of the permanent accounts from one fiscal period to another.

Contrast this to the handling of *nominal or temporary-equity accounts* (revenue, expenses, Income Summary, and Drawing), which, as you have seen, are closed at the end of each fiscal period.

If the totals of the post-closing trial balance are not equal, here's a recommended procedure for tracking down the error.

1. Re-add the trial balance columns.
2. Check to see that the figures were correctly transferred from the ledger accounts to the post-closing trial balance.
3. Verify the posting of the adjusting entries and the recording of the new balances.
4. Make sure the closing entries have been posted and all revenue, expense, Income Summary, and Drawing accounts have zero balances.

FIGURE 6-7

Paul's Auto Body
Post-Closing Trial Balance
June 30, 19–

ACCOUNT NAME	DEBIT	CREDIT
Cash	11 5 2 0 00	
Accounts Receivable	2 0 00	
Supplies	3 2 0 00	
Prepaid Insurance	3 0 6 67	
Equipment	22 9 4 0 00	
Accumulated Depreciation		2 8 6 75
Accounts Payable		2 4 0 0 00
Wages Payable		1 0 0 00
Paul Greenwalt, Capital		32 3 1 9 92
	35 1 0 6 67	35 1 0 6 67

INTERIM STATEMENTS

As we said previously, a firm's fiscal period generally consists of twelve consecutive months. However, it is understandable that the owner of the business does not want to wait until the end of the twelve-month period to find out how the company is doing financially. Instead, most owners want financial statements at the end of each month. The financial statements prepared during the fiscal year for periods of less than twelve months are called **interim statements.** (They are given this name because they are prepared in the in-between times.) For example, a business may prepare the income statement, the statement of owner's equity, and the balance sheet *monthly*. These statements provide up-to-date information about the results and status of operations. Suppose a company has a fiscal period extending from January 1 of one year through December 31 of the same year; it might have the following interim statements:

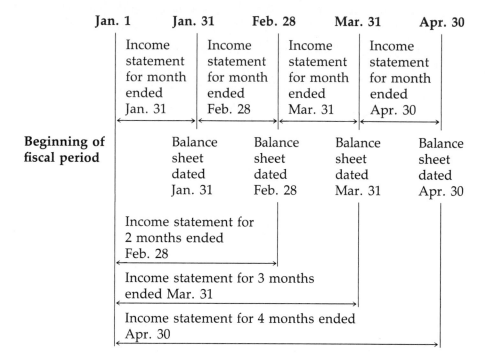

In this case, the accountant would prepare a work sheet at the end of each month. Next, based on these work sheets, he or she prepares the financial statements. *However, the remaining steps—journalizing the adjusting and closing entries and preparing the post-closing trial balance—would be performed only at the end of the year.*

Insurance Expense

(b)	240	240

Miscellaneous Expense

120	120

L.O. 2   Exe

L.O. 2,3   Exe
of tl
$27,
$11,
the
new

L.O. 2   Ex
of R

Cas
Equ
Acc
Acc
A. I
A. I

All

L.O. 2   Ex
Bor

1
2
3
4
5
6
7

SUMMARY

L.O. 1   The accounting cycle begins when the accountant analyzes source documents and records business transactions in a journal. It ends when the accountant journalizes and posts closing entries and then prepares a post-closing trial balance.

L.O. 2   The purpose of closing entries is to close off temporary-equity accounts. These accounts consist of revenues, expenses, Income Summary, and the Drawing account. In the closing process we balance off the account, making the balance equal to zero. The four steps for closing are:

1. Close the revenue accounts into Income Summary.
2. Close the expense accounts into Income Summary.
3. Close Income Summary into the Capital account by the amount of the net income or net loss.
4. Close the Drawing account into the Capital account.

Write the word *Closing* in the Item column of the ledger accounts, and extend lines through the balance columns, indicating that the balance of each account closed is zero.

L.O. 3   A post-closing trial balance consists of the final balances of the accounts remaining open. It is the final proof that the debit balances equal the credit balances before the posting for the new fiscal period commences. Many

L.O. 4   businesses prepare interim financial statements at regular intervals throughout the year. This lets managers know how the business is doing.

GLOSSARY

Closing entries   Entries made at the end of a fiscal period to close off the revenue and expense accounts; that is, to make the balances of the temporary-equity account equal to zero. This is also referred to as *clearing the accounts*.

Income Summary   An account brought into existence in order to have a debit and credit with each closing entry.

Interim statements   Financial statements prepared during the fiscal year, covering a period of time less than the entire twelve months.

Nominal or **temporary-equity accounts**   Accounts that apply to only one fiscal period and that are to be closed at the end of that fiscal period, such as revenue, expense, Income Summary, and Drawing accounts. This category may also be described as all accounts except assets, liabilities, and the Capital account.

Post-closing trial balance   The listing of the final balances of the real accounts at the end of the fiscal period.

Real or **permanent accounts**   The accounts that remain open (assets, liabilities, and the Capital account in owner's equity) and that have balances that will be carried over to the next fiscal period.

QUES

Discus

1. What i
   accoun
2. Explair
3. List the
4. For the
   sugges
   throug
   January
5. What i:
   fiscal p
   fiscal p
6. List the
7. What i:
8. What a

Exerci

L.O. 3   **Exercise**
closing tri:

a. Salaries
b. J. Barke
c. Income
d. Accoun
e. Rent E>

L.O. 1   **Exercise**
proper seq

a. Prepare
b. Comple
c. Record
d. Gather
e. Prepare
f. Analyze
g. Record
h. Post jou
i. Prepare

L.O. 2   **Exercise**
closing ent

Accumulated Depreciation

	1,600
(a)	400

The Balance Sheet columns of the work sheet contain the following:

ACCOUNT NAME	INCOME STATEMENT DEBIT	INCOME STATEMENT CREDIT	BALANCE SHEET DEBIT	BALANCE SHEET CREDIT
T. O. Borne, Capital				80 0 0 0 00
T. O. Borne, Drawing			17 0 0 0 00	

Journalize the four closing entries.

L.O. 4   **Exercise 6-8**   Selected T accounts for D. J. Minelli Company are as follows:

Income Summary

Dec. 31	90,000	Dec. 31	120,000
Dec. 31 Closing	30,000		

D. J. Minelli, Capital

Dec. 31	26,000	Jan. 1 Balance	77,000
		Dec. 31	30,000

D. J. Minelli, Drawing

Mar. 21	6,000	Dec. 31 Closing	26,000
Sept. 30	9,000		
Nov. 14	11,000		

Prepare a statement of owner's equity.

Problem Set A

L.O. 2   **Problem 6-1A**   After the adjusting entries have been posted for C. P. Stacy, Consulting Engineer, the ledger contained the following account balances on June 30:

Cash	$43,644	Income Summary	$ 0
Office Supplies	2,280	Professional Fees	45,840
Furniture and Fixtures	19,032	Salary Expense	20,256
Accum. Depreciation	13,008	Rent Expense	2,496
Accounts Payable	10,236	Telephone Expense	288
Salaries Payable	1,968	Office Supplies Expense	5,052
C. P. Stacy, Capital	38,988	Depreciation Expense	2,592
C. P. Stacy, Drawing	14,400		

Income Summary has a zero balance, because the account was not used previously.

Instructions

Journalize the closing entries with the four steps in the proper sequence.

L.O. 2   **Problem 6-2A**   Following is the partial work sheet for Garvey Upholstery for the fiscal year ending December 31 of this year:

ACCOUNT NAME	INCOME STATEMENT DEBIT	INCOME STATEMENT CREDIT	BALANCE SHEET DEBIT	BALANCE SHEET CREDIT
Cash			13 6 0 0 00	
Accounts Receivable			7 2 0 0 00	
Supplies			2 7 3 2 00	
Equipment			16 8 8 0 00	
Accumulated Depreciation, Equipment				11 7 0 4 00
Truck			12 7 6 0 00	
Accumulated Depreciation, Truck				7 8 1 6 00
Accounts Payable				2 5 6 0 00
L. Murren, Capital				70 3 9 2 00
L. Murren, Drawing			38 4 0 0 00	
Service Income		94 6 8 0 00		
Wages Expense	73 6 8 0 00			
Rent Expense	9 6 0 0 00			
Truck Operating Expense	7 4 4 0 00			
Telephone Expense	7 2 0 00			
Supplies Expense	9 0 8 00			
Depreciation Expense, Equipment	1 3 0 4 00			
Depreciation Expense, Truck	1 9 2 8 00			
	95 5 8 0 00	94 6 8 0 00	91 5 7 2 00	92 4 7 2 00
Net Loss		9 0 0 00	9 0 0 00	
	95 5 8 0 00	95 5 8 0 00	92 4 7 2 00	92 4 7 2 00

Instructions

Journalize the closing entries with the four steps in the proper sequence.

L.O. 1,2,3   **Problem 6-3A**   The completed work sheet for Gable Insurance Agency is presented in the Working Papers.

Instructions

1. Record beginning balances in ledger. Journalize and post adjusting entries.
2. Journalize and post the closing entries with the four steps in the proper sequence.
3. Prepare a post-closing trial balance.

L.O. 1,2,3   **Problem 6-4A**   The account balances of Jacobi Window-Washing Service
as of December 31, the end of the fiscal year, are as follows:

Cash	$2,524.50	R. Jacobi, Capital	$ 4,998.00
Accounts Receivable	2,685.00	R. Jacobi, Drawing	14,400.00
Cleaning Supplies	364.50	Service Income	31,461.50
Cleaning Equipment	4,455.00	Wages Expense	9,630.00
Accumulated Depreciation,		Advertising Expense	396.00
Cleaning Equipment	2,790.00	Truck Operating Expense	622.50
Truck	6,762.50	Utilities Expense	330.00
Accumulated Depreciation, Truck	2,137.50	Miscellaneous Expense	157.50
Accounts Payable	940.50		

Data for the adjustments:

a. Accrued wages, $192.
b. Inventory of cleaning supplies, $180.
c. Depreciation of cleaning equipment, $377.50.
d. Depreciation of truck, $570.

Instructions

1. Complete the work sheet.
2. Prepare an income statement.
3. Prepare a statement of owner's equity assuming that no additional investments were made during the year.
4. Prepare a balance sheet.
5. Journalize the adjusting entries.
6. Journalize the closing entries with the four steps in the proper sequence.

L.O. 2   Problem Set B

Problem 6-1B   After the adjusting entries have been posted for F. L.
Fagan, Architect, the ledger contained the following account balances on
April 30:

Cash	$36,498	Income Summary	$ 0
Office Supplies	4,239	Professional Fees	45,567
Furniture and Fixtures	25,911	Salary Expense	20,340
Accum. Depreciation	16,569	Rent Expense	3,150
Accounts Payable	8,469	Telephone Expense	468
Salaries Payable	360	Office Supplies Expense	1,080
F. L. Fagan, Capital	39,600	Depreciation Expense	684
F. L. Fagan, Drawing	15,720	Miscellaneous Expense	2,475

Income Summary has a zero balance, because the account had not been
used previously.

Instructions

Journalize the closing entries with the four steps in the proper sequence.

L.O. 2   **Problem 6-2B**   Following is the partial work sheet for Creski Veterinary Service for the fiscal year ending December 31 of this year:

ACCOUNT NAME	INCOME STATEMENT		BALANCE SHEET	
	DEBIT	CREDIT	DEBIT	CREDIT
Cash			11 852 00	
Accounts Receivable			7 124 00	
Supplies			2 620 00	
Equipment			19 656 00	
Accumulated Depreciation, Equipment				14 440 00
Truck			14 336 00	
Accumulated Depreciation, Truck				12 880 00
Accounts Payable				3 304 00
L. Creski, Capital				15 596 00
L. Creski, Drawing			41 600 00	
Service Income		102 864 00		
Wages Expense	29 680 00			
Rent Expense	9 600 00			
Truck Operating Expense	7 720 00			
Telephone Expense	960 00			
Supplies Expense	928 00			
Depreciation Expense, Equipment	1 248 00			
Depreciation Expense, Truck	1 760 00			
	51 896 00	102 864 00	97 188 00	46 220 00
Net Income	50 968 00			50 968 00
	102 864 00	102 864 00	97 188 00	97 188 00

Instructions

Journalize the closing entries with the four steps in the proper sequence.

L.O. 1,2,3   **Problem 6-3B**   The completed work sheet for Manfred Employment Agency is presented in the Working Papers.

Instructions

1. Record beginning balances in ledger. Journalize and post adjusting entries.
2. Journalize and post the closing entries with the four steps in the proper sequence.
3. Prepare a post-closing trial balance.

L.O. 1,2   **Problem 6-4B**   The account balances of Wyreski Landscape Service as of
October 31, the end of the current fiscal year, are as follows:

Cash	$ 1,947.00
Accounts Receivable	3,165.00
Supplies	639.00
Equipment	5,796.00
Accumulated Depreciation, Equipment	2,898.00
Truck	9,470.00
Accumulated Depreciation, Truck	8,180.00
Accounts Payable	1,308.50
L. Wyreski, Capital	2,758.00
L. Wyreski, Drawing	16,200.00
Service Income	37,260.00
Wages Expense	12,960.00
Advertising Expense	393.00
Truck Operating Expense	636.00
Utilities Expense	478.50
Miscellaneous Expense	720.00

Data for the adjustments:

a. Accrued wages, $174.
b. Inventory of supplies, $456.
c. Depreciation of equipment, $180.
d. Depreciation of truck, $444.

Instructions

1. Complete the work sheet.
2. Prepare an income statement.
3. Prepare a statement of owner's equity assuming that no additional investments were made during the year.
4. Prepare a balance sheet.
5. Journalize the adjusting entries.
6. Journalize the closing entries with the four steps in the proper sequence.

REVIEW OF T ACCOUNT PLACEMENT AND REPRESENTATIVE TRANSACTIONS: CHAPTERS 1 THROUGH 6
Review of T Account Placement

The following display sums up the placement of T accounts covered in Chapters 2 through 6 in relation to the fundamental accounting equation. Accounts shown in red are contra accounts.

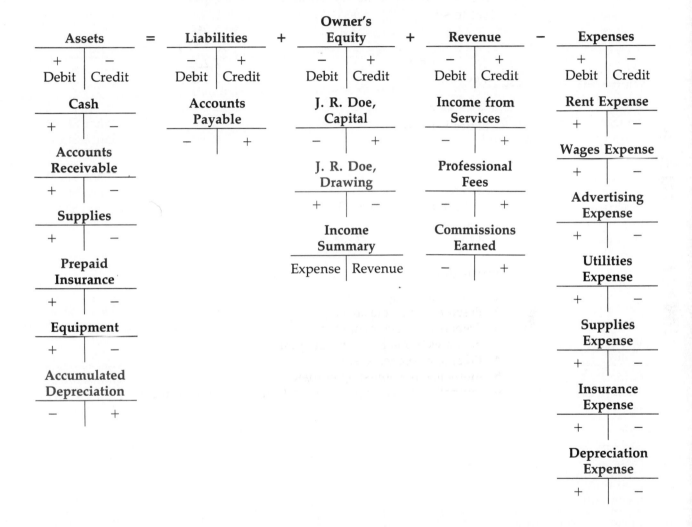

Review of Representative Transactions

The following table summarizes the recording of the various transactions described in Chapters 1–6 and the classification of the accounts involved.

Transaction	Accounts Involved	Class.	Increase or Decrease	Therefore Debit or Credit	Financial Statement
Owner invested cash in business	Cash J. R. Doe, Capital	A OE	I I	Debit Credit	Balance Sheet Statement of Owner's Equity
Bought equipment for cash	Equipment Cash	A A	I D	Debit Credit	Balance Sheet Balance Sheet
Bought supplies on account	Supplies Accounts Payable	A L	I I	Debit Credit	Balance Sheet Balance Sheet

Bought equipment paying a down payment with the remainder on account	Equipment
	  Cash
	  Accounts Payable
		A
		A
		L
			I
			D
			I
				Debit
				Credit
				Credit
					Balance Sheet
					Balance Sheet
					Balance Sheet

Paid premium for insurance policy	Prepaid Insurance Cash	A A	I D	Debit Credit	Balance Sheet Balance Sheet
Paid creditor on account	Accounts Payable Cash	L A	D D	Debit Credit	Balance Sheet Balance Sheet
Sold services for cash	Cash Income from Services	A R	I I	Debit Credit	Balance Sheet Income State.
Paid rent for month	Rent Expense Cash	E A	I D	Debit Credit	Income State. Balance Sheet
Billed customers for services performed	Accounts Receivable Income from Services	A R	I I	Debit Credit	Balance Sheet Income State.
Owner withdrew cash for personal use	J. R. Doe, Drawing Cash	OE A	I D	Debit Credit	Statement of Owner's Equity Balance Sheet

Transaction	Accounts Involved	Class.	Increase or Decrease	Therefore Debit or Credit	Financial Statement
Received cash from charge customers to apply on account	Cash Accounts Receivable	A A	I D	Debit Credit	Balance Sheet Balance Sheet
Paid wages to employees	Wages Expense Cash	E A	I D	Debit Credit	Income State. Balance Sheet
Adjusting entry for supplies used	Supplies Expense Supplies	E A	I D	Debit Credit	Income State. Balance Sheet
Adjusting entry for insurance expired	Insurance Expense Prepaid Insurance	E A	I D	Debit Credit	Income State. Balance Sheet
Adjusting entry for depreciation of assets	Depreciation Expense Accumulated Depreciation	E A	I I	Debit Credit	Income State. Balance Sheet
Adjusting entry for accrued wages	Wages Expense Wages Payable	E L	I I	Debit Credit	Income State. Balance Sheet
Closing entry for revenue accounts	Revenue accounts Income Summary	R OE	D —	Debit Credit	Income State. —
Closing entry for expense accounts	Income Summary Expense accounts	OE E	— D	Debit Credit	— Income State.
Closing entry for Income Summary account (Net Income)	Income Summary J. R. Doe, Capital	OE OE	— I	Debit Credit	— Balance Sheet
Closing entry for Drawing account	J. R. Doe, Capital J. R. Doe, Drawing	OE OE	D D	Debit Credit	Balance Sheet State. of Owner's Equity

Accounting Cycle Review Problem

This problem is designed to get you to review and apply the knowledge that you have acquired in the preceding chapters. In accounting, the ultimate test is being able to handle data in real-life situations. This problem will give you valuable experience.

Chart of Accounts

Assets
111 Cash
112 Accounts Receivable
114 Prepaid Insurance
121 Land
122 Pool Structure
123 Accumulated Depreciation, Pool Structure
124 Filter System
125 Accumulated Depreciation, Filter System
126 Bumper Boats
127 Accumulated Depreciation, Bumper Boats

Liabilities
211 Accounts Payable
212 Wages Payable
221 Mortgage Payable

Owner's Equity
311 B. Hanula, Capital
312 B. Hanula, Drawing
313 Income Summary

Revenue
411 Income from Services
412 Concession Income

Expenses
511 Bumper Boat Rental Expense
512 Wages Expense
513 Advertising Expense
514 Utilities Expense
515 Interest Expense
516 Insurance Expense
517 Depreciation Expense, Pool Structure
518 Depreciation Expense, Filter System
519 Depreciation Expense, Bumper Boats
522 Miscellaneous Expense

You are to record transactions in a two-column general journal. To get in a little more practice, assume that the fiscal period is one month. You will then be able to complete all the steps in the accounting cycle.

When you are analyzing the transactions, think them through by mentally visualizing the T accounts or by writing them down on scratch paper. In the case of unfamiliar types of transactions, specific instructions for recording them are included. However, go ahead and reason them out for yourself as well. Check off each transaction as it is recorded.

The following transactions were completed during June of this year:

June   1 Hanula deposited $83,200 in a bank account for the purpose of buying Parkland Bumper Boats, a business offering the use of bumper boats to the public.

June 2 Bought Parkland Bumper Boats in its entirety for a total price of $213,300. The assets include boats, $20,800; filter system, $8,500; pool structure, $144,000; land, $40,000. Paid $64,400 down, and signed a mortgage note for the remainder. (Debit the assets and credit Cash and the liability.)

   3 Received and paid bill for newspaper advertising, $148.

   3 Received and paid bill for property and liability insurance for the coming year, $1,036.

   3 Bought additional boats from A and M Manufacturing Co. for $6,520, paying $3,200 down, with the remainder due in thirty days.

   3 Signed a contract with a vending machine service to lease them space for their vending machines. The rental income agreed upon is 10 percent of the sales generated from their machines, with the estimated total rental income payable in advance. Received cash payment for June, $180. (Debit Cash and credit Concession Income.)

   3 Received bill from Exacto Printing for promotional handouts, $368.

   3 Signed a contract for leasing bumper boats from Kelsey Amusement Co. and paid rental fee for June, $632.

   5 Paid cash for miscellaneous expenses, $92.44.

   8 Received $2,632.50 in cash as income for the use of the boats.

   9 Bought parts for the filter system on account from Stanwood Pool Supply, $836.

  15 Paid wages to employees for the period ending June 14, $4,200.

  16 Paid the bill for promotional handouts already recorded on June 3.

  16 Hanula withdrew cash for personal use, $1,052.

  16 Bought an additional boat motor from Dunham Products, Inc., $854; payment due in thirty days.

  16 Received $3,043 in cash as income for the use of the boats.

  19 Paid cash for miscellaneous expenses, $42.64.

  20 Paid cash to A and M Manufacturing Co. as part payment on account, $480.

  22 Received $5,082 in cash as income for the use of the boats.

  23 Received an allowance from A and M Manufacturing Co. for a boat received in a damaged condition (a reduction in the outstanding bill), $452.

  24 Received and paid telephone bill, $84.

  29 Paid wages for period June 15 through 28, $4,652.

  30 Paid cash to Stanwood Pool Supply to apply on account, $418.

  30 Received and paid electric bill, $42.

  30 Paid cash as an installment payment on the mortgage, $1,880. Of this amount, $680 represents a reduction in the principal, and the remainder is interest. (Debit Mortgage Payable, debit Interest Expense, and credit Cash.)

  30 Received and paid water bill, $432.

  30 Bought additional boats from Stanski and Son for $4,852, paying $452 down, with the remainder due in thirty days.

Transaction	Accounting Basis	
	Accrual	Modified Cash
c. Bought equipment on account from Danton Company, $1,940.	Journalized	Journalized
d. Received $2,200 from charge customers previously billed.	Journalized	Journalized (Revenue recorded at this point.)
e. Paid $100 to Melton Publications owed for advertising to apply on account.	Journalized	Journalized (Expense recorded at this point.)
f. Paid wages for the period, $1,400.	Journalized (Expense recorded at this point.)	Journalized (Expense recorded at this point.)
g. Recorded depreciation of equipment for the period, $380.	Journalized (Expense recorded at this point.)	Journalized (Expense recorded at this point.)

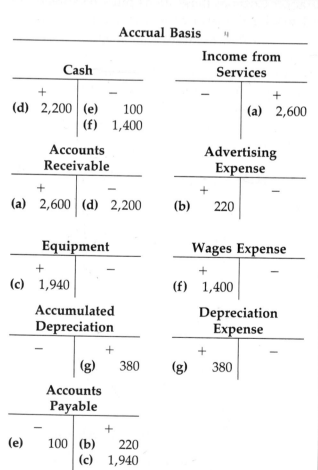

Accrual Basis

Cash

+		−	
(d) 2,200	(e)	100	
	(f)	1,400	

Accounts Receivable

+		−	
(a) 2,600	(d)	2,200	

Equipment

+	−
(c) 1,940	

Accumulated Depreciation

−	+	
	(g)	380

Accounts Payable

−	+	
(e) 100	(b)	220
	(c)	1,940

Income from Services

−	+	
	(a)	2,600

Advertising Expense

+	−
(b) 220	

Wages Expense

+	−
(f) 1,400	

Depreciation Expense

+	−
(g) 380	

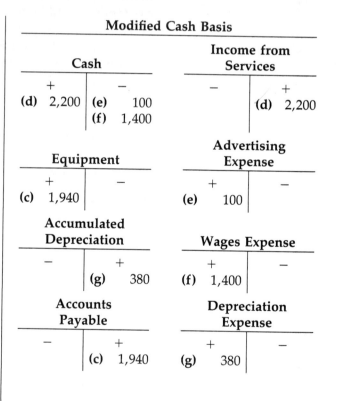

Modified Cash Basis

Cash

+		−	
(d) 2,200	(e)	100	
	(f)	1,400	

Equipment

+	−
(c) 1,940	

Accumulated Depreciation

−	+	
	(g)	380

Accounts Payable

−	+	
	(c)	1,940

Income from Services

−	+	
	(d)	2,200

Advertising Expense

+	−
(e) 100	

Wages Expense

+	−
(f) 1,400	

Depreciation Expense

+	−
(g) 380	

	Accrual Basis			Modified Cash Basis	

Income Statement

Revenue:			Revenue:		
Income from Services		$2,600	Income from Services		$2,200
Less Expenses:			Less Expenses:		
Advertising Expense	$ 220		Advertising Expense	$ 100	
Wages Expense	1,400		Wages Expense	1,400	
Depreciation Expense	380	2,000	Depreciation Expense	380	1,880
Net Income		$ 600	Net Income		$ 320

EXAMPLE: RECORDS OF A DENTIST

To understand the modified-cash system used by a professional enterprise, let us look at the records of Dr. Alan R. Palmer, a dentist. The basic records used in his office are the appointment record and the patient's ledger record. Following is the chart of accounts for the office:

Chart of Accounts

Assets

111 Cash
112 X-ray Supplies
113 Dental Supplies
114 Office Supplies
115 Prepaid Insurance
121 Dental Equipment
122 Accumulated Depreciation, Dental Equipment
123 Office Furniture and Equipment
124 Accumulated Depreciation, Office Furniture and Equipment

Liabilities

211 Notes Payable

Owner's Equity

311 A. R. Palmer, Capital
312 A. R. Palmer, Drawing
313 Income Summary

Revenue

411 Professional Fees

Expenses

511 Dental Instruments Expense
512 Laundry and Office Cleaning Expense
513 Salary Expense
514 Laboratory Expense
515 Dental Supplies Expense
516 Rent Expense
517 Depreciation Expense, Dental Equipment
518 Depreciation Expense, Office Furniture and Equipment
519 X-ray Supplies Expense
521 Office Supplies Expense
522 Insurance Expense
523 Telephone Expense
524 Utilities Expense
525 Repairs and Maintenance Expense
526 Miscellaneous Expense

Appointment Record

The dentist's receptionist keeps a daily appointment record, showing the time of appointment and the name of each patient, and gives a copy of the appointment record to the dentist the day before the scheduled appointments. Dr. Palmer's appointment record is shown in Figure 7-1.

FIGURE 7-1

APPOINTMENT RECORD

DATE ___12/1___

HOUR	PATIENT	SERVICE RENDERED	FEES	RECEIPTS
8 00	Donald Rankin			
15	Patricia Fischer			
30				
45	Cecil Hansen			
9 00				
15				
30				
45	Donna Heller			
10 00	R. C. Santos			
15				
30				
45	Ralph Simons			
11 00	Peter Smithson			
15				
30				
45				
1 00	Donald C. Kraft			
15				
30	N. C. Byers			
45				
2 00	Mrs. N. D. Silversmith			
15				
30	John F. Piper			
45	Nolan F. Sanderson			
3 00				
15	Nancy Stacy			
30				
45	C. D. Harper			
4 00				
15	Ardis Newell			
30				
45				
5 00				
15				

Patient's Ledger Record

The receptionist also maintains a patient's ledger record card for each patient. One side of this card shows a daily record of the services performed, amount of any cost estimate given, plan of payment, information regarding collections, and the like. This side of the card is shown in Figure 7-2.

FIGURE 7-2

Santos, R. C.   365-2619
1629 S. W. Arbor St.
Denver, CO 80232

DATE		SERVICE RENDERED	TIME	DEBIT	CREDIT	BALANCE
June	15	#31—M.O.D. (4)	10:00	5 0 00		5 0 00
July	4	Ck.			5 0 00	——
	16	#27—D.O. (Amal.)	9:15	4 5 00		4 5 00
Aug.	5	Ck.			4 5 00	——
Sept.	24	#25—P.J.C.	10:00	3 1 0 00		3 1 0 00
Oct.	6	Ck.			9 0 00	2 2 0 00
	18	#24—D. (Porc.)	9:00	3 5 00		2 5 5 00
Nov.	3	Ck.			9 0 00	1 6 5 00
	9	#18—full gold crown	10:00	2 7 5 00		4 4 0 00
Dec.	1	B.W. X-rays (6)	10:00	6 4 00		5 0 4 00
		Impression upper		4 8 0 00		9 8 4 00
		12/1				
	1	Ck.			1 8 0 00	8 0 4 00

PLAN OF SERVICE	PLAN OF PAYMENT	COLLECTION EFFORTS
1–2 surf. \ amalgam	30-day basis	
2–3 surf. \\ 1 full gold crown	or $90 per	
1–1 surf. / 1 ceramic crown	month	
2 anterior porcelain		

ESTIMATE IF ANY		
$480 upper denture (6 appt.)	$120 per month	

The other side of the card contains a diagram of the patient's teeth and a space for personal information about the patient.

After Dr. Palmer has completed the work, he (or an assistant) describes the services performed and writes the amount of the fees in the debit column. The card is returned to the receptionist, who records the services rendered and the fees charged on the appointment record.

When a patient sends in a payment, the receptionist records the amount on the appointment record on the day the payment was received and on the patient's ledger record in the credit column. *Remember that the fees charged are not recorded in the Professional Fees account until they are received in cash.* The record showing the amounts patients owe is much like Accounts Receivable, except that these amounts are not officially recorded in the books. The patient's ledger record for R. C. Santos is shown in Figure 7-2. As with Accounts Receivable, debits mean increases in the amounts owed by patients and credits mean decreases in the amounts owed by patients. The balance columns show the final amounts owed by patients at the time of the latest entry.

FIGURE 7-3

Alan R. Palmer, D.D.S.
1620 South Canton Place
Denver, Colorado 80226

STATEMENT

R. C. SANTOS
1629 S.W. ARBOR STREET
DENVER, CO 80232

DATE	PROFESSIONAL SERVICE	CHARGES	PAYMENTS	BALANCE
6/15	#31-MOD (4)	50.00		50.00
7/4	Ck		50.00	—
7/16	#27-DO (Amal.)	45.00		45.00
8/5	Ck		45.00	—
9/24	#25-PJC	310.00		310.00
10/6	Ck		90.00	220.00
10/18	#24-D (Porc.)	35.00		255.00
11/3	Ck		90.00	165.00
11/9	#18-full gold crown	275.00		440.00
12/1	B. W. X-rays (6)	64.00		504.00
	Impression upper	480.00		984.00
12/1	Ck		180.00	804.00

PAY LAST AMOUNT IN BALANCE COLUMN. ◆

The services to be performed may require a number of appointments. Some patients may make partial payments each time they have appointments. Others may pay the entire amount at—or after—the last appointment. Patients' bills are compiled directly from the patient's ledger record. The dentist or receptionist keeps a constant watch on the patients' ledger records to determine which accounts are past due and to take the necessary steps to speed up collections. Figure 7-3 shows the statement that was mailed to R. C. Santos at the end of the month.

Receipt of Payments from Patients

Depending on the size of the office, the person who receives payments may be the receptionist or the cashier in the accounting office. Whoever receives the payments issues a written receipt for all incoming cash, filled out in duplicate, sending the first copy to the patient and filing the second copy as evidence of the transaction. Receipts should be prenumbered so that they can all be accounted for. The payment is recorded in the Receipts column of the appointment record.

The form in Figure 7-4 on the next page is a typical appointment record for a day, showing services rendered, fees (recorded by the dentist on the patients' ledger records), and payments received (recorded by the receptionist). The receptionist deposits $833 in the bank. A journal entry would now be made debiting Cash and crediting Professional Fees for $833 each. Remember that Professional Fees are journalized only when received in cash.

Summary of Procedures

1. Patients request appointments.
2. Receptionist records appointments on appointment record: date, time, and name of patient.
3. Receptionist furnishes dentist with appointment record for the day, plus the patients' ledger records.
4. Dentist performs services and records on each patient's ledger card descriptions of the services performed and lists the fees to be charged in the Debit column.
5. Receptionist accepts payments from patients both in the office and through the mail and records receipt of payments in the Receipts column of the appointment record.
6. At the end of the day, receptionist deposits in the bank any cash received.
7. Receptionist lists the description of services and the amount charged on the appointment record.

FIGURE 7-4

APPOINTMENT RECORD

DATE *12/1*

HOUR	PATIENT	SERVICE RENDERED	FEES		RECEIPTS	
8 00	Donald Rankin	Extraction	20	00		
15	Patricia Fischer	Three amalgam fillings				
30		D.O. (3)	150	00	30	00
45	Cecil Hansen	Gold inlay filling	225	00		
9 00						
15						
30						
45	Donna Heller	Amalgam filling D.O.	45	00		
10 00	R. C. Santos	B.W. X-rays (6)	64	00	180	00
15		Denture—full upper	480	00		
30		(6 appointments)				
45	Ralph Simons	Prophylaxis	32	00	32	00
11 00	Peter Smithson	Endodontia treatment	120	00	30	00
15						
30						
45						
1 00	Donald C. Kraft	Amalgam filling M.O.D.	50	00	25	00
15						
30	N. C. Byers	Ceramco crown	310	00		
45						
2 00	Mrs. N. D. Silversmith	Extraction	20	00		
15						
30	John F. Piper	Amalgam filling 1 surf.	35	00		
45	Nolan F. Sanderson	Prophylaxis and full-	67	00		
3 00		mouth X-ray (14)				
15	Nancy Stacy	Fixed bridge 3 units	930	00	75	00
30		(Gold) (5 appointments)				
45	C. D. Harper	Prophylaxis & bitewing	44	00		
4 00		X-rays				
15	Ardis Newell	Periodontal treatment	62	00		
30						
45						
5 00						
15						
	Ronald T. McCaw				70	00
	Helen Bower				65	00
	Eugene Sampson				80	00
	Sidney Weeks				32	00
	C. D. Sanderson				110	00
	Roger Lindsay				44	00
	Gilbert Rae				60	00
			2,654	00	833	00

8. Receptionist records the payments received from patients on the patients' ledger cards in the Credit column. The source is the appointment record.

9. The receptionist compiles monthly statements directly from the patients' ledger records.

This procedure may vary, depending on the size of the office staff. It could be further shortened by describing the services rendered only once. For the sake of security or internal control, if the size of the office staff is sufficiently large, the function of accepting and depositing money should be separated from the function of recording payments.

Here is a list of Dr. Palmer's transactions for December, the last month of the fiscal period. To save time and space, cash receipts are recorded on a weekly basis.

Dec.　　1　Paid rent for the month, $1,000.
　　　　　1　Paid telephone bill, $32.
　　　　　1　Paid electric bill, $66.
　　　　　3　Issued check to First-Rate Printing for patient statement forms, $132.
　　　　　5　Bought short-term supply of drills for cash from Murdoch Dental Supply, $254.
　　　　　5　Total cash received from patients during the week, $5,524.
　　　　　8　Paid bill for repair of typewriter to Greeley Office Supply, $58.
　　　　　9　Palmer withdrew cash for personal use, $400.
　　　　11　Paid Reliable Building Maintenance Company for janitorial service, $120.

Because you are now familiar with a general journal, we will first record these transactions in general journal form (Figure 7-5 on page 198). However, since our objective is to introduce the combined journal, we will also record the same transactions also in a combined journal.

THE COMBINED JOURNAL

Objective 2

Record transactions for both a professional and a service-type enterprise in a combined journal.

The **combined journal** is designed to make the recording and posting of transactions more efficient. It is used widely by professional and service-type enterprises, where **it replaces the general journal.** Notice that no explanations are given in the combined journal. Special columns are set up to record accounts that are used frequently by a particular business. Most transactions can be recorded on one line.

Compare the recording of the first nine transactions in the combined journal in Figure 7-6 with the same transactions portrayed in the general journal in Figure 7-5. For example, in the first transaction (paid rent for

FIGURE 7-5

GENERAL JOURNAL

DATE		DESCRIPTION	POST. REF.	DEBIT	CREDIT
19–					
Dec.	1	Rent Expense		1 0 0 0 00	
		Cash			1 0 0 0 00
		Rent for December.			
	1	Telephone Expense		3 2 00	
		Cash			3 2 00
		Telephone bill for November.			
	1	Utilities Expense		6 6 00	
		Cash			6 6 00
		Electric bill for November.			
	3	Office Supplies		1 3 2 00	
		Cash			1 3 2 00
		First-Rate Printing for			
		statement forms.			
	5	Dental Instruments Expense		2 5 4 00	
		Cash			2 5 4 00
		Murdoch Dental Supply for			
		drills.			
	5	Cash		5 5 2 4 00	
		Professional Fees			5 5 2 4 00
		For period December 1 through 5.			
	8	Repairs and Maintenance Expense		5 8 00	
		Cash			5 8 00
		Greeley Office Supply,			
		typewriter.			
	9	A. R. Palmer, Drawing		4 0 0 00	
		Cash			4 0 0 00
		For personal use.			
	11	Laundry and Office Cleaning Expense		1 2 0 00	
		Cash			1 2 0 00
		Reliable Building Maintenance			
		Company.			

the month, $1,000), you determine that the entry is a debit to Rent Expense and a credit to Cash. There is a Cash Credit column, so you list $1,000 in this column; that $1,000 will be posted as a part of the column total. The Sundry columns are used to record any accounts for which there are no special columns. Since there is no Rent Expense Debit column, the $1,000 debit to Rent Expense must be recorded in the Sundry Debit column. Notice, however, that the Sundry column does not tell you where to post $1,000. Therefore, you need to write the title of the account to be posted in the Account Name column. This amount will be posted separately.

In the entry of December 5 to record professional fees received in cash, special columns are available to handle both the debit to Cash and the credit to Professional Fees. In cases where the special columns can handle both the entire debit and credit amounts, the Account Name column is left blank. Insert a dash in the Post. Ref. column. The individual amounts will be posted as parts of the totals of the special columns. The rest of the month's transactions follow:

Dec.   12   Total cash received from patients during the week, $1,842.

           16   Paid Pender Dental Supply for miscellaneous dental supplies, $432.

           16   Paid salaries of dental assistant and receptionist, $980.

           19   Bought new dental chair from Murdoch Dental Supply, $1,234; made $434 downpayment, with the balance to be paid in eight monthly payments of $100 each (Notes Payable).

           19   Total cash received from patients during the week, $620.

           22   Palmer withdrew $520 for personal use.

           23   Paid bill for laboratory expense to Nollen Dental Laboratory, $296.

           23   Paid Pender Dental Supply $320 as a contract payment (Notes Payable) on dental equipment purchased in October.

           27   Total cash received from patients during the week, $392.

           29   Palmer wrote a business check to the garage for repairing his car, $128 (to be recorded as Drawing).

           31   Paid Murdoch Dental Supply for miscellaneous dental supplies, $192.

           31   Paid salaries of dental assistant and receptionist, $980.

           31   Palmer withdrew $780 for personal use.

           31   Paid $54 to Jersey Publishers Service for magazines for the office.

           31   Paid Clement Linen Supply for laundry service, $84.

           31   Total cash received from patients this week up until last day of year, $266.

After you have added all columns at the end of the month, prove on scratch paper that the sum of the debit totals equals the sum of the credit totals, as shown in the example at the top of the next page.

Column	Debit totals	Credit totals
Sundry	$ 3,096.00	$ 800.00
Dental Supplies	624.00	
A. R. Palmer, Drawing	1,828.00	
Professional Fees		8,644.00
Laundry and Cleaning Expense	204.00	
Salary Expense	1,960.00	
Laboratory Expense	296.00	
Miscellaneous Expense	54.00	
Cash	8,644.00	7,262.00
	$16,706.00	$16,706.00

FIGURE 7-6

	DATE		ACCOUNT NAME	POST. REF.	SUNDRY DEBIT	SUNDRY CREDIT	DENTAL SUPPLIES DEBIT
1	19–						
2	Dec.	1	Rent Expense	516	1 0 0 0 00		
3		1	Telephone Expense	523	3 2 00		
4		1	Utilities Expense	524	6 6 00		
5		3	Office Supplies	114	1 3 2 00		
6		5	Dental Instruments Expense	511	2 5 4 00		
7		5		–			
8		8	Repairs and Maintenance Expense	525	5 8 00		
9		9		–			
10		11		–			
11		12		–			
12		16		–			4 3 2 00
13		16		–			
14		19	Dental Equipment	121	1 2 3 4 00		
15			Notes Payable	211		8 0 0 00	
16		19		–			
17		22		–			
18		23		–			
19		23	Notes Payable	211	3 2 0 00		
20		27		–			
21		29		–			
22		31		–			1 9 2 00
23		31		–			
24		31		–			
25		31		–			
26		31		–			
27		31		–			
28		31			3 0 9 6 00	8 0 0 00	6 2 4 00
29					(√)	(√)	(1 1 3)
30							
31							
32							

Posting from the Combined Journal

Objective 3

Post from the combined journal, determine the cash balance, and prepare a work sheet for a professional enterprise.

The person who is keeping records posts items in the Sundry columns individually, usually daily, using the specific transaction date. After posting the ledger account, the person records the ledger account number in the Post. Ref. column of the combined journal. This procedure is similar to posting from a general journal.

Special columns, used only for the debit or credit to specific accounts, are posted as totals at the end of the month. **After posting the ledger account, the accountant records the ledger account number in the special column immediately below the total.** The account number is placed in

COMBINED JOURNAL   PAGE __12__

A. R. PALMER, DRAWING — DEBIT	PROFESSIONAL FEES — CREDIT	LAUNDRY AND OFFICE CLEANING EXPENSE — DEBIT	SALARY EXPENSE — DEBIT	LABORATORY EXPENSE — DEBIT	MISCELLANEOUS EXPENSE — DEBIT	CASH — DEBIT	CASH — CREDIT	
								1
							1 0 0 0 00	2
							3 2 00	3
							6 6 00	4
							1 3 2 00	5
							2 5 4 00	6
	5 5 2 4 00					5 5 2 4 00		7
							5 8 00	8
4 0 0 00							4 0 0 00	9
		1 2 0 00					1 2 0 00	10
	1 8 4 2 00					1 8 4 2 00		11
							4 3 2 00	12
			9 8 0 00				9 8 0 00	13
								14
							4 3 4 00	15
	6 2 0 00					6 2 0 00		16
5 2 0 00							5 2 0 00	17
				2 9 6 00			2 9 6 00	18
							3 2 0 00	19
	3 9 2 00					3 9 2 00		20
1 2 8 00							1 2 8 00	21
							1 9 2 00	22
			9 8 0 00				9 8 0 00	23
7 8 0 00							7 8 0 00	24
					5 4 00		5 4 00	25
		8 4 00					8 4 00	26
	2 6 6 00					2 6 6 00		27
1 8 2 8 00	8 6 4 4 00	2 0 4 00	1 9 6 0 00	2 9 6 00	5 4 00	8 6 4 4 00	7 2 6 2 00	28
(3 1 2)	(4 1 1)	(5 1 2)	(5 1 3)	(5 1 4)	(5 2 6)	(1 1 1)	(1 1 1)	29
								30
								31
								32

parentheses. The total of the Cash Debit column in Figure 7-6 may be used as an example. After the Cash account in the general ledger has been debited for $8,644.00, the account number of Cash (111) is placed in parentheses below the total of the Cash Debit column in the combined journal. Notice that the accountant puts a check mark in parentheses below the totals of the Sundry columns. The check mark indicates that the amounts have been posted individually and should not be posted again.

Selected accounts from Dr. Palmer's completed general ledger are shown in Figure 7-7. Cash, Dental Supplies, and Rent Expense are used to illustrate the posting process.

FIGURE 7-7

GENERAL LEDGER

ACCOUNT *Cash*   ACCOUNT NO. *111*

	DATE		ITEM	POST. REF.	DEBIT	CREDIT	BALANCE DEBIT	BALANCE CREDIT	
1	19–								1
2	Dec.	1	Balance	✓			6 4 0 4 00		2
3		31		12	8 6 4 4 00		15 0 4 8 00		3
4		31		12		7 2 6 2 00	7 7 8 6 00		4
5									5

ACCOUNT *Dental Supplies*   ACCOUNT NO. *113*

	DATE		ITEM	POST. REF.	DEBIT	CREDIT	BALANCE DEBIT	BALANCE CREDIT	
1	19–								1
2	Dec.	1	Balance	✓			4 8 5 6 00		2
3		31		12	6 2 4 00		5 4 8 0 00		3
4									4

ACCOUNT *Rent Expense*   ACCOUNT NO. *516*

	DATE		ITEM	POST. REF.	DEBIT	CREDIT	BALANCE DEBIT	BALANCE CREDIT	
1	19–								1
2	Dec.	1	Balance	✓			11 0 0 0 00		2
3		1		12	1 0 0 0 00		12 0 0 0 00		3
4									4

Determining Cash Balance

The cash balance may be determined at any time during the month by taking the beginning balance of cash, adding the total cash debits so far during the month, and subtracting the total cash credits so far during the month. For example, to determine the balance of cash on December 5:

Cash

Dec. 1 Balance 6,404

COMBINED JOURNAL   PAGE 12

DATE			MISCELLANEOUS EXPENSE	CASH DEBIT	CASH CREDIT
19–					
Dec. 1					1 0 0 0 00
1					3 2 00
1					6 6 00
3					1 3 2 00
5					2 5 4 00
5				5 5 2 4 00	
				5 5 2 4 00	1 4 8 4 00

Beginning balance (Dec. 1)	$ 6,404
Add cash debits	5,524
Total	$11,928
Less cash credits	1,484
Ending balance (Dec. 5)	$10,444

Work Sheet for a Professional Enterprise

Assume that Dr. Palmer's receptionist has posted the journal entries to the ledger accounts and has recorded the trial balance in the first two columns of the work sheet. Dr. Palmer uses the modified cash basis of accounting, recording revenue only when he has received it in cash, and recording expenses only when he has paid for them in cash. In addition, when Dr. Palmer buys an item that is going to last a number of years, he records this item as an asset and writes it off or depreciates it by making an adjusting entry each year of its useful life. He also makes adjusting entries for expired insurance, as well as for supplies used.

Data for the adjustments are given on the next page.

a. Additional depreciation on dental equipment, $8,400.
b. Additional depreciation on office furniture and equipment, $1,520.
c. Inventory of x-ray supplies, $618 (ending balance).
d. Inventory of dental supplies, $1,616 (ending balance).
e. Inventory of office supplies, $196 (ending balance).
f. Insurance expired, $720.

FIGURE 7-8

	ACCOUNT NAME	TRIAL BALANCE DEBIT	TRIAL BALANCE CREDIT
1	Cash	7 7 8 6 00	
2	X-ray Supplies	2 7 6 2 00	
3	Dental Supplies	5 4 8 0 00	
4	Office Supplies	1 3 0 8 00	
5	Prepaid Insurance	8 4 8 00	
6	Dental Equipment	85 2 3 4 00	
7	Accum. Depr., Dental Equipment		17 2 0 0 00
8	Office Furniture and Equipment	7 8 0 0 00	
9	Accum. Depr., Office Furniture & Equipment		4 2 0 0 00
10	Notes Payable		7 6 0 0 00
11	A. R. Palmer, Capital		52 5 5 8 00
12	A. R. Palmer, Drawing	33 2 8 0 00	
13	Professional Fees		112 0 2 4 00
14	Dental Instruments Expense	1 9 8 2 00	
15	Laundry and Office Cleaning Expense	3 0 2 4 00	
16	Salary Expense	23 5 2 0 00	
17	Laboratory Expense	5 8 5 6 00	
18	Rent Expense	12 0 0 0 00	
19	Telephone Expense	4 1 2 00	
20	Utilities Expense	7 7 8 00	
21	Repairs and Maintenance Expense	8 8 8 00	
22	Miscellaneous Expense	6 2 4 00	
23		193 5 8 2 00	193 5 8 2 00
24	Depreciation Expense, Dental Equipment		
25	Depreciation Expense, Off. Furn. & Equip.		
26	X-ray Supplies Expense		
27	Dental Supplies Expense		
28	Office Supplies Expense		
29	Insurance Expense		
30			
31	Net Income		
32			
33			

With these adjusting entries, the rest of the work sheet can now be completed as shown in Figure 7-8. First the balances of the accounts that were adjusted are brought up to date in the Adjusted Trial Balance columns. Then these amounts are carried forward to the remaining columns.

A. R. Palmer, D.D.S.
Work Sheet
For Year Ended December 31, 19–

ADJUSTMENTS DEBIT	ADJUSTMENTS CREDIT	ADJUSTED TRIAL BALANCE DEBIT	ADJUSTED TRIAL BALANCE CREDIT	INCOME STATEMENT DEBIT	INCOME STATEMENT CREDIT	BALANCE SHEET DEBIT	BALANCE SHEET CREDIT	
		7 7 8 6 00				7 7 8 6 00		1
	(c)2 1 4 4 00	6 1 8 00				6 1 8 00		2
	(d)3 8 6 4 00	1 6 1 6 00				1 6 1 6 00		3
	(e)1 1 1 2 00	1 9 6 00				1 9 6 00		4
	(f) 7 2 0 00	1 2 8 00				1 2 8 00		5
		85 2 3 4 00				85 2 3 4 00		6
	(a)8 4 0 0 00		25 6 0 0 00				25 6 0 0 00	7
		7 8 0 0 00				7 8 0 0 00		8
	(b)1 5 2 0 00		5 7 2 0 00				5 7 2 0 00	9
			7 6 0 0 00				7 6 0 0 00	10
			52 5 5 8 00				52 5 5 8 00	11
		33 2 8 0 00				33 2 8 0 00		12
			112 0 2 4 00		112 0 2 4 00			13
		1 9 8 2 00		1 9 8 2 00				14
		3 0 2 4 00		3 0 2 4 00				15
		23 5 2 0 00		23 5 2 0 00				16
		5 8 5 6 00		5 8 5 6 00				17
		12 0 0 0 00		12 0 0 0 00				18
		4 1 2 00		4 1 2 00				19
		7 7 8 00		7 7 8 00				20
		8 8 8 00		8 8 8 00				21
		6 2 4 00		6 2 4 00				22
								23
(a)8 4 0 0 00		8 4 0 0 00		8 4 0 0 00				24
(b)1 5 2 0 00		1 5 2 0 00		1 5 2 0 00				25
(c)2 1 4 4 00		2 1 4 4 00		2 1 4 4 00				26
(d)3 8 6 4 00		3 8 6 4 00		3 8 6 4 00				27
(e)1 1 1 2 00		1 1 1 2 00		1 1 1 2 00				28
(f) 7 2 0 00		7 2 0 00		7 2 0 00				29
17 7 6 0 00	17 7 6 0 00	203 5 0 2 00	203 5 0 2 00	66 8 4 4 00	112 0 2 4 00	136 6 5 8 00	91 4 7 8 00	30
				45 1 8 0 00			45 1 8 0 00	31
				112 0 2 4 00	112 0 2 4 00	136 6 5 8 00	136 6 5 8 00	32
								33

Financial Statements

From the work sheet, Dr. Palmer's accountant prepares the financial statements shown in Figure 7-9. In this case, there was no additional investment made by A. R. Palmer during the year. However, whenever you are preparing a statement of owner's equity, always check the capital account in the general ledger to see if any additional investment was recorded.

FIGURE 7-9

A. R. Palmer, D.D.S.
Income Statement
For Year Ended December 31, 19–

Revenue:		
Professional Fees		$ 112 024 00
Expenses:		
Dental Instruments Expense	$ 1 982 00	
Laundry and Office Cleaning Expense	3 024 00	
Salary Expense	23 520 00	
Laboratory Expense	5 856 00	
Dental Supplies Expense	3 864 00	
Rent Expense	12 000 00	
Depreciation Expense, Dental Equipment	8 400 00	
Depreciation Expense, Office Furniture and Equipment	1 520 00	
X-ray Supplies Expense	2 144 00	
Office Supplies Expense	1 112 00	
Insurance Expense	720 00	
Telephone Expense	412 00	
Utilities Expense	778 00	
Repairs and Maintenance Expense	888 00	
Miscellaneous Expense	624 00	
Total Expenses		66 844 00
Net Income		$ 45 180 00

FIGURE 7-9
(continued)

A. R. Palmer, D.D.S.
Statement of Owner's Equity
For Year Ended December 31, 19–

A. R. Palmer, Capital, January 1, 19–		$52 5 5 8 00
Net Income for year	$45 1 8 0 00	
Less Withdrawals for year	33 2 8 0 00	
Increase in Capital		11 9 0 0 00
A. R. Palmer, Capital, December 31, 19–		$64 4 5 8 00

A. R. Palmer, D.D.S.
Balance Sheet
December 31, 19–

Assets			
Cash			$ 7 7 8 6 00
X-ray Supplies			6 1 8 00
Dental Supplies			1 6 1 6 00
Office Supplies			1 9 6 00
Prepaid Insurance			1 2 8 00
Dental Equipment	$85 2 3 4 00		
Less Accumulated Depreciation, Dental			
Equipment	25 6 0 0 00	59 6 3 4 00	
Office Furniture and Equipment	$ 7 8 0 0 00		
Less Accumulated Depreciation, Office			
Furniture and Equipment	5 7 2 0 00	2 0 8 0 00	
Total Assets			$72 0 5 8 00
Liabilities			
Notes Payable			$ 7 6 0 0 00
Owner's Equity			
A. R. Palmer, Capital			64 4 5 8 00
Total Liabilities and Owner's Equity			$72 0 5 8 00

Objective 4

Complete the entire accounting cycle for a professional enterprise.

Adjusting and Closing Entries

Dr. Palmer (or his receptionist) records the adjusting and closing entries in the Sundry columns of the combined journal. These entries must be posted individually, so the special columns are never used for them. For

COMBINED JOURNAL   PAGE __13__

DATE		ACCOUNT NAME	POST. REF.	SUNDRY	
				DEBIT	CREDIT
19–		*Adjusting Entries*			
Dec.	31	Depreciation Expense, Dental Equipment	517	8 4 0 0 00	
		Accumulated Depreciation, Dental Equipment	122		8 4 0 0 00
	31	Depreciation Expense, Office Furniture			
		and Equipment	518	1 5 2 0 00	
		Accumulated Depreciation, Office Furniture			
		and Equipment	124		1 5 2 0 00
	31	X-ray Supplies Expense	519	2 1 4 4 00	
		X-ray Supplies	112		2 1 4 4 00
	31	Dental Supplies Expense	515	3 8 6 4 00	
		Dental Supplies	113		3 8 6 4 00
	31	Office Supplies Expense	521	1 1 1 2 00	
		Office Supplies	114		1 1 1 2 00
	31	Insurance Expense	522	7 2 0 00	
		Prepaid Insurance	115		7 2 0 00
	31			17 7 6 0 00	17 7 6 0 00
				(√)	(√)

FIGURE 7-10

example, the adjusting and closing entries are shown in Figure 7-10, two pages of a shortened combined journal.

There are three situations in accounting for a professional enterprise among the topics we have not yet considered. We will study them in the following chapters.

1. Special funds, such as the change fund and the petty cash fund. (We shall discuss these in Chapter 8.)
2. Payroll deductions, such as withholdings for employees' income taxes, Social Security taxes, and other salary deductions. (We shall discuss these in Chapter 9.)
3. Payroll taxes levied on the employer, such as the matching for Social Security, and unemployment taxes. (We shall discuss these in Chapter 10.)

On page 13 of the combined journal shown in Figure 7-10, totals are included since it is customary to show totals of all columns of a combined journal.

				SUNDRY		
DATE		ACCOUNT NAME	POST. REF.	DEBIT	CREDIT	

COMBINED JOURNAL   PAGE __14__

DATE		ACCOUNT NAME	POST. REF.	DEBIT	CREDIT
19–		*Closing Entries*			
Dec.	31	Professional Fees	411	112 0 2 4 00	
		Income Summary	313		112 0 2 4 00
	31	Income Summary	313	66 8 4 4 00	
		Dental Instruments Expense	511		1 9 8 2 00
		Laundry and Office Cleaning Expense	512		3 0 2 4 00
		Salary Expense	513		23 5 2 0 00
		Laboratory Expense	514		5 8 5 6 00
		Dental Supplies Expense	515		3 8 6 4 00
		Rent Expense	516		12 0 0 0 00
		Depreciation Expense, Dental Equipment	517		8 4 0 0 00
		Depreciation Expense, Office Furniture and Equipment	518		1 5 2 0 00
		X-ray Supplies Expense	519		2 1 4 4 00
		Office Supplies Expense	521		1 1 1 2 00
		Insurance Expense	522		7 2 0 00
		Telephone Expense	523		4 1 2 00
		Utilities Expense	524		7 7 8 00
		Repairs and Maintenance Expense	525		8 8 8 00
		Miscellaneous Expense	526		6 2 4 00
	31	Income Summary	313	45 1 8 0 00	
		A. R. Palmer, Capital	311		45 1 8 0 00
	31	A. R. Palmer, Capital	311	33 2 8 0 00	
		A. R. Palmer, Drawing	312		33 2 8 0 00
	31			257 3 2 8 00	257 3 2 8 00
				(✓)	(✓)

FIGURE 7-10 (continued)

ACCOUNTING FOR OTHER PROFESSIONAL ENTERPRISES

Accounting records for other professional enterprises are similar to our dentist's records. Professional people often use the modified cash basis, recording revenue when received in cash and recording expenses when paid in cash. Adjusting entries may be made for supplies used, expired insurance, and depreciation on specialized equipment. Ledger cards for patients or clients are used, although they may be given special titles. Lawyers, for example, call their clients' ledger cards Collection Dockets.

Lawyers have an additional asset account, Advances for Clients, representing amounts they have paid on behalf of their clients. Advances for

Clients is a receivable, similar to Accounts Receivable. Lawyers also have an additional liability account, Collections for Clients, representing amounts they receive on behalf of their clients. Collections for Clients is a payable, similar to Accounts Payable. It's safe to say, however, that the same general accounting principles and procedures prevail in all professional enterprises.

DESIGNING A COMBINED JOURNAL

Remember

A combined journal can be used for either the accrual or the modified cash basis of accounting.

As we have said, the combined journal is widely used in professional offices and service-type business firms. It is interesting to look over the varieties of combined journals that are available at stores that sell office supplies. Some are bound journals, and others are loose-leaf type books. The number of columns vary from six to twenty, and they are available with or without column headings. Those that have printed column headings represent a "canned" type of combined journal. In other words, these combined journals are set up for a particular kind of business enterprise and describe how to channel routine transactions into the journal. These journals are available for service stations, dry cleaners, doctors' offices, and many other types of businesses.

A person with even a limited knowledge of accounting can keep books as long as the transactions are routine and fall into the established channels. In every business, however, unusual or nonroutine transactions occur from time to time. You need to have enough knowledge and background to be able to handle such transactions, and you will have to understand the entire accounting system.

Combined journals with blank columns can be customized to meet the specific requirements of a given business. Prior to labeling the columns, one first studies the operations of the business and makes up a chart of accounts. Next one identifies those accounts that are likely to be used frequently in recording typical transactions of the business. Naturally, if these accounts are used over and over, one needs to set up special columns for them.

SUMMARY

L.O. 1,2

The modified cash basis of accounting, like the cash-receipts-and-disbursements method, differs from the accrual basis by recording revenue only when the firm receives cash and recording expenses only when they are paid in cash. However, the modified cash basis makes exceptions for expenditures on items having an economic life of more than one year, which makes it appropriate for professional and service businesses. Examples in the chapter and in the Working Papers illustrate how transactions are recorded in a combined journal.

L.O. 3,4   The combined journal, which can handle all the transactions of a business, replaces the general journal. Completing the accounting cycle is exactly the same as for businesses that use a general journal except that special column totals are posted as totals. This change in the posting procedure significantly speeds the posting process.

CMPUTERS AT WORK

Pegboards—Manual and Computerized

Because almost every figure entered into a business's accounts is recorded in two or more places, short-cut "one-write" recording systems were devised long before computers became a force in the accounting world. Now at least one computer software company is using the familiarity of a particular manual system to introduce new customers to a computerized system.

A "one-write" manual pegboard speeds the recording of information through the use of carbonized strips and No-Carbon-Required (NCR) paper. Both the strips and the NCR paper serve the same purpose as carbon paper—but without the mess and bother. Forms are pegged and layered on a hard board so that an entry made on the top form gets carried through to the forms below. Someone recording a number on one form automatically fills in spaces on several other forms at the same time. Carbonized strips are used where only some of the information should appear on the layers below.

For instance, someone making out a check on a pegboard system fills in the usual spaces only once. But because of the carbonized strip on the back of the check and the special paper or carbonized strips on the layers beneath it, one press of the pen serves to fill out the check stub underneath the check, update an accounts payable ledger card beneath that, and make an entry in a cash payments journal at the bottom of the layers. Similarly, filling out a payroll check automatically enters information onto an individual earnings record and a journal. When a bookkeeper fills out a cash receipt on a pegboard, the figures are carried through to an accounts receivable customer ledger card and a cash receipts journal.

Great American Software Inc. has taken the one-write pegboard concept and incorporated it into its accounting software. Its product, "One-write plus,"™ combines the friendly, familiar sense of the manual pegboard system with the efficiency and reliability of a computerized system.

Like other general ledger software packages, "One-write plus"™ posts automatically, produces a variety of reports, and generates financial statements. But instead of presenting an array of screens and spreadsheets that could be confusing and unnerving to a traditional manual bookkeeper, "One-write plus"™ shows bookkeepers what they're used to seeing. It actually presents on the screen pictures of layered checks, receipts, and journals that mimic the components of pegboard cash payments and receipts. By providing such a bridge between manual and automated accounting systems, Great American Software may step up the pace at which businesses turn to computerized accounting.

GLOSSARY

Accrual basis   An accounting method by which revenue is recorded when it is earned, regardless of when it is received, and expenses are recorded when they are incurred, regardless of when they are paid.

Cash-receipts-and-disbursements basis   An accounting method by which revenue is recorded only when it is received in cash, and all expenses are recorded only when they are paid in cash.

Combined journal   A journal format widely used by professional and service-type enterprises in place of a general journal; designed to make the recording and posting of transactions more efficient.

Modified cash basis   An accounting method by which revenue is recorded only when it is received in cash. Expenditures classified as expenses are recorded only when they are paid in cash. Exceptions are made for expenditures on items having a useful life of more than one year and for certain prepaid items. For example, expenditures for supplies and insurance premiums can be *prorated,* or spread out over the fiscal periods covered. Expenditures for long-lived items are recorded as assets and later depreciated or written off as an expense during their useful lives.

QUESTIONS, EXERCISES, AND PROBLEMS

Discussion Questions

1. Name four columns that should always be included in a combined journal. Why?
2. How does the use of a combined journal save time and space in entering a transaction involving the payment of rent for the month?
3. What do accountants mean when they talk about the *modified cash basis of accounting*?
4. Describe the procedure followed in posting the amounts in a combined journal having the following columns: Cash Debit, Professional Fees Credit, Sundry Debit, Miscellaneous Expense Debit, Sundry Credit.
5. Where is a check mark used in a combined journal, and what does it indicate?
6. What is the meaning of the account numbers that appear in the Post. Ref. column of the combined journal?
7. Describe the process of proving the combined journal at the end of the month.
8. You have been asked to set up a combined journal for Webb's Appliance Repair. The business maintains charge accounts for customers and buys parts on account from creditors. The space occupied by the shop is rented on a monthly basis. C. Webb, the owner, makes withdrawals on a weekly basis. The firm subscribes to a telephone answering service on a monthly basis. There are no employees. What money columns would you suggest?

Exercises

L.O. 2 **Exercise 7-1** L. P. Moore's Landscape Service specializes in lawn maintenance and landscaping. Charge accounts are maintained for five apartment complexes. Frequent payments include gas and oil, supplies, wages, and owner's withdrawals. List the money columns you would suggest for a combined journal.

L.O. 2 **Exercise 7-2** The books of L. Burnett, Attorney at Law, are kept on a modified cash basis. The client record of Ruth Beck is presented below.

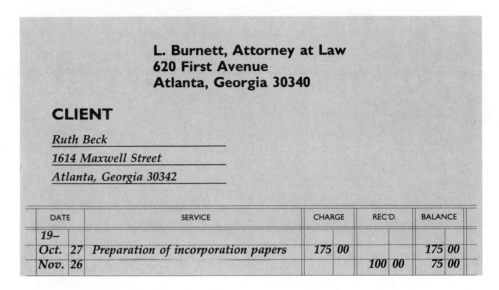

L. Burnett, Attorney at Law
620 First Avenue
Atlanta, Georgia 30340

CLIENT

Ruth Beck

1614 Maxwell Street

Atlanta, Georgia 30342

DATE		SERVICE	CHARGE		REC'D.		BALANCE	
19–								
Oct.	*27*	*Preparation of incorporation papers*	*175*	*00*			*175*	*00*
Nov.	*26*				*100*	*00*	*75*	*00*

Record the Nov. 26 transaction in the combined journal.

CASH						SUNDRY		PROF. FEES
DEPOSITS DEBIT	CHECKS CREDIT	CK. NO.	DATE	ACCOUNT NAME	POST. REF.	DEBIT	CREDIT	CREDIT

L.O. 1 **Exercise 7-3** Assume that on November 30 L. Burnett issues business check number 211, for $900, to Atlanta Furniture Company for furniture for her home. Explain how the transaction would be recorded in the combined journal illustrated in Exercise 7-2.

L.O. 1,2 **Exercise 7-4** On the appointment record for a dentist, the total of the fees column is $624, and the total of the receipts column is $386. The dentist deposits $386 in the bank at the end of the day. Record the journal entry for the deposit in general journal form. Assume the modified cash basis is used.

L.O. 3   **Exercise 7-5**   Record the proper account or classification of accounts in the blank spaces of the partial work sheet shown in this exercise. Number 1 is given as an example. (Omit the Adjustments column.)

1. Assets   5. Drawing
2. Expenses   6. Accumulated Depreciation
3. Revenue   7. Capital
4. Liabilities

Account Name	Trial Balance		Adjustments		Adjusted Trial Balance		Income Statement		Balance Sheet	
	Debit	Credit	Debit	Credit	Debit	Credit	Debit	Credit	Debit	Credit
	1	—			1	—	—	—	1	—
	—	—			—	—				
	—	—			—	—				—

L.O. 1,2,3   **Exercise 7-6**   The Eller Insurance Agency uses a combined journal, which has the following columns. Assume the accrual basis of accounting is used.

Date   Accounts Payable Debit
Account Name   Accounts Payable Credit
Post. Ref.   Commissions Income Credit
Cash Debit   Salary Expense Debit
Cash Credit   Miscellaneous Expense Debit
Accounts Receivable Debit   Sundry Debit
Accounts Receivable Credit   Sundry Credit

Answer the following.

a. Which money column totals are not posted?
b. How do you record an investment of additional cash in the business by M. R. Eller?
c. How do you determine the balance of Cash at any time during the month?
d. Which columns are used to record the payment of rent for the month?

L.O. 2,3,4   **Exercise 7-7**   Number the steps in the accounting cycle in the proper sequence.

— Prepare financial statements   — Complete the work sheet
— Prepare trial balance   — Gather the data for adjustments
— Record and post adjusting   and record on a work sheet
    entries   — Post to the ledger accounts
— Journalize transactions   — Prepare post-closing trial
— Record and post closing entries   balance

L.O. 3   **Exercise 7-8**   Determine the cash balance after September 6.

Cash

Sept. 1 Balance 941.60	

Combined Journal

Date			Cash Dr.		Cash Cr.	
19–						
Sept.	1		600	00		
	3				425	00
	4		172	60		
	4		21	52		
	5				341	58
	6		83	22		

Problem Set A

L.O. 2   **Problem 7-1A**   D. L. Martin, M.D., uses the following chart of accounts:

Assets

111 Cash
112 Medical Supplies
113 X-ray Supplies
114 Office Supplies
121 Medical Equipment
122 Accum. Deprec., Medical
     Equipment
123 Office Furniture and
     Equipment
124 Accum. Deprec., Office
     Furniture and Equipment
125 Automobile
126 Accum. Deprec., Automobile

Liabilities

211 Notes Payable

Owner's Equity

311 D. L. Martin, Capital
312 D. L. Martin, Drawing
313 Income Summary

Revenue

411 Professional Fees

Expenses

511 Nurse's Salary Expense
512 Office Salary Expense
513 Rent Expense
514 Equipment Rental Expense
515 Medical Supplies Expense
516 X-ray Supplies Expense
517 Laboratory Expense
518 Laundry and Office Cleaning
     Expense
519 Office Supplies Expense
521 Dep. Exp., Medical Equipment
522 Dep. Exp., Office Furniture
     and Equipment
523 Dep. Exp., Automobile
524 Automobile Expense
525 Insurance Expense
526 Telephone Expense
527 Utilities Expense
528 Miscellaneous Expense

Dr. Martin's records consist of an appointment record book, examination and charge reports, patients' ledger records, a combined journal, and a general ledger. The doctor fills out an examination and charge report each time a patient visits. The reports contain a description or listing of the treatments and tests administered and the amount of the charges. The charges are then recorded in the patient's ledger record. Monthly statements based on the patient's ledger record are mailed to the patient. Dr. Martin's books are kept on the modified cash basis. These transactions took place during June.

June 1 Paid rent for the month, $1,350 to Sullivan Realty.
      3 Bought medical supplies for cash from Hedges Surgical Supply, $390.
      4 Paid salary of part-time office person, $780.
      6 Received cash from patients during week, $6,240.
      10 Paid telephone bill, $81.
      12 Paid for laboratory expense to Quality Laboratories, $630.
      13 Total cash received from patients during week, $4,398.
      16 Bought x-ray supplies for cash from Garner Supply Company, $183.
      17 Dr. Martin withdrew $780 for personal use.
      19 Bought postage stamps, $9 (Miscellaneous Expense); paid cash.
      20 Received cash from patients during week, $1,776.
      23 Paid for gas and oil to Rod's Service Station, $93.

PROBLEM 7-2A

	ACCOUNT NAME	TRIAL BALANCE DEBIT	TRIAL BALANCE CREDIT
1	Cash	5 9 9 2 00	
2	Supplies	1 9 9 6 40	
3	Office Equipment	33 1 8 0 00	
4	Accum. Deprec., Office Equipment		15 2 1 8 00
5	A. C. Noyd, Capital		17 5 5 7 40
6	A. C. Noyd, Drawing	22 6 8 0 00	
7	Professional Fees		70 9 5 2 00
8	Salary Expense	26 2 0 8 00	
9	Advertising Expense	3 0 4 0 80	
10	Rent Expense	5 8 8 0 00	
11	Automobile Expense	1 2 8 8 00	
12	Travel Expense	2 0 7 2 00	
13	Entertainment Expense	7 8 9 60	
14	Miscellaneous Expense	6 0 0 60	
15		103 7 2 7 40	103 7 2 7 40
16	Deprec. Exp., Office Equipment		
17	Supplies Expense		
18			
19	Net Income		
20			
21			

June 24 Paid Timely News Service for magazines, $61.50 (Miscellaneous Expense).

27 Paid $72 for laundry service to Crystal Laundry.

30 Paid nurse's salary, $1,890, for the month.

30 Paid Johnson Janitorial Service, $123.

30 Received cash from patients (June 21 through June 30), $1,371.50.

30 Dr. Martin withdrew $1,020 for personal use.

Instructions

1. Record these transactions on page 26 of the combined journal. Insert the name of the drawing account.
2. Prove the equality of the debit and credit totals on scratch paper.

L.O. 4 **Problem 7-2A** The completed work sheet for A. C. Noyd, Psychologist is shown at the bottom of the page.

Instructions

Record the adjusting and closing entries in the combined journal. Remember to total the columns.

A. C. Noyd, Psychologist
Work Sheet
For Year Ended December 31, 19–

	ADJUSTMENTS			ADJUSTED TRIAL BALANCE			INCOME STATEMENT			BALANCE SHEET			
	DEBIT		CREDIT		DEBIT		CREDIT		DEBIT		CREDIT		DEBIT		CREDIT
				5 9 9 2 00							5 9 9 2 00			1
		(b)1 6 9 9 60	2 9 6 80							2 9 6 80			2
			33 1 8 0 00							33 1 8 0 00			3
		(a)4 7 7 4 00			19 9 9 2 00							19 9 9 2 00	4
					17 5 5 7 40							17 5 5 7 40	5
			22 6 8 0 00							22 6 8 0 00			6
					70 9 5 2 00			70 9 5 2 00					7
			26 2 0 8 00			26 2 0 8 00							8
			3 0 4 0 80			3 0 4 0 80							9
			5 8 8 0 00			5 8 8 0 00							10
			1 2 8 8 00			1 2 8 8 00							11
			2 0 7 2 00			2 0 7 2 00							12
			7 8 9 60			7 8 9 60							13
			6 0 0 60			6 0 0 60							14
													15
(a)4 7 7 4 00			4 7 7 4 00			4 7 7 4 00							16
(b)1 6 9 9 60			1 6 9 9 60			1 6 9 9 60							17
6 4 7 3 60		6 4 7 3 60	108 5 0 1 40		108 5 0 1 40		46 3 5 2 60		70 9 5 2 00		62 1 4 8 80		37 5 4 9 40	18
							24 5 9 9 40						24 5 9 9 40	19
							70 9 5 2 00		70 9 5 2 00		62 1 4 8 80		62 1 4 8 80	20
													21

L.O. 2,3   **Problem 7-3A**   Margo C. Warwick, D.C., operates the City Chiropractic Clinic. The transactions described below were completed during November of this year. Her chart of accounts is as follows:

Assets

111 Cash
112 Accounts Receivable
113 Supplies
114 Prepaid Insurance
121 Equipment
122 Accum. Deprec., Equipment

Liabilities

211 Accounts Payable

Owner's Equity

311 M. C. Warwick, Capital
312 M. C. Warwick, Drawing
313 Income Summary

Revenue

411 Professional Fees

Expenses

511 Salary Expense
512 Rent Expense
513 Laboratory Expense
514 Utilities Expense
515 Deprec. Exp., Equipment
516 Miscellaneous Expense

Nov.   2   Bought laboratory equipment on account, $1,404 from Healy Medical Supplies. (Use two lines.)

       2   Paid office rent for month, $690.

       2   Received cash on account from patients, $705: M. C. Sessions, $127.50; Agnes Milton, $222; Frank Barber, $288; Simon Russett, $67.50. (Dr. Warwick is on the accrual basis. Use four lines, recording individual amounts in both the Cash Debit column and the Accounts Receivable Credit column. List each patient's name in the Account Name column.)

       4   Received cash for professional services rendered, $1,213.

       6   Received and paid telephone bill for month, $39.

       8   Received and paid electric bill, $123.57

       9   Recorded fees charged to patients on account for professional services rendered, $703.50: C. R. Rhoades, $373.50; M. Wendt, $330. (Use two lines.)

     16   Paid salary of assistant, $502.50.

     19   Received cash for professional services, $474.

     23   Returned part of the equipment purchased on Nov. 2 and received a reduction on the bill, $63.

     27   Billed patients on account for professional services rendered, $960: N. P. Roberts, $540; Mary MacIntyre, $217.50; David Allen, $202.50.

     30   Paid salary of part-time assistant, $740.60.

     30   Paid salary of receptionist, $800.00.

     30   Dr. Warwick withdrew $1,477.50 cash for personal use.

Instructions

1. Record these transactions in the combined journal, page 37.
2. On scratch paper, prove the equality of the debit and credit totals.
3. Post to the accounts in the general ledger.
4. Prepare a trial balance.

L.O. 1,2   **Problem 7-4A**   On May 1 of this year, N. Salazar started a tree spraying business. Salazar completed the following transactions related to Salazar's Tree Spray Service:

May   1 Salazar opened an account in the Gibbs National Bank in the name of the business and deposited $12,000.

1 Paid rent for office and warehouse space, $250 (check no. 1).

2 Bought a used truck from Kelly Motors for $16,400, paying $3,000 as a downpayment, with the balance on account due in 30 days (check no. 2).

2 Bought a used sprayer from James Equipment and Chemical for $4,800, paying $2,000 as a downpayment, with the balance due in 30 days (check no. 3).

3 Received and paid bill for advertising from the *City News and Views*, $144 (check no. 4).

4 Paid Brogan Fast Service for gas and oil for the truck, $152 (check no. 5).

4 Bought two portable sprayers on account from Ken's Pump and Irrigation, $1,150.

4 Bought chemicals from J and R Distributing Company on account, $217.27.

6 Received revenue for the week, $1,128.

7 Paid wages to part-time employee, $242 (check no. 6).

7 Paid for telephone answering service for the month, $122 (check no. 7).

10 Paid Brogan Fast Service for gas and oil for the truck, $118 (check no. 8).

13 Received revenue for the week, $1,256.

17 Salazar withdrew $840 for personal use (check no. 9).

20 Received revenue for the week, $1,284.

21 Paid wages to part-time employee, $264 (check no. 10).

26 Paid utilities for the month, $116 (check no. 11).

26 Paid $48 for city business license (check no. 12).

30 Paid Kelly Motors $1,800 to apply on account (check no. 13).

30 Paid Brogan Fast Service for gas and oil for the truck, $36, plus $94 for a tune-up (check no. 14).

31 Received revenue for the week, $1,572.

31 Paid wages to part-time employee, $286 (check no. 15).

31 Salazar withdrew $650 for personal use (check no. 16).

Instructions

1. By reviewing the transactions for Salazar's Tree Spray Service, formulate a chart of accounts. Salazar will use the modified cash basis of accounting.
2. Label the appropriate columns in the combined journal. Next to the Date column, list a Check No. column and record checks beginning with number 1.
3. Record the transactions in the combined journal beginning with page 1.
4. Show proof of the equality of debits and credits.

Problem Set B

L.O. 2　**Problem 7-1B**　The following chart of accounts is used by C. A. Weiss, M.D.:

Assets

111 Cash
112 Medical Supplies
113 X-ray Supplies
114 Office Supplies
121 Medical Equipment
122 Accum. Deprec., Medical Equipment
123 Office Furniture and Equipment
124 Accum. Deprec., Office Furniture and Equipment
125 Automobile
126 Accum. Deprec., Automobile

Liabilities

211 Notes Payable

Owner's Equity

311 C. A. Weiss, Capital
312 C. A. Weiss, Drawing
313 Income Summary

Revenue

411 Professional Fees

Expenses

511 Salary Expense
512 Rent Expense
513 Equipment Rental Expense
514 Medical Supplies Expense
515 X-ray Supplies Expense
516 Laboratory Expense
517 Laundry and Cleaning Expense
518 Office Supplies Expense
519 Dep. Exp., Medical Equipment
521 Dep. Exp., Office Furniture and Equipment
522 Dep. Exp., Automobile
523 Automobile Expense
524 Insurance Expense
525 Telephone Expense
526 Utilities Expense
527 Miscellaneous Expense

Dr. Weiss' records consist of an appointment record book, examination and charge reports, patients' ledger records, a combined journal, and a general ledger. The doctor fills out an examination and charge report each time a patient visits. The reports contain a description or listing of the treatments and tests administered and the amount of the charges. The charges are then recorded in the patient's ledger record. Monthly statements based on the patients' ledger records are mailed to patients. Dr. Weiss' books are kept on the modified cash basis.

The following transactions took place during September.

Sept. 1 Bought medical supplies for cash from Reese Surgical Supply, $429.50.
　　 1 Paid Mears Realty rent for the month, $1,275.
　　 5 Paid salary of part-time office person, $885.
　　 6 Received cash from patients during the week, $7,374.
　　 7 Bought an examination table from Reese Surgical Supply, costing $630, paying $180 in cash and agreeing by contract to pay the balance in three monthly installments of $150 each (credit Notes Payable).
　　 8 Paid telephone bill, $93.
　　 9 Paid Martinez Laboratories for laboratory expense, $324.
　　13 Total cash received from patients during the week, $4,671.

Sept. 16 Bought x-ray supplies for cash from Martin Supply Company, $193.50.

16 Dr. Weiss withdrew $925 for personal use.

20 Total cash received from patients during the week, $1,833.

23 Bought postage stamps, $6 (Miscellaneous Expense); paid cash.

25 Paid for gas and oil to Peck's Service Station, $98.25.

29 Paid United Building Maintenance for janitorial service, $60.

30 Paid nurse's salary, $2,013.

30 Dr. Weiss withdrew $1,380 for personal use.

30 Paid $92.10 to Economy Laundry for laundry service through September 30.

Instructions

1. Record these transactions in the combined journal, page 26. Insert the name of the drawing account.

2. Prove the equality of the debit and credit totals on scratch paper.

L.O. 4 **Problem 7-2B** The completed work sheet for R. L. Jones, Psychologist is shown on the next two pages.

Instructions

Record the adjusting and closing entries in the combined journal. Remember to total the columns.

L.O. 2,3 **Problem 7-3B** Jane C. Clough, D.C., operates the West Chiropractic Clinic. The transactions described below were completed during November of this year. Her chart of accounts is as follows:

Assets
111 Cash
112 Accounts Receivable
113 Supplies
114 Prepaid Insurance
121 Equipment
122 Accum. Deprec., Equipment

Liabilities
211 Accounts Payable

Owner's Equity
311 J. C. Clough, Capital
312 J. C. Clough, Drawing
313 Income Summary

Revenue
411 Professional Fees

Expenses
511 Salary Expense
512 Rent Expense
513 Laboratory Expense
514 Utilities Expense
515 Deprec. Exp., Equipment
516 Miscellaneous Expense

Nov. 2 Bought laboratory equipment on account from Harvey Surgical, $1,410. (Use two lines.)

2 Paid office rent for the month, $690.

2 Received cash on account from patients, $705: Roy Cannon,

Nov. $240; Thomas Parker, $285; Anthony Anderson, $180. (Dr. Clough is on the accrual basis. Use three lines, recording individual amounts in both the Cash Debit column and the Accounts Receivable Credit column. List each patient's name in the Account Name column.)

4 Received cash for professional services rendered, $1,187.50.

6 Received and paid telephone bill for month, $36.

6 Received and paid electric bill, $127.50.

9 Recorded fees charged to patients on account for professional services rendered, $817.50: P. R. Blanchard, $390; Hubert Hastings, $427.50. (Use two lines.)

16 Paid salary of assistant, $492.00.

19 Received cash for professional services, $465.

PROBLEM 7-2B

	ACCOUNT NAME	TRIAL BALANCE	
		DEBIT	CREDIT
1	Cash	4 4 5 0 60	
2	Supplies	3 0 4 0 80	
3	Office Equipment	44 4 0 5 20	
4	Accumulated Depreciation, Office Equipment		13 6 6 4 00
5	R. L. Jones, Capital		31 4 9 5 18
6	R. L. Jones, Drawing	22 0 9 2 00	
7	Professional Fees		65 4 6 1 20
8	Salary Expense	24 0 2 9 60	
9	Advertising Expense	2 8 1 2 10	
10	Rent Expense	5 8 8 0 00	
11	Automobile Expense	1 2 4 0 66	
12	Travel Expense	1 8 0 8 80	
13	Entertainment Expense	5 8 3 14	
14	Miscellaneous Expense	2 7 7 48	
15		110 6 2 0 38	110 6 2 0 38
16	Depreciation Expense, Office Equipment		
17	Supplies Expense		
18			
19	Net Income		
20			
21			
22			
23			
24			
25			
26			

Nov.   23 Returned part of the equipment purchased on Nov. 2 and received a reduction on the bill, $90.

        27 Billed patients on account for professional services rendered, $585: N. R. Russett, $135; Neil Suter, $240; C. A. Thornton, $210.

        30 Paid salary of part-time assistant, $546.50.

        30 Paid salary of receptionist, $820, for the month.

        30 Dr. Clough withdrew $1,260 cash for personal use.

Instructions

1. Record these transactions in a combined journal, page 37.
2. On scratch paper, prove the equality of the debit and credit totals.
3. Post to the accounts in the general ledger.
4. Prepare a trial balance.

R. L. Jones, Psychologist
Work Sheet
For Year Ended December 31, 19—

	ADJUSTMENTS		ADJUSTED TRIAL BALANCE		INCOME STATEMENT		BALANCE SHEET		
	DEBIT	CREDIT	DEBIT	CREDIT	DEBIT	CREDIT	DEBIT	CREDIT	
			4 4 5 0 60				4 4 5 0 60		1
		(b)1 6 7 0 20	1 3 7 0 60				1 3 7 0 60		2
			44 4 0 5 20				44 4 0 5 20		3
		(a)4 1 7 4 80		17 8 3 8 80				17 8 3 8 80	4
				31 4 9 5 18				31 4 9 5 18	5
			22 0 9 2 00				22 0 9 2 00		6
				65 4 6 1 20		65 4 6 1 20			7
			24 0 2 9 60		24 0 2 9 60				8
			2 8 1 2 10		2 8 1 2 10				9
			5 8 8 0 00		5 8 8 0 00				10
			1 2 4 0 66		1 2 4 0 66				11
			1 8 0 8 80		1 8 0 8 80				12
			5 8 3 14		5 8 3 14				13
			2 7 7 48		2 7 7 48				14
									15
(a)4 1 7 4 80			4 1 7 4 80		4 1 7 4 80				16
(b)1 6 7 0 20			1 6 7 0 20		1 6 7 0 20				17
5 8 4 5 00		5 8 4 5 00	114 7 9 5 18	114 7 9 5 18	42 4 7 6 78	65 4 6 1 20	72 3 1 8 40	49 3 3 3 98	18
					22 9 8 4 42			22 9 8 4 42	19
					65 4 6 1 20	65 4 6 1 20	72 3 1 8 40	72 3 1 8 40	20
									21
									22
									23
									24
									25
									26

L.O. 1,2,3 **Problem 7-4B** On November 1 of this year, R. A. Dobbs decided to open a delivery business serving the local area. Dobbs completed the following transactions related to Dobbs Delivery Service:

Nov.   1 Dobbs opened an account in The First State Bank in the name of the business and deposited $32,000.

2 Bought two delivery vans from Brandon Motors for $24,900, paying $8,000 down, with the balance on account (check no. 1).

3 Bought four hand trucks from Shattuck and Torres for $454, paying cash (check no. 2).

4 Paid City Service for gas and oil for delivery vans, $168 (check no. 3).

5 Paid rent for subletting office space, $170 (check no. 4).

7 Paid wages to employee, $368 (check no. 5).

7 Received revenue for the week, $952.

9 Paid for city business license, $64 (check no. 6).

11 Paid for telephone answering service for the month, $116 (check no. 7).

14 Bought desk and filing cabinet on account from Murren Office Supply, $236.

14 Received revenue for the week, $1,176.

14 Paid wages to employee, $384 (check no. 8).

14 Dobbs withdrew $636 for personal use (check no. 9).

17 Paid Brandon Motors $1,600 as part payment on account (check no. 10).

17 Paid City Service for gas and oil for delivery vans, $232 (check no. 11).

18 Paid $124 for advertisement in the telephone directory (check no. 12).

20 Paid utilities for the month, $94 (check no. 13).

21 Received revenue for the week, $1,292.

23 Paid wages to employee, $424 (check no. 14).

25 Paid Murren Office Supply in full payment of account, $236 (check no. 15).

30 Received revenue for the week, $1,568.

30 Received bill from Newman Insurance Agency for vehicle insurance, $182.

30 Paid wages to employee, $440 (check no. 16).

30 Dobbs withdrew $850 for personal use (check no. 17).

Instructions

1. By reviewing the transactions for Dobbs Delivery Service, develop a chart of accounts. Dobbs will use the modified cash basis.
2. Label the appropriate columns in the combined journal. Next to the Date column, list a Check No. column and record checks beginning with number 1.
3. Record the transactions in the combined journal beginning with page 1.
4. Show proof of the equality of debits and credits.

8

Bank Accounts and Cash Funds

LEARNING OBJECTIVES

After you have completed this chapter, you will be able to do the following:

1. Reconcile a bank statement.
2. Record the required journal entries directly from the bank reconciliation.
3. Record journal entries to establish and reimburse Petty Cash Fund.
4. Complete petty cash vouchers and petty cash payments records.
5. Record the journal entries to establish a Change Fund.
6. Record journal entries for transactions involving Cash Short and Over.

A very important aspect of any system of financial accounting, either for an individual or for a business enterprise, is the efficient management of cash. For a business of any size, all cash received during a working day should be deposited at the end of the day, and all disbursements—with the exception of payments from Petty Cash—should be made by check. When we talk about cash, we mean currency, coins, checks, money orders, and bank drafts or bank cashier's checks. Personal checks are accepted on a conditional-payment status, that is, based on the condition that they're valid. In other words, we consider checks to be good until they are proved to be no good.

In this chapter besides discussing bank accounts, we are going to talk about **cash funds**—petty cash funds and change funds—which, in this sense, are separately held stores of cash.

USING A CHECKING ACCOUNT

Although you may be familiar with the process of opening a checking account, making deposits, and writing checks, let's review these and other procedures associated with opening and maintaining a business checking account. We will discuss signature cards, deposit slips, automated teller machines, night deposits, and ways of endorsing checks.

Signature Card

When Roger L. Langford founded Langford Company, a cycle rental firm, he opened a checking account in the name of the business. When he made his first deposit, he filled out a **signature card** for the bank's files. Langford gave his assistant the right to sign checks too, so the assistant also signed the card. This signature card gives the bank a copy of the official signatures of any persons authorized to sign checks. The bank can use it to verify any signatures on the checks of Langford Company presented for payment. Of course this helps the bank detect forgeries. In addition, as a means of preventing employee theft, many companies require more than one signature on their checks. Figure 8-1 shows a typical signature card.

FIGURE 8-1

Title: Langford Company

Account Number: 5008-287

In consideration of the acceptance by PRIME NATIONAL BANK of my/our account of the type indicated below, I/we agree to be bound by such rules and regulations and/or such schedules of interest, fees and charges applicable to such account as may now or hereafter be adopted by and in effect at said Bank, and also by the provisions printed hereon. It is understood that the acceptance by said Bank of my/our account is subject to the receipt by said Bank of satisfactory credit information.

(1) Sign Here: Roger L. Langford

(2) Sign Here: Gloria B. Neilson

Address: 2254 Fenwick Avenue

City: Oakland State: California Zip: 94614

☑ CHECKING ☐ MULTIPLE MATURITY ☐ CASH MANAGER

☐ SAVINGS ☐ GUARANTEED INTEREST (Multiple Maturity) ☐ SAFE DEPOSIT ☐ OTHER ______

IF THIS IS A JOINT ACCOUNT, BOTH OWNERS MUST SIGN ABOVE

Each of the signers guarantees the genuineness of the signature of the other. Each signer also agrees with the other and the Bank that deposits now or hereafter made to this account may be withdrawn in whole or part by either or survivor, and that each may endorse for deposit to this account any instrument payable to the order of either or both. Provisions respecting this agreement shall be modified only upon receipt by the Bank of written notice, signed by both.

Deposit Slips

The bank provides printed **deposit slips** on which customers record the amount of coins and currency they are depositing and list each individual check being deposited. A typical deposit slip is shown in Figure 8-2.

For identification purposes, each check should be listed according to its American Bankers Association (ABA) transit number. The **ABA number** is the small fraction located in the upper right corner of a check. The numerator (top of the fraction) indicates the city or state in which the bank is located and the specific bank on which the check is drawn. The

FIGURE 8-2

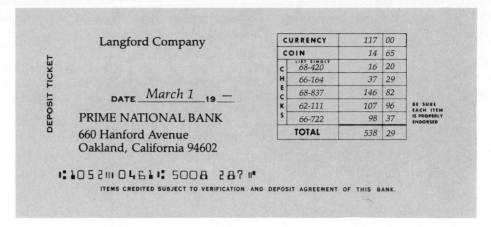

denominator (bottom of the fraction) indicates the Federal Reserve District in which the check is cleared and the routing number used by the Federal Reserve Bank. For example,

68-420

1210

The 68 identifies the city or state, and the 420 indicates the specific bank within that area. That is all you need to list on the deposit slip. However, for your information, the 12 in the denominator represents the Twelfth Federal Reserve District, and the 10 represents the routing number used by the Federal Reserve Bank.

The depositor fills out the deposit slip in duplicate, giving one copy to the bank teller and keeping the other copy. (This procedure may vary from bank to bank.)

When the bank receives the deposited checks, it prints the amount of each check on the lower right side of the check in a very distinctive script called **MICR,** which stands for *magnetic ink character recognition*. The routing number used by the Federal Reserve Bank was previously printed on the lower left side of the blank check. The reason banks use this MICR script is that the electronic equipment used to process the checks is able to read the script identifying the bank on which the check is drawn as well as the amount of the check. Clearing checks electronically speeds up the process dramatically.

Automated Teller Machines

Deposits and withdrawals can be made at all hours of the day at banks having automated teller machines. Each depositor uses a plastic card that contains a code number. This card resembles a bank credit card. The amount to be deposited or withdrawn is keyed in by the depositor and shows up on a screen. To make a deposit, the customer inserts an envelope containing cash and/or checks and a copy of the deposit slip into the

ATM. To make a withdrawal, the customer removes the cash requested from the machine. When all transactions are completed, the automated teller machine returns the customer's plastic card and prints out a slip that lists the type and amount of each transaction.

Night Deposits

Most banks also provide night depositories so that firms can make deposits after regular banking hours. Depositories are steel-lined chutes into which a firm's representative can drop a bag of cash and checks, knowing that their day's receipts will be safe until the bank opens in the morning.

Endorsements

The bank refuses to accept for deposit a check made out to a firm until someone from the firm has endorsed the check. The **endorsement** may be made by signature or by stamp. The endorsement should appear on the back of the left end of a check, as it does in Figure 8-3. The endorsement (1) transfers title to the money and (2) guarantees the payment of the check. In other words, if the check is not good, NSF (not sufficient funds), then the bank, in order to protect itself, will deduct the amount of the check from the depositor's account.

FIGURE 8-3

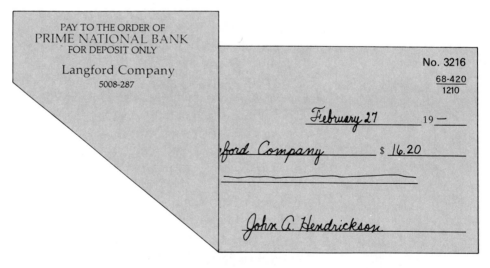

Restrictive Endorsement   Langford Company endorses all incoming checks by stamping on the back of the checks: "Pay to the Order of Prime National Bank, For Deposit Only, Langford Company." This is called a **restrictive endorsement** because it restricts or limits any further negotiation of the check; it forces the deposit of the check since the endorsement is not valid for any other purpose.

Blank Endorsement When the party to whom a check is made payable (the payee) endorses the check by signing only her or his name on the back of the check, the party makes what is known as a **blank endorsement** (Figure 8-4). With a blank endorsement, there are no restrictions attached.

Qualified Endorsement A third type of endorsement is a **qualified endorsement,** which generally includes the phrase "Pay to the order of" followed by the name of the person to whom the check is being transferred and then followed by the phrase "without recourse." Such an endorsement frees the endorser of future liability in case the drawer of the check does not have sufficient funds to cover the check.

FIGURE 8-4

Blank Endorsement

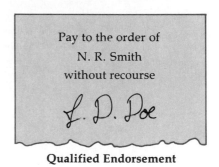

Qualified Endorsement

WRITING CHECKS

As you know, people generally use a check to withdraw money from a checking account. A check represents an order by the depositor, directing the bank to pay money to a designated person or firm: the **payee.**

The checks may be attached to check stubs. Each stub has spaces for recording the check number and amount, the date and payee, the purpose of the check, and the beginning and ending balances. _Note well:_ The information recorded on the check stub is the basis for the journal entry, so check stubs are vitally important. A person in a hurry, or working under pressure, can sometimes neglect to fill in the check stubs. Therefore, it is best to record all the information on the check stub _before making out the check._

It goes without saying that all checks should be written carefully so that no dishonest person can successfully alter them. Write the payee's name on the first long line. Write the amount of the check in figures close to the dollar sign, then write the amount in words at the extreme left of the line provided for this information. Write cents as a fraction of 100. For example, write $727.50 as "seven hundred twenty-seven and 50/100," or $69.00 as "sixty-nine and 00/100." From a legal standpoint, if there is a discrepancy between the amount in figures and the written amount, the written amount prevails. However, as a general practice, the bank gets in touch with the depositor and asks what the correct amount should be.

Many firms use a **check writer,** which is a machine used to imprint the amount in figures and in words on the check itself. Using this machine neatly prevents anyone from altering the amount of the check.

Finally, the depositor's signature on the face of the check should match that on the signature card on file at the depositor's bank.

Figure 8-5 is a check, with the accompanying stub, drawn on the account of Langford Company.

FIGURE 8-5

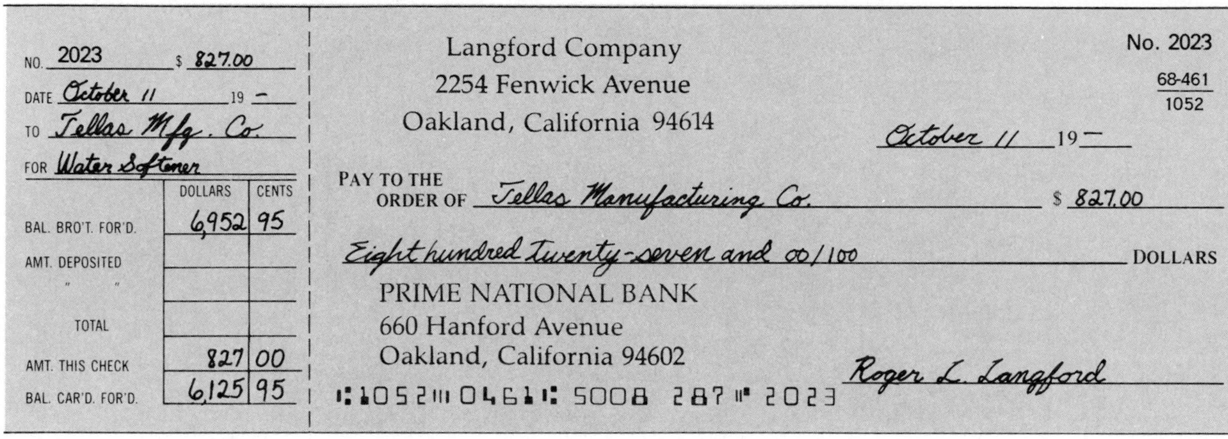

Instead of using checks with accompanying stubs, many individuals and business firms use check registers. Space is provided in the check register for recording the information contained on the check, such as date, amount, payee, number, and so on.

BANK STATEMENTS

Once a month the bank sends all its customers a **bank statement.** This statement provides the following information about customers' accounts:

- The balance at the beginning of the month
- Additions in the form of deposits and credit memos
- Deductions in the form of checks and debit memos
- The final balance at the end of the month

A bank statement for Langford Company is shown in Figure 8-6. The following code of symbols are listed on the statement:

- **CM (credit memo)** Increases or credits to the account, such as notes or accounts left with the bank for collection.
- **DM (debit memo)** Decreases or debits to the account, such as NSF checks, automated teller withdrawals, and service charges. Service charges are based on the number of items processed and the average account balance. Special charges may also be levied against the account for collections and other services performed.

FIGURE 8-6

PRIME NATIONAL BANK
660 Hanford Avenue
Oakland, California 94602

STATEMENT OF
ACCOUNT

Langford Company
2254 Fenwick Avenue
Oakland, California 94614

ACCOUNT NUMBER
5008-287
STATEMENT DATE
September 30, 19——October 31, 19–
TAX ID NUMBER
83-424 9732

SUMMARY		
	Balance Last Statement	*$6,889.13*
	Amount of Checks and Debits	*$25,158.91*
	Number of Checks	*66*
	Amount of Deposits and Credits	*$27,031.78*
	Number of Deposits	*23*
	Balance This Statement	*$8,762.00*

CHECKS/OTHER DEBITS

CHECKS

CHECK NUMBER	DATE POSTED	AMOUNT	CHECK NUMBER	DATE POSTED	AMOUNT
1952	*10-01*	*50.00*	*1988*	*10-17*	*61.22*
1953	*10-01*	*200.00*	*1989*	*10-17*	*463.29*
1954	*10-01*	*400.00*	*1990*	*10-18*	*520.00*
1955	*10-02*	*46.00*	*1991*	*10-19*	*14.57*
1956	*10-02*	*174.23*	*1992*	*10-19*	*23.98*
1957	*10-02*	*671.74*	*1993*	*10-19*	*115.16*
1958	*10-03*	*846.20*	*1994*	*10-20*	*117.37*
1984	*10-14*	*664.56*	*2018*	*10-30*	*126.70*
1985	*10-15*	*719.00*	*2019*	*10-30*	*943.64*
1986	*10-16*	*61.68*	*2020*	*10-31*	*843.17*
1987	*10-16*	*591.84*	*2021*	*10-31*	*21.92*

OTHER DEBITS

DESCRIPTION	DATE POSTED	AMOUNT
DM NSF check from C. M. Lang Company	*10-15*	*125.00*
DM Automated Teller Trans. 062142 customer N3162241 at terminal 30962—cash	*10-16*	*24.00*
DM Service charge	*10-31*	*5.00*

DEPOSITS/OTHER CREDITS

DEPOSITS

DATE POSTED	AMOUNT	DATE POSTED	AMOUNT
10-01	*921.00*	*10-17*	*873.19*
10-02	*1,476.22*	*10-18*	*946.78*
10-03	*463.62*	*10-21*	*329.49*
10-04	*789.44*	*10-22*	*1,116.27*
10-07	*1,063.14*	*10-23*	*734.13*
10-08	*1,211.96*	*10-26*	*227.69*
10-14	*992.27*	*10-28*	*439.45*
10-15	*759.41*	*10-29*	*611.12*
10-16	*641.33*	*10-30*	*764.35*

OTHER CREDITS

DESCRIPTION	DATE POSTED	AMOUNT
CM Note collected, principal $600, interest $6	*10-29*	*606.00*

PLEASE EXAMINE THIS STATEMENT CAREFULLY. REPORT ANY POSSIBLE ERRORS IN 10 DAYS.

CODE SYMBOLS

CM Credit Memo   **OD** Overdraft

DM Debit Memo   **EC** Error Correction

- **EC (error correction)**   Corrections of errors made by the bank, such as mistakes in transferring figures.
- **OD (overdraft)**   An overwithdrawal, resulting in a negative balance in the account.

The bank statement is a valuable aid to efficiency because it gives a double record of the Cash account. If a business entity deposits all cash receipts in the bank and makes all payments by check, then the bank is keeping an independent record of the firm's cash. Offhand, you might think that the two balances—the firm's and the bank's—should be equal, but this is most unlikely. Some transactions may have been recorded in the firm's account before being entered in the bank's records. In addition, there are unavoidable delays (by either the firm or the bank) in recording transactions. Ordinarily, there is a time lag of one day or more between the date a check is written and the date it is presented to the bank for payment. Also, banks usually do not record deposits until the following business day. During this time lag, deposits made or checks written are recorded in the firm's checkbook, but they are not yet listed on the bank statement.

The bank usually mails statements to its depositors shortly after the end of the month. The **canceled checks** (checks that have been cashed or cleared by the bank) and debit or credit memos are generally mailed in the same envelope with the statement. As we mentioned before, debit memos represent deductions from and credit memos represent additions to a bank account.

Recording Deposits or Withdrawals on the Bank's Books

Each business entity keeps its accounts from its *own* point of view. As far as the bank is concerned, each customer's deposits are liabilities, in that the bank owes the customer the amount of the deposits. Using T accounts, it looks like this:

Liabilities		Deposits Payable	
−	+	−	+
Debits	Credits	Debits	Credits
		Checks written	Deposits
	Debit memos	Service charges	Notes collected
		NSF checks	
		Automated teller machine withdrawals	

(Debits: Checks written, Service charges, NSF checks, Automated teller machine withdrawals } Debit memos)
(Credits: Deposits, Notes collected } Credit memos)

When the bank receives a cash deposit from its customer, the bank credits its Deposits Payable because it owes more to its customer. When the bank cashes a check (pays out) for its customer, the bank debits Deposits Payable because it owes less to its customer.

Recording Deposits or Withdrawals on the Customer's Books

The customer uses the account titled Cash, or Cash in Bank, or simply the name of the bank. Deposits are recorded as debits, and withdrawals are recorded as credits in the account. On a bank reconciliation, the balance of the account is listed as the **book balance of cash.**

Need for Reconciling Bank Balance and Book Balance

Objective I

Reconcile a bank statement.

Since the bank statement balance and the book balance are not equal, a firm makes a **bank reconciliation** to uncover the reasons for the difference between the two balances and to correct any errors that may have been made by either the bank or the firm. This makes it possible to wind up with the same balance in each account, which is called the _adjusted balance,_ or _true balance,_ of the Cash account.

There are a variety of reasons for differences between the bank statement balance and the customer's cash balance. Here are some of the more usual ones:

- **Outstanding checks** Checks that have been written but not yet received for payment by the time the bank sends out its statement. The depositor, when writing out his or her checks, deducted the amounts from the Cash account in the company's books, which explains the difference.
- **Deposit in transit** A deposit made after the bank statement was issued. The depositor has naturally already added the amount to the Cash account in his or her books, but the deposit has not been recorded by the bank.
- **Service charge** A bank charge for services rendered: for issuing checks, for collecting money, for receiving payment of notes turned over to it by the customer for collection, and for other such services. The bank notifies the depositor with a debit memorandum, and immediately deducts the fee from the balance of the bank account.
- **Collections** When the bank acts as a collection agent for its customers by accepting payments on promissory notes, installment accounts, and charge accounts, it adds the proceeds to the customer's bank account and sends a credit memorandum to notify the customer of the transaction.
- **NSF (Not Sufficient Funds) checks** When a bank customer deposits a check, she or he counts it as cash. Occasionally, however, a check is

not paid (bounces), and then the bank notifies the customer. The customer must then make a deduction from the Cash account.

- **Errors** In spite of internal control and systems designed to double-check against errors, sometimes either the customer or the bank makes a mistake. Often these errors do not become evident until the bank reconciliation is performed.

Steps in Reconciling the Bank Statement

Follow these steps in reconciling a bank statement:

1. **Canceled checks** Compare the amount of each canceled check with the bank statement, and note any discrepancies. The amount of the *proof mark* in machine-readable characters at the bottom of the check, which is the amount that will appear on the bank statement, should match the amount written on the check. Also, on the stub that matches each canceled check, list the date of the bank statement. In some cases, a bank may not pay a check until one or two months after it was written. If a question arises as to whether or not you have paid a particular bill, you can look at the check stub. Then, you can refer directly to the bank statement to pick up the canceled checks as proof of payment.

2. **Deposits** Look over the deposits in transit, or unrecorded deposits listed on the bank reconciliation of the previous month. Compare these with the deposits listed on this month's bank statement. These deposits should all be accounted for; note any discrepancy. Now compare the remaining deposits listed on the current bank statement with deposits written in the firm's accounting records. Consider any deposits not shown on the bank statement as deposits in transit.

3. **Outstanding checks** Next, arrange the canceled checks in the order of the check numbers. Look over the list of outstanding checks left over from the bank reconciliation of the previous month, and note the checks that have now been returned. Compare each canceled check with the entry in the journal. If the journal is not available, then compare the canceled checks with the check stubs. In either case, use a check mark (√) to indicate that the check has been paid and that the amount is correct. To further verify that money has been sent to the right payee, review the endorsements on the backs of the checks. Any payments that have *not* been checked off, including the outstanding checks from the previous bank reconciliation, are the present outstanding checks. In other words, they were not presented for payment by the time of the cutoff date of the bank statement.

4. **Bank memorandums** Trace the credit memos and the debit memos to the journal. If the memos have not been recorded, make separate journal entries for them.

As you can see, a bank can be an accountant's best friend. A large firm should require that the reconciliation be prepared by an employee who is not involved in recording business transactions or in handling cash receipts and disbursements.

Examples of Bank Reconciliations

Let's go through the reconciliation process for two firms. First we will take the case of R. L. Pearson Company, then we will look at Langford Company.

R. L. Pearson Company   The bank statement of R. L. Pearson Company indicates a balance of $2,119 as of March 31. The balance of the Cash account in Pearson's ledger as of that date is $1,552. Pearson's accountant has taken the following steps:

1. Verified that canceled checks were recorded correctly on the bank statement
2. Noted the deposit made on March 31 that was not recorded on the bank statement, $762
3. Noted outstanding checks: no. 921, $626; no. 985, $69; no. 986, $438
4. Noted credit memo: note collected by the bank from S. Cater, $200, not recorded in the journal
5. Noted debit memo: collection charge and service charge not recorded in the journal, $4

The note received from S. Cater is called a **promissory note.** A promissory note is a written promise to pay a definite amount at a definite future time. Let's assume that R. L. Pearson Company received the sixty-day non-interest-bearing note from S. Cater for services performed. In recording the transaction, Pearson's accountant debited Notes Receivable and credited Income from Services. The account, Notes Receivable, is similar to Accounts Receivable. However, Accounts Receivable is reserved for customer charge accounts with payments usually due in thirty days. Next, R. L. Pearson Company turned the note over to its bank for collection.

The bank will use a credit memo form to notify R. L. Pearson Company that the note has been collected and that the company's bank account has been increased by the amount of the note. Based on the credit memo, Pearson's accountant will make a journal entry debiting Cash and crediting Notes Receivable.

Think of the bank reconciliation in terms of the following:

1. Bring the bank statement balance up to date by recording the events we knew about but the bank did not know about when it prepared the statement (deposits in transit and outstanding checks as shown in our checkbook, for example).

2. Bring the balance of the Cash account up to date by recording the events the bank knew about but we did not know about until we received the statement (debit memos and credit memos as shown on the bank statement, for example).

The bank reconciliation may be made on a separate sheet of paper or on the back of the bank statement, since some banks print the main headings on the form. Figure 8-7 shows Pearson's bank reconciliation. The items in the reconciliation that require journal entries are shown in color, and the entries are on the next page.

FIGURE 8-7

R. L. Pearson
Bank Reconciliation
March 31, 19–

Bank Statement Balance		$2,119.00
Add: Deposit in transit (March 31)		762.00
		$2,881.00
Deduct: Outstanding checks		
No. 921	$626.00	
No. 985	69.00	
No. 986	438.00	1,133.00
Adjusted Balance		$1,748.00
Book Balance of Cash		$1,552.00
Add: Note collected by bank		200.00
		$1,752.00
Deduct: Bank service		
and collection charges		4.00
Adjusted Balance		$1,748.00

Events we knew about but the bank did not know about

Events the bank knew about but we did not know about

Require journal entries

Objective 2

Record the required journal entries directly from the bank reconciliation.

Note that journal entries should be based on the items used to adjust the book balance of Cash. According to the bank reconciliation the true balance of Cash is $1,748, which is the balance we wish to show on the firm's books. We can't change the balance of an account unless we first make a journal entry and then post the entry to the accounts involved. **Consequently, we have to make journal entries for items in the book balance of cash section of the bank reconciliation.** Debit additions to Cash and credit deductions from Cash. R. L. Pearson Company records the entries in its general journal.

Here service and collection charges are both recorded in Miscellaneous Expense because the amounts are relatively small. However, some accountants use a separate expense account, such as Bank Charge Expense.

GENERAL JOURNAL				PAGE _____	
DATE	DESCRIPTION	POST. REF.	DEBIT	CREDIT	
19–					
Mar. 31	Cash		2 0 0 00		
	Notes Receivable			2 0 0 00	
	Non-interest-bearing note signed				
	by S. Cater was collected by				
	the bank.				
31	Miscellaneous Expense		4 00		
	Cash			4 00	
	Service charge and collection				
	charge levied by the bank.				

After the above entries have been posted, the T account for Cash looks like this:

Cash

Balance	1,552	Mar. 31		4
Mar. 31	200			
	1,752			
Bal. 1,748				

Note that the balance in the T account is now equal to the adjusted balance on the bank reconciliation.

Form of Bank Reconciliation

Now that you have seen an example of a bank reconciliation, let's look at the standard form of a bank reconciliation for a hypothetical company.

Bank Statement Balance (last figure on the statement)		$4,000
Add		
Deposits in transit (deposits in transit already added to the Cash account)	$300	
Bank errors (that understate balance)	20	320
		$4,320
Deduct		
Outstanding checks (they have already been deducted from the Cash account)	$960	
Bank errors (that overstate balance)	40	1,000
Adjusted balance (the true balance of Cash)		$3,320

Book balance of cash (the latest balance of the Cash account if it has been posted up to date; otherwise take the beginning balance of Cash, plus cash receipts and minus cash payments)		$2,850
Add		
Credit memos (additions by the bank not recorded in the Cash account, such as collections of notes)	$500	
Book errors (that understate balance)	40	540
		$3,390
Deduct		
Debit memos (deductions by the bank not recorded in the Cash account, such as service charges or collection charges)	$ 20	
Book errors (that overstate balance)	50	70
Adjusted balance (the true balance of Cash)		$3,320

Langford Company The bank statement of Langford Company shows a final balance of $8,762 as of October 31 (see Figure 8-6). The present balance of the Cash account in the ledger, after Langford's accountant has posted from the journal, is $7,830.50. The accountant took the following steps:

1. Verified that canceled checks were recorded correctly on the bank statement.
2. Discovered that a deposit of $1,003 made on October 31 was not recorded on the bank statement.
3. Noted outstanding checks: no. 1916, $461; no. 2022, $119; no. 2023, $827; no. 2024, $67.
4. Noted that a credit memo for a note collected by the bank from Helm and Sutor, $600 principal plus $6 interest, was not recorded in the journal.
5. Found that check no. 2001 for $523, payable to Moran, Inc., on account was recorded in the journal as $532. (The correct amount is $523.)
6. Noted that a debit memo for a collection charge and service charge of $5.50 was not recorded in the journal.
7. Noted that debit memo for an NSF check for $125 from C. M. Nash Company was not recorded.
8. Noted that a $24 personal withdrawal by Roger L. Langford, the owner, using an automated teller, was not recorded.

Look at Figure 8-8 to see how each step relates to the bank reconciliation.

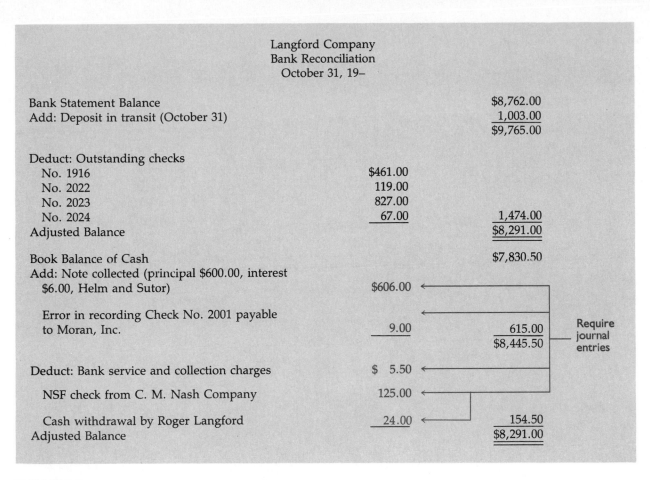

Langford Company
Bank Reconciliation
October 31, 19–

Bank Statement Balance		$8,762.00
Add: Deposit in transit (October 31)		1,003.00
		$9,765.00
Deduct: Outstanding checks		
No. 1916	$461.00	
No. 2022	119.00	
No. 2023	827.00	
No. 2024	67.00	1,474.00
Adjusted Balance		$8,291.00
Book Balance of Cash		$7,830.50
Add: Note collected (principal $600.00, interest $6.00, Helm and Sutor)	$606.00	
Error in recording Check No. 2001 payable to Moran, Inc.	9.00	615.00
		$8,445.50
Deduct: Bank service and collection charges	$ 5.50	
NSF check from C. M. Nash Company	125.00	
Cash withdrawal by Roger Langford	24.00	154.50
Adjusted Balance		$8,291.00

Require journal entries

FIGURE 8-8

The accountant makes journal entries for the items indicated in Figure 8-8 to change the Cash account from the present balance of $7,830.50 to the true balance of $8,291. Again, those items that require journal entries are highlighted in Figure 8-8 and shown in Figure 8-9.

The account, Interest Income, is classified as a revenue account. It represents the amount received on the promissory note that is over and above the face value of the note.

Regarding the NSF check, upon being notified by the bank, Langford Company calls its customer (C. M. Nash). C. M. Nash can now take steps to cover the check. Let's back up and review Langford's transaction with C. M. Nash. In return for services, Langford received Nash's check for $125. At that time Langford's accountant recorded the transaction as a debit to Cash for $125 and a credit to Rental Income for $125. Now, assume that the bank, through its debit memorandum, notifies Langford about Nash's NSF check. To avoid overdrawing its own bank account, Langford makes an entry crediting Cash (to take the amount out of Cash) and debiting Accounts Receivable (to put the amount back into Accounts

FIGURE 8-9

GENERAL JOURNAL   PAGE_____

DATE		DESCRIPTION	POST. REF.	DEBIT	CREDIT
19–					
Oct.	31	Cash		6 0 6 00	
		Notes Receivable			6 0 0 00
		Interest Income			6 00
		Bank collected note signed by			
		Helm and Sutor.			
	31	Cash		9 00	
		Accounts Payable			9 00
		Error in recording check no.			
		2001 payable to Moran, Inc.			
	31	Miscellaneous Expense		5 50	
		Cash			5 50
		Bank service charge and			
		collection charge.			
	31	Accounts Receivable		1 2 5 00	
		Cash			1 2 5 00
		NSF check received from			
		C. M. Nash.			
	31	R. L. Langford, Drawing		2 4 00	
		Cash			2 4 00
		Withdrawal for personal use.			

Remember

When you are reconciling a bank statement, always double-check for any outstanding checks or deposits from previous statements that have been carried forward. Also, double-check for any bank service charges.

Receivable). Since C. M. Nash still owes the money, it is logical to add the amount to Accounts Receivable.

A bank reconciliation form is ordinarily printed on the back of the bank statement. In a typical form, it is assumed that the adjusted balance of the book balance of cash has already been determined. Consequently, the bank form only provides for calculating the adjusted bank statement balance of the bank reconciliation. The bank form for Langford is shown in Figure 8-10.

THE PETTY CASH FUND

Day after day, business firms are confronted with transactions involving small immediate payments, such as the cost of a telegram, delivery charges, a birthday card, or a new typewriter ribbon. If the firm had to

**THIS FORM IS PROVIDED TO HELP YOU BALANCE
YOUR BANK STATEMENT**

CHECKS OUTSTANDING—NOT
CHARGED TO ACCOUNT

No. 1916	$	461	00
2022		119	00
2023		827	00
2024		67	00
TOTAL	$	1,474	00

BEFORE YOU START—

PLEASE BE SURE YOU HAVE ENTERED IN YOUR CHECKBOOK ALL AUTO-
MATIC TRANSACTIONS SHOWN ON THE FRONT OF YOUR STATEMENT.

YOU SHOULD HAVE ADDED IF
ANY OCCURRED:

1. Loan advances.
2. Credit memos.
3. Other automatic deposits.

YOU SHOULD HAVE SUBTRACTED
IF ANY OCCURRED:

1. Automatic loan payments.
2. Automatic savings transfers.
3. Service charges.
4. Debit memos.
5. Other automatic deductions and
   payments.

BANK BALANCE SHOWN
ON THIS STATEMENT $ 8,762.00 _____

ADD
DEPOSITS NOT SHOWN
ON THIS STATEMENT
(IF ANY) $ 1,003.00 _____

_____

_____

TOTAL $ 9,765.00 _____

SUBTRACT—

▸CHECKS OUTSTANDING $ 1,474.00 _____

BALANCE $ 8,291.00 _____

SHOULD AGREE WITH YOUR CHECKBOOK
BALANCE AFTER DEDUCTING SERVICE CHARGE
(IF ANY) SHOWN ON THIS STATEMENT.

Please examine immediately and report if incorrect. If no reply
is received within 15 days the account will be considered correct.

FIGURE 8-10

go through the usual procedure of making all payments by check, the
time consumed would be frustrating and the whole process unduly expensive. For many firms, the cost of writing each check is more than
$.50; this includes the cost of an employee's time in writing and reconcil-
ing the check. Suppose you buy stamps from an employee for $.27. You

must reimburse her for that money. To write a check would be ridiculous. It only makes sense to pay in cash, out of the **Petty Cash Fund**. *Petty* means small, so the firm sets a maximum amount that can be paid immediately out of petty cash. Payments that exceed this maximum must be processed by regular check through the journal.

Establishing the Petty Cash Fund

After the firm has decided on the maximum amount of a payment from petty cash, the next step is to estimate how much cash will be needed during a given period of time, such as a month. Small payments are made during the month from the Petty Cash Fund.

It is also important to consider the element of security when keeping cash in the office. If the risk is great, the amount kept in the fund should be small, and the fund should be reimbursed at intervals of perhaps one or two weeks.

Objective 3

Record journal entries to establish and reimburse Petty Cash Fund.

Langford Company decided to establish a Petty Cash Fund of $50 and put it under the control of the secretary. Accordingly, their accountant writes a check, cashes it at the bank, and records this transaction in the journal as follows:

GENERAL JOURNAL   PAGE _____

DATE	DESCRIPTION	POST. REF.	DEBIT	CREDIT
19–				
Sept. 1	Petty Cash Fund		5 0 00	
	Cash			5 0 00
	Established a Petty Cash Fund.			

T accounts for the entry look like this:

Petty Cash Fund			Cash	
+	–		+	–
50				50

Because the Petty Cash Fund is an asset account, it is listed in the balance sheet immediately below Cash.

Remember

The Petty Cash Fund account is debited only once, and this happens when the fund is established initially.

Once the fund has been created, it is not debited again unless the original amount is not large enough to handle the necessary transactions. In that case, the accountant has to make the Petty Cash Fund bigger—perhaps increasing the amount of the fund from $50 to $75. But, barring such a change in the size of the fund, Petty Cash Fund is debited only once.

After the accountant cashes that original $50 check, he or she converts it into convenient **denominations,** which are varieties of coins and currency, such as quarters and dimes and $1 and $5 bills. Then the accountant puts the money in a locked drawer in the secretary's desk, telling the secretary not to pay anything larger than $5 out of petty cash.

Payments from the Petty Cash Fund

Objective 4

Complete petty cash vouchers and petty cash payments records.

The secretary now takes the responsibility for the petty cash fund. He or she is designated as the only person who can make payments from it. In case of his or her illness, some other employee should be named as stand-in. A **petty cash voucher** must be used to account for every payment from the fund. The voucher constitutes a receipt signed by the person who authorized the payment and by the person receiving payment. Thus, even for small payments of $5 or less, there would have to be collusion between the payee and the secretary for any theft to occur. Figure 8-11 shows what a petty cash voucher looks like.

FIGURE 8-11

PETTY CASH VOUCHER

No. *1*   Date *September 2, 19–*

Paid to *Crosby Delivery Service* $ *2.00*

For *Delivery*

Account *Delivery Expense*

Approved by *R. Jason*   Payment received by *C. J. Comstock*

Petty Cash Payments Record

Some firms prefer to have a written record on one sheet of paper, so they keep a **petty cash payments record,** with columns in the Distribution of Payments section labeled with the types of expenditures they make most often.

Langford Company made the following payments from its petty cash fund during September:

Sept.   2 Paid $2 to Crosby Delivery Service, voucher no. 1.
       3 Bought pencils and pens, $3.09, voucher no. 2.
       5 Paid local newspaper for advertising, $5, voucher no. 3.
       7 Paid for mailing packages, $2.90, voucher no. 4.
    10 Roger L. Langford, the owner, withdrew $5 for personal use, voucher no. 5.
    14 Reimbursed employee for stamps, $.27, voucher no. 6.
    21 Bought typewriter ribbons, $4.10, voucher no. 7.
    22 Paid $3 to Crosby Delivery Service, voucher no. 8.
    26 Paid for mailing packages, $3.80, voucher no. 9.

PETTY CASH PAYMENTS RECORD
Month of September 19–

DATE		VOU. NO.	EXPLANATION	PAYMENTS	
1	Sept. 1		Established fund, check no. 88, $50		
2	2	1	Crosby Delivery Service	2	00
3	3	2	Pencils and pens	3	09
4	5	3	Local newspaper	5	00
5	7	4	Reimburse employee for stamps	2	90
6	10	5	Roger L. Langford	5	00
7	14	6	Postage on incoming mail		27
8	21	7	Typewriter ribbons	4	10
9	22	8	Crosby Delivery Service	3	00
10	26	9	Postage for mailings	3	80
11	27	10	Fast Way Delivery	3	50
12	29	11	Memo pads	4	40
13	29	12	Making duplicate keys	2	60
14	30	13	Crosby Delivery Service	3	20
15	30	14	Trash removal	5	00
16	30		Totals	4 7	86
17			Balance in Fund $ 2.14		
18			Reimbursed check no. 136 47.86		
19			Total $50.00		
20					
21					
22					
23					

Sept.   27   Paid $3.50 to Fast Way Delivery, voucher no. 10.
        29   Bought memo pads, $4.40, voucher no. 11.
        29   Paid for making duplicate keys, $2.60, voucher no. 12.
        30   Paid $3.20 to Crosby Delivery Service, voucher no. 13.
        30   Paid for trash removal, $5, voucher no. 14.

Figure 8-12 shows how these payments are recorded.

Reimbursement of the Petty Cash Fund

When the fund is nearly exhausted, for example, at the end of the month, the accountant reimburses the fund for expenditures made to

PAGE ___1___

OFFICE SUPPLIES		DELIVERY EXPENSE		MISCELLANEOUS EXPENSE		SUNDRY				
						DISTRIBUTION OF PAYMENTS				
						ACCOUNT	AMOUNT			
										1
		2	00							2
3	09									3
						Advertising Expense		5	00	4
		2	90							5
						R. L. Langford, Drawing		5	00	6
					27					7
4	10									8
		3	00							9
		3	80							10
		3	50							11
4	40									12
				2	60					13
		3	20							14
				5	00					15
1 1	59	1 8	40	7	87			1 0	00	16
										17
										18
										19
										20
										21
										22
										23

FIGURE 8-12

bring the fund back up to the original amount. Consequently, the Petty Cash Fund may be considered a revolving fund. If the amount initially put in the Petty Cash Fund is $50 and at the end of the month only $2.14 is left, the accountant puts $47.86 in the fund as a reimbursement, thereby bringing the fund back up to $50 to start the new month.

Bear in mind that the petty cash payments record is only a supplementary record for gathering information. A less formal way of compiling the information concerning petty cash payments might consist of collecting one month's petty cash vouchers, then sorting them by accounts, such as Office Supplies, Delivery Expense, and the like. Next, run a calculator tape for each account.

At any rate, the petty cash payments record or calculator tapes are not journals; they are simply used as a basis for compiling information for the journal entry. Remember, to change an account, we have to make a journal entry. At the end of the month, the accountant makes a summarizing entry to officially journalize the transactions that have taken place. The journal and T accounts of Langford Company are shown below.

	DATE	DESCRIPTION	POST. REF.	DEBIT	CREDIT	
1	19–					1
2	Sept. 30	Office Supplies		1 1 59		2
3		Delivery Expense		1 8 40		3
4		Miscellaneous Expense		7 87		4
5		Advertising Expense		5 00		5
6		R. L. Langford, Drawing		5 00		6
7		Cash			4 7 86	7
8		Reimbursed the Petty Cash Fund				8
9		check no. 136.				9
10						10

GENERAL JOURNAL   PAGE _____

Cash	
+	–
	47.86

R. L. Langford, Drawing	
+	–
5.00	

Miscellaneous Expense	
+	–
7.87	

Office Supplies	
+	–
11.59	

Delivery Expense	
+	–
18.40	

Advertising Expense	
+	–
5.00	

Note that in the summarizing entry the accountant debits the accounts on whose behalf the payments were made and credits the Cash account. She or he leaves the Petty Cash Fund strictly alone. Then the accountant cashes a check for $47.86 and puts the cash in the secretary's desk drawer, thereby restoring the amount in the Petty Cash Fund to the original $50.

THE CHANGE FUND

Anyone who has ever tried to pay for a small item by handing a clerk a $20 bill knows that any firm that carries out numerous cash transactions needs a **Change Fund.**

Establishing the Change Fund

Before setting up a change fund, one has to decide two things: (1) how much money needs to be in the fund, and (2) what denominations of

Objective 5

Record the journal entries to establish a Change Fund.

bills and coins are needed. Like the Petty Cash Fund, **the Change Fund is debited only once: when it is established.** It is left at the initial figure unless the person in charge decides to make it larger. The Change Fund account, like the Petty Cash account, is an asset. It is recorded in the balance sheet immediately below Cash. If the Petty Cash account is larger than the Change Fund account, it precedes the Change Fund.

The owner of Langford Company, Mr. Langford, decides to establish a change fund; he decides this at the same time he sets up the company's petty cash fund. The entries for both transactions look like this:

	DATE		DESCRIPTION	POST. REF.	DEBIT	CREDIT	
	GENERAL JOURNAL					PAGE _____	
1	*19–*						1
2	*Sept.*	*1*	*Petty Cash Fund*		5 0 00		2
3			*Cash*			5 0 00	3
4			*Established a petty cash fund.*				4
5							5
6		*1*	*Change Fund*		1 0 0 00		6
7			*Cash*			1 0 0 00	7
8			*Established a change fund.*				8
9							9
10							10
11							11
12							12

The T accounts for establishing the fund are as follows:

Change Fund		Cash	
+	−	+	−
100			100

So Langford cashes a check for $100 and gets the money in several denominations. He is now prepared to make change in any normal business transactions.

Depositing Cash

At the end of each business day, Langford deposits the cash taken in during the day, but he holds back the amount of the Change Fund, being sure that it is in convenient denominations.

When he makes up the Change Fund depends on what time his shop closes for the day and what time the bank closes. Let's say that on September 1, Langford Company has $325 on hand at the end of the day.

$325 Total cash count
− 100 Change fund
$225 New cash

The T accounts look like this.

Cash		Rental Income	
+	−	−	+
225			225

The day's receipts are journalized as follows:

			GENERAL JOURNAL						PAGE _____		
	DATE		DESCRIPTION	POST. REF.	DEBIT			CREDIT			
1	19–										1
2	Sept.	1	Cash		2 2 5	00					2
3			Rental Income					2 2 5	00		3
4			To record revenue earned during								4
5			the day.								5
6											6

Now recall that the amount of the cash deposit is the total cash count less the amount of the Change Fund, so that's how the deposit happens to be $225.

On another day, the cash count is $327. So Langford deposits $227 ($327 − $100). Langford's accountant makes the following entry to record the day's receipts:

			GENERAL JOURNAL						PAGE _____		
	DATE		DESCRIPTION	POST. REF.	DEBIT			CREDIT			
1	19–										1
2	Sept.	9	Cash		2 2 7	00					2
3			Rental Income					2 2 7	00		3
4			To record revenue earned during								4
5			the day.								5
6											6

Some business firms label the Cash account *Cash in Bank* and label the Change Fund *Cash on Hand*.

CASH SHORT AND OVER

There is an inherent danger in making change: Human beings make mistakes, especially when there are many customers to be waited on or when the business is temporarily short-handed. Ideally, mistakes should be eliminated. However, because mistakes do happen, accounting records must be set up to cope with the situation. One reason that a business uses a cash register is to detect mistakes in the handling of cash. If, after removing the change fund, the day's receipts are less than the machine reading, then a cash shortage exists. Conversely, when the day's receipts are greater than the machine reading, a cash overage exists. Both shortages and overages are recorded in the same account, which is called Cash Short and Over. (The Cash Short and Over account may also be used to handle shortages and overages in the Petty Cash Fund.) Shortages are considered to be an expense of operating a business and, therefore, are recorded on the debit side of the account. Overages are treated as another form of revenue and so are recorded on the credit side of the account.

Objective 6

Record journal entries for transactions involving Cash Short and Over.

For example, let's say that on September 14 Langford Company is faced with the following situation:

		Amount of the
Cash Register Tape	**Cash Count**	**Change Fund**
$281	$378	$100

After deducting the $100 in the Change Fund, Langford will deposit $278 ($378 − $100). Note that this amount is less than the amount indicated by the cash register; therefore, a $3 cash shortage exists ($281 − $278). The following T accounts show how Langford entered this transaction into the books.

Cash		Rental Income		Cash Short and Over	
+	−	−	+		
278			281	3	

The next day, September 15, the pendulum happens to swing in the other direction:

		Amount of the
Cash Register Tape	**Cash Count**	**Change Fund**
$356	$457	$100

The amount to be deposited is $357 ($457 − $100). This figure is $1 greater than the $356 in rental income indicated by the cash register tape. Thus, there is a $1 cash overage ($357 − $356). The analysis of this transaction is shown in the following T accounts:

Cash		Rental Income		Cash Short and Over	
+	−	−	+		
357			356		1

Langford Company's revenue for September 14 and 15 is recorded in the general journal as follows:

GENERAL JOURNAL   PAGE _____

	DATE	DESCRIPTION	POST. REF.	DEBIT	CREDIT	
1	19–					1
2	Sept. 14	Cash		2 7 8 00		2
3		Cash Short and Over		3 00		3
4		Rental Income			2 8 1 00	4
5		To record revenue earned during				5
6		the day involving a cash				6
7		shortage of $3.00.				7
8						8
9	15	Cash		3 5 7 00		9
10		Rental Income			3 5 6 00	10
11		Cash Short and Over			1 00	11
12		To record revenue earned during				12
13		the day involving a cash				13
14		overage of $1.00.				14
15						15
16						16

As far as errors are concerned, one would think that shortages would be offset by overages. However, customers receiving change are more likely to report shortages than overages. **Consequently, to the firm shortages predominate.** A firm may set a tolerance level for the cashiers. If the shortages consistently exceed the level of tolerance, either fraud is considered or somebody is making entirely too many careless mistakes.

Now let's summarize our discussion of the Cash Short and Over account by drawing the following conclusions from the illustration:

1. At the close of the business day, the firm deposits the difference between the amount in the cash drawer and the amount in the Change Fund.
2. The firm records its rental income as being the amount shown on the cash register tape.
3. If the amount of the cash deposit disagrees with the record of receipts, Cash Short and Over takes up the difference. In the first situation just described, there was a shortage of $3, so there was a debit to Cash Short and Over. In the second situation, there was an overage of $1, so there was a credit to Cash Short and Over. It is apparent that as a result of these transactions the account looks like this:

Cash Short and Over

Shortage	3	Overage	1

Throughout any fiscal period, the accountant must continually record shortages and overages in the Cash Short and Over account. Let's say that Langford's final balance is $21 on the debit side. Langford winds up with a net shortage of $21.

At the end of the fiscal period, **if the account has a debit balance or net shortage, the accountant classifies it as an expense and puts it in the income statement under Miscellaneous Expense.** The T account would look like this:

Cash Short and Over

Short		Over	
Short	3	Over	1
	4		1
	3		2
	7		2
	5		1
	2		2
	3		1
	4		10
	31		
Bal. 21			

Conversely, **if the account has a credit balance or net overage, the accountant classifies it as a revenue account and puts it in the income statement under Miscellaneous Income.** This is an exception to the policy of recording accounts under their exact account title in financial statements. Rather than attaching plus and minus signs to the Cash Short and Over account immediately, we wait until we find out its final balance.

SUMMARY

A business firm has a valuable ally in its bank because the bank maintains a record of cash independent of the firm's record of cash. That is, the bank does this if the business deposits all incoming cash in the bank and makes all cash payments by check. The only exception to this—and it is a minor one—is the case of transactions involving Petty Cash.

The bank sends its statement accompanied by canceled checks, debit memos, and credit memos. Debit memos cover service and collection charges, automated teller withdrawals, and NSF checks. Credit memos cover the collection of notes or other items left for collection.

L.O. 1,2   Each month the firm's accountant has to make a reconciliation between the bank account balance and the firm's Cash account balance because some transactions might not have been recorded by either the bank or the depositor, or errors might have been made by either.

L.O. 3,4,5   In this chapter we discussed two special funds: the Petty Cash Fund and the Change Fund. A fund, in every case, is a separate kitty of cash. When one establishes a fund, one makes a check payable to the particular fund, then cashes it, and converts it into convenient denominations. The original entry in each case is a debit to the fund account and a credit to Cash. The journal entry to reimburse Petty Cash is a debit to the accounts for which the money was expended (as shown by the petty cash payments record or a summary of the petty cash vouchers) and a credit to Cash. The Petty Cash Fund account is debited only at the time it is established, and remains at the same level, unless the firm decides to change the account's size. Whenever a firm makes a bank deposit, it holds back the amount of the Change Fund and converts it into the proper denominations.

L.O. 6   The Cash Short and Over account takes care of errors in making change. A debit to Cash Short and Over denotes a shortage; a credit to Cash Short and Over denotes an overage.

GLOSSARY

ABA number   The number assigned by the American Bankers Association to a given bank. The first part of the numerator denotes the city or state in which the bank is located; the second part denotes the bank on which the check is drawn. The denominator indicates the Federal Reserve District in which the check is cleared and the routing number used by the Federal Reserve Bank.

Bank reconciliation   A process by which an accountant determines whether there is a difference between the balance shown on the bank statement and the balance of the Cash account in the firm's general ledger. The object is to determine the adjusted (or true) balance of the Cash account.

Bank statement   Periodic statement that a bank sends to the holder of a checking account listing deposits received and checks paid by the bank, debit and credit memorandums, and beginning and ending balances.

Blank endorsement   An endorsement in which the holder (payee) of a check simply signs her or his name on the back of the check. There are no restrictions attached.

Book balance of cash   The balance of the Cash account in the general ledger before it is reconciled with the bank statement.

Canceled checks   Checks issued by the depositor that have been paid (cleared) by the bank and listed on the bank statement. They are called canceled checks because they are canceled by a stamp or perforation, indicating that they have been paid.

Cash funds   Sums of money set aside for specific purposes.

Change Fund   A cash fund used by a firm to make change for customers who pay cash for goods or services.

Check writer   A machine used to imprint the amount in figures and words on the check itself.

Denominations   Varieties of coins and currency, such as quarters, dimes, and nickels and $1 and $5 bills.

Deposit in transit   A deposit not recorded on the bank statement because the deposit was made between the time of the bank's closing date for compiling items for its statement and the time the statement is received by the depositor; also known as a *late deposit*.

Deposit slips Printed forms provided by a bank so that customers can list all items being deposited; also known as a *deposit ticket*.

Endorsement The process by which the payee transfers ownership of the check to a bank or another party. A check must be endorsed when deposited in a bank because the bank must have legal title to it in order to collect payment from the drawer of the check (the person or firm who wrote the check). In case the check cannot be collected, the endorser guarantees all subsequent holders (*Exception:* an endorsement "without recourse").

MICR Magnetic ink character recognition; the characters the bank uses to print the number of the depositor's account and the bank's number at the bottom of checks and deposit slips. The bank also prints the amount of the check in MICR when the check is deposited. A number written in these characters can be read by electronic equipment used by banks in clearing checks.

NSF (Not Sufficient Funds) check A check drawn against an account in which there are *Not Sufficient Funds:* this check is returned by the depositor's bank to the drawer's bank because of nonpayment; also known as a *dishonored check*.

Outstanding checks Checks that have been written by the depositor and deducted on his or her records but have not reached the bank for payment and are not deducted from the bank balance by the time the bank issues its statement.

Payee The person to whom a check is payable.

Petty Cash Fund A cash fund used to make small immediate cash payments.

Petty cash payments record A record indicating the amount of each petty cash voucher and the accounts to which they should be charged.

Petty cash voucher A form stating who got what from the Petty Cash Fund, signed by (1) the person in charge of the fund, and (2) the person who received the cash.

Promissory note A written promise to pay a definite sum at a definite future time.

Qualified endorsement An endorsement in which the holder (payee) of a check avoids future liability in case the drawer of the check does not have sufficient funds to cover the check by adding the words "without recourse" to the endorsement on the back of the check.

Restrictive endorsement An endorsement, such as "Pay to the order of (name of bank), for deposit only," that restricts or limits any further negotiation of a check. If forces the check's deposit since the endorsement is not valid for any other purpose.

Service charge The fee the bank charges for handling checks, collections, and other items. It is in the form of a debit memorandum.

Signature card The form a depositor signs to give the bank a sample of the official signatures of any persons authorized to sign checks. The bank can use it to verify the depositor's signature on checks, on cash items that the depositor(s) may endorse for deposit, and on other business papers that the depositor(s) may present to the bank.

QUESTIONS, EXERCISES, AND PROBLEMS

Discussion Questions

1. Why is it important to fill in the check stub before writing the actual check?
2. What is the purpose of a bank reconciliation?
3. Explain why it is necessary to make journal entries for items relating to the bank reconciliation.
4. Describe in order the steps in reconciling a bank statement.
5. What is the difference between outstanding checks and deposits in transit?
6. What is the purpose of a petty cash payments record? Is it necessary to maintain a petty cash payments record?
7. If there is cash remaining in the Petty Cash Fund at the end of the fiscal year, why is it necessary to reimburse it? Describe the journal entry.
8. What does a debit balance in Cash Short and Over represent? Where does it appear in the financial statements? What does a credit balance in Cash Short and Over represent? Where does it appear in the financial statements?

Exercises

L.O. 1   **Exercise 8-1**   In reconciling a bank statement, indicate the placement of the following items:

	Add to Bank Statement	Subtract from Bank Statement	Add to Book Balance	Subtract from Book Balance
a. A deposit in transit	____	____	____	____
b. A bank service charge	____	____	____	____
c. An outstanding check	____	____	____	____
d. A collection charge the bank made for a note it collected for its depositor	____	____	____	____
e. A check written for $17.98 and recorded in the check stubs as $19.78	____	____	____	____
f. A check printing charge	____	____	____	____
g. A check written for $365.50 and recorded in the check stubs as $356.50	____	____	____	____

L.O. 2   **Exercise 8-2**   The Dobrinski Company made the following bank reconciliation on April 30 of this year. Record the necessary entries in general journal form.

Bank Statement Balance		$2,598.00
Add: Deposit in transit (April 30)		203.00
		$2,801.00
Deduct: Outstanding checks		
No. 191	$280.00	
No. 192	210.00	490.00
Adjusted Balance		$2,311.00
Book Balance of Cash		$1,932.00
Add: Note collected by bank		420.00
		$2,352.00
Deduct: NSF check from Thomas Thorp	$ 38.00	
Collection charge for note	3.00	41.00
Adjusted Balance		$2,311.00

L.O. 1 **Exercise 8-3** When the bank statement is received on June 3, it shows a balance of $1,856 on May 29 before reconciliation. After reconciliation, the adjusted balance is $1,651. If there was one deposit in transit amounting to $145, what was the total amount of the outstanding checks, assuming there were no other adjustments to be made to the bank statement?

L.O. 1 **Exercise 8-4** The Waldon Company's Cash account shows a balance of $3,489 as of May 31 of this year. The balance on the bank statement on that date is $5,063.52. Checks for $61.50, $531, and $110.60 are outstanding. The bank statement shows a charge for a check issued by another depositor for $125. The statement also shows a credit of $1,000 for a customer's note that had been left with the bank for collection. Service charges for the month were $3.58. What is the true balance of cash as of May 31?

L.O. 3,4 **Exercise 8-5** Make entries in general journal form to record the following:

a. Established a Petty Cash Fund, $80.
b. Reimbursed the Petty Cash Fund for expenditures of $78: store supplies, $21; office supplies, $18; miscellaneous expense, $39.
c. Increased the amount of the fund by an additional $20.

L.O. 5,6 **Exercise 8-6** Describe the nature of the entries that have been posted to the following accounts after the Change Fund was established.

Change Fund		Sales		Cash	
200			948	946	
			940	941	
			1,036	1,032	

Cash Short and Over	
2	1
4	

L.O. 3,6   **Exercise 8-7**   J. Dennis, the petty cashier, decides to reimburse the Petty Cash Fund. The petty cash payments record reveals the following information: supplies, $31.23; travel, $46.20; withdrawals by the owner, R. Stennick, $10; miscellaneous, $2.52. The Petty Cash Fund account shows a balance of $100, and the petty cash drawer contains $9.55 in currency and coins. Record the entry to reimburse the Petty Cash Fund in the general journal.

L.O. 6   **Exercise 8-8**   The cash register tape for today indicates $882.16 in sales for the day. The cash count, including a $200 Change Fund, is $1,080.72. Make the entry to record how much cash you will deposit in the bank today.

Problem Set A

L.O. 1,2   **Problem 8-1A**   The Mallon Company deposits all receipts in the bank and makes all payments by check. On November 30 its Cash account has a balance of $2,829.42. The bank statement on November 30 shows a balance of $2,999.42. You are given the following information with which to reconcile the bank statement:

a. A deposit of $319.23 was placed in the night depository on November 30 and did not appear on the bank statement.

b. The reconciliation for October, the previous month, showed three checks outstanding on October 31: no. 727 for $81.30, no. 730 for $127.40, and no. 732 for $38.46. Checks no. 727 and 730 were returned with the November bank statement; however, check no. 732 was not returned.

c. Checks no. 742 for $31, no. 743 for $19.20, no. 744 for $106, and no. 745 for $14.56 were written during November but were not returned by the bank.

d. You compare the canceled checks with the entries in the checkbook and find that check no. 737 for $48 was written correctly, payable to C. R. Mallon, the owner, for her personal use. However, the check was recorded in the checkbook as $84.

e. Included in the bank statement was a bank debit memo for service charges, $2.99.

f. A bank credit memo was also enclosed for the collection of a note signed by L. B. Leman, $247, including $244 principal and $3 interest.

Instructions

1. Prepare a bank reconciliation as of November 30, assuming that the debit and credit memos have not been recorded.
2. Record the necessary entries in general journal form.

L.O. 3,4   **Problem 8-2A**   On March 1 of this year, the Stenn Company established a Petty Cash Fund, and the following petty cash transactions took place during the month:

Mar.   1 Cashed check no. 314 for $60 to establish a Petty Cash Fund, and put the $60 in a locked drawer in the office.
        4 Issued voucher no. 1 for taxi fare, $4 (Miscellaneous Expense).

Mar. 7 Issued voucher no. 2 for typewriter ribbons, $6.20.
       9 Paid $7.50 for an advertisement in college basketball program, voucher no. 3.
      16 Bought postage stamps, $6, voucher no. 4 (Miscellaneous Expense).
      20 Paid $8.50 to have snow removed from office front sidewalk, voucher no. 5 (Miscellaneous Expense).
      25 Issued voucher no. 6 for delivery charge, $4.45.
      28 R. C. Stenn, the owner, withdrew $9 for personal use, voucher no. 7.
      29 Paid $1.72 for postage, voucher no. 8 (Miscellaneous Expense).
      30 Paid $5.40 for delivery charge, voucher no. 9.
      31 Issued for cash check no. 372 for $52.77 to reimburse Petty Cash Fund.

Instructions

1. Journalize the entry establishing the Petty Cash Fund in the general journal.
2. Record the disbursements of petty cash in the petty cash payments record.
3. Journalize the summarizing entry to reimburse the Petty Cash Fund.

L.O. 6 **Problem 8-3A** Betty Rice, owner of Betty's Beauty Salon, makes bank deposits in the night depository at the close of each business day. The following information for the first three days of April is available.

	April		
	1	2	3
Cash register tape	$304.75	$480.25	$428.00
Cash count	373.50	551.25	496.00

Instructions

In general journal form, record the cash deposit for each day, assuming that there is a $70 Change Fund.

L.O. 1,2 **Problem 8-4A** On August 2, Northway Hotel receives its bank statement. The company deposits its receipts in the bank and makes all payments by check. The NSF check was written by T. N. Rankin. Check no. 1617 for $72.50, payable to Melville Company (a creditor), was incorrectly recorded in the checkbook and journal as $27.50.

The balance of the Cash account as of July 31 is $1,482.46. Outstanding checks as of July 31 are: no. 1631, $110; no. 1632, $71.19; no. 1633, $163.20. The accountant notes that the July 31 deposit of $165.69 did not appear on the bank statement.

STANTON NATIONAL BANK

Northway Hotel
410 W. Lang Street
Rockford, Illinois 61104

ACCOUNT NO.
761-145-792
STATEMENT DATE
July 1–31, 19—

SUMMARY

Balance Last Statement	$1,153.80
Amount of Checks and Debits	$2,105.91
Number of Checks	14
Amount of Deposits and Credits	$2,528.17
Number of Deposits	7
Balance This Statement	$1,576.06

CHECKS/OTHER DEBITS

CHECKS	CHECK NUMBER	DATE POSTED	AMOUNT	CHECK NUMBER	DATE POSTED	AMOUNT
	1617	7-03	72.50	1624	7-08	120.00
	1618	7-03	167.00	1625	7-09	429.60
	1619	7-03	124.20	1626	7-12	37.40
	1620	7-05	137.20	1627	7-14	38.49
	1621	7-06	236.25	1628	7-22	182.71
	1622	7-06	159.89	1629	7-25	96.87
	1623	7-08	244.50	1630	7-26	19.20

OTHER DEBITS	DESCRIPTION	DATE POSTED	AMOUNT
	DM NSF check	7-22	37.00
	DM Service charge	7-31	3.10

DEPOSITS/OTHER CREDITS

DEPOSITS	DATE POSTED	AMOUNT	DATE POSTED	AMOUNT
	7-03	491.50	7-15	291.76
	7-06	415.72	7-18	142.90
	7-09	439.16	7-28	368.93
	7-11	378.20		

PLEASE EXAMINE THIS STATEMENT CAREFULLY. REPORT ANY POSSIBLE ERRORS IN 10 DAYS.

CODE SYMBOLS

CM Credit Memo	**OD Overdraft**
DM Debit Memo	**EC Error Correction**

Instructions

1. Prepare a bank reconciliation as of July 31, assuming that the debit memos have not been recorded.
2. Record the necessary journal entries.
3. Complete the bank form to determine the adjusted balance of cash.

Problem Set B

L.O. 1,2 **Problem 8-1B**   Mario's Men's Shop deposits all receipts in the bank each evening and makes all payments by check. On November 30 its Cash in Bank account has a balance of $1,967.65. The bank statement of November 30 shows a balance of $2,122.25. The following information pertains to reconciling the bank statement:

a. The reconciliation for October, the previous month, showed three checks outstanding on October 31: no. 1416 for $85, no. 1419 for $76.50, and no. 1420 for $126. Checks no. 1416 and 1420 were returned with the November bank statement; however, check no. 1419 was not returned.

b. Checks no. 1499 for $39, no. 1516 for $21.60, no. 1517 for $101.50, and no. 1518 for $17 were written during November and have not been returned by the bank.

c. A deposit of $410 was placed in the night depository on November 30 and did not appear on the bank statement.

d. The canceled checks were compared with the entries in the checkbook, and it was observed that check no. 1487, for $78, was written correctly, payable to M. A. Gallo, the owner, for personal use, but was recorded in the checkbook as $87.

e. A bank debit memo for service charges, $3.

f. A bank credit memo for collection of a note signed by T. R. Schultz, $303, including $300 principal and $3 interest.

Instructions

1. Prepare a bank reconciliation as of November 30, assuming that the debit and credit memos have not been recorded.
2. Record the necessary entries in general journal form.

L.O. 3,4 **Problem 8-2B**   On May 1 of this year, Berger and Company established a Petty Cash Fund. The following petty cash transactions took place during the month:

May   1 Cashed check no. 956 for $70 to establish a Petty Cash Fund, and put the $70 in a locked drawer in the office.
         3 Bought postage stamps, $6, voucher no. 1 (Miscellaneous Expense).
         4 Issued voucher no. 2 for taxi fare, $4 (Miscellaneous Expense).
         6 Issued voucher no. 3 for delivery charges on outgoing parts, $8.
         9 N. Berger withdrew $9.50 for personal use, voucher no. 4.
        13 Paid $7 for postage, voucher no. 5.
        19 Bought pens for office, $7.74, voucher no. 6.
        23 Paid $2 for a box of staples, voucher no. 7 (Miscellaneous Expense).
        28 Paid $9 for window cleaning service, voucher no. 8.
        29 Paid $1.82 for pencils for office, voucher no. 9.
        31 Issued for cash check no. 1098 for $55.06 to reimburse Petty Cash Fund.

Instructions

1. Journalize the entry establishing the Petty Cash Fund in the general journal.
2. Record the disbursements of petty cash in the petty cash payments record.
3. Journalize the summarizing entry to reimburse the Petty Cash Fund.

L.O. 6   **Problem 8-3B**   Errol Horn, owner of Horn's Dry Cleaners, makes bank deposits in the night depository at the close of each business day. The following information for the last three days of July is available.

| | July | | |
	29	30	31
Cash register tape	$867.20	$724.50	$ 921.60
Cash count	965.50	823.60	1,023.40

Instructions

In general journal form, record the cash deposit for each day, assuming that there is a $100 Change Fund.

L.O. 1,2   **Problem 8-4B**   On August 31, Bronski and Company receives its bank statement. The company deposits its receipts in the bank and makes all payments by check. The debit memo for $49 is for an NSF check written by N. Collins. Check no. 924 for $37, payable to Johnson Company (a creditor), was recorded in the checkbook and journal as $73.

    The balance of the Cash account as of August 31 is $1,237. Outstanding checks as of August 31 are: no. 928, $119; no. 929, $243. The accountant notes that the deposit of August 31 for $261 did not appear on the bank statement.

Instructions

1. Prepare a bank reconciliation as of August 31, assuming that the debit memos have not been recorded.
2. Record the necessary journal entries.
3. Complete the bank form to determine the adjusted balance of cash.

PEABODY NATIONAL BANK

Bronski and Company
416 Seneca Avenue
Kansas City, Missouri 64102

ACCOUNT NO.
152-6 55-217
STATEMENT DATE
August 1–31, 19—

SUMMARY		
Balance Last Statement	$ 961.00
Amount of Checks and Debits	$2,289.00
Number of Checks	11
Amount of Deposits and Credits	$2,651.00
Number of Deposits	7
Balance This Statement	$1,323.00

CHECKS/ OTHER DEBITS

CHECKS	CHECK NUMBER	DATE POSTED	AMOUNT	CHECK NUMBER	DATE POSTED	AMOUNT
	917	8-04	172.00	923	8-09	621.00
	918	8-04	76.00	924	8-17	37.00
	919	8-05	146.00	925	8-17	14.00
	920	8-07	206.00	926	8-23	533.00
	921	8-07	139.00	927	8-28	94.00
	922	8-08	200.00			

OTHER DEBITS	DESCRIPTION	DATE POSTED	AMOUNT
	DM NSF check	8-31	49.00
	DM Service charge	8-31	2.00

DEPOSITS/ OTHER CREDITS

DEPOSITS	DATE POSTED	AMOUNT	DATE POSTED	AMOUNT
	8-02	326.00	8-18	419.00
	8-05	412.00	8-24	398.00
	8-09	437.00	8-28	291.00
	8-14	368.00		

PLEASE EXAMINE THIS STATEMENT CAREFULLY. REPORT ANY POSSIBLE ERRORS IN 10 DAYS.

CODE SYMBOLS

CM Credit Memo   OD Overdraft

DM Debit Memo   EC Error Correction

PROBLEM 8-4B

APPENDIX B
Bad Debts

After you have completed this appendix, you will be able to do the following:

1. Prepare the adjusting entry for bad debts using the allowance method, based on a percentage of credit sales.
2. Prepare the entry to write off an account as uncollectible when the allowance method is used.
3. Prepare the entry to write off an account as uncollectible when the specific charge-off method is used.

As you know, not all credit customers pay their bills. In this appendix we turn our attention to the accounts receivable that will not be collected. There are two basic methods of providing for writing or charging off credit customers' accounts that are considered uncollectible. They are the allowance method and the specific charge-off method.

ALLOWANCE METHOD

The allowance method attempts to provide for bad debt losses in advance. In order to provide for bad debt losses, an estimate must be made. While there are a number of ways to estimate the amount of future losses from open accounts, we will base our estimate on a percentage of income or revenue from services on account.

As an illustration, based on its experience with bad debt losses, the Palmer Company estimates that 1 percent of its revenue from services on account for the year will prove to be uncollectible. Obviously Palmer does not know which credit customers will not pay their bills. If the company was certain that a particular customer would not pay his or her bill, then it wouldn't perform the services in the first place.

Adjusting Entry

Palmer's total income from services on account for last year amounted to $192,000. One percent of $192,000 is $1,920. On its work sheet, Palmer makes an adjusting entry. We'll show this in T account form.

Bad Debts Expense	
+	−
Dec. 31 Adjusting 1,920	

Allowance for Doubtful Accounts	
−	+
	Dec. 31 Adjusting 1,920

Allowance for Doubtful Accounts is treated as a deduction from Accounts Receivable. Consequently, Allowance for Doubtful Accounts is a contra account. The adjusting entry is similar to the entry for depreciation in that there is a debit to an expense account and a credit to a contra account. In T account form it looks like this:

Depreciation Expense, Equipment		Accumulated Depreciation, Equipment	
+	−	−	+
Adjusting 3,500			Adjusting 3,500

Assume Palmer Company's balance of Accounts Receivable is $207,000 and its balance of Equipment is $70,000. Let's show the accounts and the adjusting entries in T account form.

				Owner's				
Assets		**= Liabilities +**		**Equity**	**+ Revenue −**		**Expenses**	
+	−	−	+	−	+	−	+	+	−

Accounts Receivable

+	−
Bal. 207,000	

Bad Debts Expense

+	−
Adj. 1,920	

Allowance for Doubtful Accounts

−	+
	Bal. 170
	Adj. 1,920
	Bal. 2,090

Income from Services

−	+
Bal. 192,000	

Deprec. Expense, Equipment

+	−
Adj. 3,500	

Equipment

+	−
Bal. 70,000	

Accumulated Deprec., Equipment

−	+
	Bal. 7,000
	Adj. 3,500
	Bal. 10,500

As you know, the Depreciation Expense, Equipment account comes into existence as an adjusting entry at the end of the year. It is closed immediately after being brought into existence. The same thing happens to Bad Debts Expense; it comes into existence as an adjusting entry, and then it is immediately closed.

As certain charge customers' accounts are definitely determined to be uncollectible and are written off, the losses are taken out of Allowance for

Doubtful Accounts. We can think of the Allowance for Doubtful Accounts as a reservoir. By the medium of the adjusting entry, the account is filled up at the end of the year and then is gradually drained off or consumed during the next year by write-offs of charge customer accounts. The $170 balance in Allowance for Doubtful Accounts at the end of the year indicates that the account was not fully used up. In other words, the reservoir had not been entirely drained by write-offs during the year. Incidentally, most companies generally have a credit balance left in the Allowance account.

Let's go on to the next year. On January 2, the Palmer Company finally gives up its attempts to collect $650 from its credit customer A. N. Smith, which is included in Accounts Receivable. The Palmer Company now writes off the account in the amount of $650 as shown below in T account form.

Accounts Receivable				Allowance for Doubtful Accounts			
+		−		−		+	
Balance	207,000	Jan. 2 (write-off)	650	Jan. 2 (write-off)	650	Balance	2,090
Bal.	206,350					Bal.	1,440

As you can see, the write-off has reduced both the balance of Accounts Receivable and the balance of Allowance for Doubtful Accounts. The general journal entry is shown below.

	DATE		DESCRIPTION	POST. REF.	DEBIT	CREDIT	
1	19–						1
2	Jan.	2	Allowance for Doubtful Accounts		6 5 0 00		2
3			Accounts Receivable			6 5 0 00	3
4			Wrote off the account of				4
5			A. N. Smith as uncollectible.				5
6							6

Advantage of the Allowance Method

The allowance method is consistent with the accrual basis of accounting of matching revenues of one year with expenses of the same year. The bad-debt loss potential is provided in the same year in which the revenue is earned.

Disadvantage of the Allowance Method

The allowance method cannot be used for federal income tax purposes. This means that if the allowance method is used by a business, the company's net income shown on its income statement will differ from its net income shown on its federal income tax return.

SPECIFIC CHARGE-OFF METHOD

Under the specific charge-off method, when a credit customer's account is definitely determined to be uncollectible, the account is simply written off. Incidentally, the terms *write-off* and *charge-off* mean the same thing. As an illustration, Hiller Company uses the specific charge-off method. On May 5 Hiller Company writes off the account of L. C. Johnson, $341. For the purpose of this example, we will use a separate Accounts Receivable account for L. C. Johnson. T accounts pertaining to Johnson's account look like this:

Accounts Receivable			Bad Debts Expense	
+	−	+	−
Balance 341	May 5 (write-off) 341	May 5 (write-off) 341	

The general journal entry is shown below.

	DATE	DESCRIPTION	POST. REF.	DEBIT	CREDIT	
1	19–					1
2	May 5	Bad Debts Expense		3 4 1 00		2
3		Accounts Receivable			3 4 1 00	3
4		Wrote off the account of				4
5		L. C. Johnson as uncollectible.				5
6						6

Under this method, entries will be made directly into the Bad Debts Expense account during the year. In addition, no adjusting entry is needed, and Allowance for Doubtful Accounts is not used.

Advantage of the Specific Charge-off Method

The main advantage is that the method may be used for federal income tax purposes. It is not necessary to make an adjusting entry. Also, one less account (Allowance for Doubtful Accounts) is required.

Disadvantage of the Specific Charge-off Method

This method is not consistent with the accrual basis of accounting (recognizing revenue when it is earned and expenses when they are incurred). The method does not match up the revenue of one year with the expense of the same year. For example, the sale of services on account to L. C. Johnson could have been made four years ago. Since the account receivable will never by collected, the revenue of that year was too high (overstated). Consequently, net income is also overstated during that year. Now, four years later, $341 is chalked up as an expense. So net income for this year is too low (understated) because of the added expense.

PROBLEMS

L.O. 1,2 **Problem B-1** Shannon Company's total sales on account for 1990 amounted to $246,000. The company estimated bad debts at 1 percent of its charge sales. Journalize the following selected entries:

1990
Dec. 31 Record the adjusting entry.
1991
Mar. 2 Wrote off the account of S. T. Nevers as uncollectible, $66.
June 6 Wrote off the account of L. O. Hanes as uncollectible, $124.

L.O. 1,2 **Problem B-2** Robinson Building Maintenance Company's total revenue on account for 1989 amounted to $398,740. The company estimates bad debts at ½ percent of total revenue on account. Journalize the following selected entries:

1989
Dec. 12 Performed services on account for R. T. Hughes, $124.
      31 Record the adjusting entry.
      31 Record the closing entry.
1992
Feb. 18 Wrote off the account of R. T. Hughes as uncollectible, $124.

L.O. 3 **Problem B-3** Drexel Equipment Rental uses the specific charge-off method for recording bad debts. Journalize the following selected entries:

1991
Apr. 6 Wrote off the account of R. A. Rand as uncollectible, $68.
July 21 Wrote off the account of U. R. Stuck as uncollectible, $109.

9 Payroll Accounting: Employee Earnings and Deductions

LEARNING OBJECTIVES

After you have completed this chapter, you will be able to do the following:

1. Calculate total earnings based on an hourly, piece-rate, or commission basis.
2. Determine deductions from tables of employees' income tax withholding.
3. Complete a payroll register.
4. Journalize the payroll entry from a payroll register.
5. Maintain employees' individual earnings records.

Up to now, we've been recording employees' wages as a debit to Salaries or Wages Expense and a credit to Cash, but we've really been talking only about **gross pay**. We haven't said a word about the various deductions that we all know are taken out of our gross pay before we get to the **net pay** or take-home pay. In this chapter we will be talking about types and amounts of deductions and how to enter them in payroll records as well as journal entries for recording the payroll and paying the employees.

OBJECTIVES OF PAYROLL RECORDS AND ACCOUNTING

There are two primary reasons for maintaining accurate payroll records. First, we must collect the necessary data to compute the compensation for each employee for each payroll period.

Second, we must provide information needed to complete the various government reports—federal and state—that are required of all employers. All business enterprises, both large and small, are required by law to withhold certain amounts from employees' pay for taxes, to make payments to government agencies by specified deadlines, and to submit reports on official forms. Because governments impose penalties if the requirements are not met, employers are vitally concerned with payroll accounting. Anyone going into accounting, or involved with the management of any business, should be thoroughly acquainted with payroll accounting.

EMPLOYER/EMPLOYEE RELATIONSHIPS

Payroll accounting is concerned only with employees and their compensations, withholdings, records, reports, and taxes. *Note:* There is a distinction between an employee and an independent contractor. An **employee** is one who is under the direction and control of the employer, such as a secretary, bookkeeper, salesclerk, vice president, controller, and so on. An **independent contractor,** on the other hand, is someone who is engaged for a definite job or service who may choose her or his own means of doing the work (*examples:* an appliance repair person, a plumber, a CPA firm). Payments made to independent contractors are in the form of fees or charges. Independent contractors submit bills or invoices for the work they do. The invoice is paid in a lump sum and is not subject to any withholding or payroll taxes by the person or firm paying that invoice.

LAWS AFFECTING EMPLOYEES' PAY

Both federal and state laws require the employer to act as a collecting agent and deduct specified amounts from employees' gross earnings. The employer sends the withholdings to the appropriate government agencies, along with reports substantiating the figures. Let's look at some of the more important laws that pertain to employees' pay.

Federal Income Tax Withholding

The **Current Tax Payment Act** requires employers not only to withhold the tax and then pay it to the Internal Revenue Service but to keep records of the names and addresses of persons employed, their earnings and withholdings, and the amounts and dates of payment. The employer has to submit reports to the Internal Revenue Service on a quarterly basis (Form 941) and to the employee on an annual basis (W-2 form). With few exceptions, this requirement applies to employers of one or more persons. We will discuss these reports and the related deposits in Chapter 10.

State and City Income Tax Withholding

Besides requiring employers to deduct money from employees' earnings for federal income taxes, two-thirds of the states require employers to deduct money to pay state income taxes. A number of cities also require withholding for *city* income taxes. When these laws are in effect, the employer handles the reporting and payments in much the same way as for federal income taxes. Separate liability accounts may be set up for employees' state and city income taxes withheld.

FICA Tax Withholding

The **Federal Insurance Contributions Act** provides for retirement pensions after a worker reaches age 62, disability benefits for any worker who becomes disabled (and for her or his dependents), and a health insurance program or Medicare after age 65. Both the employee and the employer have to pay **FICA taxes,** which are commonly referred to as Social Security taxes. The employer withholds FICA taxes from employees' wages and pays them to the Internal Revenue Service.

FICA tax rates apply to the gross earnings of an employee during the calendar year (January 1 through December 31). After an employee has paid FICA tax on the maximum taxable earnings, the employer stops deducting FICA tax until the next calendar year begins. Congress has frequently changed the schedule of rates and taxable incomes. Taxable income increases automatically with growth in average earnings. In this text, for the examples and problems we will assume a rate of 7.6 percent of the first $45,000 of earnings of each employee during the calendar year.

The employer is required to keep records of the following information:

1. **Personal data on employee**   Name, address, Social Security number, date of birth
2. **Data on wage payments**   Dates and amounts of payments, and payroll periods
3. **Amount of taxable wages paid**   Total amount earned so far during the year
4. **Amount of tax withheld from each employee's earnings**

Fair Labor Standards Act

The **Fair Labor Standards Act (Wages and Hours Law)** specifies that employers engaged in interstate commerce must pay their employees overtime at the rate of 1½ times the regular rate (time-and-a-half) for hours worked in excess of 40 per week. Frequently, union contracts stipulate additional overtime pay for work performed on Sundays and holidays. The act provides that certain management and supervisory employees are exempt from its regulations—these exempt employees are usually referred to as salaried personnel. Minimum wages are also specified in the act.

LAWS AFFECTING EMPLOYER'S PAYROLL TAXES (PAYROLL TAX EXPENSE)

Certain payroll taxes, based on the total wages paid to employees, are levied on the employer. Let's look at some of the more important laws that pertain to the pay of employees.

FICA Tax (Employer's Share)

The employer has to match the amount of FICA tax withheld from the employees' wages, and the employer's share is recorded under Payroll Tax Expense. Every three months the employer has to submit reports to the Internal Revenue Service, recording the information on Form 941, the same form that is used to report the income tax withheld. The employer's payment to the Internal Revenue Service consists of (1) the employee's share of the FICA tax, (2) the employer's matching portion of the FICA tax, and (3) the employee's income tax withheld. We will talk about this in detail in Chapter 10.

Federal Unemployment Tax Act (FUTA)

The purpose of the Federal Unemployment Tax Act is to provide financial support for the maintenance of government-run employment offices throughout the country. **FUTA taxes are paid by employers only.** Generally this includes all employers except nonprofit schools and institutions.

   The federal unemployment tax is based on the total earnings of each employee during the calendar year. Congress has frequently changed the rates and the taxable income base.

   For the examples and problems in this text, we will assume that employers pay an effective federal unemployment tax rate of .8 percent (.008) of the first $7,000 of earnings of each employee during the calendar year.

   Reports to the federal government (Form 940) must be submitted annually. We will discuss these reports in Chapter 10.

State Unemployment Taxes (SUTA)

Each state is responsible for paying its own unemployment compensation benefits. The revenue provided by **state unemployment taxes** is used exclusively for this purpose. However, there is considerable variation among the states concerning the tax rates and the amount of taxable income. **This tax is paid by employers only.** Most states, under a State Unemployment Tax Act, charge their employers 5.4 percent based on the taxable income stipulated in the Federal Unemployment Tax Act. States require employers to file reports on a quarterly, or three-month, basis. Included in these reports are a listing of employees' names, Social Security numbers, amounts of wages paid to each employee, and computations of unemployment taxes. We will discuss these reports in Chapter 10.

Our example of payroll accounting deals with the firm of Gilbert and Associates. The business is located in the state of South Dakota, which has an assumed unemployment tax rate of 5.4 percent of the first $7,000 of wages paid to each employee during the calendar year. Note that the assumed state taxable base ($7,000) is the same as the taxable base for the federal unemployment tax.

Workers' Compensation Laws

Workers' compensation laws protect employees and their dependents against losses due to death or injury incurred on the job. Most states require employers either to contribute to a state compensation insurance fund or to buy similar insurance from a private insurance company. The employer ordinarily pays the cost of the insurance premiums. The premium rates vary according to the degree of danger inherent in each job category and the employer's number of accidents. The employer has to keep records of job descriptions and classifications as well as claims of insured persons.

HOW EMPLOYEES GET PAID

Employees may be paid a salary or wages, depending on the type of work and the period of time covered. Money paid to a person for managerial or administrative services is usually called a salary, and the time period covered is generally a month or a year. Money paid for either skilled or unskilled labor is usually called wages, and the time period covered is hours or weeks. Wages may also be paid on a piecework basis. In practice, the words *salaries* and *wages* are somewhat interchangeable. A company may supplement an employee's salary or wage by commissions, bonuses, cost-of-living adjustments, and profit-sharing plans. As a rule, employees are paid by check or in cash. However, their compensation may take the form of merchandise, lodging, meals, or other property as well. When the compensation is in these forms, one has to determine the fair value of property or service given in payment for an employee's labor.

Calculating Total Earnings

Objective 1

Calculate total earnings based on an hourly, piece-rate, or commission basis.

When compensation is based on the amount of time worked, the accountant of course has to have a record of the number of hours worked by each employee. When there are only a few employees, this can be accomplished by means of a book record. When there are many employees, time clocks are the traditional method. Nowadays, for computer-operated time-keeping systems, employers use punched cards.

Wages

Let's take the case of Arnold L. Lacey, who works for Gilbert and Associates. His regular rate of pay is $12 per hour. The company pays time-and-a-half for hours worked in excess of 40 per week. In addition, it pays him double time for any work he does on Sundays and holidays. Lacey has a ½-hour lunch break during an 8½-hour day. He is not paid for the lunch break. His time card for the week is shown in Figure 9-1.

FIGURE 9-1

TIME CARD

Name   Lacey, Arnold L.
Week ending   Nov. 7, 19–

Day	In	Out	In	Out	Regular	Overtime
M	7⁵⁷	12⁰⁰	12²⁰	4³²	8	
T	7⁵⁶	12⁰⁶	12³⁶	4³⁷	8	
W	7⁵⁷	12⁰²	12³¹	4³¹	8	
T	8⁰⁰	12¹¹	12⁴⁰	6³²	8	2
F	8⁰⁰	12⁰³	12³³	5³³	8	1
S	7⁵⁹	1⁰²				5
S	7⁵⁵	12⁰⁴				4

Lacey's gross wages can be computed by one of two methods. The first method works like this:

40 hours at straight time	40 × $12 per hour = $480
2 hours overtime on Thursday	2 × $18 per hour = 36
1 hour overtime on Friday	1 × $18 per hour = 18
5 hours overtime on Saturday	5 × $18 per hour = 90
4 hours overtime on Sunday	4 × $24 per hour = 96
Total gross wages	$720

The second method of calculating gross wages is often used when machine accounting is involved:

52 hours at straight time: 52 × $12 per hour = $624
Overtime premium:
8 hours × $ 6 per hour premium = $48
4 hours × $12 per hour premium = $\underline{48}$
Total overtime premium $\underline{96}$
Total gross wages $\underline{\underline{\$720}}$

Salaries

Employees who are paid a regular salary may also be entitled to premium pay for overtime. It is necessary to figure out their regular hourly rate of pay before you can determine their overtime rate. Let's consider the case of Margo N. Day, who gets a salary of $1,872 per month. She is entitled to overtime pay for all hours worked in excess of 40 during a week at the rate of 1½ times her regular hourly rate. This past week she worked 44 hours, so we calculate her overtime pay as follows:

$1,872 per month × 12 months = $22,464 per year
  $22,464 per year ÷ 52 weeks = $432 per week
    $432 per week ÷ 40 hours = $10.80 per regular hour

Earnings for 44 hours:
40 hours at straight time   40 × $10.80 = $432.00
 4 hours overtime   4 × $16.20 = $\underline{64.80}$
Total gross earnings $\underline{\underline{\$496.80}}$

Piece Rate

Workers under the piece-rate system are paid at the rate of so much per unit of production. For example, Peter Ryan, an apple picker, gets paid $8 for picking a bin of apples. If he picks 6 bins during the day, his total earnings are 6 × $8 = $48.

Commissions and Bonuses

Some salespersons are paid on a purely commission basis. However, a more common arrangement is a salary plus a commission or bonus. Assume that Mary Pomeroy receives an annual salary of $12,000. Her employer agrees to pay her a 5 percent commission on all sales during the year in excess of $120,000. Her sales for the year total $260,000. Her bonus amounts to $7,000 ($140,000 × .05). Therefore her total earnings amount to $19,000 ($12,000 + $7,000).

DEDUCTIONS FROM TOTAL EARNINGS

Anyone who has ever earned a paycheck has encountered some of the many types of deductions that account for the shrinkage. The most usual deductions are for the following reasons:

1. Federal income tax withholding
2. State income tax withholding
3. FICA tax (Social Security), employee's share
4. Purchase of U.S. savings bonds
5. Union dues
6. Medical and life insurance premiums
7. Contributions to a charitable organization
8. Repayment of personal loans from the company credit union
9. Savings through the company credit union

Employees' Federal Income Tax Withholding

The amount of federal income tax withheld from an employee's wages depends on the amount of her or his total earnings and the number of exemptions claimed. An **exemption** is the amount of an individual's earnings that is exempt from income taxes (nontaxable). An employee is entitled to one personal exemption, plus an additional exemption for each dependent. Each employee has to fill out an **Employee's Withholding Allowance Certificate (Form W-4),** shown in Figure 9-2.

The employer retains this form, as authorization to withhold money for the employee's federal income tax.

FIGURE 9-2

Form **W-4** Department of the Treasury Internal Revenue Service	**Employee's Withholding Allowance Certificate** ▶ **For Privacy Act and Paperwork Reduction Act Notice, see instructions.**	OMB No. 1545-0010

1 Type or print your full name
   Arnold L. Lacey

2 Your social security number
   543-24-1680

Home address (number and street or rural route)
   6242 Harold Drive

City or town, state, and ZIP code
   Mercer, South Dakota 57814

3 Marital Status
☐ Single   ☒ Married
☐ Married, but withhold at higher Single rate
Note: *If married, but legally separated, or spouse is a nonresident alien, check the Single box.*

4 Total number of allowances you are claiming (from the Worksheet on page 3)   3

5 Additional amount, if any, you want deducted from each pay (see Step 4 on page 2) . . . . $

6 I claim exemption from withholding because (see Step 2 above and check boxes below that apply):

  a ☐ Last year I did not owe any Federal income tax and had a right to a full refund of **ALL** income tax withheld, **AND**

  b ☐ This year I do not expect to owe any Federal income tax and expect to have a right to a full refund of **ALL** income tax withheld. If both a and b apply, enter the year effective and "EXEMPT" here . . . ▶ | Year 19

  c If you entered "EXEMPT" on line 6b, are you a full-time student? . . . . ☐ Yes ☐ No

Under penalties of perjury, I certify that I am entitled to the number of withholding allowances claimed on this certificate or, if claiming exemption from withholding, that I am entitled to claim the exempt status.

Employee's signature ▶   *Arnold L. Lacey*   Date ▶ February 1   , 19 --

7 Employer's name and address (**Employer: Complete 7, 8, and 9 only if sending to IRS**) | **8** Office code | **9** Employer identification number

Circular E, Employer's Tax Guide

Circular E contains withholding tables for federal income and FICA taxes as well as the rules for depositing these taxes. It is regularly updated to

FIGURE 9-3

MARRIED Persons–WEEKLY Payroll Period

And the wages are–		And the number of withholding allowances claimed is–										
At least	But less than	0	1	2	3	4	5	6	7	8	9	10
		The amount of income tax to be withheld shall be–										
290	300	37	31	26	20	15	9	4	0	0	0	0
300	310	38	33	27	22	16	11	6	1	0	0	0
310	320	40	34	29	23	18	12	7	3	0	0	0
320	330	41	36	30	25	19	14	8	4	0	0	0
330	340	43	37	32	26	21	15	10	5	1	0	0
340	350	44	39	33	28	22	17	11	6	2	0	0
350	360	46	40	35	29	24	18	13	7	3	0	0
360	370	47	42	36	31	25	20	14	9	4	0	0
370	380	49	43	38	32	27	21	16	10	5	1	0
380	390	50	45	39	34	28	23	17	12	6	2	0
390	400	52	46	41	35	30	24	19	13	8	3	0
400	410	53	48	42	37	31	26	20	15	9	4	0
410	420	55	49	44	38	33	27	22	16	11	6	2
420	430	56	51	45	40	34	29	23	18	12	7	3
430	440	58	52	47	41	36	30	25	19	14	8	4
440	450	59	54	48	43	37	32	26	21	15	10	5
450	460	61	55	50	44	39	33	28	22	17	11	6
460	470	62	57	51	46	40	35	29	24	18	13	7
470	480	64	58	53	47	42	36	31	25	20	14	9
480	490	65	60	54	49	43	38	32	27	21	16	10
490	500	67	61	56	50	45	39	34	28	23	17	12
500	510	68	63	57	52	46	41	35	30	24	19	13
510	520	70	64	59	53	48	42	37	31	26	20	15
520	530	71	66	60	55	49	44	38	33	27	22	16
530	540	73	67	62	56	51	45	40	34	29	23	18
690	700	112	102	92	82	75	69	64	58	53	47	42
700	710	115	105	95	84	76	71	65	60	54	49	43
710	720	118	108	97	87	78	72	67	61	56	50	45
720	730	121	110	100	90	80	74	68	63	57	52	46
730	740	123	113	103	93	83	75	70	64	59	53	48
740	750	126	116	106	96	85	77	71	66	60	55	49
750	760	129	119	109	98	88	78	73	67	62	56	51
760	770	132	122	111	101	91	81	74	69	63	58	52
770	780	135	124	114	104	94	84	76	70	65	59	54
780	790	137	127	117	107	97	86	77	72	66	61	55
790	800	140	130	120	110	99	89	79	73	68	62	57
800	810	143	133	123	112	102	92	82	75	69	64	58
810	820	146	136	125	115	105	95	84	76	71	65	60
820	830	149	138	128	118	108	98	87	78	72	67	61
830	840	151	141	131	121	111	100	90	80	74	68	63
840	850	154	144	134	124	113	103	93	83	75	70	64
850	860	157	147	137	126	116	106	96	85	77	71	66
860	870	160	150	139	129	119	109	98	88	78	73	67
870	880	163	152	142	132	122	112	101	91	81	74	69
880	890	165	155	145	135	125	114	104	94	84	76	70
890	900	168	158	148	138	127	117	107	97	86	77	72
900	910	171	161	151	140	130	120	110	99	89	79	73
910	920	175	164	153	143	133	123	112	102	92	82	75
920	930	178	166	156	146	136	126	115	105	95	85	76
930	940	182	169	159	149	139	128	118	108	98	87	78
940	950	185	173	162	152	141	131	121	111	100	90	80
950	960	189	176	165	154	144	134	124	113	103	93	83
960	970	192	180	167	157	147	137	126	116	106	96	86
970	980	196	183	170	160	150	140	129	119	109	99	88
980	990	199	187	174	163	153	142	132	122	112	101	91
990	1,000	203	190	177	166	155	145	135	125	114	104	94
1,000	1,010	206	194	181	168	158	148	138	127	117	107	97
1,010	1,020	210	197	184	171	161	151	140	130	120	110	100
1,020	1,030	213	201	188	175	164	154	143	133	123	113	102
1,030	1,040	217	204	191	178	167	156	146	136	126	115	105
1,040	1,050	220	208	195	182	169	159	149	139	128	118	108
1,050	1,060	224	211	198	185	173	162	152	141	131	121	111
1,060	1,070	227	215	202	189	176	165	154	144	134	124	114
1,070	1,080	231	218	205	192	180	168	157	147	137	127	116
1,080	1,090	234	222	209	196	183	170	160	150	140	129	119

Determine deductions from tables of employees' income tax withholding.

reflect changes in tax laws and withholding rates. Filing requirements for official employer reports are also described. Circular E is provided free of charge by the Internal Revenue Service. Accountants responsible for preparation of payroll registers and forms should be familiar with the contents of Circular E.

The wage-bracket tax tables cover monthly, semimonthly, biweekly, weekly, and daily payroll periods. The tables are also subdivided on the basis of married and unmarried persons. To determine the tax to be withheld from an employee's gross wages, first locate the wage bracket in the first two columns of the table. Next, find the column for the number of exemptions claimed and read down this column until you get to the appropriate wage-bracket line. A portion of the weekly federal income tax withholding table for married persons is reproduced in Figure 9-3.

Assume that Arnold L. Lacey, who claims three exemptions, has gross wages of $720 for the week. At first it appears that $720 could fall in either the $710–$720 bracket or the $720–$730 bracket. However, note the headings of the bracket columns: "At least" and "But less than." A strict interpretation of the $710–$720 bracket really means $710–$719.99. Therefore $720 must be included in the $720–$730 bracket. As can be seen from the table, $90 should be withheld.

Employees' State Income Tax Withholding

Many states that levy state income taxes also furnish employers with withholding tables. Other states use a fixed percentage of the federal income tax withholding as the amount to be withheld for state taxes. In our illustration, we will assume that the amount of each employee's state income tax deduction amounts to 20 percent of that employee's federal income tax deduction.

Employees' FICA Tax Withholding (Social Security)

To determine the FICA tax for each employee, simply multiply the FICA taxable wages by the FICA tax rate.

Let's get back to Arnold L. Lacey, who had gross wages of $720 for the week ending October 7. Suppose that his total accumulated gross wages earned this year prior to this payroll period were $23,316. Lacey's total gross wages including this payroll period were $24,036 ($23,316 + $720), which is well below the $45,000 assumed maximum taxable income. Therefore, multiply the FICA taxable wages ($720) by the FICA tax rate (7.6 percent).

$720 × .076 = $54.72

Of course, if Lacey's gross earnings prior to this payroll period had been greater than $45,000, then there would be *no* FICA tax deduction. (Tables for FICA tax withholding are published in the Internal Revenue Service's *Circular E, Employer's Tax Guide*.)

PAYROLL REGISTER

The payroll register is a form that summarizes the information about employees' wages and salaries for a given payroll period. In Figure 9-4 on the next page we see a payroll register that shows the data for each employee on a separate line. This would be suitable for a firm, like Gilbert and Associates, which has a small number of employees.

Steps in Completing Payroll Register

Objective 3

Complete a payroll register.

1. Determine and record each employee's total hours worked during the payroll period. Take data from the time cards.
2. Record each employee's cumulative earnings at the beginning of the payroll period. Take the amount listed on each individual employee's earnings record.
3. Calculate each employee's regular, overtime, and total earnings for the payroll period—use time cards and hourly rates.
4. Calculate each employee's cumulative earnings at the end of the payroll period (beginning cumulative earnings + total earnings = ending cumulative earnings).
5. Complete the two Taxable Earnings columns. By the term *taxable earnings* we mean the amount of this week's (payroll period's) earnings that are subject to the tax.
   a. Unemployment—in our example, the first $7,000 is taxable for each employee. (If beginning cumulative earnings is less than $7,000, record the present payroll period's earnings without going over $7,000.)
   b. FICA—in our example, the first $45,000 is taxable for each employee. (If beginning cumulative earnings is less than $45,000, record the present payroll period's earnings without going over $45,000.)
6. Complete the Federal Income Tax Deduction. Find each employee's total earnings for the payroll period on the withholding tables to determine the deduction.
7. Complete the State Income Tax Deduction. Take each employee's total earnings for the payroll period multiplied by a fixed percentage of the federal income tax (we assume 20 percent in our example), or use state withholding tables.

Employees' Cumulative Earnings Before This Week Were Less Than $7,000 and After This Week Are More Than $7,000 Next, look at the line for Robert Berry. Notice that his cumulative earnings before this week were $6,760. Berry's new cumulative earnings (ending) are $7,235 ($6,760 + $475), putting him over the $7,000 maximum. Therefore, to bring Berry up to the $7,000 limit, $240 ($7,000 − $6,760) of his earnings for the week are taxable. After this week, none of Berry's earnings for the remainder of this calendar year will be taxable for unemployment.

Remember

Unemployment taxable earnings are used for calculating the amount of the unemployment tax, which is paid by the employer only. We will use the taxable earnings in Chapter 10 to figure the employer's Payroll Tax Expense.

Employees' Cumulative Earnings Before This Week Were More Than $7,000 After an employee's earnings top $7,000 during the calendar year, the employer no longer pays either state or federal unemployment for that employee. A dash is recorded in the Unemployment Taxable Earnings column to indicate that the column has not been forgotten or overlooked. For example, Arnold Lacey's total earnings before the payroll period ended October 7 (beginning) were $23,316 (as shown in his individual earnings record in Figure 9-7). Since he had previously earned more than $7,000 this year, we record a dash in the Unemployment Taxable Earnings column.

FICA Taxable Earnings Column

We have assumed a FICA tax rate of 7.6 percent of the first $45,000 paid to each employee during the calendar year.

Employees' Cumulative Earnings Including This Pay Period Have Not Reached $45,000 When an employee's cumulative earnings so far during the year are less than $45,000, we record the total earnings for the payroll period in the FICA Taxable Earnings column. For example, Donald Allen's cumulative earnings this year amount to $6,852. Because Allen's total earnings are less than $45,000, the entire $392 of wages earned during this pay period is listed in the FICA Taxable Earnings column. Note that this is true of all the employees except Anthony Garcia.

Employees' Cumulative Earnings Before the Week Were More Than $45,000 After an employee's earnings top $45,000 during the calendar year, neither the employer nor the employee has to pay the FICA tax. A dash is used to indicate that the column has not been forgotten or overlooked. (The same procedure was used for Unemployment Taxable Earnings column.) For example, Anthony Garcia's cumulative earnings before the payroll period ended October 7 were $45,200. Since he had previously earned more than $45,000, we record a dash in the FICA Taxable Earnings column.

As we said earlier, the two taxable earnings columns are used to calculate the employer's payroll tax expense, which we will discuss in the next chapter. However, since employees are also subject to the FICA tax, the FICA Taxable Earnings column is used to determine the amount of each employee's FICA tax deduction. For example, to find Allen's FICA deduction, multiply his FICA taxable earnings of $392 by the assumed FICA tax rate of 7.6 percent: $392 × .076 = $29.79. As another example, Lacey's FICA deduction is $54.72 ($720 FICA taxable × .076). Note that these are the same amounts entered in the payroll register FICA Deductions column.

Deductions Columns

The federal and state income tax withholdings and the FICA (Social Security) deductions are employee deductions required by law; the others are usually voluntary. One could set up special columns for any frequently used deductions. Here, United Way and Accounts Receivable are included as other deductions.

Net Amount and Salary Expense Columns

The Net Amount column represents the employee's take-home pay. The last two columns show the distribution of the salary accounts to be debited. Gilbert and Associates uses Sales Salary Expense and Office Salary Expense. The sum of these two columns equals the total earnings.

Objective 4

Journalize the payroll entry from a payroll register.

THE PAYROLL ENTRY

Because the payroll register summarizes the payroll data for the period, it seems logical that it should be used as the basis for recording the payroll

FIGURE 9-5

	DATE		DESCRIPTION	POST. REF.	DEBIT	CREDIT	
1	19–						1
2	Oct.	7	Sales Salary Expense		5 0 3 3 00		2
3			Office Salary Expense		2 0 1 0 00		3
4			Employees' Federal Income Tax				4
5			Payable			9 2 3 00	5
6			Employees' State Income Tax				6
7			Payable			1 8 4 60	7
8			FICA Tax Payable			4 5 5 47	8
9			Employees' Medical Insurance				9
10			Payable			2 6 4 00	10
11			Employees' United Way				11
12			Payable			2 4 00	12
13			Accounts Receivable			4 0 00	13
14			Salaries Payable			5 1 5 1 93	14
15			Payroll register, page 68,				15
16			for week ended October 7.				16

GENERAL JOURNAL   PAGE 31

Remember

The totals from the payroll register are the amounts used in the payroll entry.

in the ledger accounts. Since the payroll register does not have the status of a journal, a journal entry is necessary. Figure 9-5 shows the entry in general journal form.

Note that a firm records the total cost to the company for services of employees as debits to the salary expense accounts. To pay the employees, the firm now makes the following journal entry:

18	8	*Salaries Payable*	5 1 5 1 93		18
19		*Cash*		5 1 5 1 93	19
20		*Paid salaries for week*			20
21		*ended October 7. Issued*			21
22		*check no. 667, payable to*			22
23		*special payroll bank*			23
24		*account.*			24
25					25

Remember

The amount shown as Salaries Payable is the employees' take-home pay.

In the two journal entries, the debit and credit to the Salaries Payable account cancel each other. It would be possible to combine the two entries by making one credit to Cash. If a combined journal were in use, both of the above entries would be recorded in it, instead of in the general journal.

Special Payroll Bank Account

A firm having a large number of employees would probably open a special payroll account with its bank. One check drawn on the regular bank

FIGURE 9-6

EMPLOYEE	TOTAL HOURS	O.T. HOURS	REG. PAY RATE	REG. PAY	O.T. PREM. PAY	GROSS PAY	FED. INC. TAX	STATE INC. TAX	FICA	MED. INS.	OTHER	TOTAL DED.	NET PAY
Arnold L. Lacey	52	12	12.00	480.00	240.00	720.00	90.00	18.00	54.72	25.00	UW3.00	190.72	529.28

CENTRAL NATIONAL BANK   98-461/252

Payroll Account
GILBERT AND ASSOCIATES
201 FIFTH STREET
MERCER, NEW JERSEY 08651   October 8   19 —   No. 937

PAY TO THE ORDER OF Arnold L. Lacey $ 529.28

Five hundred twenty-nine and 28/100------------------------------------- DOLLARS

Francis C. Gilbert

⑈252⑈0461⑈

account is made payable to the special payroll account for the amount of the total net pay for a payroll period. All payroll checks for the period are then written on the special payroll account. With the use of the special payroll account, if employees delay cashing their paychecks, then the checks do not have to be listed on the bank reconciliation of the firm's regular bank account. Balances of Employees' Medical Insurance Payable, Employees' United Way Payable, and other employee deductions are paid out of the firm's regular bank account.

Small businesses that have just a few workers will not find it worthwhile to use a special payroll bank account. Instead, these firms will use their regular bank account to write the employees' payroll checks, crediting Cash directly rather than crediting Salaries Payable.

PAYCHECK

All the data needed to make out a payroll check are available in the payroll register. Arnold L. Lacey's paycheck is shown in Figure 9-6.

Employees' Individual Earnings Records

Objective 5

Maintain employees' individual earnings records.

To comply with government regulations, a firm has to keep current data on each employee's accumulated earnings, deductions, and net pay. The information contained in the payroll register is recorded in each **employee's individual earnings record** each payday. Figure 9-7 on the next page shows a portion of the earnings record for Arnold L. Lacey.

SUMMARY

L.O. 1,2 Payroll accounting is concerned with the following:

- Computing compensation for employees
- Taking out required and voluntary deductions
- Paying employees
- Paying various government agencies
- Submitting required reports to government agencies
- Paying private agencies for employees' deductions for contributions, etc.

In this chapter we discussed important provisions of federal and state laws pertaining to employment. In earlier chapters we showed the entry recording compensation of employees as a debit to Salaries or Wages Expense and a credit to Cash. We have now made the transition from this simplified entry to the complete entry.

L.O. 3,4 First, we record the information for the payroll period in the payroll register. Next, using the payroll register as the source of information, we record payroll entries in the general journal or combined journal. The complete

FIGURE 9-7

EMPLOYEE'S INDIVIDUAL

NAME *Arnold L. Lacey*

ADDRESS *6242 Harold Drive*

Mercer, South Dakota 57814

MALE *X*   FEMALE _____

MARRIED *X*   SINGLE _____

PHONE NO. *663-2556*   DATE OF BIRTH *9/19/51*

LINE NO.	PERIOD ENDED	DATE PAID	HOURS WORKED REG.	HOURS WORKED O.T.	EARNINGS REGULAR	EARNINGS OVERTIME	EARNINGS TOTAL	ACCUMULATED EARNINGS
40	9/3	9/4	40	8	4 8 0 00	1 4 4 00	6 2 4 00	21 1 6 2 00
41	9/10	9/11	40	2	4 8 0 00	3 6 00	5 1 6 00	21 6 7 8 00
42	9/17	9/18	40	2	4 8 0 00	3 6 00	5 1 6 00	22 1 9 4 00
43	9/24	9/25	40	5	4 8 0 00	9 0 00	5 7 0 00	22 7 6 4 00
44	9/30	10/1	40	4	4 8 0 00	7 2 00	5 5 2 00	23 3 1 6 00
45	10/7	10/8	40	12	4 8 0 00	2 4 0 00	7 2 0 00	24 0 3 6 00

payroll entry consists of debits to the salary expense accounts, credits to the various deductions payable, and finally a credit to Salaries Payable, or Cash. If the payroll entry involves a credit to Salaries Payable, then a second journal entry is recorded debiting Salaries Payable and crediting Cash. As a result, the Salaries Payable account is canceled out.

L.O. 5   To comply with the employment laws, any business firm should maintain a payroll register and an employee's individual earnings record.

GLOSSARY

Current Tax Payment Act   Requires employers to withhold employees' federal income tax as well as to pay and report the tax.

Employee   One who works for compensation under the direction and control of the employer.

Employee's individual earnings record   A supplementary record for each employee showing personal payroll data and yearly cumulative earnings and deductions.

Employee's Withholding Allowance Certificate (Form W-4)   This form specifies the number of exemptions claimed by each employee and gives the employer the authority to withhold money for an employee's income taxes and FICA taxes.

EARNINGS RECORD

EMPLOYEE NO. _5_ DATE EMPLOYED _2/1/—_

SOC. SEC. NO. _543-24-1680_ NO. OF EXEMPTIONS _3_

PAY RATE _$12.00_ PER HOUR _X_ PER DAY _____

EQUIVALENT HOURLY RATE _$12.00_ PER WEEK _____ PER MONTH _____

DATE TERMINATED _____

CLASSIFICATION FOR WORKERS' COMPENSATION INSURANCE _Sales floor_

				DEDUCTIONS						PAID	
FEDERAL INCOME TAX	STATE INCOME TAX	FICA	MEDICAL INSURANCE	OTHER CODE	OTHER AMOUNT	TOTAL	NET AMOUNT	CK. NO.
70 00	14 00	47 42	25 00	UW	3 00	159 42	464 58	877
53 00	10 60	39 22	25 00	UW	3 00	130 82	385 18	889
53 00	10 60	39 22	25 00	UW	3 00	130 82	385 18	901
62 00	12 40	43 32	25 00	UW	3 00	145 72	424 28	913
59 00	11 80	41 95	25 00	UW	3 00	140 75	411 25	925
90 00	18 00	54 72	25 00	UW	3 00	190 72	529 28	937

Exemption An amount of an employee's annual earnings not subject to income tax. The term is also called a *withholding allowance*.

Fair Labor Standards Act (Wages and Hours Law) An act requiring employers whose products are involved in interstate commerce to pay their employees time-and-a-half for all hours worked in excess of 40 per week.

FICA taxes Social Security taxes paid by both employers and employees under the provisions of the Federal Insurance Contributions Act. The proceeds are used to pay old-age and disability pensions.

FUTA taxes Taxes paid only by employers under the provisions of the Federal Unemployment Tax Act. The proceeds are used to provide financial support for the maintenance of government-run employment offices throughout the country.

Gross pay The total amount of an employee's pay before any deductions.

Independent contractor Someone who is engaged for a definite job or service who may choose her or his own means of doing the work. This person is not an employee of the firm for which the service is provided. (*Examples:* appliance repair person, plumber, freelance artist, CPA firm.)

Net pay Gross pay minus deductions. Also called take-home pay.

State unemployment taxes Taxes paid by employers only. The proceeds are used to pay unemployment benefits.

Workers' compensation laws State laws guaranteeing benefits for employees who are injured or killed on the job.

C**O**MPUTERS AT WORK

The Payroll Application

Computerizing payroll activities can save businesses a great deal of time and improve the accuracy of their records. Today's software can produce payroll registers, employee earnings records, and checks and stubs as well as a variety of reports and tax forms. Reports may include an employee directory, payroll information by department, tax liability reports, and a posting summary that lists the general ledger accounts that change when payroll figures are integrated into them. Some programs will also fill in tax forms such as W-2, 941, and 940 forms.

Because payroll is such a sensitive issue, businesses must take special care to insure accuracy and confidentiality. All parties involved—employers, employees, and local, state, and federal agencies—demand accuracy and timeliness. Accurate time keeping and accurate data entry procedures are the keys to the success of any payroll system, computerized or manual.

Computer programs vary in their ease of entry and the sophistication of their output. Regardless of the program's complexity, however, it is imperative that a brief manual summary be maintained to crosscheck the computerized system. Some payroll programs will integrate with a general ledger package. That is, as the payroll information is entered into the payroll module, it posts the totals to the general ledger accounts involved. Integration saves time by eliminating the separate compiling and keying of payroll entries to the general ledger.

Thus, payroll accounting software can save time by streamlining completion of repetitive, sometimes tedious tasks involved in manual payroll preparation. It can cut down on errors by reducing the number of times the same data are entered and by carrying out calculations automatically. This popular tool can also update cumulative records, produce required tax reports, and provide vital management information.

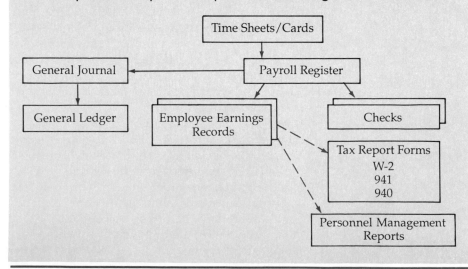

QUESTIONS, EXERCISES, AND PROBLEMS
Discussion Questions

1. What are the objectives of the Federal Insurance Contributions Act? Who pays the FICA taxes?
2. Suggest three required deductions and four voluntary deductions from employees' total earnings.
3. What is the purpose of the payroll register?
4. Distinguish between an employee and an independent contractor.
5. Describe how a special payroll bank account is useful in paying the wages of employees.
6. What information is included in an employee's individual earnings record?
7. Explain the requirements of the Fair Labor Standards Act.
8. What is the difference between an employee's gross pay and net pay?

Exercises

L.O. 1,2 **Exercise 9-1**   Clara C. Petrillo works for Downing, Inc., which must abide by the Fair Labor Standards Act. It must pay its employees time-and-a-half for all hours worked in excess of 40 per week. Petrillo's pay rate is $14.50 per hour. Her wages are subject to federal income tax and to FICA tax deductions at the rate of 7.6 percent. She claims four tax exemptions. Petrillo has a ½-hour lunch break during an 8½-hour day. Her time card is shown below:

TIME CARD

Name   *Petrillo, Clara C.*
Week ending   *March 11, 19–*

Day	In	Out	In	Out	Hours Worked Regular	Hours Worked Overtime
M	7⁵⁶	12⁰⁹	12³⁹	4³²	8	
T	7⁵²	12⁰⁵	12³⁵	5⁰⁴	8	½
W	7⁵⁹	12²⁰	12⁴⁰	5⁰³	8	½
T	8⁰⁰	12⁰⁸	12³⁸	4³⁴	8	
F	7⁵⁶	12⁰⁹	12³⁹	6³³	8	2
S	8⁰⁰	11⁰¹				3
S						

Complete the following:

a. _____ hours at straight time × $14.50 per hour $_____
b. _____ hours overtime × $21.75 per hour   _____
c. Total gross wages $_____

d. Federal income tax withholding
(from tax tables in Figure 9-3, page 275) $_____
e. FICA withholding at 7.6 percent   _____
f. Total withholding   _____
g. Net pay $_____

L.O. 1   **Exercise 9-2**   Carol Weister's salary is $1,664 per month. If she works more than 40 hours in one week, she is entitled to overtime pay at the rate of 1½ times her regular hourly rate. During the current week, she worked 46 hours. Calculate her gross pay.

L.O. 2   **Exercise 9-3**   Using the table in Figure 9-3, determine the amount of federal income tax an employer should withhold weekly for married employees with the following wages and exemptions:

	Total Weekly Wages	Number of Exemptions	Amount of Withholding
a.	$321.48	0	_____
b.	$733.16	5	_____
c.	$856.25	2	_____
d.	$951.00	1	_____
e.	$1,080.00	4	_____

L.O. 1   **Exercise 9-4**   Henry Mills works for Steigler Pottery, a company engaged in interstate commerce, which is subject to the provisions of the Fair Labor Standards Act. Steigler has just adopted a four-day, 40-hour workweek. Mills' pay rate is $8.88 per hour. During the four-day week, his working hours were as follows: Monday, 12 hours; Tuesday, 10 hours; Wednesday, 11½ hours; Thursday, 10½ hours. Compute the amount of his gross earnings for the week.

L.O. 2,3,4   **Exercise 9-5**   The following information for the week ended January 7 was taken from the records of Tires Galore, a company that is subject to the Fair Labor Standards Act.

NAME	HOURLY RATE	HOURS WORKED REG.	O.T.	TOTAL EARNINGS	FEDERAL INCOME TAX	FICA	SAVINGS BONDS	MEDICAL INSURANCE	TOTAL	NET PAY
Lee, M.	8.40	40	6				4 00	26 00		
Ott, L.	14.10	40	8				10 00	28 00		

Using the table in Figure 9-3, determine the income tax withheld. The FICA tax rate is 7.6 percent. Lee and Ott claim two exemptions each. In general journal form, record the payroll entry, debiting Wages Expense for the amount of the total earnings and crediting Cash for the net pay.

L.O. 2,3,4 **Exercise 9-6** On January 31, Salinger Auto Sales' column totals of its payroll register showed that its sales employees had earned $6,840 and its office employees had earned $1,440. FICA taxes were withheld at an assumed rate of 7.6 percent. Other deductions consisted of federal income tax, $842.60; U.S. savings bonds, $220; medical insurance, $480. Determine the amount of FICA taxes to be withheld and record the general journal entry for the payroll, crediting Salaries Payable for the net pay.

L.O. 5 **Exercise 9-7** Goldstein Optical has two employees. The information shown below was taken from their individual earnings record cards for the month of August. Determine the missing amounts, assuming that the FICA tax is 7.6 percent.

	March	Reiner
Regular earnings	$?	$1,130.00
Overtime earnings	46.00	?
Total earnings	$?	$1,368.00
Federal income tax withheld	142.00	254.00
FICA taxes withheld	?	103.97
State income tax withheld	28.40	?
Medical insurance withheld	96.00	105.00
Total deductions	$340.27	$ 513.77
Net pay	$631.73	$?

L.O. 3,4 **Exercise 9-8** Assume the employees in Exercise 9-7 are paid from the firm's regular bank account. Record the payroll entry in general journal form dated August 31.

Problem Set A

L.O. 1,2 **Problem 9-1A** Earl Dailey, an employee of Harris Distributing Company, worked 46 hours during the week of July 12 to 18. His rate of pay is $8.10 per hour, and he receives time-and-a-half for all work in excess of 40 hours per week. Dailey is married and claims two exemptions on his W-4 form. His wages are subject to the following deductions:

a. Federal income tax (use the table in Figure 9-3).
b. FICA tax at 7.6 percent.
c. Union dues, $9.60.
d. Medical insurance, $27.20.

Instructions

Compute his regular pay, overtime pay, gross pay, and net pay.

L.O. 3,4   **Problem 9-2A**   Schumansky Dairy has the following payroll information for the week ended February 21:

Name	Earnings at End of Previous Week	Daily Time							Pay Rate	Federal Income Tax	Union Dues
		S	M	T	W	T	F	S			
Alvarez, Thomas C.	1,824.00	8	8	8	8	8			7.60	39.00	6.00
Berg, Peter R.	2,016.00			8	8	8	8	8	8.40	30.00	6.00
Church, Pamela N.	1,824.00	8	8	8			8	8	7.60	39.00	6.00
Dunham, Steven A.	466.00				8	8			6.00	6.00	
Mack, Teresa P.	2,084.00	8	8	8			8	8	8.40	30.00	6.00
Roy, Milton D.	1,892.00	8	8		8	8	8	8	7.60	54.00	6.00

Taxable earnings for FICA are based on the first $45,000. Taxable earnings for federal and state unemployment insurance are based on the first $7,000. Federal income tax withholdings and deductions for union dues are given. Employees are paid time-and-a-half for hours worked in excess of 40 per week.

Instructions

1. Complete the payroll register, using 7.6 percent for calculating FICA tax withholding.
2. Prepare a general journal entry to record the payroll. The firm's general ledger contains a Wages Expense account and a Wages Payable account.
3. Assuming that the firm transfers funds from its regular bank account to its special payroll bank account, make the entry in the general journal to record the payment of wages, check no. 54. In the payroll register, begin payroll checks with no. 172.

L.O. 2,3,4   **Problem 9-3A**   The Caswell Company is subject to the Fair Labor Standards Act. Accordingly, it pays its employees time-and-a-half for hours worked in excess of 40 per week. The information available from time cards and employees' individual earnings records for the period ended October 7 is shown in the chart at the top of the next page. Taxable earnings for FICA are based on the first $45,000. Taxable earnings for federal and state unemployment insurance are based on the first $7,000.

Instructions

1. Complete the payroll register, using the wage-bracket income tax withholding tables in Figure 9-3. The FICA tax rate is 7.6 percent. Assume that all employees are married.
2. Prepare a general journal entry to record the payroll. The firm's general ledger contains a Wages Expense account and a Wages Payable account.
3. Assume that the firm transfers funds from its regular bank account to its

| Name | Earnings at End of Previous Week | Daily Time | | | | | | Pay Rate | Income Tax Exempt. | Union Dues | Medical Ins. |
		M	T	W	T	F	S				
Cook, Monte C.	12,642.00	8	8	8	8	8	0	8.70	2	9.00	22.00
Cooper, Frank L.	13,210.00		8	8	8	10	0	9.50	1	9.00	20.00
Dye, Ira N.	12,916.00	8	8	10	8	8	0	8.70	2	9.00	22.00
Elmer, John R.	19,296.00	8	8	8	8	8	0	13.40	4		28.00
Fox, Linda D.	13,942.00	8	8	8	8	8	4	9.50	3	9.00	26.00
Hobbs, Jean A.	11,008.00	8	8	8	8	8	0	7.90	1	9.00	20.00
Lane, Dale M.	6,246.80	8	8	8	8	8	4	7.90	1	9.00	20.00
Ramos, Jose A.	13,784.00	8	8	8	8	8	4	9.50	3	9.00	26.00

special payroll bank account. Make the entry in the general journal to record the payment of wages, check no. 143. In the payroll register, begin payroll checks with no. 912.

L.O. 3,4 **Problem 9-4A** The Kingsley Company is subject to the Fair Labor Standards Act. Accordingly, its employees, including Davey L. Day, are paid time-and-a-half for all hours worked in excess of 40 per week. The following information is available from Kingsley's time books and the employees' individual earnings records for the payroll period ended December 22:

Name	Hours Worked	Earnings at End of Previous Week	Pay Rate	Class.	Federal Income Tax	Medical Ins.	Other Deduct.
Bell, Alan L.	44	21,427.00	$10.50 per hour	Sales	60.00	22.00	UW 4.00
Byrd, Roy A.	40	27,735.00	$12.50 per hour	Sales	57.00	26.00	AR 64.00
Carr, Mary C.	40	25,920.00	$12.50 per hour	Sales	63.00	22.00	UW 4.00
Day, Davey L.	44	27,200.00	$500 per week	Office	62.00	30.00	UW 4.00
Davis, Fred N.	48	6,714.00	$9.00 per hour	Sales	51.00	26.00	
Ellis, Gene R.	40	47,500.00	$950 per week	Office	144.00	34.00	UW 6.00
Eng, Lee Y.	40	26,440.00	$12.50 per hour	Sales	52.00	30.00	UW 4.00
Gray, Gary P.	40	6,250.00	$290 per week	Office	31.00	22.00	
Hurd, Gwen B.	44	25,654.00	$12.50 per hour	Sales	62.00	30.00	AR 50.00
Perry, Dora D.	40	44,625.00	$875 per week	Sales	132.00	30.00	UW 6.00

Taxable earnings for FICA are based on the first $45,000. Taxable earnings for federal and state unemployment insurance are based on the first $7,000.

Instructions

1. Complete the payroll register using a FICA tax rate of 7.6 percent. Concerning the Other Deductions, AR refers to Accounts Receivable, and UW refers to United Way.
2. Prepare a general journal entry to record the payroll and the payment to employees. Assume the company transfers funds from its regular bank account to its special payroll bank account and issues check no. 544. In the payroll register, begin the payroll checks with check no. 4171.

Problem Set B

L.O. 1,2 **Problem 9-1B** Jana C. White, an employee of C and R Freight, worked 47 hours during the week of June 14 to 20. Her rate of pay is $8.60 per hour, and she gets time-and-a-half for work in excess of 40 hours per week. She is married and claims one exemption on her W-4 form. Her wages are subject to the following deductions:

a. Federal income tax (use the table in Figure 9-3).
b. FICA tax at 7.6 percent.
c. Union dues, $7.50.
d. Medical insurance, $16.25.

Instructions

Compute her regular pay, overtime pay, gross pay, and net pay.

L.O. 3,4 **Problem 9-2B** Saunders Bakery has the following payroll information for the week ended May 12:

| Name | Earnings at End of Previous Week | Daily Time | | | | | | Pay Rate | Federal Income Tax | Union Dues |
		M	T	W	T	F	S			
Abbey, Laura A.	6,442.00	8	8	8	8	8	0	8.40	37.00	6.00
Booth, Carl R.	6,716.00	8	8	8	8	8	0	7.20	42.00	6.00
Clark, Dennis M.	5,140.00	0	8	8	8	8	8	7.20	42.00	6.00
Green, Anna D.	8,520.00	8	8	8	0	8	8	9.50	45.00	6.00
Merta, Terry L.	5,140.00	8	8	8	8	8	8	7.20	48.00	6.00
Tuttle, Ross B.	7,296.00	0	8	8	8	8	8	8.40	37.00	6.00

Taxable earnings for FICA are based on the first $45,000. Taxable earnings for federal and state unemployment insurance are based on the first $7,000.

Federal income tax withholdings and deductions for union dues are given. Employees are paid time-and-a-half for hours worked in excess of 40 per week.

Instructions

1. Complete the payroll register, using 7.6 percent for calculating FICA tax withholding.
2. Prepare a general journal entry to record the payroll. The firm's general ledger contains a Wages Expense account and a Wages Payable account.
3. Assuming that the firm transfers funds from its regular bank account to its special payroll bank account, make the entry in the general journal to record the payment of wages, check no. 51. Begin payroll checks with no. 114.

L.O. 2,3,4 **Problem 9-3B** The Bradford Company is subject to the Fair Labor Standards Act. Accordingly, it pays its employees time-and-a-half for hours worked in excess of 40 per week. The following information is available from time cards and employees' individual earnings records for the pay period ended September 22:

| Name | Earnings at End of Previous Week | Daily Time | | | | | | Pay Rate | Income Tax Exempt. | Union Dues | Medical Ins. |
		M	T	W	T	F	S				
Beech, Earl D.	5,412.00	8	8	8	10	0	0	8.60	1	9.00	24.00
Evans, John R.	14,446.00	8	8	8	8	8	0	9.20	2	9.00	30.00
Faris, Gary C.	13,120.00	8	10	8	8	8	0	8.60	2	9.00	30.00
Faw, Agnes N.	15,912.00	8	8	8	8	8	4	9.20	2	9.00	30.00
Hall, Jack L.	13,380.00	8	8	8	8	8	0	12.00	3	9.00	34.00
Kibby, Mary M.	14,760.00	8	8	9	8	8	0	9.20	3	9.00	34.00
Main, Victor A.	6,312.00	8	8	8	9	9	4	7.80	2	9.00	30.00
Pinto, Rafael C.	15,364.00	8	8	10	8	8	0	9.20	2	9.00	30.00

Taxable earnings for FICA are based on the first $45,000. Taxable earnings for federal and state unemployment insurance are based on the first $7,000.

Instructions

1. Complete the payroll register, using the wage-bracket income tax withholding tables in Figure 9-3. The FICA tax rate is 7.6 percent. Assume that all employees are married.
2. Prepare a general journal entry to record the payroll. The firm's general ledger contains a Wages Expense account and a Wages Payable account.
3. Assume that the firm transfers funds from its regular bank account to its special payroll bank account. Make the entry in the general journal to record the payment of wages, check no. 97. In the payroll register, begin payroll checks with no. 714.

L.O. 3,4   **Problem 9-4B**   The Brighton Company is subject to the Fair Labor Standards Act. Accordingly, employees, including Debra M. Hart, are paid time-and-a-half for all hours worked in excess of 40 per week. The following information is available from the time books and employees' individual earnings records for the pay period ended December 7:

Name	Hours Worked	Earnings at End of Previous Week	Pay Rate	Class.	Federal Income Tax	Medical Ins.	Other Deduct.
Bennett, Rita C.	46	24,120.00	$11.50 per hour	Sales	66.00	30.00	AR 50.00
Cox, James N.	40	46,080.00	$960 per week	Office	147.00	36.00	UW 5.00
Coe, Pearl D.	40	22,140.00	$11.50 per hour	Sales	51.00	30.00	UW 4.00
Drake, Karl L.	40	6,750.00	$11.50 per hour	Sales	57.00	30.00	UW 3.00
Green, Lloyd K.	40	22,080.00	$11.50 per hour	Sales	51.00	30.00	UW 3.00
Hart, Debra M.	44	30,260.00	$600 per week	Office	82.00	30.00	UW 4.00
Kirk, May P.	40	27,190.00	$14 per hour	Sales	66.00	33.00	AR 75.00
Mack, Nila B.	46	4,430.00	$10 per hour	Sales	61.00	30.00	
Noll, Dale W.	40	9,660.00	$200 per week	Office	18.00	30.00	
Roy, John N.	40	44,472.00	$872 per week	Sales	132.00	33.00	UW 4.00

Taxable earnings for FICA are based on the first $45,000. Taxable earnings for federal and state unemployment insurance are based on the first $7,000.

Instructions

1. Complete the payroll register using a FICA tax rate of 7.6 percent. Concerning the Other Deductions, AR refers to Accounts Receivable and UW refers to United Way.
2. Prepare a general journal entry to record the payroll and the payment of the employees. Assume the company transfers funds from its regular bank account to its special bank account and issues check no. 416. In the payroll register, begin the payroll checks with check no. 3114.

10

Payroll Accounting: Employer's Taxes, Payments, and Reports

LEARNING OBJECTIVES

After you have completed this chapter, you will be able to do the following:

1. Journalize the entry to record payroll tax expense.
2. Journalize the entry for the deposit of employees' federal income taxes withheld and FICA taxes (both employees' withheld and employer's matching share).
3. Journalize the entries for the payment of employer's state and federal unemployment taxes.
4. Journalize the entry for the deposit of employees' state income taxes withheld.
5. Complete Employer's Quarterly Federal Tax Return, Form 941.
6. Prepare W-2 forms and W-3 forms.
7. Calculate the premium for workers' compensation insurance, and prepare the entry for payment in advance.
8. Determine the amount of adjustment for workers' compensation insurance at end of year, and record the adjustment.

In Chapter 9, we talked about the computing and recording of such payroll data as gross pay, employees' income tax withheld, employees' FICA tax withheld, and various deductions requested by employees. Now we will pay these withholdings and the taxes levied on the employer based on total payroll.

EMPLOYER'S IDENTIFICATION NUMBER

Everyone who works must have a Social Security number, a number that is a vital part of his or her federal income tax returns. For an employer, a counterpart to the Social Security number is the **employer identification number.** Each employer of one or more persons is required to have such a number, and it must be listed on all reports and payments of employees' federal income tax withholding and FICA taxes.

EMPLOYER'S PAYROLL TAXES

An employer's payroll taxes are levied on the employer on the basis of the gross wages paid to the employees. Payroll taxes—like property taxes—are an expense of doing business. Gilbert and Associates records these taxes in the Payroll Tax Expense account and debits the account for the company's FICA taxes as well as for state and federal unemployment taxes. In T account form, Payroll Tax Expense for Gilbert and Associates would look like the following example.

Payroll Tax Expense

+	−
FICA (employer's matching portion)	Closed at the end of the year along with
Federal Unemployment Tax	all other expense accounts
State Unemployment Tax	

As you can see, **FICA tax (employer's share),** federal unemployment tax, and state unemployment tax **are included under the umbrella of Payroll Tax Expense.** The unemployment taxes are levied on the employer only.

Employer's Matching Portion of FICA Tax

The FICA tax is imposed on both employer and employee. The firm's accountant deducts the employee's share from gross wages and records it in the payroll entry under FICA Tax Payable (the same liability account as shown in Chapter 9). Next, he or she determines the employer's share by multiplying the employer's FICA tax rate (assumed to be 7.6 percent) times the total FICA-taxable earnings (gross annual earnings for the calendar year for each employee up to an assumed $45,000). In this text, we shall assume that the same tax rate applies to both the employer and the employee. **The accountant gets the FICA-taxable earnings figure from the payroll register.** In Figure 10-1 we take another look at the Taxable Earnings columns from the payroll register for the week ended October 7, 19–, shown in Figure 9-4.

FIGURE 10-1

Amount of employees' earnings that are less than $7,000 per employee for the year

Amount of employees' earnings that are less than $45,000 per employee for the year

	NAME	TOTAL HOURS	TOTAL	CUMULATIVE EARNINGS	TAXABLE EARNINGS	
					UNEMPL.	FICA
1	Allen, Donald C.	46	3 9 2 00	6 8 5 2 00	3 9 2 00	3 9 2 00
2	Berry, Robert A.	45	4 7 5 00	7 2 3 5 00	2 4 0 00	4 7 5 00
3	Dennis, Virginia L.	49	5 3 5 00	23 6 3 5 00	———	5 3 5 00
4	Dillon, Nancy B.	40	3 6 0 00	16 2 0 0 00	———	3 6 0 00
5	Fuller, Harold A.	40	3 8 4 00	6 5 1 0 00	3 8 4 00	3 8 4 00
6	Garcia, Anthony R.	40	1 0 5 0 00	46 2 5 0 00	———	———
7	Lacey, Arnold L.	52	7 2 0 00	24 0 3 6 00	———	7 2 0 00
8	Lee, Opal D.	40	6 0 0 00	27 0 0 0 00	———	6 0 0 00
9	McKee, Grace E.	44	5 0 6 00	22 2 6 8 00	———	5 0 6 00
10	Olivera, Mario B.	45	4 7 5 00	19 8 0 9 00	———	4 7 5 00
11	Pyle, Marvin W.	40	8 5 0 00	38 2 5 0 00	———	8 5 0 00
12	Taylor, Leona J.	52	6 9 6 00	28 4 0 8 00	———	6 9 6 00
13			7 0 4 3 00	266 4 5 3 00	1 0 1 6 00	5 9 9 3 00

Employer's state unemployment tax $1,016 × .054 = $54.86

Employer's federal unemployment tax $1,016 × .008 = $8.13

Employer's FICA tax $5,993 × .076 = $455.47

By T accounts, the entry to record the employer's portion of the FICA tax looks like this:

Payroll Tax Expense

+		−
(5,993 × .076)	455.47	

FICA Tax Payable

−		+	
	Balance	455.47	(employees' share of FICA tax as posted from the payroll entry)
	(5,993 × .076)	455.47	(employer's share of FICA tax)

Note particularly that the FICA Tax Payable account is often used for the tax liability of both the employer and the employee. This is logical because both FICA taxes are paid at the same time and the same place. There might be a slight difference between the employer's and the employee's share of FICA taxes, because of the rounding-off process. In our example, the accountant calculates the employee's share by taking 7.6 percent (assumed rate) of the taxable earnings of each worker, then adding these figures to find the total amount due for all employees. At the same time, she or he determines the employer's share by taking 7.6 percent of the total taxable earnings of all the employees. The two figures may vary, but only by a few cents.

Employer's Federal Unemployment Tax (FUTA)

The employer's federal unemployment tax is levied on the employer only. Congress may from time to time change the rate. But for now, let's assume a rate of .8 percent (.008) of the first $7,000 earned by each employee during the calendar year. For the weekly payroll period for Gilbert and Associates, the tax liability is $8.13 ($1,016 of unemployment taxable earnings taken from the payroll register multiplied by .008, the tax rate). By T accounts, the entry is as follows:

Payroll Tax Expense		Federal Unemployment Tax Payable	
+	−	−	+
(1,016 × .008) 8.13			(1,016 × .008) 8.13

Employer's State Unemployment Tax

This tax, like the federal unemployment tax, is paid by the employer only. The rate of the state unemployment tax varies considerably among the states. However, as we stated in Chapter 9, assume that Gilbert and Associates is subject to a rate of 5.4 percent of the first $7,000 of each employee's earnings (same base amount as federal unemployment insurance). As shown in the portion of the payroll register illustrated in Figure 10-1, $1,016 of earnings are subject to the state unemployment tax. Accordingly, by T accounts, the state unemployment tax based on taxable earnings is as follows:

Payroll Tax Expense		State Unemployment Tax Payable	
+	−	−	+
(1,016 × .054) 54.86			(1,016 × .054) 54.86

To make things clearer in the foregoing discussion, figures for the three employer's payroll taxes have been presented separately. Now let's com-

Objective 1

Journalize the entry to record payroll tax expense.

bine this information into one entry, which follows the regular payroll entry. Gilbert and Associates pays its employees weekly, so it also makes its Payroll Tax Expense entry weekly.

	DATE		DESCRIPTION	POST. REF.	DEBIT	CREDIT	
			GENERAL JOURNAL			PAGE _____	
17	*19–*						17
18	*Oct.*	*7*	*Payroll Tax Expense*		*5 1 8 46*		18
19			*FICA Tax Payable*			*4 5 5 47*	19
20			*Federal Unemployment Tax*				20
21			*Payable*			*8 13*	21
22			*State Unemployment Tax Payable*			*5 4 86*	22
23			*To record employer's share of*				23
24			*FICA tax and employer's*				24
25			*federal and state*				25
26			*unemployment taxes.*				26

JOURNAL ENTRIES FOR RECORDING PAYROLL

At this point let us restate in general journal form the entries that have been recorded, using the payroll register illustrated in Chapter 9 (Figure 9-4) as the source of information. We'll do this so that you can see the sequence of the payroll entries. First, the entry to record the payroll is journalized.

	DATE		DESCRIPTION	POST. REF.	DEBIT	CREDIT	
1	*19–*						1
2	*Oct.*	*7*	*Sales Salary Expense*		*5 0 3 3 00*		2
3			*Office Salary Expense*		*2 0 1 0 00*		3
4			*Employees' Federal Income Tax*				4
5			*Payable*			*9 2 3 00*	5
6			*Employees' State Income Tax*				6
7			*Payable*			*1 8 4 60*	7
8			*FICA Tax Payable*			*4 5 5 47*	8
9			*Employees' Medical Insurance*				9
10			*Payable*			*2 6 4 00*	10
11			*Employees' United Way Payable*			*2 4 00*	11
12			*Accounts Receivable*			*4 0 00*	12
13			*Salaries Payable*			*5 1 5 1 93*	13
14			*Payroll register, page 68*				14
15			*for week ended October 7.*				15
16							16

Next, the entry to record the employer's payroll taxes is journalized.

	DATE	DESCRIPTION	POST. REF.	DEBIT	CREDIT	
17	Oct. 7	*Payroll Tax Expense*		5 1 8 46		17
18		*FICA Tax Payable*			4 5 5 47	18
19		*Federal Unemployment Tax*				19
20		*Payable*			8 13	20
21		*State Unemployment Tax Payable*			5 4 86	21
22		*To record employer's share*				22
23		*of FICA tax and employer's*				23
24		*federal and state unemployment*				24
25		*taxes.*				25
26						26

Finally, the entry to pay the employees is journalized. Gilbert and Associates issues one check payable to a payroll bank account. To pay its employees, it will draw separate payroll checks on this payroll bank account.

	DATE	DESCRIPTION	POST. REF.	DEBIT	CREDIT	
27	Oct. 7	*Salaries Payable*		5 1 5 1 93		27
28		*Cash*			5 1 5 1 93	28
29		*Paid salaries for week*				29
30		*ended October 7. Issued*				30
31		*check no. 667, payable to*				31
32		*special payroll bank*				32
33		*account.*				33

As stated previously, in the first payroll entry, small employers will credit Cash directly instead of Salaries Payable. These employers will issue separate checks out of their regular bank accounts for each employee.

Next, we will describe the entries for paying withholdings for employees' federal income tax and FICA tax and the employer's matching share of FICA tax. We will also show the entries paying the federal and state unemployment taxes as well as the withholdings for employees' state income tax.

PAYMENTS OF FICA TAX AND EMPLOYEES' FEDERAL INCOME TAX WITHHOLDING

After paying employees, the employer must make payments in the form of federal tax deposits. A deposit includes the combined total of three items: (1) employees' federal income taxes withheld, plus (2) employees'

Objective 2

Journalize the entry for the deposit of employees' federal income taxes withheld and FICA taxes (both employees' withheld and employer's matching share).

FICA taxes withheld, plus (3) employer's share of FICA taxes. These deposits put employers on a pay-as-you-go basis.

Deposits are made to authorized commercial banks or Federal Reserve banks. The deposits are forwarded to the U.S. Treasury. The timing of these deposits depends on the amounts owed. In this regard, employers are divided into three classes.

Small-Sized Employers

These are employers whose total of undeposited employees' federal income taxes and FICA taxes at the end of any calendar **quarter** (three months) is less than an assumed $500. **These employers are not required to make deposits until they submit their quarterly return, Form 941.** Now remember that we are talking about a quarter of a year. The due dates for filing Form 941, Employer's Quarterly Tax Return, are:

Quarter	Ending Date of Quarter	Due Date of Form 941
January-February-March	March 31	April 30
April-May-June	June 30	July 31
July-August-September	September 30	October 31
October-November-December	December 31	January 31

We will show a Form 941 later in this chapter.

Medium-Sized Employers

These are employers whose total undeposited employees' federal income taxes and FICA taxes at the end of the month is between an assumed $500 and $2,999.99. **These employers must make deposits within fifteen days after the end of the month.** For example, on April 30 an employer has undeposited taxes amounting to $640; the deposit must be made by May 15.

Large-Sized Employers

These are employers whose total of undeposited employees' federal income taxes and FICA taxes is an assumed $3,000 or more for an eighth-of-a-month period (approximately three or four days). **Deposits must be made within three banking days after the end of the payroll period** and must include 95 percent of the tax liability. Note that these amounts are cumulative (described below). These **eighth-of-a-month periods** end on the 3rd, 7th, 11th, 15th, 19th, 22nd, 25th, and last day of any month. For example, assume that an employer has $5,140 of undeposited taxes for an eighth-of-a-month period ending on Friday, August 14. Since banks are traditionally closed on Saturday and Sunday, the employer would have to make the deposit by Wednesday, August 19.

Let's go back to Gilbert and Associates, where taxes were previously paid up to date. From the payroll of October 7, the following federal taxes are owed:

Employees' federal income taxes withheld	$ 923.00
Employees' FICA taxes withheld	455.47
Employer's share of FICA taxes	455.47
Total federal undeposited taxes	$1,833.94

Because Gilbert's tax liability is less than $3,000, it is not necessary for Gilbert to make a deposit at this time.

We continue on for the next payroll period ended October 14:

	Oct. 7	Oct. 14	Total
Employees' federal income taxes withheld	$ 923.00	$1,089.14	$2,012.14
Employees' FICA taxes withheld	455.47	537.45	992.92
Employer's share of FICA taxes	455.47	537.45	992.92
Total federal undeposited taxes	$1,833.94	$2,164.04	$3,997.98

Because Gilbert's cumulative tax liability is now more than $3,000, it is necessary to make a deposit within three banking days after October 14. (Using our example, we will say October 17.)

Gilbert and Associates previously received a federal tax deposit card (preprinted with the company's name and tax number) from the Internal Revenue Service. The accountant records the amount of the deposit and the name of the bank where the deposit is submitted. The entry in general journal form to record the deposit of three weeks' taxes looks like this:

DATE		DESCRIPTION	POST. REF.	DEBIT	CREDIT
19–					
Oct.	17	*Employees' Federal Income Tax*			
		Payable		2 0 1 2 14	
		FICA Tax Payable		1 9 8 5 84	
		Cash			3 9 9 7 98
		Issued check for federal tax			
		deposit.			

T accounts, including the posting of the payroll entries (employees' income and FICA taxes withheld) and recording of the payroll tax expense (employer's share of FICA taxes) for the three weekly payroll periods look like this:

Employee's Federal Income Tax Payable					FICA Tax Payable		
−		+			−		+
Oct. 17 2,012.14		Oct. 7 923.00			Oct. 17 1,985.84		Oct. 7 455.47
		14 1,089.14					7 455.47
							14 537.45
Cash							14 537.45
+		−					
		Oct. 17 3,997.98					

PAYMENTS OF STATE UNEMPLOYMENT INSURANCE

Objective 3

Journalize the entries for the payment of employer's state and federal unemployment taxes.

As we stated previously, states differ with regard to both the rate and the taxable base for unemployment insurance. In our example, we have assumed the state tax is 5.4 percent of the first $7,000 paid to each employee during the calendar year. The state tax is usually paid quarterly (every three months) and is due by the end of the month following the end of the quarter (same as the due dates for Form 941). Here's the entry in general journal form made by Gilbert and Associates for the first quarter (covering the months of January, February, and March). We will assume that $59,142 was taxable for the quarter. The amount of the tax is $3,193.67 ($59,142 × .054).

DATE		DESCRIPTION	POST. REF.	DEBIT	CREDIT
19–					
Apr.	30	*State Unemployment Tax Payable*		3 1 9 3 67	
		Cash			3 1 9 3 67
		Issued check for payment of			
		state unemployment tax.			

The T accounts are as follows:

Cash					State Unemployment Tax Payable		
+		−			−		+
		Apr. 30 3,193.67			Apr. 30 3,193.67		Mar. 31 Balance 3,193.67

The balance in State Unemployment Tax Payable is the result of weekly entries recording the state unemployment portion of payroll tax expense.

PAYMENTS OF FEDERAL UNEMPLOYMENT INSURANCE

The FUTA tax is calculated quarterly, during the month following the end of each calendar quarter. **If the accumulated tax liability is greater than an assumed $100, the tax is deposited in a commercial bank or Federal Reserve bank, accompanied by a preprinted federal tax deposit card,** like the form used to deposit employees' federal income tax withholding and FICA taxes. The due date for this deposit is the last day of the month following the end of the quarter, the same as the due dates for the Employer's Quarterly Federal Tax Return and for state unemployment taxes.

Here is the entry in general journal form made by Gilbert and Associates for the first quarter. In our example, since the FUTA and state unemployment taxable earnings are the same (the first $7,000 for each employee), we will assume that $59,142 was taxable for the quarter. The amount of the tax is $473.14 ($59,142 × .008).

DATE	DESCRIPTION	POST. REF.	DEBIT	CREDIT
19–				
Apr. 30	*Federal Unemployment Tax Payable*		4 7 3 14	
	Cash			4 7 3 14
	Issued check for deposit of			
	federal unemployment tax.			

The T accounts are as follows:

Cash				Federal Unemployment Tax Payable			
+		–		–		+	
		Apr. 30 473.14		Apr. 30 473.14		Mar. 31 Balance 473.14	

The balance in Federal Unemployment Tax Payable is the result of weekly entries recording the federal unemployment portion of payroll tax expense.

DEPOSITS OF EMPLOYEES' STATE INCOME TAX WITHHOLDING

Objective 4

Journalize the entry to deposit employees' state income taxes withheld.

Assume the withholdings for employees' state income tax are deposited on a quarterly basis, payable at the same time as state unemployment insurance. Also, as of March 31, the credit balance of Employees' State Income Tax Payable is $1,550.14. The entry in general journal form to record the payment for the first quarter looks like this:

	DATE		DESCRIPTION	POST. REF.	DEBIT	CREDIT
	19–					
	Apr.	*30*	*Employees' State Income Tax*			
			Payable		1 5 5 0 14	
			Cash			1 5 5 0 14
			Issued check for state income			
			tax deposit.			

The T accounts are as follows:

Cash			
+		–	
		Apr. 30 1,550.14	

Employees' State Income Tax Payable			
–		+	
Apr. 30 1,550.14		Mar. 31 Balance 1,550.14	

EMPLOYER'S QUARTERLY FEDERAL TAX RETURN (FORM 941)

Objective 5

Complete employer's quarterly federal tax return, Form 941.

The purpose of **Form 941** is to report the tax liability for withholdings of employees' federal income tax and FICA tax as well as the employer's share of FICA taxes. Total tax deposits are also listed. As the title implies, the time period is three months. As we stated previously, the due dates for the calendar year are: first quarter, April 30; second quarter, July 31; third quarter, October 31; fourth quarter, January 31.

A completed Form 941 for Gilbert and Associates is shown in Figure 10-2 on page 306. Referring to the form, there are three main sections, which may be completed in the order presented below. Bear in mind that the Internal Revenue Service has frequently changed the arrangement and questions on Form 941.

Heading

Once an employer has secured an identification number and has filed her or his first return, the Internal Revenue Service sends forms directly to the employer. These forms have the employer's name, address, and identification number filled in.

Record of Federal Tax Liability

For each payroll period, list the combined total of employees' federal income and FICA taxes withheld and employer's share of FICA. Gilbert and Associates pays the full amount due rather than using the 95 percent rule, so the box is not checked. Gilbert and Associates pays wages every

FIGURE 10-2

Form **941**

Department of the Treasury
Internal Revenue Service

4141

Employer's Quarterly Federal Tax Return

▶ **For Paperwork Reduction Act Notice, see page 2.**
Please type or print.

OMB No. 1545-0029

Your name, address, employer identification number, and calendar quarter of return. (If not correct, please change.)

Name (as distinguished from trade name)

Trade name, if any
Gilbert and Associates

Address and ZIP code
201 Fifth Avenue
Mercer, South Dakota 57814

Date quarter ended
December 31, 19--

Employer identification number
64-7218463

| T |
| FF |
| FD |
| FP |
| I |
| T |

If address is different from prior return, check here ▶ ☐

IRS Use

1 1 1 1 1 1 1 1 1 1 1   2   3 3 3 3 3 3   4 4 4

5 5 5   6   7   8 8 8 8 8 8   9 9 9   10 10 10 10 10 10 10 10 10

If you are not liable for returns in the future, check here . . . ▶ ☐   Date final wages paid . . . . . ▶

Complete for First Quarter Only

1a	Number of employees (except household) employed in the pay period that includes March 12th ▶	**1a**	
b	If you are a subsidiary corporation AND your parent corporation files a consolidated Form 1120, enter parent corporation employer identification number (EIN) . . ▶ **1b** ☐ –		
2	Total wages and tips subject to withholding, plus other compensation . . . . ▶	**2**	100,238 00
3	Total income tax withheld from wages, tips, pensions, annuities, sick pay, gambling, etc. . . . ▶	**3**	14,012 00
4	Adjustment of withheld income tax for preceding quarters of calendar year (see instructions) . . ▶	**4**	------- --
5	Adjusted total of income tax withheld	**5**	14,012 00
6	Taxable social security wages paid . . . . $ _____82,138 00_ × 15.2%(.152)	**6**	12,484 98
7a	Taxable tips reported . . . . $ _____ × 15.2%(.152)	**7a**	------- --
b	Taxable hospital insurance wages paid . . . $ _____ × 2.9% (.029). .	**7b**	------- --
8	Total social security taxes (add lines 6, 7a, and 7b)	**8**	12,484 98
9	Adjustment of social security taxes (see instructions for required explanation)	**9**	------- --
10	Adjusted total of social security taxes (see instructions) . . . . ▶	**10**	12,484 98
11	Backup withholding (see instructions)	**11**	------- --
12	Adjustment of backup withholding tax for preceding quarters of calendar year . . . . . . ▶	**12**	------- --
13	Adjusted total of backup withholding	**13**	------- --
14	Total taxes (add lines 5, 10, and 13)	**14**	26,496 98
15	Advance earned income credit (EIC) payments, if any . . . . ▶	**15**	------- --
16	Net taxes (subtract line 15 from line 14). **This must equal line IV below** (plus line IV of Schedule A (Form 941) if you have treated backup withholding as a separate liability).	**16**	26,496 98
17	Total deposits for quarter, including overpayment applied from a prior quarter, from your records ▶	**17**	26,496 98
18	Balance due (subtract line 17 from line 16). This should be less than $500. Pay to IRS . . . ▶	**18**	0
19	If line 17 is more than line 16, enter overpayment here ▶ $ _____ and check if to be: ☐ Applied to next return **OR** ☐ Refunded.		

Record of Federal Tax Liability (Complete if line 16 is $500 or more.) See the instructions under rule 4 for details before checking these boxes.

Check only if you made eighth-monthly deposits using the 95% rule ▶ ☐   Check only if you are a first time 3-banking-day depositor ▶ ☐

	Date wages paid	Tax liability ▼ *Do NOT Show Federal Tax Deposits Below* ▼						
			First month of quarter		Second month of quarter		Third month of quarter	
	1st through 3rd	A		I		Q	2,171.30	
	4th through 7th	B	1,833.94	J	1,932.51	R		
	8th through 11th	C		K	2,004.12	S	2,173.94	
	12th through 15th	D	2,164.04	M			2,172.40	
	16th through 19th	E		M	2,126.47			
	20th through 22nd	F	2,012.16	N		V		
	23rd through 25th	G		O	2,140.32	W	1,939.06	
	26th through the last	H	2,059.48	P		X	1,767.24	
	Total liability for month	I	8,069.62	II	8,203.42	III	10,223.94	

(watermark: Do Not Show Tax Deposits Here)

IV Total for quarter (add lines **I, II,** and **III**). **This must equal line 16 above** . . . . . . ▶   26,496.98

Under penalties of perjury, I declare that I have examined this return, including accompanying schedules and statements, and to the best of my knowledge and belief, it is true, correct, and complete.

Signature ▶ *James M. Gilbert*   Title ▶ Owner   Date ▶ 1/31/--

week, resulting in 13 paydays during the three-month period, as follows: October 7, 14, 21, 28, November 4, 11, 18, 25, December 2, 9, 16, 23, 30.

Questions Listed on Form 941

Read each question line by line.

1. Total number of employees during first quarter.
2. Total wages and tips subject to federal tax withholding.
3. Total federal income tax withheld—shown as credits in the Employees' Federal Income Tax Payable account.
4. Adjustments of federal income tax withheld—used to record corrections in income tax withheld in earlier quarters of the same calendar year.
6. Taxable Social Security wages paid—total of the FICA Taxable Earnings listed in the payroll register for the three-month quarter. 15.2 percent equals the employees' 7.6 percent plus the employer's 7.6 percent.
7. a. Taxable tips—refers to customer tips reported by employees; the employer withholds 7.6 percent.
   b. Taxable hospital insurance—pertains to federal government employees only.
9. Adjustment of Social Security taxes—used to record corrections in Social Security taxes reported on earlier returns.
11. Backup withholding—applies to payers (not employers) of interest, and dividends to recipients who have not given their Social Security numbers.
15. Advance earned income credit payments—pertains to payments made in advance to qualified employees for earned income credit. To be eligible for this credit, the filing status must be married filing a joint return, qualifying widow(er) with a dependent child, or head of household. Other requirements are having a child living in the home, having a twelve-month tax year, and earnings less than $15,432.
16. Net taxes—equals the total federal tax liability for the quarter (same amount as the total of the record of federal tax liability section).
17. Total deposits for quarter—total of the debits to the Employees' Federal Income Tax Payable and the FICA Tax Payable accounts for the three-month quarter.

Wage Withholding Statements for Employees (Forms W-2)

Objective 6

Prepare W-2 forms and W-3 forms.

After the end of a year (December 31) and by the following January 31, the employer must furnish each employee a Wage and Tax Statement known as **Form W-2**. This form contains information about the employee's earnings and tax deductions for the year. The source of information for completing Form W-2 is the employee's individual earnings record. Arnold L. Lacey's earnings record with his earnings up to October 7 was presented in Chapter 9 on page 284. The amounts used to complete Lacey's W-2 form (in Figure 10-3) represent the amounts taken from his earnings record at the end of the calendar year, December 31.

FIGURE 10-3

1 Control Number		22222	For Paperwork Reduction Act Notice, see back of Copy D. OMB No. 1545-0008	For Official Use Only ▶		
2 Employer's Name, Address, and ZIP Code Gilbert and Associates 201 Fifth Avenue Mercer, South Dakota 57814				**3 Employer's Identification Number** 64-7218463		**4 Employer's State I.D. Number** 464-729
				5 Statutory Employee ☐ Deceased ☐ Pension Plan ☐ Legal Rep. ☐	942 Emp. ☐ Subtotal ☐ Deferred Compensation ☐ Void ☐	
				6 Allocated Tips 0		**7 Advance EIC Payment** 0
8 Employee's Social Security Number 543-24-1680		**9 Federal Income Tax Withheld** $3,739.00		**10 Wages, Tips, Other Compensation** $32,516.00		**11 Social Security Tax Withheld** $2,417.22
12 Employee's Name (First, Middle, Last) Arnold L. Lacey				**13 Social Security Wages** $32,516.00		**14 Social Security Tips** 0
6242 Harold Drive Mercer, South Dakota 57814				**16 ***		**16a** Fringe Benefits Incl. in Box 10 0
				17 State Income Tax $747.80	**18 State Wages, Tips, Etc.** $32,516.00	**19 Name of State** So. Dakota
				20 Local Income Tax	**21 Local Wages, Tips, Etc.**	**22 Name of Locality**
15 Employee's Address and ZIP Code						

Form **W-2 Wage and Tax Statement 1987**
36-2515832 I.R.S. APP.

COPY A For Social Security Administration
*See Instructions for Form W-2 and W-2P

Department of the Treasury
Internal Revenue Service

Notice the squares in block 5. Statutory employees are life insurance and traveling salespersons; legal representatives include attorneys and parents; 942 employees include household workers; subtotal is used if the employer is submitting more than forty-one W-2 forms. Block 7 shows the total paid to employees as advance earned income credit payments. For qualifying low-income taxpayers, the earned income credit is a deduction from income tax owed. Block 16 is used for miscellaneous items, such as sick pay not included in income, because the employee contributed to the sick pay plan. This block is also used for employer-provided group term life insurance of over $50,000. Block 16a shows the value on noncash fringe benefits, such as providing a vehicle for the employee.

The accountant will prepare at least four copies of W-2 forms for each employee.

Copy A—Employer sends to the Social Security Administration.

Copy B—Employer gives to employee to be attached to the employee's individual federal income tax return.

Copy C—Employer gives to employee to be kept for his or her personal records.

Copy D—Employer keeps this copy as a record of payments made.

If state and local income taxes are withheld, the employer prepares additional copies to be sent to the appropriate tax agency.

Employer's Annual Federal Income Tax Reports (Forms W-3)

Accompanying copy A of the employees' W-2 forms, Gilbert and Associates sends Form W-3, Transmittal of Income and Tax Statements, to the Social Security Administration. This form is due on February 28, following the end of the calendar year.

For all employees, Form W-3 shows the total wages and tips, total federal income tax withheld, total FICA taxable wages, total FICA tax withheld, and other information. These amounts must be the same as the grand totals of the W-2 forms and the four quarterly 941 forms for the year. Gilbert and Associates' completed Form W-3 is presented in Figure 10-4.

To sum up thus far: The employer must submit the following at the end of the calendar year: Employer's Quarterly Federal Tax Return, Form 941, for the fourth quarter by January 31; Wage and Tax Statements, Form W-2, for all employees by January 31; Transmittal of Income and Tax Statements, Form W-3, by February 28.

FIGURE 10-4

DO NOT STAPLE

1 Control number	33333	For Official Use Only ▶ OMB No. 1545-0008			
☐ **Kind of Payer** ▶	2 941/941E ☒ Military ☐ 943 ☐ CT-1 ☐ 942 ☐ Medicare gov't. emp. ☐		3	4	5 Number of statements attached 12
6 Allocated tips 0	7 Advance EIC payments 0		8		
9 Federal income tax withheld $46,184.00	10 Wages, tips, and other compensation $352,412.00		11 Social security tax withheld $25,224.71		
12 Employer's state I.D. number 464-729	13 Social security wages $332,562.00		14 Social security tips 0		
15 Employer's identification number 64 7218463			16 Establishment number 0		
17 Employer's name Gilbert and Associates 201 Fifth Street Mercer, South Dakota 57814			18 Gross annuity, pension, etc. (Form W-2P) 0		
			20 Taxable amount (Form W-2P) 0		
			21 Income tax withheld by third-party payer 0		
19 Employer's address and ZIP code (If available, place label over boxes 15, 17, and 19.)					

Under penalties of perjury, I declare that I have examined this return and accompanying documents, and to the best of my knowledge and belief they are true, correct, and complete. In the case of documents without recipients' identifying numbers, I have complied with the requirements of the law in attempting to secure such numbers from the recipients.

Signature ▶ *James M. Gilbert*   Title ▶ Owner   Date ▶ 2/26/--

Form **W-3 Transmittal of Income and Tax Statements**   Department of the Treasury Internal Revenue Service

REPORTS AND PAYMENTS OF FEDERAL UNEMPLOYMENT INSURANCE

As we stated previously, generally all employers are subject to the Federal Unemployment Tax Act. These employers must submit an Employer's Annual Federal Unemployment Tax Return, **Form 940,** not later than January 31 following the close of the calendar year. This deadline may be extended until February 10 if the employer has made deposits paying the FUTA tax liability in full. The FUTA tax is calculated quarterly, during the month following the end of each calendar quarter. **If the accumulated tax liability is greater than $100, the tax is deposited in a commercial bank or Federal Reserve bank, accompanied by a preprinted federal tax deposit card.** The due date for this deposit is the last day of the month following the end of the quarter, the same as the dates for the Employer's Quarterly Federal Tax Return and state unemployment taxes.

Using Gilbert and Associates as our example, federal unemployment taxable earnings by quarter are as follows:

Federal Unemployment Tax	1st Quarter	2nd Quarter	3rd Quarter	4th Quarter	Cumulative Total
Taxable earnings	$59,142	$9,158	$14,046	$1,654	$84,000
Tax rate	× .008	× .008	× .008	×.008	× .008
Tax liability	$473.14	$73.26	$112.37	$13.23	$672.00

We now repeat the journal entry for the first quarter, as shown on page 304, in which $473.14 was deposited on April 30.

DATE		DESCRIPTION	POST. REF.	DEBIT	CREDIT
19–					
Apr.	30	Federal Unemployment Tax Payable		4 7 3 14	
		Cash			4 7 3 14
		Issued check for deposit of			
		federal unemployment tax.			

During the second quarter, many employees' total earnings had passed the $7,000 limit of taxable earnings, and the firm's tax liability was reduced accordingly. However, due to an expansion of the company, three new employees were hired during the middle of the quarter. Since Gilbert's total accumulated liability ($73.26) was less than $100, a deposit was not made covering that quarter.

For the third quarter, the tax liability amounted to $112.37. The total cumulative tax liability was now $185.63 ($73.26 second quarter plus $112.37 third quarter). Consequently, $185.63 was deposited on October 31.

By the end of the fourth quarter, each of the twelve employee's earnings has passed the $7,000 mark. The total liability for the quarter is $13.23. This amount will be paid by January 31, accompanied by the completed Employer's Annual Federal Unemployment Tax Return, Form 940.

The T account for Federal Unemployment Tax Payable is presented below. The credits to the account were part of the entries recording the federal unemployment tax portion of Payroll Tax Expense for each payroll period (like the entry on page 299).

Federal Unemployment Tax Payable

−		+	
April 30 deposit	473.14	1st quarter (liability)	473.14
Oct. 31 deposit	185.63	2nd quarter (liability)	73.26
		3rd quarter (liability)	112.37
Jan. 31 deposit	13.23	4th quarter (liability)	13.23

Employer's Annual Federal Unemployment (FUTA) Tax Return (Form 940)

Figure 10-5 on the next page shows a completed Form 940 for Gilbert and Associates. Referring to the form, we are concerned with three sections. Bear in mind that this form has been changed from time to time.

Part I   Line 1 Record total wages paid.

Line 3 Record exempt wages paid—wages paid to each employee over and above $7,000 for the calendar year.

Line 2 Record certain other exempt wages—includes such items as agricultural labor, family employment, value of meals and lodging.

Line 5 Record the difference between total wages paid and exempt wages, which amount to the taxable wages (earnings).

Line 6 For certain states, multiply taxable wages by the specified decimal. This adjustment increases the FUTA tax.

Part II   Line 1 Multiply taxable wages by .008 to determine amount of tax owed.

Line 4 Record the total amount of deposits made during the year—shown as debits in the Federal Unemployment Tax Payable account. As we stated previously, when the amount exceeds $100 at the end of any calendar quarter, the money must be deposited in an authorized financial institution (same as banks use for federal income and FICA taxes).

Line 5 Balance due—credit balance in Federal Unemployment Tax Payable account as of December 31.

Part IV Record the tax liability for each quarter—total credits in the Federal Unemployment Tax Payable account for each three-month period.

FIGURE 10-5

Form **940** Department of the Treasury Internal Revenue Service	**Employer's Annual Federal Unemployment (FUTA) Tax Return** ▶ For Paperwork Reduction Act Notice, see page 2.	OMB No. 1545-0028

	T	
	FF	
	FD	
	FP	
	I	
	T	

If incorrect, make any necessary change. ▶

Name (as distinguished from trade name)   Calendar year 19--

Trade name, if any
Gilbert and Associates
Address and ZIP code
201 Fifth Avenue
Mercer, South Dakota 57814

Employer identification number
64-7218463

A   Did you pay all required contributions to state unemployment funds by the due date of Form 940? (See instructions if none required.) . . . . [X] **Yes** ☐ **No**
     If you checked the "Yes" box, enter the amount of contributions paid to state unemployment funds . . . . ▶ $ _____ 4,536 00
B   Are you required to pay contributions to only one state? . . . . [X] **Yes** ☐ **No**
     If you checked the "Yes" box: (1) Enter the name of the state where you are required to pay contributions . . . . . . ▶ _____ South Dakota
     (2) Enter your state reporting number(s) as shown on state unemployment tax return. ▶ _____ 463-227 _____
C   If any part of wages taxable for FUTA tax is exempt from state unemployment tax, check the box. (See the Specific Instructions on page 2.) . . . . ☐

Part I   Computation of Taxable Wages and Credit Reduction (to be completed by all taxpayers)

1	Total payments (including exempt payments) during the calendar year for services of employees	1	352,412	00
2	Exempt payments. (Explain each exemption shown, attaching additional sheets if necessary.) ▶ _____	Amount paid **2**			
3	Payments for services of more than $7,000. Enter only the excess over the first $7,000 paid to individual employees not including exempt amounts shown on line 2. Do not use the state wage limitation.	**3** 268,412 00			
4	Total exempt payments (add lines 2 and 3)	4	268,412	00
5	**Total taxable wages** (subtract line 4 from line 1). (If any part is exempt from state contributions, see instructions.)▶	5	84,000	00
6	Additional tax resulting from credit reduction for unpaid advances to the state listed below (by two-letter Postal Service abbreviation). Enter the wages included on line 5 above for that state and multiply by the rate shown. (See the instructions.) Enter the credit reduction amount here and in Part II, line 2, or Part III, line 4: PA _____ x .015= ▶	6		

Part II   Tax Due or Refund (Complete if you checked the "Yes" boxes in both questions A and B and did not check the box in C, above.)

1	FUTA tax. Multiply the wages in Part I, line 5, by .008 and enter here	1	672	00
2	Enter amount from Part I, line 6	2	---	--
3	**Total FUTA tax** (add lines 1 and 2)	3	672	00
4	Minus: Total FUTA tax deposited for the year, including any overpayment applied from a prior year (from your records)	4	658	77
5	**Balance due** (subtract line 4 from line 3). This should be $100 or less. Pay to IRS . . . . ▶	5	13	23
6	**Overpayment** (subtract line 3 from line 4). Check if it is to be: ☐ Applied to next return, or ☐ Refunded ▶	6		

Part III   Tax Due or Refund (Complete if you checked the "No" box in either question A or B or you checked the box in C, above. Also complete Part V.)

1	Gross FUTA tax. Multiply the wages in Part I, line 5, by .062	1	
2	Maximum credit. Multiply the wages in Part I, line 5, by .054	**2**	
3	Enter the smaller of the amount in Part V, line 11, or Part III, line 2 . . .	**3**	
4	Enter amount from Part I, line 6	4	
5	**Credit allowable** (subtract line 4 from line 3). (If zero or less, enter 0.) . . .	5	
6	**Total FUTA tax** (subtract line 5 from line 1)	6	
7	Minus: Total FUTA tax deposited for the year, including any overpayment applied from a prior year (from your records)	7	
8	**Balance due** (subtract line 7 from line 6). This should be $100 or less. Pay to IRS . . . . ▶	8	
9	**Overpayment** (subtract line 6 from line 7). Check if it is to be: ☐ Applied to next return, or ☐ Refunded ▶	9	

Part IV   Record of Quarterly Federal Tax Liability for Unemployment Tax (Do not include state liability.)

Quarter	First	Second	Third	Fourth	Total for Year
Liability for quarter	473.14	73.26	112.37	13.23	672.00

If you will not have to file returns in the future, write "Final" here (see general instruction "Who Must File") and sign the return. ▶

Under penalties of perjury, I declare that I have examined this return, including accompanying schedules and statements, and to the best of my knowledge and belief, it is true, correct, and complete, and that no part of any payment made to a state unemployment fund claimed as a credit was or is to be deducted from the payments to employees.

Signature ▶ *James M. Gilbert*   Title (Owner, etc.) ▶ Owner   Date ▶ 1/31/--

Form **940**

WORKERS' COMPENSATION INSURANCE

As we said in Chapter 9 when we were describing the law affecting employment, most states require employers to provide **workers' compensation insurance** or industrial accident insurance, either through plans administered by the state or through private insurance companies authorized by the state. The employer usually has to pay all the premiums. The premium rate varies with the amount of risk the job entails and the company's number of accidents. For example, handling molten steel ingots is much more dangerous than typing reports. So it is very important that employees be identified properly according to the insurance premium classifications. For example, the rates as percentages of the payroll may be .15 percent for office work, .5 percent for sales work, and 3.5 percent for industrial labor in heavy manufacturing. These same rates may be expressed as 15¢ per $100 of the salaries or wages for office work, 50¢ per $100 for sales work, and $3.50 per $100 for industrial labor.

Generally, the employer pays a premium in advance, based on the estimated payrolls for the year. After the year ends, the employer knows the exact amounts of the payrolls and can calculate the exact premium. At this time, depending on the difference between the estimated and the exact premium, the employer either pays an additional premium or gets a credit for overpayment.

At Gilbert and Associates, there are two types of work classifications: office work and sales work. At the beginning of the year, the firm's accountant computed the estimated annual premium, based on the predicted payrolls for the year, as follows:

Classification	Predicted Payroll	Rate (Percent)	Estimated Premium
Office work	$ 76,000	.15	$ 76,000 × .0015 = $ 114
Sales work	270,000	.5	270,000 × .005 = 1,350
			Total estimated premium $1,464

As shown by T accounts, the acountant made the following entry.

Prepaid Insurance, Workers' Compensation			Cash	
+	−		+	−
Jan. 10 1,464				Jan. 10 1,464

Then, at the end of the calendar year, the accountant calculated the exact premium.

Classification	Exact Payroll	Rate (Percent)	Exact Premium
Office work	$ 78,000	.15	$ 78,000 × .0015 = $ 117.00
Sales work	274,412	.5	274,412 × .005 = 1,372.06
			Total exact premium $1,489.06

Therefore, the amount of the unpaid premium is

$1,489.06	Total exact premium
1,464.00	Less total estimated premium paid
$ 25.06	Additional premium owed

Objective 8

Determine the amount of adjustment for workers' compensation insurance at end of year, and record adjustment.

Now the accountant makes an adjusting entry, similar to the adjusting entry for expired insurance; this entry appears on the work sheet. The accountant then makes an additional adjusting entry for the extra premium owed. By T accounts, the entries are as follows:

Prepaid Insurance, Workers' Compensation

+		−	
Jan. 10 Bal.	1,464	Dec. 31 Adj.	1,464

Workers' Compensation Insurance Payable

−		+	
		Dec. 31 Adj.	25.06

Workers' Compensation Insurance Expense

+		−
Dec. 31 Adj.	1,464.00	
Dec. 31 Adj.	25.06	

Gilbert and Associates will pay $25.06, the amount of unpaid premium, in January, together with the estimated premium for the next year.

ADJUSTING FOR ACCRUED SALARIES AND WAGES

Assume that $800 of salaries accrue for the time between the last payday and the end of the year. The adjusting entry is the same as that introduced in Chapter 5.

	DATE		DESCRIPTION	POST. REF.	DEBIT	CREDIT	
1			*Adjusting Entry*				1
2	*Dec.*	*31*	*Salary Expense*		8 0 0 00		2
3			*Salaries Payable*			8 0 0 00	3
4							4

Salaries Payable is considered a liability account, as are employees' withholding taxes and deductions payable. Actually, federal income tax and FICA tax levied on employees do not legally become effective until the employees are paid. Therefore, for the purpose of recording the adjusting entry, one includes the entire liability of the gross salaries and wages under Salaries Payable or Wages Payable. In other words, in the adjusting entry such accounts as Employees' Income Tax Payable, FICA Tax Payable (employees' share), and Employees' Union Dues Payable, are not used at this time.

Adjusting Entry for Accrual of Payroll Taxes

As we have seen, the following taxes come under the umbrella of the Payroll Tax Expense account: the employer's share of the FICA tax, the state unemployment tax, and the federal unemployment tax. The employer becomes liable for these taxes only when the employees are actually paid, rather than at the time the liability to the employees is incurred. From the standpoint of legal liability, there should be no adjusting entry for Payroll Tax Expense. From the standpoint of the income statement, however, failure to make this entry means that this accrued expense for payroll taxes is not included; thus the expenses are understated and the net income is overstated, although by a rather inconsequential amount. Although the legal element is not consistent with good accounting practice, we have to abide by the law.

TAX CALENDAR

Now let's put it all together: Assume that the employer's combined monthly totals of employees' FICA tax, employer's FICA tax, and employees' income tax withheld are usually greater than $500 and less than $3,000. So to keep up with the task of paying and reporting the various taxes, the accountant compiles a chronological list of the due dates. We are including only the payroll taxes here; however, sales taxes and property taxes should also be listed. When you think about the penalties for nonpayment of taxes by the due dates, this chronological list seems to be well worth the trouble.

Jan.   10   Pay estimated annual premium for workers' compensation insurance. (This is an approximate date, as it varies among the states.)

          31   Complete Employer's Quarterly Federal Tax Return, Form 941, for the fourth quarter and pay employees' income tax withholding, employees' FICA tax withholding, and employer's FICA tax for wages paid during the month of December.

          31   Issue copies B and C of Wage and Tax statement, Form W-2, to employees.

          31   Pay state unemployment tax liability for the previous quarter and submit state return, employer's tax report.

          31   Pay any remaining federal unemployment tax liability for the previous year and submit Form 940, Employer's Annual Federal Unemployment Tax Return.

Feb.   15   Make federal tax deposit for employees' income tax withholding, employees' FICA tax withholding, and employer's FICA tax for wages paid during the month of January.

          28   Complete Transmittal of Income and Tax Statements, Form W-3, and attach copy A of W-2 forms for employees.

Mar.   15   Make federal tax deposit for employees' income tax withholding, employees' FICA tax withholding, and employer's FICA tax for wages paid during the month of February.

Apr.   30   Pay state unemployment tax liability for the previous quarter and submit state return, employer's tax report.

          30   Complete Employer's Quarterly Federal Tax Return, Form 941, for the first quarter, and pay employees' income tax withholding, employees' FICA tax withholding, and employer's FICA tax for wages paid during the month of March.

          30   Make federal tax deposit for federal unemployment tax liability if it exceeds $100.

          30   Make state deposit for employees' state income tax withholding.

SUMMARY

An employer's taxes with their assumed rates based on the payroll are as follows. Remember that rates are always subject to change.

1. FICA tax is 7.6 percent of the first $45,000 for each employee.
2. Federal unemployment tax is .8 percent of the first $7,000 in taxable income for each employee.
3. State unemployment tax varies from state to state but is approximately 5.4 percent of approximately the first $7,000 in taxable income for each employee.

L.O. 1   After recording each payroll entry from the payroll register, the accountant makes the following type of entry to record the employer's payroll taxes:

DATE		DESCRIPTION	POST. REF.	DEBIT	CREDIT
19–					
Oct.	7	*Payroll Tax Expense*		5 18 46	
		FICA Tax Payable			4 55 47
		Federal Unemployment Tax			
		Payable			8 13
		State Unemployment Tax Payable			5 4 86
		To record employer's share of			
		FICA tax and employer's			
		federal and state unemployment			
		taxes.			

Payment of the tax liabilities and sample journal entries are as follows:

L.O. 2 1. Payment of the combined amounts of employees' federal income tax withheld, employees' FICA tax withheld, and employer's FICA tax falls into three brackets:

   a. **Large**   If at the end of any eighth of a month (approximately three or four days) the cumulative amount of undeposited taxes so far for the calendar quarter (three months) is $3,000 or more, deposit the taxes within three banking days after the end of the deposit period. The Internal Revenue Service divides any month into eight deposit periods ending on the 3rd, 7th, 11th, 15th, 19th, 22nd, 25th, and last day of the month.

   b. **Medium**   If at the end of any month (except the last month of a quarter) the cumulative amount of undeposited taxes for the quarter is at least $500 but less than $3,000, deposit the taxes within fifteen days after the end of the month. For the last month of the quarter, make the payment by the end of the next month.

   c. **Small**   If at the end of a calendar month or calendar quarter (three months) the total amount of undeposited taxes is less than $500, make the payment when submitting the Employer's Quarterly Federal Tax Return.

DATE		DESCRIPTION	POST. REF.	DEBIT	CREDIT
19–					
Oct.	17	*Employees' Federal Income Tax*			
		Payable		2 0 12 14	
		FICA Tax Payable		1 9 85 84	
		Cash			3 9 97 98
		Issued check for federal tax			
		deposit.			

L.O. 3   2. State unemployment tax is paid on a quarterly basis. Payment is due by the end of the next month following the end of the calendar quarter.

	DATE		DESCRIPTION	POST. REF.	DEBIT	CREDIT	
1	19–						1
2	Apr.	30	State Unemployment Tax Payable		3 1 9 3 67		2
3			Cash			3 1 9 3 67	3
4			Issued check for payment of				4
5			state unemployment tax.				5
6							6

3. If the amount of the accumulated federal unemployment tax liability exceeds $100, pay the tax by the end of the next month following the end of the quarter. If the federal unemployment tax payable is less than $100 at the end of the year, pay it by January 31 of the next year.

	DATE		DESCRIPTION	POST. REF.	DEBIT	CREDIT	
1	19–						1
2	Apr.	30	Federal Unemployment Tax Payable		4 7 3 14		2
3			Cash			4 7 3 14	3
4			Issued check for deposit of				4
5			federal unemployment tax.				5
6							6

L.O. 4   4. Employees' state income taxes withheld are paid on a quarterly basis. Payment is due by the end of the next month following the end of the calendar quarter.

	DATE		DESCRIPTION	POST. REF.	DEBIT	CREDIT	
1	19–						1
2	Apr.	30	Employees' State Income Tax				2
3			Payable		1 5 5 0 14		3
4			Cash			1 5 5 0 14	4
5			Issued check for state income				5
6			tax deposit.				6
7							7

L.O. 7,8   5. Workers' compensation insurance is based on a state plan or private insurance. At the beginning of the year, pay the premium in advance based on the estimated annual payroll. At the end of the year, when you know the actual payroll, adjust for the exact amount of the premium.

GLOSSARY

Eighth-of-a-month periods   Periods used to determine the due date of tax deposits, designated by the Internal Revenue Service as follows: from the 1st to the 3rd of the month, from the 4th to the 7th of the month, from the 8th to the 11th of the month, from the 12th to the 15th of the month, from the 16th to the 19th of the month, from the 20th to the 22nd of the month, from the 23rd to the 25th of the month, and from the 26th to the last day of the month. (All dates are inclusive.)

Employer identification number   The number assigned each employer by the Internal Revenue Service for use in the submission of reports and payments for FICA taxes and federal income tax withheld.

Federal unemployment tax   A tax levied on the employer only, amounting to .8 percent of the first $7,000 of total earnings paid to each employee during the calendar year. This tax is used to supplement state unemployment benefits.

Form 940   An annual report filed by employers showing total wages paid to employees, total wages subject to federal unemployment tax, total federal unemployment tax, and other information. Also called the *Employer's Annual Federal Unemployment Tax Return.*

Form 941   A report showing the tax liability for withholdings of employees' federal income tax and FICA tax as well as the employer's share of FICA tax. Total tax deposits made in the quarter are also listed on this Employer's Quarterly Federal Tax Return.

Form W-2   A form containing information about employee earnings and tax deductions for the year. Also called *Wage and Tax Statement.*

Form W-3   An annual report sent to the Social Security Administration listing the total wages and tips, total federal income tax withheld, total FICA taxable wages, total FICA tax withheld, and other information for all employees of a firm. Also called the *Transmittal of Income and Tax Statements.*

Payroll Tax Expense   A general expense account used for recording the employer's matching portion of the FICA tax, the federal unemployment tax, and the state unemployment tax.

Quarter   A three-month interval of the year, also referred to as a *calendar quarter,* as follows: first quarter, January, February, and March; second quarter, April, May, and June; third quarter, July, August, and September; fourth quarter, October, November, and December.

State unemployment tax   A tax levied on the employer only. Rates differ among the various states; however, they are generally 5.4 percent or higher of the first $7,000 of total earnings paid to each employee during the calendar year. The proceeds are used to pay subsistence benefits to unemployed workers.

Workers' compensation insurance   This insurance, usually paid for by the employer, provides benefits for employees injured or killed on the job. The rates vary according to the degree of risk inherent in the job. The plans may be sponsored by states or by private firms. The employer pays the premium in advance at the beginning of the year, based on the estimated payroll. The rates are adjusted after the exact payroll is known.

QUESTIONS, EXERCISES, AND PROBLEMS
Discussion Questions

1. List the correct sequence of steps for recording payroll entries and identify the source of information for each entry. Assume that the company uses a special payroll bank account.
2. What is the purpose of the W-2, W-3, and W-4 forms? To whom are the copies given?
3. What is meant by an eighth-of-a-month period, and why is it important?
4. What is the purpose of Form 941? How often is it prepared, and what are the due dates?
5. Explain the deposit requirement for federal unemployment insurance.
6. What payroll taxes are included under Payroll Tax Expense?
7. Generally, what is the time schedule for payment of premiums of workers' compensation insurance?
8. Explain the advantage of establishing a tax calendar.

Exercises

L.O. 1   **Exercise 10-1**   King Company's payroll for the week ended December 15 is as follows:

Gross earnings of employees	$154,000
FICA taxable earnings	142,000
Federal unemployment taxable earnings	41,000
State unemployment taxable earnings	41,000

Assuming that the payroll is subject to a FICA tax of 7.6 percent (.076), a federal unemployment tax of .8 percent (.008), and a state unemployment tax of 5.4 percent (.054), give the entry in general journal form to record the payroll tax expense.

L.O. 1,2,3   **Exercise 10-2**   The earnings for the calendar year for the employees of Brandon Office Machines are as follows:

Employee	Cumulative Earnings
Belko, C. P.	$ 19,200
Kerry, N. R.	31,500
Nowell, M. E.	46,400
Woods, D. N.	6,800
	$103,900

The employees had to pay FICA tax during the year at the rate of 7.6 percent on the first $45,000 of their earnings; the employer had to pay a matching FICA tax. Unemployment insurance rates were .8 percent for the federal government and 5.4 percent for the state on the first $7,000 of an employee's earnings.

a. Determine the taxable earnings for FICA, federal unemployment, and state unemployment.

b. Determine the amount of tax paid by the employees.

c. Determine the total amount of payroll taxes paid by the employer.

d. What percentage of the employer's total payroll of $103,900 was represented by payroll taxes?

L.O. 1 **Exercise 10-3** On January 7, at the end of the first weekly pay period during the year, the totals of Dowell Taxi's payroll register showed its driver employees had earned $11,000 and its office employees had earned $2,900. The employees were to have FICA taxes withheld at the rate of 7.6 percent of the first $45,000, plus $1,290 of federal income taxes, and $440 of union dues.

a. Calculate the amount of FICA taxes to be withheld, and write the general journal entry to record the payroll. Assume the company uses a special payroll bank account.

b. Write the general journal entry to record the employer's payroll taxes, assuming that the federal unemployment tax is .8 percent of the first $7,000 and the state unemployment tax rate is 5.4 percent of the same base.

L.O. 1,2 **Exercise 10-4** Martin Company's payroll register for the month of January had the following payroll deductions and employer FICA taxes:

Payment Date	Employees' Fed. Inc. Tax	Employees' FICA Tax	Employer's FICA Tax
Jan. 7	1,260	1,060	1,060
14	1,480	1,250	1,250
21	1,530	1,290	1,290
28	1,530	1,290	1,290

Federal taxes are to be paid three days after the payroll payment date. Record the entry for the first payment of federal taxes in general journal form. Assume that a deposit must be made if the federal tax liability exceeds $3,000.

L.O. 1 **Exercise 10-5** Romanoff Construction had the following payroll data for the week ended March 14:

	EMPLOYEE DEDUCTIONS			
TOTAL EARNINGS	FEDERAL INCOME TAX	STATE INCOME TAX	FICA	MEDICAL INSURANCE
3 2 6 0 00	3 5 8 60	1 9 5 60	2 4 7 76	1 5 0 00

a. Record the payroll entry as of March 14 in general journal form. The firm uses a special payroll bank account.

b. Journalize the entry to record the employer's payroll taxes as of March 14. The employer matches the employee deductions for FICA. Assume rates of .8 percent for federal unemployment insurance and 5.4 percent for state unemployment insurance based on the first $7,000 for each employee. No employee has earned over $7,000.

L.O. 2,3   **Exercise 10-6**   On June 30, Anderson Company's selected payroll accounts are as follows:

FICA Tax Payable			State Unemployment Tax Payable		
	June 30	1,960.08		June 30	1,513.89
	June 30	1,960.07			

Federal Unemployment Tax Payable			Employees' Federal Income Tax Payable		
	June 30	224.28		June 30	3,143.26

Prepare general journal entries to record payment of the taxes.

July   3   Record payment of federal tax deposit of FICA and income tax.
        31   Record payment of state unemployment tax.
        31   Record deposit of federal unemployment tax.

L.O. 1   **Exercise 10-7**   The following information on earnings and deductions for the pay period ended December 21 is from Wysocki Company's payroll records:

Name	Gross Pay	Earnings at End of Previous Week
Gamble, J. C.	$210	$ 6,800
Miner, A. R.	620	27,300
Wyatt, S. T.	950	44,900
Yates, T. L.	740	39,400

Prepare a general journal entry to record the employer's payroll taxes. The FICA tax is 7.6 percent of the first $45,000 of earnings for each employee. The federal unemployment tax is .8 (.008) percent of the first $7,000 of earnings of each employee, and the state unemployment tax is 5.4 percent (.054) of the same base.

L.O. 7,8   **Exercise 10-8**   Suppose that you are an accountant for a small business, and you get a premium notice on January 2 for workers' compensation insurance, stating the rates for the new year. You have estimated employees' earnings for the year as follows:

Classification	Estimated Wages and Salaries	Rate, %	Estimated Premium	
Sales work	$64,000	.84		$537.60
Warehouse work	16,000	1.90		304.00
			Total estimated premium	$841.60

a. Record the entry in general journal form for payment of the estimated premium. At the end of the year, the exact figures for the payroll are as follows:

Classification	Estimated Wages and Salaries	Rate, %	Premium	
Sales work	$69,000	.84		$579.60
Warehouse work	17,000	1.90		323.00
			Total actual premium	$902.60
			Less estimated premium paid	841.60
			Balance of premium due	$ 61.00

b. Record the adjusting entries on December 31 for the insurance expired as well as for the additional premium due.

Problem Set A

L.O. 1 **Problem 10-1A** The Backstrom Dental Laboratory had the following payroll for the week ended May 7:

Salaries		Deductions	
Technicians' salaries	$5,580	Federal income tax withheld	$ 861
Office salaries	1,170	FICA tax withheld	513
Total	$6,750	U.S. savings bonds	480
		Medical insurance	540
		Total	$2,394

Assumed tax rates are as follows:

a. FICA tax, 7.6 percent (.076) on the first $45,000 on each employee
b. Federal unemployment tax, .8 percent (.008) on the first $7,000 for each employee
c. State unemployment tax, 5.4 percent (.054) on the first $7,000 for each employee

Instructions

Record the following entries in general journal form:

1. The payroll entry as of May 7, assuming that Backstrom uses a payroll bank account.
2. The entry to record the employer's payroll taxes as of May 7, assuming that the total payroll is subject to the FICA tax and that $4,200 is subject to unemployment taxes.
3. The payment of the employees as of May 9.

L.O. 1 **Problem 10-2A** Myron's Electric has the following payroll information for the week ended December 21:

NAME	EARNINGS AT END OF PREVIOUS WEEK	TOTAL EARNINGS	DEDUCTIONS FEDERAL INCOME TAX	STATE INCOME TAX	MEDICAL INSURANCE
Gaines, S. T.	23 6 4 0 00	7 5 0 00	8 6 00	1 7 20	2 0 00
Howe, J. R.	27 8 2 0 00	7 9 0 00	1 2 0 00	2 4 00	2 5 00
King, C. L.	44 7 0 0 00	1 0 7 0 00	2 0 9 00	4 1 80	2 5 00
Lang, D. E.	6 9 0 0 00	4 3 0 00	6 5 00	1 3 00	1 5 00
Moore, B. A.	15 3 5 0 00	5 9 0 00	7 6 00	1 5 20	1 5 00
Olsen, M. P.	34 7 1 0 00	8 4 0 00	1 3 4 00	2 6 80	2 5 00
	153 1 2 0 00	4 4 7 0 00	6 9 0 00	1 3 8 00	1 2 5 00

Assumed tax rates are as follows:

a. FICA tax, 7.6 percent (.076) on the first $45,000 for each employee
b. Federal unemployment tax, .8 percent (.008) on the first $7,000 for each employee
c. State unemployment tax, 5.4 percent (.054) on the first $7,000 for each employee

Instructions

1. Complete the payroll register.
2. Prepare a general journal entry to record the payroll as of December 21. The company's general ledger contains a Salary Expense account and a Salaries Payable account.
3. Prepare a general journal entry to record the payroll taxes as of December 21.
4. Assuming that the firm uses a special payroll bank account, make the entry in general journal to record payment of salaries, check no. 614 as of December 23. Payroll checks begin with no. 992.

L.O. 5 **Problem 10-3A** For the third quarter of the year, Emerson Property Management, of 516 Ellis Boulevard, San Francisco, California 94159, received Form 941 from the Director of the Internal Revenue Service. The identification number for Emerson Property Management is 79-639112. Its payroll for the quarter ended September 30 is as follows:

| NAME | TOTAL EARNINGS | TAXABLE EARNINGS | | DEDUCTIONS | |
		UNEMPLOYMENT INSURANCE	FICA	INCOME TAX	FICA
Curtis, D. B.	2 9 7 2 00	1 0 5 6 00	2 9 7 2 00	2 7 0 00	2 2 5 87
Farr, W. A.	6 4 2 7 00		6 4 2 7 00	7 2 0 00	4 8 8 45
Griggs, K. M.	7 5 0 0 00		7 5 0 0 00	8 1 3 00	5 7 0 00
Kerr, V. S.	5 9 4 6 00		5 9 4 6 00	6 4 8 00	4 5 1 90
Peck, S. K.	3 2 0 0 00	6 0 0 00	3 2 0 0 00	3 0 6 00	2 4 3 20
Taylor, M. B.	9 6 0 0 00		9 6 0 0 00	1 2 3 6 00	7 2 9 60
	35 6 4 5 00	1 6 5 6 00	35 6 4 5 00	3 9 9 3 00	2 7 0 9 02

The company has had six employees throughout the year. Assume that the FICA tax payable by the employees is 7.6 percent of the first $45,000 of their earnings, and that the FICA tax payable by the employer is also 7.6 percent of the first $45,000 paid to the employees. There are no taxable tips, adjustments, backup withholding, or earned income credits. Emerson Property Management has submitted the following federal tax deposits and written the accompanying checks:

On August 3 for the July Payroll	On September 3 for the August Payroll	On October 3 for the September Payroll
Employees' income tax withheld $1,312.22 Employees' FICA tax withheld 890.26 Employer's FICA tax 890.26 $3,092.74	Employees' income tax withheld $1,335.97 Employees' FICA tax withheld 906.38 Employer's FICA tax 906.38 $3,148.73	Employees' income tax withheld $1,344.81 Employees' FICA tax withheld 912.38 Employer's FICA tax 912.38 $3,169.57

Instructions

Complete Form 941 dated October 28 for the owner Charles Emerson.

L.O. 1,2,3,4

Problem 10-4A The Ruiz Company has the following balances in its general ledger as of June 1 of this year:

a. FICA tax payable (liability for May), $1,218.44
b. Employees' federal income tax payable (liability for May), $961.92
c. Federal unemployment tax payable (liability for April and May), $128.26
d. State unemployment tax payable (liability for April and May), $865.76
e. Medical insurance payable (liability for April and May), $1,080

The company completed the following transactions involving the payroll during June and July:

June   14 Issued check for $2,180.36 payable to the Prudent Bank for the monthly deposit of May FICA taxes and employees' federal income tax withheld.

June   30 Recorded the payroll entry in the general journal from the payroll register for June. The payroll register has the following column totals:

Sales salaries	$6,720.00	
Office salaries	1,296.00	
Total earnings		$8,016.00
Employees' federal income tax deductions	$ 961.92	
Employees' FICA tax deductions	609.22	
Employees' medical insurance	540.00	
Total deductions		2,111.14
Net pay		$5,904.86

     30 Recorded payroll taxes in the general journal. Employees' FICA tax is 7.6 percent, employer's is 7.6 percent, state unemployment insurance is 5.4 percent, and federal unemployment insurance is .8 percent. At this time, all employees' earnings are taxable for FICA and unemployment taxes.

     30 Issued check for $5,904.86 payable to a payroll bank account.

July   14 Issued check for $1,620, payable to Stable Insurance Company, in payment of employees' medical insurance for April, May, and June.

     14 Issued check for $2,180.36, payable to the Prudent Bank for the monthly deposit of June FICA taxes and employees' federal income tax withheld.

     31 Issued check for $1,298.63 payable to the State Tax Commission, for state unemployment tax for April, May, and June. The check was accompanied by the quarterly tax return.

     31 Issued check for $192.39 payable to the Prudent Bank for the deposit of federal unemployment tax for the months of April, May, and June.

Instructions

Record the transactions in the general journal.

Problem Set B

L.O. 1   **Problem 10-1B**   Goldschmidt and Company had the following payroll for the week ended May 21:

Salaries		**Deductions**	
Sales salaries	$4,920	Federal income tax withheld	$ 690.00
Office salaries	840	FICA tax withheld	437.76
Total	$5,760	U.S. savings bonds	450.00
		Medical insurance	480.00
		Total	$2,057.76

Assume tax rates are as follows:

a. FICA tax, 7.6 percent (.076) on the first $45,000 for each employee
b. Federal unemployment tax, .8 percent (.008) on the first $7,000 for each employee
c. State unemployment tax, 5.4 percent (.054) on the first $7,000 for each employee

Instructions

Record the following entries in general journal form:

1. The payroll entry as of May 21, assuming that Goldschmidt uses a payroll bank account.
2. The entry to record the employer's payroll taxes as of May 21, assuming that the total payroll is subject to the FICA tax and that $4,230 is subject to unemployment taxes.
3. The payment of the employees as of May 23.

L.O. 1   **Problem 10-2B**   Hinds Delicatessen has the following payroll information for the week ended December 14:

NAME	EARNINGS AT END OF PREVIOUS WEEK	TOTAL EARNINGS	DEDUCTIONS FEDERAL INCOME TAX	STATE INCOME TAX	MEDICAL INSURANCE
Aiken, D. R.	4 9 0 0 00	4 2 0 00	6 2 00	1 2 40	2 0 00
Ball, C. M.	6 6 0 0 00	5 6 0 00	7 2 00	1 4 40	2 0 00
Coe, R. R.	31 4 0 0 00	8 3 0 00	1 3 1 00	2 6 20	3 0 00
Drake, L. A.	23 2 0 0 00	7 4 0 00	8 4 00	1 6 80	2 7 00
Evers, C. P.	45 5 0 0 00	1 0 9 0 00	2 1 0 00	4 2 00	3 0 00
Flynn, N. H.	19 3 0 0 00	6 7 0 00	8 6 00	1 7 20	2 7 00
	130 9 0 0 00	4 3 1 0 00	6 4 5 00	1 2 9 00	1 5 4 00

Assumed tax rates are as follows:

a. FICA tax, 7.6 percent (.076) on the first $45,000 for each employee
b. Federal unemployment tax, .8 percent (.008) on the first $7,000 for each employee
c. State unemployment tax, 5.4 percent (.054) on the first $7,000 for each employee

Instructions

1. Complete the payroll register.
2. Prepare a general journal entry to record the payroll as of December 14. The company's general ledger contains a Salary Expense account and a Salaries Payable account.
3. Prepare a general journal entry to record the payroll taxes as of December 14.
4. Assuming that the firm uses a special payroll bank account, make the entry in the general journal to record payment of salaries, check no. 522, as of December 16. Payroll checks begin with no. 882.

L.O. 5   **Problem 10-3B**   For the second quarter of the year, Ennis Company, 7334 Baldwin Avenue, Chicago, IL 60649, received Form 941 from the Director of Internal Revenue Service. The identification number of Ennis Company is 72-419368. Its payroll for the quarter ended June 30 is as follows:

		TAXABLE EARNINGS		DEDUCTIONS	
NAME	TOTAL EARNINGS	UNEMPLOYMENT INSURANCE	FICA	INCOME TAX	FICA
Brown, R. N.	5 4 6 0 00	1 5 4 0 00	5 4 6 0 00	5 7 6 00	4 1 4 96
Cross, C. A.	8 4 0 0 00		8 4 0 0 00	9 5 7 00	6 3 8 40
Dailey, J. F.	4 9 1 2 00	2 1 7 6 00	4 9 1 2 00	5 6 9 00	3 7 3 31
Hall, J. F.	3 4 3 6 00	3 4 3 6 00	3 4 3 6 00	3 9 9 00	2 6 1 14
Lyon, D. B.	7 5 0 0 00	2 0 3 0 00	7 5 0 0 00	9 3 6 00	5 7 0 00
Pope, B. H.	5 0 1 0 00		5 0 1 0 00	5 2 2 00	3 8 0 76
	34 7 1 8 00	9 1 8 2 00	34 7 1 8 00	3 9 5 9 00	2 6 3 8 57

The company has had six employees throughout the year. Assume that the FICA tax payable by the employees is 7.6 percent of the first $45,000 of their earnings, and that the FICA tax payable by the employer is also 7.6 percent of the first $45,000 paid to the employees. There are no taxable tips, adjustments, backup withholding, or earned income credits. Ennis Company has submitted the following federal tax deposits and written the accompanying checks:

On May 3 for the April Payroll		On June 3 for the May Payroll		On July 3 for the June Payroll	
Employees' income tax withheld	$1,314.00	Employees' income tax withheld	$1,298.00	Employees' income tax withheld	$1,347.00
Employees' FICA tax withheld	875.75	Employees' FICA tax withheld	865.08	Employees' FICA tax withheld	897.74
Employer's FICA tax	875.75	Employer's FICA tax	865.08	Employer's FICA tax	897.74
Total deposit	$3,065.50	Total deposit	$3,028.16	Total deposit	$3,142.48

For each month of the quarter, tax liabilities and deposits are the same amounts.

Instructions

Complete Form 941 dated July 20 for the owner Alicia Ennis.

L.O. 1,2,3,4   **Problem 10-4B**   The Pruitt Company has the following balances in its general ledger as of March 1 of this year:

a. FICA tax payable (liability for February), $1,378.94
b. Employees' federal income tax payable (liability for February), $1,088

    c. Federal unemployment tax payable (liability for the months of January and February), $145.16

    d. State unemployment tax payable (liability for the months of January and February), $979.83

    e. Medical insurance payable (liability for January and February), $920

The company completed the following transactions involving the payroll during March and April:

Mar. 14 Issued check for $2,466.94 payable to Main Bank and Trust, for monthly deposit of February FICA taxes and employees' federal income tax withheld.

      31 Recorded the payroll entry in the general journal from the payroll register for March. The payroll register had the following column totals:

Sales salaries	$6,942.00	
Office salaries	2,130.00	
Total earnings		$9,072.00
Employees' federal income tax deductions	$1,088.00	
Employees' FICA tax deductions	689.47	
Employees' medical insurance deductions	460.00	
Total deductions		2,237.47
Net pay		$6,834.53

      31 Recorded payroll taxes. Employer's FICA tax is 7.6 percent. State unemployment tax is 5.4 percent. Federal unemployment tax is .8 percent. At this time, all employees' earnings are taxable for FICA and unemployment taxes.

      31 Issued check for $6,834.53, payable to a payroll bank account.

Apr.   3 Issued check for $1,380, payable to Armour Insurance Company, in payment of employees' medical insurance for January, February, and March.

      14 Issued check for $2,466.94, payable to Main Bank and Trust, for monthly deposit of March FICA taxes and employees' federal income tax withheld.

      30 Issued check payable to Main Bank and Trust for deposit of federal unemployment tax for January, February, and March, $217.74.

      30 Issued check for $1,469.72, payable to the State Tax Commission, for state unemployment tax for January, February, and March. The check was accompanied by the quarterly tax return.

Instructions

Record the transactions in the general journal.

REVIEW OF T ACCOUNT PLACEMENT AND REPRESENTATIVE TRANSACTIONS: CHAPTERS 7 THROUGH 10

Review of T Account Placement

The following sums up the placement of T accounts covered in Chapters 7 through 10 in relation to the fundamental accounting equation.

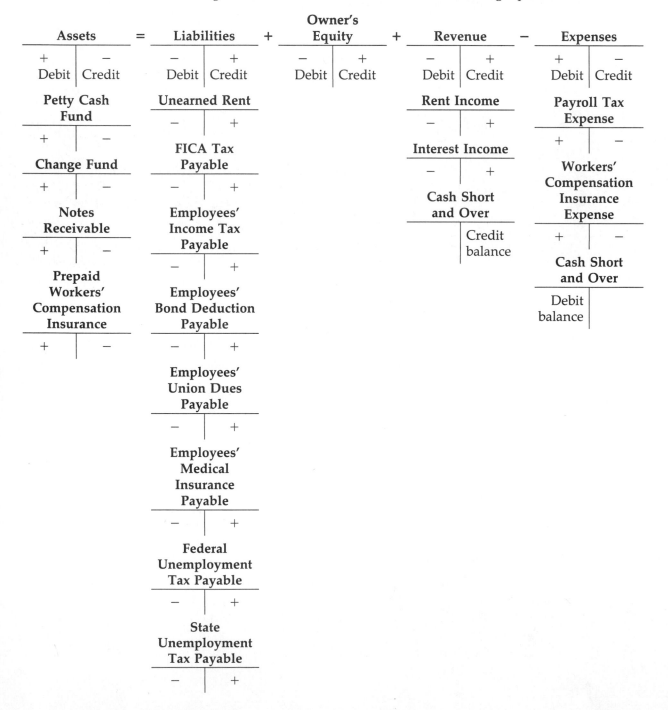

Review of Representative Transactions

The following summarizes the recording of transactions covered in Chapters 7 through 10, along with a classification of the accounts involved.

Transaction	Accounts Involved	Class.	Increase or Decrease	Therefore Debit or Credit	Financial Statement
Established a Petty Cash Fund	Petty Cash Fund	A	I	Debit	Balance Sheet
	Cash	A	D	Credit	Balance Sheet
Reimbursed Petty Cash Fund	Expenses or	E,	I	Debit	Income State.
	Assets or	A,		Debit	Balance Sheet
	Drawing	OE		Debit	State. of O.E.
	Cash	A	D	Credit	Balance Sheet
Established a Change Fund	Change Fund	A	I	Debit	Balance Sheet
	Cash	A	D	Credit	Balance Sheet
Recorded cash sales (amount on cash register tape was larger than cash count)	Cash	A	I	Debit	Balance Sheet
	Cash Short and Over	E	—	Debit	Income State.
	Sales	R	I	Credit	Income State.
Recorded cash sales (amount on cash register tape was less than cash count)	Cash	A	I	Debit	Balance Sheet
	Sales	R	I	Credit	Income State.
	Cash Short and Over	R	—	Credit	Income State.
Recorded service charges on bank account	Miscellaneous Expense	E	I	Debit	Income State.
	Cash	A	D	Credit	Balance Sheet
Recorded NSF check received from customer	Accounts Receivable	A	I	Debit	Balance Sheet
	Cash	A	D	Credit	Balance Sheet
Recorded interest-bearing note receivable collected by our bank	Cash	A	I	Debit	Balance Sheet
	Notes Receivable	A	D	Credit	Balance Sheet
	Interest Income	R	I	Credit	Income State.

Transaction	Accounts Involved	Class.	Increase or Decrease	Therefore Debit or Credit	Financial Statement
Recorded the payroll entry from the payroll register	Sales Salary Expense	E	I	Debit	Income State.
	Office Salary Expense	E	I	Debit	Income State.
	FICA Tax Payable	L	I	Credit	Balance Sheet
	Employees' Income Tax Payable	L	I	Credit	Balance Sheet
	Employees' Bond Deduction Payable	L	I	Credit	Balance Sheet
	Employees' Union Dues Payable	L	I	Credit	Balance Sheet
	Salaries Payable	L	I	Credit	Balance Sheet
Issued check payable to payroll bank account	Salaries Payable	L	D	Debit	Balance Sheet
	Cash	A	D	Credit	Balance Sheet
Recorded employer's payroll taxes	Payroll Tax Expense	E	I	Debit	Income State.
	FICA Tax Payable	L	I	Credit	Balance Sheet
	State Unemployment Tax Payable	L	I	Credit	Balance Sheet
	Federal Unemployment Tax Payable	L	I	Credit	Balance Sheet
Recorded deposit of FICA taxes and employees' income tax withheld	Employee's Income Tax Payable	L	D	Debit	Balance Sheet
	FICA Tax Payable	L	D	Debit	Balance Sheet
	Cash	A	D	Credit	Balance Sheet
Recorded deposit of federal unemployment tax	Federal Unemployment Tax Payable	L	D	Debit	Balance Sheet
	Cash	A	D	Credit	Balance Sheet
Paid state unemployment tax	State Unemployment Tax Payable	L	D	Debit	Balance Sheet
	Cash	A	D	Credit	Balance Sheet
Paid for workers' compensation insurance in advance	Prepaid Workers' Compensation Insurance	A	I	Debit	Balance Sheet
	Cash	A	D	Credit	Balance Sheet
Adjusting entry for workers' compensation insurance, assuming an additional amount is owed	Workers' Compensation Insurance Expense	E	I	Debit	Income State.
	Prepaid Workers' Compensation Insurance	A	D	Credit	Balance Sheet
	Workers' Compensation Insurance Payable	L	I	Credit	Balance Sheet

11

Accounting for Merchandise: Sales

LEARNING OBJECTIVES

After you have completed this chapter, you will be able to do the following:

1. Prepare a sales invoice.
2. Record transactions in sales journals.
3. Post from sales journals to an accounts receivable ledger and a general ledger.
4. Prepare a schedule of accounts receivable.
5. Record sales returns and allowances, including credit memorandums and returns involving sales tax.
6. Locate errors.
7. Post directly from sales invoices to an accounts receivable ledger and a general ledger.

By now you have had enough experience to complete the full accounting cycle for service-type and professional enterprises. To enlarge your accounting knowledge, let us now introduce accounting systems for merchandising enterprises. The same general principles of double-entry accounting prevail. This chapter describes specific accounts of merchandising firms; such a merchandising firm could be anything from a dress shop to a supermarket. The sales journal and the accounts receivable ledger are also presented. Just as we used Paul's Auto Body as a continuous example of a service-type business, we shall use City-Wide Electric Supply as an example of a merchandising business.

SPECIAL JOURNALS

In our previous descriptions of the accounting process, we have intentionally shown the entire procedure. In other words, we have taken the long way home, but there are certain shortcuts available. Moreover, as far as understanding accounting is concerned, if you fully understand the long way, it's relatively easy to learn the shortcuts. The reverse is not true: you cannot readily understand the entire system if you are exposed to shortcuts only.

Any accounting system must be as efficient as possible. As a matter of fact, accounting is a means, or tool, by which to measure efficiency in a business. Consequently, one should take shortcuts wherever one can do so without sacrificing internal control, which we will discuss in detail in Chapter 12.

As we shall see, **special journals** provide one shortcut. Using a two-column general journal for recording transactions that take place day after day is extremely time-consuming because each individual debit and credit entry must be posted separately. Special journals make it easier to handle specialized repetitive transactions and delegate work. The following table lists the four special journals that we shall introduce separately in the next few chapters.

Chapter	Special Journal	Letter Designation	Specialized Transaction
11	Sales journal	S	Sales of merchandise on account only
12	Purchases journal	P	Purchases of merchandise on account only
13	Cash receipts journal	CR	All cash received from any source
13	Cash payments journal	CP	All cash paid out for any purpose

When any of these four journals are used, the general journal must also be used to record any *non*specialized transactions—in other words, any transactions that the special journals cannot handle. The letter designation for the general journal is J. When more than one journal is used in a business, it is necessary to use a letter with the page number of the journal when posting to the ledger. For example, a business would use J4 to identify page 4 of the general journal and S6 to identify page 6 of the sales journal. By following this method, the source of each entry is easily identified.

For an overview of special journals, look over the chart in Figure 13-7 showing the types of transactions recorded in these journals.

SPECIFIC ACCOUNTS FOR MERCHANDISING FIRMS

A service or professional enterprise, such as the ones we have encountered, depends for its revenue on the rendering of services. A service or professional enterprise uses such accounts as Income from Services or Professional Fees. A merchandising business, on the other hand, depends for its revenue on the sale of goods or merchandise and records the amount of the sale under the account titled Sales.

Merchandise inventory consists of a stock of goods that a firm buys and intends to resell, in the same physical condition, at a profit. Merchandise should be differentiated from other assets, such as equipment and supplies, that are acquired for use in the business and are not for resale.

Because the merchandising firm has to record transactions involving the purchase, handling, and sale of its merchandise, it uses accounts and procedures that we have not yet discussed. Let's look at the fundamental accounting equation with the new T accounts that are introduced in this chapter as well as the T accounts that will be introduced in Chapters 12 and 13.

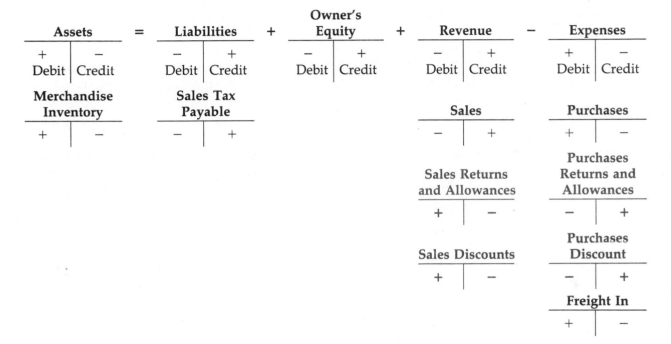

The **Sales** account, as we have said, is a revenue account used for recording sales of merchandise.

The **Purchases** account is used to record the cost of merchandise bought for resale. Remember that the Purchases account is used strictly for the buying of merchandise. The plus and minus signs are the same as the signs for Merchandise Inventory. Purchases is placed under the heading of Expenses only because the accountant closes it, along with the expense accounts, at the end of the fiscal period. We will cover Purchases in Chapter 12.

The **Sales Returns and Allowances** account is used to record the physical returns of merchandise by customers or a reduction in a bill because merchandise was damaged. It is treated as a deduction from Sales.

The **Purchases Returns and Allowances** account is used to record the firm's returns of merchandise it has purchased or reductions in bills because of damaged merchandise. It is treated as a deduction from Purchases. We will talk about this account in Chapter 12.

The **Sales Discount** and **Purchases Discount** accounts are used to record cash discounts granted for prompt payments, in accordance with the credit terms. We will discuss these accounts along with cash journals in Chapter 13.

The **Freight In** account is used to record the transportation charges on incoming merchandise intended for resale. Debits to this account increase the cost of purchases. The T accounts for returns and allowances and for discounts are shown in red to emphasize that we are treating them as deductions from the related accounts placed above them. We list these accounts as deductions because they appear as deductions in the financial statements. Their relationship is similar to that between the Drawing account and the Capital account; remember that we deduct Drawing from Capital in the statement of owner's equity.

The firm's accountant makes entries involving Merchandise Inventory only when the firm takes an actual physical count of the goods in stock; otherwise the accountant leaves this account strictly alone. Changing the balance of the Merchandise Inventory account requires adjusting entries made at the end of the fiscal period. We will show these adjusting entries in Chapter 14.

The type of transaction most frequently encountered in a merchandising business is the sale of merchandise. Some businesses sell on a cash-and-carry basis only; others sell only on credit. Many firms offer both arrangements. The same general types of entries pertain to retail and wholesale enterprises. Here are some examples.

Sale of merchandise for cash, $100. Debit Cash and credit Sales; record this in the cash receipts journal.

	Cash				Sales	
+		−		−		+
	100					100

Sale of merchandise on account, $200. Debit Accounts Receivable and credit Sales; record this in the sales journal.

	Accounts Receivable				Sales	
+		−		−		+
	200					200

HANDLING SALES ON ACCOUNT

Objective 1

Prepare a sales invoice.

Sales are recorded only in response to a customer order. The routines for processing orders and recording sales vary with the type and size of the business.

In a retail business, a salesperson usually prepares a sales ticket—either in duplicate or triplicate—for a sale on account. One copy is given to the customer, and another to the accounting department, where it will serve as the basis for an entry in the sales journal. A third copy may be used as a record of sales—when one is computing sales commissions or is involved in inventory control, for example.

In a wholesale business, the company usually receives a written order from a customer or from a salesperson who obtained the order from the customer. The order must then be approved by the credit department, after which it is sent to the billing department, where the sales invoice is prepared.

Invoices are prepared in multiple copies. For example, Figure 11-1 shows a possible distribution of sales invoice copies to various parties.

FIGURE 11-1

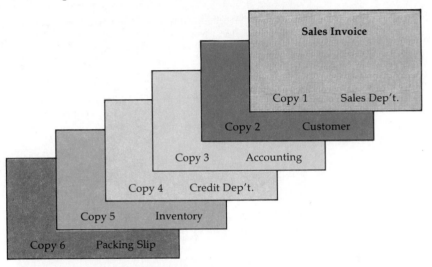

For our model business, we shall use City-Wide Electric Supply, a wholesaler. One of its invoices is shown in Figure 11-2.

We shall introduce the sales journal by looking at three transactions on the books of City-Wide Electric Supply.

Aug. 1 Sold merchandise on account to L. A. Long Company, invoice no. 320, $424.

3 Sold merchandise on account to Maier, Inc., invoice no. 321, $116.

6 Sold merchandise on account to A. and L. Construction, invoice no. 322, $94.

We can use T accounts to visualize these transactions:

Accounts Receivable		Sales	
+	−	−	+
424			424
116			116
94			94

FIGURE 11-2

CITY-WIDE ELECTRIC SUPPLY
1968 N.E. Allen Street
Portland, OR 97201

INVOICE

SOLD TO: L. A. Long Co.
620 S.W. Kennedy Street
Portland, OR 97110

DATE: *August 1, 19–*
INVOICE NO.: *320*
ORDER NO.: *5384*
SHIPPED BY: *Their truck*
TERMS: *2/10, n/30*

QUANTITY	DESCRIPTION	UNIT PRICE	TOTAL
1,000	Ivory duplex outlet cover	32	320 00
50	Ceiling junction box	96	48 00
40	Junction box (stud mount)	1 40	56 00
	TOTAL		424 00

If the transactions were recorded in a general journal, they would appear as they do in Figure 11-3.

FIGURE 11-3

GENERAL JOURNAL   PAGE ___23___

	DATE		DESCRIPTION	POST. REF.	DEBIT	CREDIT	
1	19–						1
2	Aug.	1	Accounts Receivable	113	4 2 4 00		2
3			Sales	411		4 2 4 00	3
4			Invoice no. 320, L. A. Long				4
5			Company.				5
6							6
7		3	Accounts Receivable	113	1 1 6 00		7
8			Sales	411		1 1 6 00	8
9			Invoice no. 321, Maier, Inc.				9
10							10
11		6	Accounts Receivable	113	9 4 00		11
12			Sales	411		9 4 00	12
13			Invoice no. 322, A. and L.				13
14			Construction.				14
15							15
16							16

Next, the journal entries would be posted to the accounts in the general ledger. As the last step in the posting process, the ledger account numbers would be recorded in the Post. Ref. column of the journal. (In each of the following ledger accounts, assume there were no beginning balances.)

GENERAL LEDGER

ACCOUNT _Accounts Receivable_   ACCOUNT NO. _113_

	DATE	ITEM	POST. REF.	DEBIT	CREDIT	BALANCE DEBIT	BALANCE CREDIT	
1	19–							1
2	Aug. 1		23	4 2 4 00		4 2 4 00		2
3	3		23	1 1 6 00		5 4 0 00		3
4	6		23	9 4 00		6 3 4 00		4
5								5
6								6
7								7

ACCOUNT _Sales_   ACCOUNT NO. _411_

	DATE	ITEM	POST. REF.	DEBIT	CREDIT	BALANCE DEBIT	BALANCE CREDIT	
1	19–							1
2	Aug. 1		23		4 2 4 00		4 2 4 00	2
3	3		23		1 1 6 00		5 4 0 00	3
4	6		23		9 4 00		6 3 4 00	4
5								5
6								6
7								7

Obviously, there is a great deal of repetition in both journalizing and posting. The credit sales require three separate journal entries, three debit postings to Accounts Receivable, and three credit postings to Sales. We have presented all of this to show the advantages of the sales journal. Using a sales journal eliminates all this repetition.

THE SALES JOURNAL

Objective 2

Record transactions in sales journals.

The **sales journal** records sales of merchandise _on account only_. This specialized type of transaction calls for debits to Accounts Receivable and credits to Sales. Let's see how to record the three transactions for City-Wide Electric Supply in the sales journal _instead of_ in the general journal.

SALES JOURNAL   PAGE 38

	DATE	INV. NO.	CUSTOMER'S NAME	POST. REF.	ACCOUNTS RECEIVABLE DR., SALES CR.	
1	19–					1
2	Aug. 1	320	L. A. Long Company		4 2 4 00	2
3	3	321	Maier, Inc.		1 1 6 00	3
4	6	322	A. and L. Construction		9 4 00	4
5						5

Because *one* money column is headed *Accounts Receivable Debit and Sales Credit*, each transaction requires only a single line. Repetition is avoided, and all entries for sales of merchandise on account are found in one place. Listing the invoice number makes it easier to check the details of a particular sale at a later date.

Objective 3

Post from sales journals to an accounts receivable ledger and a general ledger.

Posting from the Sales Journal

Using the sales journal also saves time and space in posting to the ledger accounts. The transactions involving the sales of merchandise on account for the entire month of August are shown in Figure 11-4.

FIGURE 11-4

SALES JOURNAL   PAGE 38

	DATE	INV. NO.	CUSTOMER'S NAME	POST. REF.	ACCOUNTS RECEIVABLE DR., SALES CR.	
1	19–					1
2	Aug. 1	320	L. A. Long Company		4 2 4 00	2
3	3	321	Maier, Inc.		1 1 6 00	3
4	6	322	A. and L. Construction		9 4 00	4
5	9	323	Manning Service Company		9 6 1 00	5
6	11	324	Chavez Hardware		8 6 00	6
7	16	325	Home Hardware Company		2 1 5 00	7
8	20	326	Harrells Electric		2 9 3 00	8
9	23	327	Baker Building Supplies		5 6 0 00	9
10	24	328	Chavez Hardware		2 8 6 00	10
11	28	329	Home Hardware Company		7 5 00	11
12	30	330	Baker Building Supplies		3 8 7 00	12
13	31	331	L. A. Long Company		5 6 00	13
14	31	332	Robert D. Bishop, Inc.		8 7 1 00	14
15	31				4 4 2 4 00	15
16					(113)(411)	16
17						17
18						18

Because all the entries are a debit to Accounts Receivable and a credit to Sales, one can now make a single posting to these accounts for the amount of the total as of the last day of the month. This entry is called a **summarizing entry** because it summarizes one month's transactions. In the Post. Ref. columns of the ledger accounts, the letter S designates the sales journal.

GENERAL LEDGER

ACCOUNT _Accounts Receivable_   ACCOUNT NO. _113_

	DATE	ITEM	POST. REF.	DEBIT	CREDIT	BALANCE DEBIT	BALANCE CREDIT	
1	19–							1
2	Aug. 31		S38	4 4 2 4 00		4 4 2 4 00		2
3								3
4								4
5								5

ACCOUNT _Sales_   ACCOUNT NO. _411_

	DATE	ITEM	POST. REF.	DEBIT	CREDIT	BALANCE DEBIT	BALANCE CREDIT	
1	19–							1
2	Aug. 31		S38		4 4 2 4 00		4 4 2 4 00	2
3								3
4								4
5								5

After posting to the Accounts Receivable account, go back to the sales journal and record the account number in parentheses directly below the total. The account number for the account being debited (Accounts Receivable) goes on the left. The account number for the account being credited (Sales) goes on the right of the account number being debited. Again, as a precaution, don't record these account numbers until you have completed the postings.

If you should find an error, do not erase it. The same procedure for error correction described in Chapter 4 applies to special journals. If you catch the error in the journal entry before it is posted to the ledger, simply draw a single line through the error (with a ruler), write in the correct information, and add your initials. If an amount is entered incorrectly in the ledger (although the journal entry is correct), follow the same procedure. However, if an entry has been posted to the wrong accounts in the ledger, then you must prepare a new journal entry correcting the first one.

Sales Journal Provision for Sales Tax

Most states and some cities levy a **sales tax** on retail sales of goods and services. The retailer collects the sales tax from customers and later pays it to the tax authorities.

When goods or services are sold on credit, the sales tax is charged to the customer and recorded at the time of the sale. The sales journal must be designed to handle this type of transaction. For example, if a retail store sells an item for $100 and the sales tax is 4 percent, the transaction would be recorded in T accounts like this:

Accounts Receivable		Sales		Sales Tax Payable	
+	−	−	+	−	+
104			100		4

Incidentally, when the sales tax is paid to the government, the accountant debits Sales Tax Payable and credits Cash.

Right now, because we want to illustrate a sales journal for a retail merchandising firm operating in a state having a sales tax, we shall talk about the transactions of another company, Melnor Gift Shop. Its sales journal is presented below.

SALES JOURNAL   PAGE 96

	DATE	INV. NO.	CUSTOMER'S NAME	POST. REF.	ACCOUNTS RECEIVABLE DEBIT	SALES TAX PAYABLE CREDIT	SALES CREDIT	
1	19–							1
2	Apr. 1	9382	B. T. Lawson		16 64	64	16 00	2
3	1	9383	Culver Apartments		22 88	88	22 00	3
4	1	9384	Richard Gladdon		52 00	2 00	50 00	4
5	2	9385	T. R. Sears		12 48	48	12 00	5
6								6
7								7
8	30	10121	Paul Murphy		1 24 80	4 80	1 20 00	8
9	30				25 16 80	96 80	24 20 00	9
10					(113)	(214)	(411)	10
11								11
12								12
13								13

Remember

With a sales journal having more than one column, using the column totals, prove that the total debits equal the total credits.

Each column is posted to the ledger accounts as a total at the end of the month. After posting the figures, the accountant records the account numbers in parentheses immediately below the totals. Note that Melnor Gift Shop's charge customers owe the total amount of the sales plus the sales tax, $2,516.80 ($2,420 + $96.80 = $2,516.80).

GENERAL LEDGER

ACCOUNT _Accounts Receivable_   ACCOUNT NO. _113_

	DATE	ITEM	POST. REF.	DEBIT	CREDIT	BALANCE DEBIT	BALANCE CREDIT	
1	19–							1
2	Apr. 30		S96	2 5 1 6 80		2 5 1 6 80		2
3								3
4								4

ACCOUNT _Sales Tax Payable_   ACCOUNT NO. _214_

	DATE	ITEM	POST. REF.	DEBIT	CREDIT	BALANCE DEBIT	BALANCE CREDIT	
1	19–							1
2	Apr. 30		S96		9 6 80		9 6 80	2
3								3
4								4

ACCOUNT _Sales_   ACCOUNT NO. _411_

	DATE	ITEM	POST. REF.	DEBIT	CREDIT	BALANCE DEBIT	BALANCE CREDIT	
1	19–							1
2	Apr. 30		S96		2 4 2 0 00		2 4 2 0 00	2
3								3
4								4
5								5

THE ACCOUNTS RECEIVABLE LEDGER

Accounts Receivable, as we have seen, represents the total amount owed to a business by its charge customers.

There is a major lack of information with this account, however. The business can't tell at a glance _how much each_ individual charge customer owes, which handicaps the credit department. To correct this shortcoming, businesses keep a separate account for each charge customer.

When a business has very few charge customers, it is possible to have a separate Accounts Receivable account in the general ledger for each charge customer. However, when there are many charge customers, which is the usual case, this arrangement is too cumbersome. Listing each charge customer's account makes the trial balance very long. In addition, there is a greater likelihood of errors.

It is more practical to have a separate book containing a list of all the charge customers with their respective balances. This is called the **accounts receivable ledger.** In the accounts receivable ledger, the individual charge customer accounts are listed in alphabetical order. Most accountants prefer a loose-leaf binder so they can insert accounts for new customers and remove other accounts; they don't use account numbers.

The Accounts Receivable account should still be maintained in the general ledger; when all the postings are up to date, the balance of this account should equal the total of all the individual balances of the charge customers. The Accounts Receivable account in the general ledger is called a **controlling account.** The accounts receivable *ledger,* containing the accounts or listing of all the charge customers, is really a special ledger, called a **subsidiary ledger.** Figure 11-5 diagrams the interrelationship of these books.

FIGURE 11-5

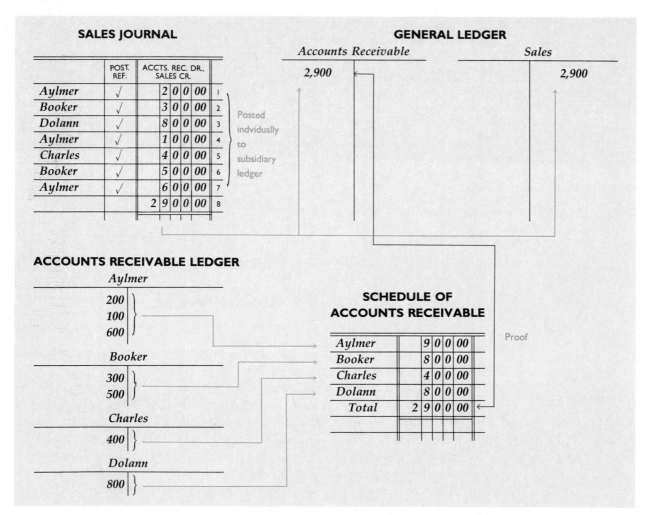

The accountant posts the individual amounts to the accounts receivable ledger every day, so that this ledger will have up-to-date information. At the end of the month, the accountant posts the total of the sales journal (in Figure 11-5 it happens to be $2,900) to the general ledger accounts as a debit to the Accounts Receivable controlling account and a credit to the Sales account. *As indicated in Figure 11-5, the balance of the Accounts Receivable controlling account at the end of the month must equal the total of the balances of the charge customer accounts in the accounts receivable ledger.* The schedule of accounts receivable is merely a listing of charge customers' individual balances.

In the simplified illustration in Figure 11-5, it just so happens that since no payments were received from charge customers, the total of the sales journal equals the balance of Accounts Receivable. On the other hand, if Melnor Gift Shop had received, say, $1,200 from its charge customers, the balance of both the Accounts Receivable controlling account and the total of the schedule of accounts receivable would be $1,700 ($2,900 − $1,200). The total of the sales journal would still be $2,900.

After you post the amount from the sales journal to the charge customer's account in the accounts receivable ledger, put a check mark (√) in the Post. Ref. column of the sales journal.

Let's get back to the sales journal of City-Wide Electric Supply for August. We will cover the daily postings that its accountant has made to the accounts receivable ledger. Then we'll see the schedule of accounts receivable. These entries are shown in Figure 11-6 and the ledger accounts that follow. Note that the ruling consists of a single line under the amount column and double lines extended through the Date, Post. Ref., and Amount columns. The last day of the month is recorded on the same line as the total.

FIGURE 11-6

SALES JOURNAL
PAGE 38

	DATE	INV. NO.	CUSTOMER'S NAME	POST. REF.	ACCOUNTS RECEIVABLE DR., SALES CR.	
1	19–					1
2	Aug. 1	320	L. A. Long Company	√	4 2 4 00	2
3	3	321	Maier, Inc.	√	1 1 6 00	3
4	6	322	A. and L. Construction	√	9 4 00	4
5	9	323	Manning Service Company	√	9 6 1 00	5
6	11	324	Chavez Hardware	√	8 6 00	6
7	16	325	Home Hardware Company	√	2 1 5 00	7
8	20	326	Harrells Electric	√	2 9 3 00	8
9	23	327	Baker Building Supplies	√	5 6 0 00	9
10	24	328	Chavez Hardware	√	2 8 6 00	10
11	28	329	Home Hardware Company	√	7 5 00	11
12	30	330	Baker Building Supplies	√	3 8 7 00	12
13	31	331	L. A. Long Company	√	5 6 00	13
14	31	332	Robert D. Bishop, Inc.	√	8 7 1 00	14
15	31				4 4 2 4 00	15
16					(113) (411)	16

ACCOUNTS RECEIVABLE LEDGER

NAME   *A. and L. Construction*

ADDRESS   *1015 Broadway, S.W.*

Seattle, WA 98102

DATE		ITEM	POST. REF.	DEBIT	CREDIT	BALANCE
19–						
Aug.	6		S38	9 4 00		9 4 00

NAME   *Baker Building Supplies*

ADDRESS   *17 No. Second St.*

Renton, WA 98055

DATE		ITEM	POST. REF.	DEBIT	CREDIT	BALANCE
19–						
Aug.	23		S38	5 6 0 00		5 6 0 00
	30		S38	3 8 7 00		9 4 7 00

NAME   *Robert D. Bishop, Inc.*

ADDRESS   *2168 Main St.*

Kent, WA 98031

DATE		ITEM	POST. REF.	DEBIT	CREDIT	BALANCE
19–						
Aug.	31		S38	8 7 1 00		8 7 1 00

NAME   *Chavez Hardware*

ADDRESS   *2005 N. Powder St.*

Everett, WA 98201

DATE		ITEM	POST. REF.	DEBIT	CREDIT	BALANCE
19–						
Aug.	11		S38	8 6 00		8 6 00
	24		S38	2 8 6 00		3 7 2 00

NAME ___ *Harrells Electric*
ADDRESS ___ *21680 S.E. Twelfth Ave.*
Portland, OR 97208

DATE	ITEM	POST. REF.	DEBIT	CREDIT	BALANCE
19—					
Aug. 20		S38	2 9 3 00		2 9 3 00

NAME ___ *Home Hardware Company*
ADDRESS ___ *7810 N.W. Cherburg St.*
Portland, OR 97206

DATE	ITEM	POST. REF.	DEBIT	CREDIT	BALANCE
19—					
Aug. 16		S38	2 1 5 00		2 1 5 00
28		S38	7 5 00		2 9 0 00

NAME ___ *L. A. Long Company*
ADDRESS ___ *620 S.W. Kennedy St.*
Portland, OR 97110

DATE	ITEM	POST. REF.	DEBIT	CREDIT	BALANCE
19—					
Aug. 1		S38	4 2 4 00		4 2 4 00
31		S38	5 6 00		4 8 0 00

NAME ___ *Maier, Inc.*
ADDRESS ___ *1720 Ninth St., N.W.*
Seattle, WA 98107

DATE	ITEM	POST. REF.	DEBIT	CREDIT	BALANCE
19—					
Aug. 3		S38	1 1 6 00		1 1 6 00

NAME ___ *Manning Service Company*
ADDRESS ___ *2720 N.W. 43rd Ave.*
Portland, OR 97210

DATE	ITEM	POST. REF.	DEBIT	CREDIT	BALANCE
19—					
Aug. 9		S38	9 6 1 00		9 6 1 00

Assuming that these were the only transactions involving charge customers, the accountant prepares a schedule of accounts receivable, listing
the balance of each charge customer.

City-Wide Electric Supply Schedule of Accounts Receivable August 31, 19–		
A. and L. Construction	$	9 4 00
Baker Building Supplies		9 4 7 00
Robert D. Bishop, Inc.		8 7 1 00
Chavez Hardware		3 7 2 00
Harrells Electric		2 9 3 00
Home Hardware Company		2 9 0 00
L. A. Long Company		4 8 0 00
Maier, Inc.		1 1 6 00
Manning Service Company		9 6 1 00
Total Accounts Receivable	$ 4 4 2 4 00	

Again we assume that there were no previous balances in the customers' accounts. Under this circumstance, the Accounts Receivable controlling account in the general ledger will have the same balance, $4,424,
as the schedule of accounts receivable.

GENERAL LEDGER

ACCOUNT *Accounts Receivable*   ACCOUNT NO. *113*

	DATE	ITEM	POST. REF.	DEBIT	CREDIT	BALANCE DEBIT	BALANCE CREDIT	
1	19–							1
2	Aug. 31		S38	4 4 2 4 00		4 4 2 4 00		2
3								3
4								4

SALES RETURNS AND ALLOWANCES

Objective 5

Record sales returns
and allowances,
including credit
memorandums and
returns involving sales
tax.

The Sales Returns and Allowances account handles two types of transactions having to do with merchandise that has previously been sold. A *return* is a physical return of the goods. An *allowance* is a reduction from
the original price because the goods were defective or damaged. It may
not be economically worthwhile to have customers return the goods;
each situation is a special case. To avoid writing a separate letter each
time to inform customers of their account adjustments, businesses use a
special form called a **credit memorandum**. A credit memorandum is

FIGURE 11-7

CITY-WIDE ELECTRIC SUPPLY
1968 N.E. Allen St.
Portland, OR 97201

CREDIT MEMORANDUM   No. *69*

CREDIT TO *Chavez Hardware*
2005 N. Powder St.
Everett, WA 98201

DATE: *September 2, 19–*

WE CREDIT YOUR ACCOUNT AS FOLLOWS:

1 *Entrance panel circuit breaker, 100 amp*
120 v—12 circuits   **$45.00**

shown in Figure 11-7. A credit memorandum is a written statement indicating a seller's willingness to reduce the amount of a buyer's debt.

The Sales Returns and Allowances account is considered to be a deduction from Sales. Using an account separate from Sales provides a better record of the total returns and allowances. Accountants deduct Sales Returns and Allowances from Sales in the income statement, as we shall see later.

Using T accounts, here's an example of a return. The original sale is shown first and is followed by the issuance of a credit memorandum.

Transaction (a)   On August 24, City-Wide Electric Supply sold merchandise on account to Chavez Hardware, $286, and recorded the sale in the sales journal.

Transaction (b)   On September 2, Chavez Hardware returned $45 worth of the merchandise. City-Wide Electric Supply issued credit memorandum no. 69 (see Figure 11-7).

Assets		=	Liabilities		+	Owner's Equity		+	Revenue		–	Expenses	
+	–		–	+		–	+		–	+		+	–
Debit	Credit		Debit	Credit		Debit	Credit		Debit	Credit		Debit	Credit

Accounts Receivable

+	–
(a) 286	(b) 45

Sales

–	+
	(a) 286

Sales Returns and Allowances

+	–
(b) 45	

Since Sales Returns and Allowances is a deduction from Sales, the plus and minus signs are switched around.

City-Wide Electric's accountant debits Sales Returns and Allowances because City-Wide Electric has more returns and allowances than it did before. The accountant credits Accounts Receivable because the charge customer (Chavez Hardware) owes less than before.

One uses the word *credit* in "credit memorandum" because the seller has to credit Accounts Receivable. Suppose that during September, City-Wide Electric Supply issues two credit memorandums and makes the following entries in the general journal:

GENERAL JOURNAL   PAGE __27__

	DATE	DESCRIPTION	POST. REF.	DEBIT	CREDIT	
1	*19–*					1
2	*Sept. 2*	*Sales Returns and Allowances*		*4 5 00*		2
3		*Accounts Receivable, Chavez*				3
4		*Hardware*			*4 5 00*	4
5		*Credit memo no. 69.*				5
6						6
7	*2*	*Sales Returns and Allowances*		*1 1 6 00*		7
8		*Accounts Receivable, Home*				8
9		*Hardware Company*			*1 1 6 00*	9
10		*Credit memo no. 70.*				10
11						11
12						12
13						13
14						14
15						15
16						16

The general journal entry serves as the posting source for crediting the Accounts Receivable controlling account in the general ledger. It also serves as the posting source for updating the accounts receivable ledger and therefore includes the name of the charge customer. If the balance of the Accounts Receivable controlling account is to equal the total of the individual balances in the accounts receivable ledger, one must post to *both* the Accounts Receivable account in the general ledger *and* the account of Chavez Hardware in the accounts receivable ledger. To take care of this double posting, one puts a slant line in the Post. Ref. column. When the amount has been posted as a credit to the general ledger account, the accountant puts the account number of Accounts Receivable in the left part of the Post. Ref. column. After the account of Chavez Hardware has been posted as a credit, the accountant puts a check mark in the right portion of the Post. Ref. column. Sales Returns and Allowances is posted in the usual manner. Here are the entries after posting is complete:

GENERAL JOURNAL   PAGE 27

	DATE	DESCRIPTION	POST. REF.	DEBIT	CREDIT	
1	19–					1
2	Sept. 2	Sales Returns and Allowances	412	4 5 00		2
3		Accounts Receivable, Chavez				3
4		Hardware	113/√		4 5 00	4
5		Credit memo no. 69.				5
6						6
7	2	Sales Returns and Allowances	412	1 1 6 00		7
8		Accounts Receivable, Home				8
9		Hardware Company	113/√		1 1 6 00	9
10		Credit memo no. 70.				10
11						11

GENERAL LEDGER

ACCOUNT Accounts Receivable   ACCOUNT NO. 113

	DATE	ITEM	POST. REF.	DEBIT	CREDIT	BALANCE DEBIT	BALANCE CREDIT	
1	19–							1
2	Aug. 31		S38	4 4 2 4 00		4 4 2 4 00		2
3	Sept. 2		J27		4 5 00	4 3 7 9 00		3
4	2		J27		1 1 6 00	4 2 6 3 00		4
5								5

ACCOUNT Sales Returns and Allowances   ACCOUNT NO. 412

	DATE	ITEM	POST. REF.	DEBIT	CREDIT	BALANCE DEBIT	BALANCE CREDIT	
1	19–							1
2	Sept. 2		J27	4 5 00		4 5 00		2
3	2		J27	1 1 6 00		1 6 1 00		3

ACCOUNTS RECEIVABLE LEDGER

NAME Chavez Hardware
ADDRESS 2005 N. Powder St.
Everett, WA 98201

DATE	ITEM	POST. REF.	DEBIT	CREDIT	BALANCE
19–					
Aug. 11		S38	8 6 00		8 6 00
24		S38	2 8 6 00		3 7 2 00
Sept. 2		J27		4 5 00	3 2 7 00

NAME	Home Hardware Company
ADDRESS	7810 N.W. Cherburg St.
	Portland, OR 97206

DATE		ITEM	POST. REF.	DEBIT	CREDIT	BALANCE
19–						
Aug.	16		S38	2 1 5 00		2 1 5 00
	28		S38	7 5 00		2 9 0 00
Sept.	2		J27		1 1 6 00	1 7 4 00

Sales Return Involving a Sales Tax

If a customer who returns merchandise to a retail store was originally charged a sales tax, the sales tax must be returned to the customer. To illustrate, first, refer to the sales journal of Melnor Gift Shop on page 342 involving sales taxes. On April 3, assume that B. T. Lawson returns the merchandise bought on April 1 for $16 plus $.64 sales tax. Following is the general journal entry required for this type of return:

	DATE		DESCRIPTION	POST. REF.	DEBIT	CREDIT	
			GENERAL JOURNAL			PAGE _12_	
1	19 –						1
2	Apr.	3	Sales Returns and Allowances		1 6 00		2
3			Sales Tax Payable		64		3
4			Accounts Receivable, B. T. Lawson			1 6 64	4
5			Credit memorandum no. 371.				5
6							6
7							7

Procedure for Locating Errors

Objective 6

Locate errors.

Suppose you are facing a situation where the total of the schedule of accounts receivable does not equal the balance of the Accounts Receivable controlling account. As we stated before, to locate possible errors, do everything in reverse. Here is a suggested order:

1. Re-add the schedule of accounts receivable.
2. Check the balances transferred from the customer accounts in the accounts receivable ledger to the schedule of accounts receivable.

3. Verify the postings from the sales and general journals to the Accounts Receivable controlling account.
4. Re-add the sales journal.
5. Verify the balances of the customer accounts in the accounts receivable ledger.
6. Check the postings from the sales and general journals to the customer accounts in the accounts receivable ledger.

POSTING DIRECTLY FROM SALES INVOICES (AN ALTERNATIVE TO USING A SALES JOURNAL)

Objective 7

Post directly from sales invoices to an accounts receivable ledger and a general ledger.

Companies that have a large volume of sales on account sometimes use duplicate copies of their sales invoices as a sales journal. The accountant posts daily to the charge customer accounts in the accounts receivable ledger, working directly from the duplicate copies of the sales invoices or sales slips. He or she writes the invoice number rather than the journal page in the Posting Reference column of the customer's account. A file is maintained for the copies of the sales invoices. Then at the end of the month, the accountant brings the Accounts Receivable controlling account up to date by totaling all the sales invoices for the month and then making a general journal entry debiting Accounts Receivable and crediting Sales.

Let's use a different firm to show how this procedure works. The Cobb Sports Equipment Company posts directly from its sales invoices; the total of its sales invoices for December is $17,296. Its accountant journalizes and posts the entry as follows:

	DATE	DESCRIPTION	POST. REF.	DEBIT	CREDIT	
1	*19–*					1
2	*Dec.* 31	*Accounts Receivable*	113	17 2 9 6 00		2
3		*Sales*	411		17 2 9 6 00	3
4		*Summarizing entry for the total*				4
5		*of the sales invoices for the*				5
6		*month.*				6
7						7
8						8
9						9
10						10
11						11

GENERAL JOURNAL   PAGE __36__

GENERAL LEDGER

ACCOUNT _Accounts Receivable_   ACCOUNT NO. _113_

	DATE	ITEM	POST. REF.	DEBIT	CREDIT	BALANCE DEBIT	BALANCE CREDIT	
1	19–							1
2	Dec. 31		J36	17 2 9 6 00		17 2 9 6 00		2
3								3
4								4

ACCOUNT _Sales_   ACCOUNT NO. _411_

	DATE	ITEM	POST. REF.	DEBIT	CREDIT	BALANCE DEBIT	BALANCE CREDIT	
1	19–							1
2	Dec. 31		J36		17 2 9 6 00		17 2 9 6 00	2
3								3
4								4

The above journal entry can be recognized as a _summarizing entry_ because it summarizes the credit sales for one month. Because the company's accountant posts the entry to the accounts in the general ledger, there is no need for a sales journal; the one summarizing entry in the general journal records the total sales for the month.

FIGURE 11-8

COBB SPORTS EQUIPMENT COMPANY
1610 Alhambra Blvd.
San Diego, CA 92002

INVOICE

SOLD TO _Parker and Cranston, Sporting Goods_
1600 Santa Clara Ave.
San Francisco, CA 94133

DATE: _Dec. 4, 19–_
INVOICE NO.: _6075_
ORDER NO.: _359_
SHIPPED BY: _Express Collect_
TERMS: _2/10, n/30_

QUANTITY	DESCRIPTION	UNIT PRICE	TOTAL
10	_Molded unicellular foam ski/life vest (Davis) lg._	16 80	168 00

ACCOUNTS RECEIVABLE LEDGER

NAME *Parker and Cranston, Sporting Goods*

ADDRESS *1600 Santa Clara Ave.*
San Francisco, CA 94133

DATE	ITEM	POST. REF.	DEBIT	CREDIT	BALANCE
19–					
Dec. 4		6075	1 6 8 00		1 6 8 00

One invoice and the corresponding entry in the accounts receivable ledger might look like Figure 11-8 and the ledger account shown above. The $168 would of course be posted to the general ledger as a part of the total comprising the monthly summarizing entry.

SUMMARY

Keeping special journals is a shortcut in the accounting process that makes it possible to record a transaction on one line and to post column totals rather than individual figures. This chapter introduced three new kinds of accounts: Sales, Sales Returns and Allowances, and Sales Tax Payable. *Sales* is a revenue account like Income from Services. *Sales Returns and Allowances* is a deduction from Sales. *Sales Tax Payable* is a liability account since the company has to pay the balance to a state or local government. It also describes how to make out a sales invoice.

L.O. I

The sales journal takes care of sales of merchandise on account only. The entries are posted *daily* to the accounts receivable ledger. At the end of the month the total is posted to the general ledger as a debit to the Accounts Receivable controlling account and a credit to the Sales account. The accountant then prepares a schedule of accounts receivable, which is a listing of the individual balances of the charge customers.

L.O. 2
L.O. 3

L.O. 4

When a customer returns merchandise that he or she has bought or when his or her bill is reduced due to an allowance for defective or damaged merchandise, the Sales Returns and Allowances account is increased and the Accounts Receivable account is decreased. The entry is recorded in the general journal and posted to both the general ledger and the accounts receivable ledger. If at the end of the month the balance of the Accounts Receivable controlling account does not equal the total of the schedule of accounts receivable, accountants must retrace their steps to locate the errors.

L.O. 5

L.O. 6

Another shortcut is using sales invoices or sales slips as a sales journal, thereby doing away with the sales journal. One posts to the charge customer accounts in the accounts receivable ledger directly from the sales invoices. At the end of the month, one adds all the sales invoices and makes a summarizing entry in the general journal for the amount of the total. This entry is a debit to Accounts Receivable and a credit to Sales.

L.O. 7

C◉MPUTERS AT WORK

Integrating Sales and Inventory

Companies involved in the sale of merchandise—manufacturers, distributers, retailers—have traditionally had to cope with an information lag. Sales figures used to take so long to get back to company management that many businesses had to make decisions about inventory based on guesses or projections from old data. Computers and bar code readers are changing that.

Most Americans first became aware of this new aspect of accounting technology when black-line bar codes began appearing on various products. Soon supermarket clerks started to pass items over a magic eye instead of punching prices into a register. Most people noticed that the register receipt from these bar code readers listed, often in considerable detail, the exact items purchased. Few customers think, however, about the advantages for the retailer in knowing exactly what products are leaving the store at any given moment. These point-of-sale terminals can relay sales information instantaneously to a central computer that performs most of a company's accounting functions, including keeping track of inventory. Store managers can make their purchases and projections based on truly up-to-the-minute information.

Gradually the bar codes have spread from supermarkets to other retailers, many of whom use hand-held "guns" to read information off coded tags or labels and feed it into the computer. Retailers and accountants are working to make the use of the code—officially known as *universal product code*—more uniform so that information can be passed on more quickly and automatically. Some retailing giants have already hooked up their computers with those of their major suppliers, thus making a direct link between the cash register and the manufacturer. New computer software allows managers to make the best use of the information provided by bar codes and scanners. With the push of a button, managers can get numbers, graphs, and full reports on such things as the cost, profitability, and brand shares of certain products.

Because computers track information constantly, they spot trends rapidly. A manufacturer can discover that sales of a formerly profitable product are dropping sharply and cut down on production instead of getting stuck with unsalable inventory. Smaller companies can cut drastically the number of people needed to handle an order. They don't have to put customers on hold while someone runs out back to see if the giant rubber sharks are still in stock. And retailers—from the giants like Wal-Mart to smaller chains like Designs, Inc., which sells Levi Strauss products exclusively—can cut down on overall inventory and still be sure that they have needed items in stock. Everyone from manufacturer to retailer to customer can get accurate information rapidly. And that makes everyone happy.

Sources: Isadore Barmash, "Retailers Seek to Use Scanners More," *New York Times,* January 11, 1988, D1–D2; David Mehegan, "A Levi Connection Sure Sells Jeans," *Boston Globe,* May 3, 1988, 33, 40; Nielsen Marketing Research, "Nielsen Marketing Research Introduces New Personal Computer Software for Managing Supermarket Scanning Data," November 23, 1987; Mark Stevens, "Six Small-Business Problems Computers Can Solve," *Working Woman,* September 1987, 33–42.

GLOSSARY

Accounts receivable ledger A subsidiary ledger that lists the individual accounts of charge customers in alphabetical order.

Controlling account An account in the general ledger that summarizes the balances of a subsidiary ledger.

Credit memorandum A written statement indicating a seller's willingness to reduce the amount of a buyer's debt. The seller records the amount of the credit memorandum under the Sales Returns and Allowances account.

Freight In The account used to record transportation charges on incoming merchandise intended for resale.

Merchandise inventory A stock of goods that a firm buys and intends to resell, in the same physical condition, at a profit.

Purchases An account for recording the cost of merchandise acquired for resale.

Purchases Discount An account that records cash discounts granted by suppliers in return for prompt payment; it is treated as a deduction from Purchases.

Purchases Returns and Allowances An account that records a company's return of merchandise it has purchased or a reduction in the bill because of damaged merchandise; it is treated as a deduction from Purchases.

Sales A revenue account for recording the sale of merchandise.

Sales Discount An account that records a deduction from the original price, granted by the seller to the buyer for the prompt payment of an invoice.

Sales journal A special journal for recording the sale of merchandise on account only.

Sales Returns and Allowances The account a seller uses to record the physical return of merchandise by customers or a reduction in the bill because merchandise was damaged. Sales Returns and Allowances is treated as a deduction from Sales. This account is usually evidenced by a credit memorandum issued by the seller.

Sales tax A tax levied by a state or city government on the retail sale of goods and services. The tax is paid by the consumer but collected by the retailer.

Special journals Books of original entry in which one records specialized types of repetitive transactions.

Subsidiary ledger A group of accounts representing individual subdivisions of a controlling account.

Summarizing entry An entry made to post the column totals of the special journals to the appropriate accounts in the general ledger. It is also used when individual sales invoices are posted directly to the accounts receivable ledger. The summarizing entry represents the one entry made in the general journal to record the total sales on account for a period of time and posted to the general ledger.

QUESTIONS, EXERCISES, AND PROBLEMS
Discussion Questions

1. How is a special sales journal more efficient than a general journal for recording sales of merchandise on account?
2. Why is it necessary to post to individual charge customer accounts on a daily basis?
3. What information typically appears on a sales invoice?
4. What kind of ledger is an accounts receivable ledger? Are account numbers used? Why or why not?
5. What is a schedule of accounts receivable?
6. What is the difference between a sales return and a sales allowance?
7. Why does a business with a large number of charge customer accounts need an accounts receivable ledger?
8. Describe the method of posting directly from sales invoices.

Exercises

L.O. 1 **Exercise 11-1**   Prepare a sales invoice to Callan Company, 240 Alhambra Avenue, El Paso, TX 79947, for a sale made on November 2, 19–; invoice number 421C; terms 2/10, n/30. Callan's order number is 9941. Items sold to Callan Company:

24 Persona Executive Billfolds at $21.50 each
12 Persona Organizer Clutch Purses at $19.72 each
24 Persona Calculator Checkbook Clutch Purses at $23.64 each

Items shipped via FPS.

L.O. 2,3,5 **Exercise 11-2**   Record the following transactions in general journal form.

a. Sold merchandise on account to L. C. Mason, $236, invoice no. 421.
b. Issued credit memo no. 19 to L. C. Mason for merchandise returned, $42.
c. Received full payment from L. C. Mason.

L.O. 2,5, **Exercise 11-3**   Record the following transactions in general journal form.

a. Sold merchandise for cash to R. A. Johnson, $282 plus 6 percent sales tax.
b. Johnson returned $50 of the merchandise. Issued credit memo no. 127 and paid Johnson $53 in cash; $50 for the amount of the return plus $3 for the amount of the sales tax.

L.O. 7 **Exercise 11-4**   A business firm uses duplicate copies of its sales invoices to record sales of merchandise on account and duplicate copies of its credit memos to record sales returns and allowances. During September, the firm issued 217 invoices for $98,452.69 and 14 credit memos for $2,116.44. Present the summarizing entries, dated September 30, in general journal form, to record the sales and sales returns for the month.

L.O. 3 **Exercise 11-5**   Describe how the following sales journal of Berthold Company would be posted to the ledgers:

					SALES JOURNAL		PAGE 26					
	DATE		INV. NO.	CUSTOMER'S NAME		POST. REF.	ACCOUNTS RECEIVABLE DR., SALES CR.					
1	19–											1
2	Nov.	2	723	Sanderson Company				2	2	1	62	2
3		6	724	J. C. Farnsworth			1	6	4	2	00	3
4		12	725	A. R. Dombroski			1	2	6	8	71	4
5		20	726	Bannion and Worthy			3	6	8	4	00	5
6		30	727	Craig and Luckman			1	8	7	4	68	6
7		30					8	6	9	1	01	7
8												8

L.O. 3,5 **Exercise 11-6** Describe the transactions recorded in the following T accounts.

Cash		Accounts Receivable		Sales Returns and Allowances
(c) 168		(a) 210 | (b) 42		(b) 40
		(c) 168		

Sales		Sales Tax Payable
(a) 200		(b) 2 | (a) 10

L.O. 5 **Exercise 11-7** Post the following entry to the general ledger and subsidiary ledger accounts:

			GENERAL JOURNAL			PAGE 43						
	DATE		DESCRIPTION	POST. REF.	DEBIT				CREDIT			
1	19–											1
2	May	1	Sales Returns and Allowances		1	2	1	16				2
3			Accounts Receivable, J. Converse						1	2	1	16	3
4			Issued credit memo no. 129.										4
5													5

GENERAL LEDGER

ACCOUNT Accounts Receivable   ACCOUNT NO. 113

	DATE		ITEM	POST. REF.	DEBIT	CREDIT	BALANCE		
							DEBIT	CREDIT	
1	19–								1
2	May	1	Balance	✓			6 3 2 1 70		2
3									3
4									4

ACCOUNT	*Sales Returns and Allowances*						ACCOUNT NO. *412*		

			POST. REF.	DEBIT	CREDIT	BALANCE			
	DATE	ITEM				DEBIT		CREDIT	
1	*19–*								1
2	*May* 1	*Balance*	√	*3 2 9 80*		*3 2 9 80*			2
3									3

ACCOUNTS RECEIVABLE LEDGER

ACCOUNT	*J. Converse*
	P.O. Box 25
	Grantham, N.H. 03753

	DATE	INVOICE NO.	ITEM	POST. REF.	DEBIT	CREDIT	BALANCE	
1	*19–*							1
2	*Apr.* 30	*761*		*S26*	*4 9 2 60*		*4 9 2 60*	2

L.O. 6 **Exercise 11-8** An accountant made the following errors in journalizing sales of merchandise on account in a single-column sales journal and posting to the general ledger and accounts receivable ledger. The errors were discovered at the end of the month before the closing entries were journalized and posted. Describe how to correct the errors.

a. The sales journal was footed correctly as $26,960, but it was posted as a debit and credit of $26,690.
b. A sale correctly recorded at $48 to C. D. Rose was posted to his account as $4.80.
c. A sale correctly recorded at $76 to D. Arnold was posted to Arnold's account as $67.

Problem Set A

L.O. 2,3,4,5 **Problem 11-1A** Marvin Wholesale Beauty Supplies had the following sales of merchandise on account and sales returns and allowances during November:

Nov. 2 Sold merchandise on account to Wanda's Hairitage, invoice no. 91, $158.62.
   8 Sold merchandise on account to Shear Touch Styling Salon, invoice no. 92, $327.50.
   10 Sold merchandise on account to Rhonda's Coiffure Center, invoice no. 93, $428.42.
   15 Sold merchandise on account to Piedmont Hair Design, invoice no. 94, $126.90.

Nov. 16 Issued credit memo no. 12, $64.21, to Shear Touch Styling Salon for merchandise returned.

21 Sold merchandise on account to Wanda's Hairitage, invoice no. 95, $322.74.

23 Issued credit memo no. 13, $119.52, to Rhonda's Coiffure Center for merchandise returned.

26 Sold merchandise on account to Shear Touch Styling Salon, invoice no. 96, $126.47.

28 Sold merchandise on account to Piedmont Hair Design, invoice no. 97, $215.44.

29 Sold merchandise on account to Wanda's Hairitage, invoice no. 98, $49.77.

30 Issued credit memo no. 14, $29.47, to Rhonda's Coiffure Center for merchandise damaged in transit.

Instructions

1. Record these sales of merchandise on account in the sales journal (page 34). Record the sales returns and allowances in the general journal (page 59).
2. Immediately after recording each transaction, post to the accounts receivable ledger.
3. Post the amounts from the general journal daily. Post the sales journal amount as a total at the end of the month.
4. Prepare a schedule of accounts receivable. Compare the balance of the Accounts Receivable controlling account with the total of the schedule of accounts receivable.

L.O. 2,3,4,5
C•
Problem 11-2A C. H. Brighton Company sells electrical supplies on a wholesale basis. The following transactions took place during April of this year:

Apr. 3 Sold merchandise on account to Mayfair Company, invoice no. 822, $641.20.

7 Sold merchandise on account to L. R. Friedman Company, invoice no. 823, $378.53.

8 Sold merchandise on account to Danforth Hardware, invoice no. 824, $193.25.

13 Issued credit memo no. 61 to L. R. Friedman Company for merchandise returned $46.50.

15 Sold merchandise on account to Berg and Hobart, invoice no: 825, $814.77.

21 Sold merchandise on account to Poe and Roberts, invoice no. 826, $681.64.

24 Issued credit memo no. 62 to Berg and Hobart for merchandise returned, $78.31.

26 Sold merchandise on account to Overmeier Company, invoice no. 827, $587.16.

28 Issued credit memo no. 63 to Danforth Hardware for damage to merchandise, $43.67.

30 Sold merchandise on account to Danforth Hardware, invoice no. 828, $740.04.

Instructions

1. Record these sales of merchandise on account in the sales journal (page 39). Record the sales returns and allowances in the general journal (page 74).
2. Immediately after recording each transaction, post to the accounts receivable ledger.
3. Post the amounts from the general journal daily. Post the sales journal amount as a total at the end of the month.
4. Prepare a schedule of accounts receivable. Compare the balance of the Accounts Receivable controlling account with the total of the schedule of accounts receivable.

L.O. 2,3,4,5   **Problem 11-3A**   Mancini Florists sells flowers on a retail basis. Most of the sales are for cash; however, a few steady customers have charge accounts. Mancini's sales staff fills out sales slips for each sale. The state government levies a 5 percent retail sales tax, which is collected by the retailer. Mancini Florists' charge sales for March are as follows:

Mar.   4   Sold floral arrangement on account to R. Drake, sales slip no. 236, $32, plus sales tax of $1.60, total $33.60.

7   Sold potted plant on account to C. Mills, sales slip no. 272, $18, plus sales tax of $.90, total $18.90.

12   Sold wreath on account to American Legion for $64, plus sales tax, sales slip no. 294.

17   Town Funeral Home bought several floral arrangements on account, sales slip no. 299, $180 plus sales tax.

20   Town Funeral Home returned a flower spray. Delivery of the spray occurred after the funeral was over. Mancini allowed full credit on the sale of $36 and the sales tax of $1.80.

21   Peninsula Savings and Loan Association bought flower arrangements on account for their anniversary for $236, plus sales tax, sales slip no. 310.

22   Allowed Peninsula Savings and Loan Association credit, $20 plus tax, because of withered blossoms in floral arrangements.

27   Sold corsage on account to B. Cater, sales slip no. 332, $16.80, plus sales tax.

Instructions

1. Record these transactions in either the sales journal (page 23) or the general journal (page 57).
2. Immediately after recording each transaction, post to the accounts receivable ledger.
3. Post the amounts from the general journal daily. Post the sales journal amount as a total at the end of the month.
4. Prepare a schedule of accounts receivable.

L.O. 4,7   **Problem 11-4A**   Rogers Sporting Goods Supply uses duplicate copies of its charge sales invoices as a sales journal and posts to the accounts receivable ledger directly from the sales invoices. The invoices are totaled at the end of the month, and an entry is made in the general journal to summarize the charge sales for the month. The charge sales invoices for December are as follows:

Dec.   4 R. A. Flanders Company, invoice no. 5216, $451.
         9 Smith Athletic Supply, invoice no. 5240, $666.
     11 C. T. Brandon, invoice no. 5242, $341.
     18 Howard and Rule, Inc., invoice no. 5267, $269.
     24 Bauer and Low, invoice no. 5287, $402.
     27 Sadler Specialty Company, invoice no. 5294, $569.
     28 Rowland and Company, invoice no. 5311, $334.
     31 Smith Athletic Supply, invoice no. 5317, $293.

Instructions

1. Post to the accounts receivable ledger directly from the sales invoices, listing the invoice number in the Posting Reference column.
2. Record the summarizing entry in the general journal (page 33) for the total amount of the sales invoices.
3. Post the general journal entry to the appropriate accounts in the general ledger.
4. Prepare a schedule of accounts receivable.

Problem Set B

L.O. 2,3,4,5   **Problem 11-1B** Marvin Wholesale Beauty Supplies had the following sales of merchandise on account and sales returns and allowances during November:

Nov.   5 Sold merchandise on account to Wanda's Hairitage, invoice no. 71, $141.60.
      9 Sold merchandise on account to Shear Touch Styling Salon, invoice no. 72, $212.72.
    11 Sold merchandise on account to Rhonda's Coiffure Center, invoice no. 73, $326.41.
    15 Sold merchandise on account to Piedmont Hair Design, invoice no. 74, $340.50.
    16 Issued credit memo no. 14, $72.14, to Shear Touch Styling Salon for merchandise returned.
    21 Sold merchandise on account to Wanda's Hairitage, invoice no. 75, $417.92.
    22 Issued credit memo no. 15, $27.15, to Rhonda's Coiffure Center for merchandise returned.
    26 Sold merchandise on account to Piedmont Hair Design, invoice no. 76, $271.96.
    28 Sold merchandise on account to Shear Touch Styling Salon, invoice no. 77, $284.71.
    29 Sold merchandise on account to Wanda's Hairitage, invoice no. 78, $97.52.

Nov.   30 Issued credit memo no. 16 to Piedmont Hair Design for damage done to merchandise during shipping, $27.12.

Instructions

1. Record these sales of merchandise on account in the sales journal (page 34). Record the sales returns and allowances in the general journal (page 59).
2. Immediately after recording each transaction, post to the accounts receivable ledger.
3. Post the amounts from the general journal daily. Post the sales journal amount as a total at the end of the month.
4. Prepare a schedule of accounts receivable. Compare the balance of the Accounts Receivable controlling account with the total of the schedule of accounts receivable.

L.O. 2,3,4,5   **Problem 11-2B**   C. H. Brighton Company sells electrical supplies on a wholesale basis. The following transactions took place during April of this year:

Apr.   1 Sold merchandise on account to Mayfair Company, invoice no. 761, $561.24.

       5 Sold merchandise on account to L. R. Friedman Company, invoice no. 762, $297.11.

       6 Issued credit memo no. 50 to Mayfair Company for merchandise returned, $42.72.

      10 Sold merchandise on account to Danforth Hardware, invoice no. 763, $193.35.

      14 Sold merchandise on account to Berg and Hobart, invoice no. 764, $740.16.

      17 Sold merchandise on account to Poe and Roberts, invoice no. 765, $472.12.

      21 Issued credit memo no. 51 to Berg and Hobart for merchandise returned, $67.77.

      24 Sold merchandise on account to Overmeier Company, invoice no. 766, $482.87.

      26 Sold merchandise on account to Danforth Hardware, invoice no. 767, $761.19.

      30 Issued credit memo no. 52 to Danforth Hardware for damage to merchandise, $91.50.

Instructions

1. Record these sales of merchandise on account in the sales journal (page 39). Record the sales returns and allowances in the general journal (page 74).
2. Immediately after recording each transaction, post to the accounts receivable ledger.
3. Post the amounts from the general journal daily. Post the sales journal amount as a total at the end of the month.
4. Prepare a schedule of accounts receivable. Compare the balance of the Accounts Receivable controlling account with the total of the schedule of accounts receivable.

L.O. 2,3,4,5 **Problem 11-3B** Mancini Florists sells flowers on a retail basis. Most of the sales are for cash; however, a few steady customers have charge accounts. Mancini's sales staff fill out sales slips for each sale. The state government levies a 5 percent retail sales tax, which is collected by the retailer. The following represent Mancini Florists' charge sales for March:

Mar. 4 Sold potted plant on account to C. Mills, sales slip no. 242, $18, plus sales tax of $.90, total $18.90.

6 Sold floral arrangement on account to R. Drake, sales slip no. 267, $36, plus sales tax of $1.80, total $37.80.

12 Sold corsage on account to B. Cater, sales slip no. 279, $14, plus sales tax of $.70.

16 Sold wreath on account to American Legion for $68, plus sales tax, sales slip no. 296.

18 Town Funeral Home bought several floral arrangements on account. Sales slip no. 314, $240 plus sales tax.

21 Town Funeral Home returned a flower spray. Delivery of the spray occurred after the funeral was over. Mancini allowed full credit on the sale of $44 and the sales tax of $2.20.

23 Peninsula Savings and Loan Association bought flower arrangements on account for their anniversary for $160 plus sales tax, sales slip no. 337.

24 Allowed Peninsula Savings and Loan Association credit, $18, plus tax, because of withered blossoms in floral arrangements.

Instructions

1. Record these transactions in either the sales journal (page 23) or the general journal (page 57).
2. Immediately after recording each transaction, post to the accounts receivable ledger.
3. Post the amounts from the general journal daily. Post the sales journal amount as a total at the end of the month.
4. Prepare a schedule of accounts receivable.

L.O. 4,7 **Problem 11-4B** Rogers Sporting Goods Supply uses duplicate copies of its charge sales invoices as a sales journal and posts to the accounts receivable ledger directly from the sales invoices. At the end of the month, the accountant totals the invoices and makes an entry in the general journal summarizing the charge sales for the month. The charge sales invoices are as follows:

Dec. 3 R. A. Flanders Company, invoice no. 5214, $450.

9 C. T. Brandon, invoice no. 5237, $681.

11 Smith Athletic Supply, invoice no. 5245, $215.

13 Bauer and Low, invoice no. 5261, $1,026.

17 Howard and Rule, Inc., invoice no. 5277, $644.

19 Sadler Specialty Company, invoice no. 5291, $485.

23 Rowland and Company, invoice no. 5309, $945.

30 Smith Athletic Supply, invoice no. 5322, $1,327.

Instructions

1. Post to the accounts receivable ledger directly from the sales invoices, listing the invoice number in the Posting Reference column.
2. Record the summarizing entry in the general journal (page 33) for the total amount of the sales invoices.
3. Post the general journal entry to the appropriate accounts in the general ledger.
4. Prepare a schedule of accounts receivable.

12 Accounting for Merchandise: Purchases

LEARNING OBJECTIVES

After you have completed this chapter, you will be able to do the following:

1. Record transactions in a three-column purchases journal.
2. Post from a three-column purchases journal to an accounts payable ledger and a general ledger.
3. Record transactions involving purchases returns and allowances in a general journal.
4. Prepare a schedule of accounts payable.
5. Record transactions in a multicolumn purchases journal.
6. Post directly from purchase invoices to an accounts payable ledger and a general ledger.

We have been talking about the procedures, accounts, and special journals used to record the *selling* of merchandise. Now let's talk about those same elements as they apply to the *buying* of merchandise. We will be dealing with the Purchases account and with Purchases Returns and Allowances. In this chapter you'll see that Accounts Payable is a controlling account, just as you saw in Chapter 11 that Accounts Receivable is a controlling account.

PURCHASING PROCEDURES

When you think of the great variety in types and sizes of merchandising firms, it comes as no surprise to learn that there is also considerable variety in the procedures used to buy goods for resale. Some purchases may be for cash; however, in most cases, purchases are on a credit basis. In a small retail store, the owner may do the buying. In large retail and wholesale concerns, department heads or division managers do the buying, after which the Purchasing Department goes into action: placing purchase orders, following up the orders, receiving the goods, and seeing that deliveries are made to the right departments. The Purchasing Department also acts as a source of information on current prices, price trends, quality of goods, prospective suppliers, and reliability of suppliers.

The Purchasing Department normally requires that any buying orders be in writing, in the form of a **purchase requisition**. After the purchase requisition is approved, the Purchasing Department sends a **purchase order** to the supplier. A purchase order is the company's written offer to buy certain goods. The accountant does not make any entry at this point, because the supplier has not yet indicated acceptance of the order. A purchase order with at least five copies is made out. One copy goes to the supplier, one stays in the Purchasing Department (as proof of what was ordered), one goes to the department that sent out the requisition (telling them that the goods they wanted have been ordered), one goes to the Accounting Department, and a blind copy (with quantities omitted) goes to Receiving.

To continue with the accounts of City-Wide Electric Supply: The Cable Department submits a purchase requisition to the Purchasing Department as shown in Figure 12-1.

FIGURE 12-1

CITY-WIDE ELECTRIC SUPPLY   No. C-726
1968 N.E. Allen Street
Portland, OR 97201

PURCHASE REQUISITION

DEPARTMENT   _Cable_   DATE OF REQUEST   _July 2, 19–_
ADVISE ON DELIVERY   _Mr. Holloway_   DATE REQUIRED   _Aug. 5, 19–_

QUANTITY	DESCRIPTION
1,000'	Jacketed copper cable, 6 ga., 65 amp. (100' roll)

APPROVED BY _R. C. Schmidt_   REQUESTED BY _J. H. Holloway_

FOR PURCHASING DEPT. USE ONLY

PURCHASE ORDER NO. _7918_
DATE _July 5, 19–_   ISSUED TO: _Draper, Inc._
                                                 1616 Madera Ave.
                                                 Los Angeles, CA 90026

The Purchasing Department completes the rest of the purchase requisition and then sends out the purchase order shown in Figure 12-2.

FIGURE 12-2

CITY-WIDE ELECTRIC SUPPLY
1968 N.E. Allen Street
Portland, OR 97201

PURCHASE ORDER

TO: Draper, Inc.
1616 Madera Ave.
Los Angeles, CA 90026

DATE: July 5, 19–
ORDER NO.: 7918
SHIPPED BY: Freight Truck
TERMS: 2/10, n/30

QUANTITY	DESCRIPTION	UNIT PRICE	TOTAL
1,000'	Jacketed copper cable, 6 ga., 65 amp. (100' roll)	39	390 00

R.C. Schmidt

FIGURE 12-3

DRAPER, INC.
1616 Madera Ave.
Los Angeles, CA 90026

No. 2706

INVOICE

SOLD TO: City-Wide Electric Supply
1968 N.E. Allen St.
Portland, OR 97201

DATE: July 31, 19–
ORDER NO.: 7918
SHIPPED BY: Western Freight Line
TERMS: 2/10, n/30

YOUR ORDER NO.	SALESPERSON	TERMS
7918	C. L.	2/10, n/30
DATE SHIPPED	SHIPPED BY	FOB
July 31, 19–	Western Freight Line	Los Angeles

QUANTITY	DESCRIPTION	UNIT PRICE	TOTAL
1,000'	Jacketed copper cable, 6 ga., 65 amp. (100' roll)	39	390 00
	Freight		30 00
	Total		420 00

The seller then sends an **invoice** to the buyer. This invoice should arrive in advance of the goods (or at least *with* the goods). From the seller's point of view, this is a sales invoice. If the sale is on credit, as we saw in Chapter 11, the seller's accountant makes an entry debiting Accounts Receivable and crediting Sales. To the buyer, this is a purchase invoice. Customarily, when the merchandise is received, the buyer's accountant makes an entry debiting Purchases and crediting Accounts Payable. City-Wide Electric Supply receives the invoice shown in Figure 12-3 from Draper, Inc.

Let us review the fundamental accounting equation with the T accounts involved in buying and selling merchandise introduced in Chapter 11. As before, color is used to emphasize the contra accounts that are deductions from Purchases and Sales.

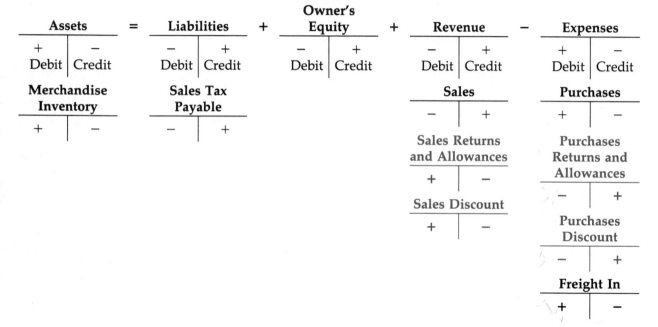

Bear in mind that the Purchases account is used exclusively for the buying of merchandise intended for resale. *If the firm buys anything else, the accountant records the amount under the appropriate asset or expense account.* At the end of the fiscal period, the balance in the Purchases account represents the total cost of merchandise bought during the period. As we said in Chapter 11, Purchases is classified as an expense only for the sake of convenience. The classification is permissible because Purchases is closed at the end of the fiscal period along with the expense accounts.

Purchases Returns and Allowances is a deduction from Purchases. A separate account is set up to keep track of the amount of the returns and the reductions in bills because of damaged merchandise. On the income statement, we treat Purchases Returns and Allowances and Purchases Discount as deductions from Purchases; so, for consistency they are presented below Purchases in the fundamental accounting equation just shown.

Freight Charges on Incoming Merchandise

Freight In is an expense account used to record the transportation costs of merchandise purchased for resale. Companies use this account to keep a record of all separately charged delivery costs on incoming merchandise. Some accountants call this account *Transportation In.*

Freight costs are expressed as FOB (free on board) destination or shipping point. (Destination is the buyer's location; shipping point is the seller's location.) In both cases, the supplier loads the goods free on board the carrier. Beyond that point, there must be an understanding as to who is responsible for ultimately paying the freight charges. If the seller assumes the entire cost of transportation, without any reimbursement from the buyer, the terms are **FOB destination.** If the buyer is responsible for paying the freight cost, the shipping terms are called **FOB shipping point.**

Briefly, in FOB destination the freight charges are not stated, and the buyer simply pays the amount of the bill. For example, City-Wide Electric (remember it's in Portland) buys conduit from a supplier in Chicago with shipping terms of FOB Portland listed on the invoice. The total of the invoice is $1,740, and there is no separate listing of freight charges. In other words, the seller has included the transportation costs in the price.

On the other hand, FOB shipping point, where the buyer is responsible for paying the freight charges, may come in two ways.

1. The freight charges may be paid separately by the buyer to the transportation company. For example, an automobile dealer in Houston buys cars FOB Detroit. In this case, the automobile dealer makes one check payable to the manufacturer and another check payable to the carrier for the freight charges.
2. The transportation costs may be listed separately on the invoice. For example, suppose a person orders a refrigerator from a mail order company like Sears. The freight charges are listed on the bill or invoice, and the mail order company has prepaid (paid in advance) the freight charges as a favor or convenience for the buyer. However, the buyer is still responsible for reimbursing the mail order company for the freight charges.

Getting back to the invoice of Draper, Inc., note that the freight cost is listed separately, so the terms are FOB shipping point. Draper paid the transportation cost, but City-Wide must reimburse Draper for this cost. Incidentally, unless the title to the goods is expressly reserved by the seller, whoever pays the freight charges customarily has title to the goods.

Let's proceed with three other transactions for City-Wide Electric. As in Chapter 11, we will first record the transactions in a general journal. Then, as a means of reemphasizing the advantages of special journals as opposed to a general journal, we will record the same transactions in a special journal.

During the first week in August, the following transactions took place:

Aug. 2 Bought merchandise on account from Draper, Inc., $390, their invoice no. 2706, dated July 31; terms 2/10, n/30, FOB Los Angeles; freight prepaid and added to the invoice, $30 (total $420).

3 Bought merchandise on account from Reilly and Peters Company, $708, their invoice no. 982, dated August 2; terms net 30 days; FOB Seattle; freight prepaid and added to the invoice, $52 (total $760).

5 Bought merchandise on account from Adkins Manufacturing Company, $692, their invoice no. 10611, dated August 3; terms 2/10, n/30, FOB Cleveland.

Notice that the transactions with Draper, Inc., and Reilly and Peters are both FOB shipping point, with the freight charges listed separately. Consequently, the buyer (City-Wide) must reimburse the sellers for the trans-

FIGURE 12-4

GENERAL JOURNAL   PAGE 22

	DATE		DESCRIPTION	POST. REF.	DEBIT	CREDIT	
1	19–						1
2	Aug.	2	Purchases	511	3 9 0 00		2
3			Freight In	514	3 0 00		3
4			Accounts Payable	212		4 2 0 00	4
5			Draper, Inc., their invoice				5
6			no. 2706, dated July 31,				6
7			terms 2/10, n/30.				7
8							8
9		3	Purchases	511	7 0 8 00		9
10			Freight In	514	5 2 00		10
11			Accounts Payable	212		7 6 0 00	11
12			Reilly and Peters, their				12
13			invoice no. 982, dated				13
14			August 2, terms net 30				14
15			days.				15
16							16
17		5	Purchases	511	6 9 2 00		17
18			Accounts Payable	212		6 9 2 00	18
19			Adkins Manufacturing Co.,				19
20			their invoice no. 10611, dated				20
21			August 3, terms 2/10, n/30.				21
22							22

portation costs by paying the total of the invoices. However, in the transaction with Adkins Manufacturing, which is FOB Cleveland without freight charges listed, the buyer (City-Wide) must pay the freight costs separately, perhaps when the goods are delivered. We will discuss paying the freight charges directly in Chapter 13, when we introduce the cash payments journal.

For the present, we are concerned with recording the three purchases. Let's visualize these transactions in terms of T accounts.

Purchases		Freight In		Accounts Payable	
+	−	+	−	−	+
Aug. 2 390		Aug. 2 30			Aug. 2 420
3 708		3 52			3 760
5 692					5 692

If these transactions are recorded in a general journal, they look like Figure 12-4. Next the general journal entries would be posted to the general ledger.

GENERAL LEDGER

ACCOUNT _Accounts Payable_   ACCOUNT NO. _212_

	DATE	ITEM	POST. REF.	DEBIT	CREDIT	BALANCE DEBIT	BALANCE CREDIT	
1	19–							1
2	Aug. 1	Balance	√				3 5 6 00	2
3	2		J22		4 2 0 00		7 7 6 00	3
4	3		J22		7 6 0 00		1 5 3 6 00	4
5	5		J22		6 9 2 00		2 2 2 8 00	5
6								6
7								7

ACCOUNT _Purchases_   ACCOUNT NO. _511_

	DATE	ITEM	POST. REF.	DEBIT	CREDIT	BALANCE DEBIT	BALANCE CREDIT	
1	19–							1
2	Aug. 1	Balance	√			20 6 1 2 00		2
3	2		J22	3 9 0 00		21 0 0 2 00		3
4	3		J22	7 0 8 00		21 7 1 0 00		4
5	5		J22	6 9 2 00		22 4 0 2 00		5
6								6
7								7

ACCOUNT   _Freight In_   ACCOUNT NO. _514_

	DATE		ITEM	POST. REF.	DEBIT	CREDIT	BALANCE DEBIT	BALANCE CREDIT	
1	19–								1
2	Aug.	1	Balance	✓			1 5 0 2 00		2
3		2		J22	3 0 00		1 5 3 2 00		3
4		3		J22	5 2 00		1 5 8 4 00		4
5									5
6									6

Let's take a minute to explain the terms in the transactions. The notation "net 30 days" or "n/30" means that the bill is due within 30 days after the date of the invoice. The notation "2/10, n/30" refers to the **purchases discount** or cash discount. It means that the seller offers a 2 percent discount if the bill is paid within 10 days after the date of the invoice. Otherwise the whole bill must be paid within 30 days after the invoice date. We will be working with these credit terms in Chapter 13.

PURCHASES JOURNAL (THREE-COLUMN)

Objective 1

Record transactions in a three-column purchases journal.

The repetition illustrated in our example can be avoided if the accountant uses a **purchases journal** instead of the general journal. This purchases journal is used to record the purchase of merchandise _on account only_.

PURCHASES JOURNAL   PAGE _29_

	DATE		SUPPLIER'S NAME	INVOICE NO.	INVOICE DATE	TERMS	POST. REF.	ACCOUNTS PAYABLE CREDIT	FREIGHT IN DEBIT	PURCHASES DEBIT	
1	19–										1
2	Aug.	2	Draper, Inc.	2706	7/31	2/10, n/30		4 2 0 00	3 0 00	3 9 0 00	2
3		3	Reilly and Peters Company	982	8/2	n/30		7 6 0 00	5 2 00	7 0 8 00	3
4		5	Adkins Manufacturing Co.	10611	8/3	2/10, n/30		6 9 2 00		6 9 2 00	4
5											5
6											6

Posting from the Purchases Journal to the General Ledger

Objective 2

Post from a three-column purchases journal to an accounts payable ledger and a general ledger.

Figure 12-5 shows the journal entries for all transactions involving the purchase of merchandise on account for August and the related ledger accounts for the same time period. In the Post. Ref. column of the ledger accounts, P designates the purchases journal. After posting to the ledger accounts, the accountant goes back to the purchases journal and records the account numbers in parentheses directly below the total.

PURCHASES JOURNAL

PAGE 29

	DATE	SUPPLIER'S NAME	INVOICE NO.	INVOICE DATE	TERMS	POST. REF.	ACCOUNTS PAYABLE CREDIT	FREIGHT IN DEBIT	PURCHASES DEBIT	
1	19–									1
2	Aug. 2	Draper, Inc.	2706	7/31	2/10, n/30		4 2 0 00	3 0 00	3 9 0 00	2
3	3	Reilly and Peters Company	982	8/2	n/30		7 6 0 00	5 2 00	7 0 8 00	3
4	5	Adkins Manufacturing Co.	10611	8/3	2/10, n/30		6 9 2 00		6 9 2 00	4
5	9	Sullivan Products Co.	B643	8/6	1/10, n/30		1 6 5 00	1 0 00	1 5 5 00	5
6	18	T. R. Wetzel	46812	8/17	n/60		2 2 8 00		2 2 8 00	6
7	25	Donaldson and Farr	1024	8/23	2/10, n/30		3 7 6 00	1 4 00	3 6 2 00	7
8	26	Draper, Inc.	2801	8/25	2/10, n/30		4 0 6 00	2 2 00	3 8 4 00	8
9	31						3 0 4 7 00	1 2 8 00	2 9 1 9 00	9
10							(2 1 2)	(5 1 4)	(5 1 1)	10
11										11
12										12

FIGURE 12-5

Remember

Transactions involving the buying of supplies or other assets should not be recorded in the three-column purchases journal, because this purchases journal may be used only for the purchases of merchandise for resale.

GENERAL LEDGER

ACCOUNT Accounts Payable ACCOUNT NO. 211

	DATE	ITEM	POST. REF.	DEBIT	CREDIT	BALANCE DEBIT	BALANCE CREDIT	
1	19–							1
2	Aug. 1	Balance	✓				3 5 6 00	2
3	31		P29		3 0 4 7 00		3 4 0 3 00	3
4								4

ACCOUNT Purchases ACCOUNT NO. 511

	DATE	ITEM	POST. REF.	DEBIT	CREDIT	BALANCE DEBIT	BALANCE CREDIT	
1	19–							1
2	Aug. 1	Balance	✓			20 6 1 2 00		2
3	31		P29	2 9 1 9 00		23 5 3 1 00		3
4								4

ACCOUNT Freight In ACCOUNT NO. 514

	DATE	ITEM	POST. REF.	DEBIT	CREDIT	BALANCE DEBIT	BALANCE CREDIT	
1	19–							1
2	Aug. 1	Balance	✓			1 5 0 2 00		2
3	31		P29	1 2 8 00		1 6 3 0 00		3
4								4

THE ACCOUNTS PAYABLE LEDGER

In Chapter 11 we called the Accounts Receivable account in the general ledger a *controlling* account, and we saw that the accounts receivable ledger consists of an individual account for each charge customer. We also saw that the accountant posts to the accounts receivable ledger every day.

Accounts Payable is a parallel case; it, too, is a controlling account in the general ledger. The accounts payable ledger is a subsidiary ledger, and it consists of individual accounts for all the creditors. Again, in the accounts payable ledger, posting is usually done daily. After posting to the individual creditors' accounts, the accountant puts a check mark ($\sqrt{}$) in the Post. Ref. column of the purchases journal. After the accountant has finished all the posting to the controlling account at the end of the period, the total of the schedule of accounts payable should equal the balance of the Accounts Payable (controlling) account. Incidentally, one always uses the three-column form for the accounts payable ledger. Below is a side-by-side comparison of the T account for Accounts Payable and the three-column form.

Remember

Increases in Accounts Payable are recorded in the Credit column. Decreases in Accounts Payable are recorded in the Debit column.

Accounts Payable

Debit	Credit
−	+

ACCOUNTS PAYABLE LEDGER
Individual Account of a Creditor

DATE	ITEM	DEBIT	CREDIT	BALANCE
		−	+	

Now let's see the purchases journal (Figure 12-6) and the postings to the ledger (Figure 12-7).

FIGURE 12-6

PURCHASES JOURNAL   PAGE __29__

	DATE		SUPPLIER'S NAME	INVOICE NO.	INVOICE DATE	TERMS	POST. REF.	ACCOUNTS PAYABLE CREDIT	FREIGHT IN DEBIT	PURCHASES DEBIT	
1	19–										1
2	Aug.	2	Draper, Inc.	2706	7/31	2/10, n/30	$\sqrt{}$	4 2 0 00	3 0 00	3 9 0 00	2
3		3	Reilly and Peters Company	982	8/2	n/30	$\sqrt{}$	7 6 0 00	5 2 00	7 0 8 00	3
4		5	Adkins Manufacturing Co.	10611	8/3	2/10, n/30	$\sqrt{}$	6 9 2 00		6 9 2 00	4
5		9	Sullivan Products Co.	B643	8/6	1/10, n/30	$\sqrt{}$	1 6 5 00	1 0 00	1 5 5 00	5
6		18	T. R. Wetzel	46812	8/17	n/60	$\sqrt{}$	2 2 8 00		2 2 8 00	6
7		25	Donaldson and Farr	1024	8/23	2/10, n/30	$\sqrt{}$	3 7 6 00	1 4 00	3 6 2 00	7
8		26	Draper, Inc.	2801	8/25	2/10, n/30	$\sqrt{}$	4 0 6 00	2 2 00	3 8 4 00	8
9		31						3 0 4 7 00	1 2 8 00	2 9 1 9 00	9
10								(2 1 2)	(5 1 4)	(5 1 1)	10
11											11

Note that in the accounts payable ledger—as in the accounts receivable ledger—the accounts of the individual creditors are listed in alphabetical order.

FIGURE 12-7

ACCOUNTS PAYABLE LEDGER

NAME _Adkins Manufacturing Company_

ADDRESS _140 S. Ellsworth Avenue_
Cleveland, OH 44101

DATE		ITEM	POST. REF.	DEBIT	CREDIT	BALANCE
_19–_						
Aug.	5		P29		6 9 2 00	6 9 2 00

NAME _Draper, Inc._

ADDRESS _1616 Madera Ave._
Los Angeles, CA 90026

DATE		ITEM	POST. REF.	DEBIT	CREDIT	BALANCE
_19–_						
Aug.	2		P29		4 2 0 00	4 2 0 00
	26		P29		4 0 6 00	8 2 6 00

NAME _Donaldson and Farr_

ADDRESS _1600 Farrow Blvd._
San Jose, CA 95101

DATE		ITEM	POST. REF.	DEBIT	CREDIT	BALANCE
_19–_						
Aug.	25		P29		3 7 6 00	3 7 6 00

NAME _Reilly and Peters Company_

ADDRESS _21325 186th Ave. No._
Seattle, WA 98101

DATE		ITEM	POST. REF.	DEBIT	CREDIT	BALANCE
_19–_						
July	27		P28		1 8 0 00	1 8 0 00
Aug.	3		P29		7 6 0 00	9 4 0 00

(continued)

FIGURE 12-7
(continued)

NAME _Sullivan Products Company_
ADDRESS _1068 Casino Ave._
Los Angeles, CA 90023

DATE	ITEM	POST. REF.	DEBIT	CREDIT	BALANCE
19–					
Aug. 9		P29		1 6 5 00	1 6 5 00

NAME _T. R. Wetzel_
ADDRESS _1620 Minard St._
San Francisco, CA 94130

DATE	ITEM	POST. REF.	DEBIT	CREDIT	BALANCE
19–					
July 29		P28		1 7 6 00	1 7 6 00
Aug. 18		P29		2 2 8 00	4 0 4 00

PURCHASES RETURNS AND ALLOWANCES

As its title implies, the Purchases Returns and Allowances account handles either a return of merchandise previously purchased or an allowance made for merchandise that arrived in damaged condition. In both cases there is a reduction in the amount owed to the supplier. The buyer sends a letter or printed form to the supplier, who acknowledges the reduction by sending a **credit memorandum**. The buyer should wait for notice of the agreed deduction before making an entry.

The Purchases Returns and Allowances account is considered to be a deduction from Purchases. Using a separate account provides a better record of the total returns and allowances. Purchases Returns and Allowances is deducted from the Purchases account on the income statement. (We'll talk about this point later.) For now, let's look at an example consisting of two entries on the books of City-Wide Electric Supply.

Transaction (a) On August 5, bought merchandise on account from Adkins Manufacturing Company, $692, their invoice no. 10611 of August 3; terms 2/10, n/30, FOB Cleveland. Recorded this as a debit to Purchases and a credit to Accounts Payable. On August 6, returned $70 worth of the merchandise. Made no entry.

Transaction (b)   On August 8, received credit memorandum no. 629 from Adkins Manufacturing Company for $70. Recorded this as a debit to Accounts Payable and a credit to Purchases Returns and Allowances.

Assets	=	Liabilities	+	Owner's Equity	+	Revenue	−	Expenses
+ −		− +		− +		− +		+ −
Debit Credit		Debit Credit		Debit Credit		Debit Credit		Debit Credit

Accounts Payable

−	+
(b) 70	(a) 692

Purchases

+	−
(a) 692	

Purchases Returns and Allowances

−	+
	(b) 70

Purchases Returns and Allowances is credited because City-Wide Electric has more returns and allowances than before. Accounts Payable is debited because City-Wide Electric owes less than before.

During August, suppose that City-Wide Electric Supply also received a credit memo from Sullivan Products Company as an allowance for damaged merchandise. The entries in the general journal for recording the two credit memos are shown below.

Objective 3

Record transactions involving purchases returns and allowances in a general journal.

GENERAL JOURNAL   PAGE 27

	DATE	DESCRIPTION	POST. REF.	DEBIT	CREDIT	
1	19–					1
2	Aug. 8	Accounts Payable, Adkins				2
3		Manufacturing Company		7 0 00		3
4		Purchases Returns and Allowances			7 0 00	4
5		Credit memo 629 for return				5
6		of merchandise.				6
7						7
8						8
9	12	Accounts Payable, Sullivan				9
10		Products Company		3 6 00		10
11		Purchases Returns and Allowances			3 6 00	11
12		Credit memo 482 as an				12
13		allowance for damaged				13
14		merchandise.				14
15						15

In these entries, Accounts Payable is followed by the name of the individual creditor's account. **The accountant must post to both the Accounts Payable controlling account and the individual creditor's account in the accounts payable ledger.** The journal entries are shown below as they appear when the posting is completed. The account numbers in the Post. Ref. column indicate postings to the accounts in the general ledger, and the check marks indicate postings to the accounts in the accounts payable ledger.

GENERAL JOURNAL PAGE __27__

	DATE		DESCRIPTION	POST. REF.	DEBIT	CREDIT	
1	19–						1
2	Aug.	8	Accounts Payable, Adkins				2
3			Manufacturing Company	212/√	7 0 00		3
4			Purchases Returns and Allowances	512		7 0 00	4
5			Credit memo 629 for return				5
6			of merchandise.				6
7							7
8							8
9		12	Accounts Payable, Sullivan				9
10			Products Company	212/√	3 6 00		10
11			Purchases Returns and Allowances	512		3 6 00	11
12			Credit memo 482 as an				12
13			allowance for damaged				13
14			merchandise.				14
15							15

GENERAL LEDGER

ACCOUNT *Accounts Payable* ACCOUNT NO. 212

	DATE		ITEM	POST. REF.	DEBIT	CREDIT	BALANCE DEBIT	BALANCE CREDIT	
1	19–								1
2	Aug.	1	Balance	√				3 5 6 00	2
3		8		J27	7 0 00			2 8 6 00	3
4		12		J27	3 6 00			2 5 0 00	4
5									5

ACCOUNT *Purchases Returns and Allowances* ACCOUNT NO. 512

	DATE		ITEM	POST. REF.	DEBIT	CREDIT	BALANCE DEBIT	BALANCE CREDIT	
1	19–								1
2	Aug.	1	Balance	√				6 4 0 00	2
3		8		J27		7 0 00		7 1 0 00	3
4		12		J27		3 6 00		7 4 6 00	4
5									5

Remember

From the viewpoint of the buyer, a credit memo is recorded as a debit to Accounts Payable and a credit to Purchases Returns and Allowances. From the viewpoint of the seller, a credit memo is recorded as a debit to Sales Returns and Allowances and a credit to Accounts Receivable.

ACCOUNTS PAYABLE LEDGER

NAME _Adkins Manufacturing Company_

ADDRESS _140 S. Ellsworth Avenue_
Cleveland, OH 44101

DATE	ITEM	POST. REF.	DEBIT	CREDIT	BALANCE
19–					
Aug. 5		P29		6 9 2 00	6 9 2 00
8		J27	7 0 00		6 2 2 00

NAME _Sullivan Products Company_

ADDRESS _1068 Casino Ave._
Los Angeles, CA 90023

DATE	ITEM	POST. REF.	DEBIT	CREDIT	BALANCE
19–					
Aug. 9		P29		1 6 5 00	1 6 5 00
12		J27	3 6 00		1 2 9 00

Schedule of Accounts Payable

Objective 4

Prepare a schedule of accounts payable.

Assuming that no other transactions involved Accounts Payable, the schedule of accounts payable would appear as follows. Note that the balances of the creditors' accounts, with the exception of the accounts for Adkins Manufacturing Company and Sullivan Manufacturing Company, are taken from the accounts payable ledger shown in Figure 12-7.

City-Wide Electric Supply
Schedule of Accounts Payable
August 31, 19–

Adkins Manufacturing Company	$ 6 2 2	00
Draper, Inc.	8 2 6	00
Donaldson and Farr	3 7 6	00
Reilly and Peters Company	9 4 0	00
Sullivan Products Company	1 2 9	00
T. R. Wetzel, Inc.	4 0 4	00
Total Accounts Payable	$3 2 9 7	00

The Accounts Payable controlling account in the general ledger at the top of the next page is now posted up to date.

GENERAL LEDGER

ACCOUNT _Accounts Payable_   ACCOUNT NO. _212_

	DATE	ITEM	POST. REF.	DEBIT	CREDIT	BALANCE DEBIT	BALANCE CREDIT	
1	19–							1
2	Aug. 1	Balance	√				3 5 6 00	2
3	8		J27	7 0 00			2 8 6 00	3
4	12		J27	3 6 00			2 5 0 00	4
5	31		P29		3 0 4 7 00		3 2 9 7 00	5
6								6
7								7

MULTICOLUMN PURCHASES JOURNAL (INVOICE REGISTER)

Objective 5

Record transactions in a multicolumn purchases journal.

Instead of the three-column purchases journal we have shown, some businesses prefer to use a multicolumn purchases journal or invoice register, which will handle not only freight charges and purchases of merchandise but anything bought on account. Items other than merchandise usually consist of supplies and equipment acquired for use in the firm. The advantage of a multicolumn purchases journal is that all types of purchases on account are recorded in one journal.

As an illustration, we will use another company, Helen's Gift Shop. Here are three transactions occurring during the first week in May recorded in the T accounts on the next page.

FIGURE 12-8

PURCHASES JOURNAL

	DATE	SUPPLIER'S NAME	INVOICE NO.	INVOICE DATE	TERMS	POST. REF.	ACCOUNTS PAYABLE CREDIT
1	19–						
2	May 2	Chase Specialty Company	L311	5/1	2/10, n/30	√	6 4 6 00
3	4	HH Paper Products	962D	5/4	n/30	√	9 8 00
4	5	Craig Cabinet Shop	4273	5/5	n/30	√	6 2 9 00
5	9	R. P. Klaus Company	C-349	5/7	1/10, n/30	√	4 1 6 00
6	16	Gable and Son	124-9	5/15	2/10, n/30	√	3 9 2 00
7	24	Moore Office Machines	N92	5/23	n/30	√	5 1 5 71
8	27	C. B. Baird, Inc.	517R	5/26	1/15, n/60	√	3 0 4 00
9	30	Coe Office Supplies	5119	5/30	n/30	√	4 2 36
10	31	Brice Corporation	D274	5/29	2/10, n/30	√	2 7 7 20
11	31						3 3 2 0 27
12							(2 1 2)
13							

May 2 Bought merchandise on account from Chase Specialty Company, $610, their invoice no. L311, dated May 1; terms 2/10, n/30, FOB shipping point, freight prepaid and added to the invoice $36 (total $646).

Purchases		Freight In		Accounts Payable	
+	−	+	−	−	+
610		36			646

May 4 Bought paper sacks on account from HH Paper Products, their invoice no. 962D, dated May 4, terms n/30, $98.

Store Supplies		Accounts Payable	
+	−	−	+
98			98

May 5 Bought a display case on account from Craig Cabinet Shop, their invoice no. 4273, dated May 5; terms n/30, $629.

Store Equipment		Accounts Payable	
+	−	−	+
629			629

These transactions, as well as other transactions during the month, are now recorded in the multicolumn purchases journal shown in Figure 12-8.

PAGE 62

FIGURE 12-8
(continued)

PURCHASES DEBIT	FREIGHT IN DEBIT	STORE SUPPLIES DEBIT	SUNDRY ACCOUNTS DEBIT		
			ACCOUNT	POST. REF.	AMOUNT
6 1 0 00	3 6 00				
		9 8 00			
			Store Equipment	125	6 2 9 00
4 0 4 00	1 2 00				
3 9 2 00					
			Office Equipment	127	5 1 5 71
3 0 4 00					
			Office Supplies	115	4 2 36
2 6 4 20	1 3 00				
1 9 7 4 20	6 1 00	9 8 00			1 1 8 7 07
(5 1 1)	(5 1 4)	(1 1 4)			(✓)

For each transaction recorded in the multicolumn purchases journal, the amount to be credited is entered in the Accounts Payable Credit column. The next three columns are used to record the particular accounts most frequently affected. These are called special columns because one special account is involved. The final set of columns, under the heading Sundry Accounts Debit, is used to record the buying of items not provided for in the special debit columns. The term *sundry* means "miscellaneous."

Posting from the Multicolumn Purchases Journal

Posting to the creditors' accounts in the accounts payable ledger is similar to posting from a three-column purchases journal. Posting is done daily, and the check marks (√) in the Post. Ref. column indicate that the amounts have been posted separately.

The amounts listed in the Sundry Accounts Debit column are posted separately—usually on a daily basis. The posting process is the same as that for posting from a general journal. The account numbers recorded in the Post. Ref. column indicate that the amounts have been posted.

At the end of the month, first prove that the sum of the debit totals equals the total of the Accounts Payable Credit column. This process is referred to as **crossfooting** the journal.

	Debit Totals		Credit Total
Purchases	$1,974.20	Accounts Payable	$3,320.27
Freight In	61.00		
Store Supplies	98.00		
Sundry Accounts	1,187.07		
	$3,320.27		

Next, the accountant posts the special columns as totals. After posting the total amount, he or she records the ledger account number in parentheses below the total in the appropriate column. The check mark (√) placed below the total of the Sundry column means "do not post"—since the figures have already been posted separately.

POSTING DIRECTLY FROM PURCHASE INVOICES (AN ALTERNATIVE TO USING A PURCHASES JOURNAL)

Objective 6

Post directly from purchase invoices to an accounts payable ledger and a general ledger.

Posting from purchase invoices is a shortcut like posting from sales invoices (described in Chapter 11). The accountant posts to the individual creditors' accounts daily, directly from the purchase invoices. The suppliers' invoice numbers rather than journal page numbers are recorded in the Post. Ref. column. The Accounts Payable controlling account in the general ledger is brought up to date at the end of the month by making a summarizing entry in the general journal. The accountant debits Purchases and Freight In, as well as any assets the company bought on account, and credits Accounts Payable.

Since posting directly from purchase invoices is a variation of the accounting system, we shall use a different example: Mel's Towing and Trailer Service. This firm sorts its invoices for the month and finds that the totals are as follows: purchases of merchandise, $8,354; freight charges on merchandise, $256; store supplies, $168; office supplies, $126; store equipment, $520. The accountant then makes a summarizing entry in the general journal, as follows.

GENERAL JOURNAL   PAGE _37_

	DATE		DESCRIPTION	POST. REF.	DEBIT	CREDIT	
1	19–						1
2	Oct.	31	Purchases	511	8 3 5 4 00		2
3			Freight In	514	2 5 6 00		3
4			Store Supplies	114	1 6 8 00		4
5			Office Supplies	115	1 2 6 00		5
6			Store Equipment	121	5 2 0 00		6
7			Accounts Payable	212		9 4 2 4 00	7
8			Summarizing entry for total				8
9			purchase of goods on account.				9
10							10

The accountant posts the above entry to the general ledger accounts.

GENERAL LEDGER

ACCOUNT _Store Supplies_   ACCOUNT NO. _114_

	DATE	ITEM	POST. REF.	DEBIT	CREDIT	BALANCE DEBIT	BALANCE CREDIT	
1	19–							1
2	Oct. 31		J37	1 6 8 00		1 6 8 00		2
3								3

ACCOUNT _Office Supplies_   ACCOUNT NO. _115_

	DATE	ITEM	POST. REF.	DEBIT	CREDIT	BALANCE DEBIT	BALANCE CREDIT	
1	19–							1
2	Oct. 31		J37	1 2 6 00		1 2 6 00		2
3								3

	DATE	ITEM	POST. REF.	DEBIT	CREDIT	BALANCE DEBIT	BALANCE CREDIT	
1	19–							1
2	Oct. 31		J37	5 2 0 00		5 2 0 00		2
3								3
4								4
5								5

ACCOUNT **Store Equipment** ACCOUNT NO. **121**

	DATE	ITEM	POST. REF.	DEBIT	CREDIT	BALANCE DEBIT	BALANCE CREDIT	
1								1
2	Oct. 31		J37		9 4 2 4 00		9 4 2 4 00	2
3								3
4								4

ACCOUNT **Accounts Payable** ACCOUNT NO. **212**

	DATE	ITEM	POST. REF.	DEBIT	CREDIT	BALANCE DEBIT	BALANCE CREDIT	
1	19–							1
2	Oct. 31		J37	8 3 5 4 00		8 3 5 4 00		2
3								3
4								4

ACCOUNT **Purchases** ACCOUNT NO. **511**

	DATE	ITEM	POST. REF.	DEBIT	CREDIT	BALANCE DEBIT	BALANCE CREDIT	
1	19–							1
2	Oct. 31		J37	2 5 6 00		2 5 6 00		2
3								3
4								4

ACCOUNT **Freight In** ACCOUNT NO. **514**

This procedure does away with the need for a purchases journal, and it also includes the buying of any assets on account in the same summarizing entry. An example of an invoice is shown in Figure 12-9.

FIGURE 12-9

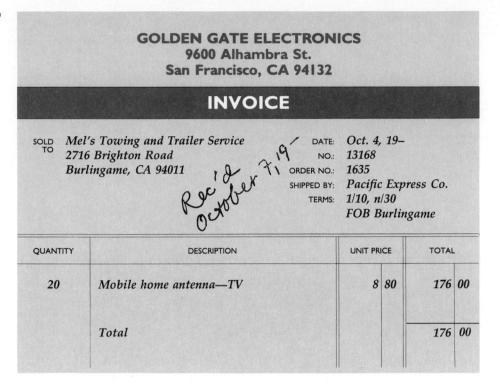

Mel's Towing and Trailer Service posts the amount of the invoice to the account of the supplier in the accounts payable ledger:

ACCOUNTS PAYABLE LEDGER

NAME   *Golden Gate Electronics*

ADDRESS   *9600 Alhambra St.*

        San Francisco, CA 94132

DATE		ITEM	POST. REF.	DEBIT	CREDIT	BALANCE
19–						
Oct.	*7*		*13168*		*1 7 6 00*	*1 7 6 00*

Mel's Towing and Trailer Service will also include the $176 figure in the summarizing entry recorded in the general journal, debiting Purchases and crediting Accounts Payable. Note that the supplier's invoice number is recorded in the Post. Ref. column in the Golden Gate Electronics account.

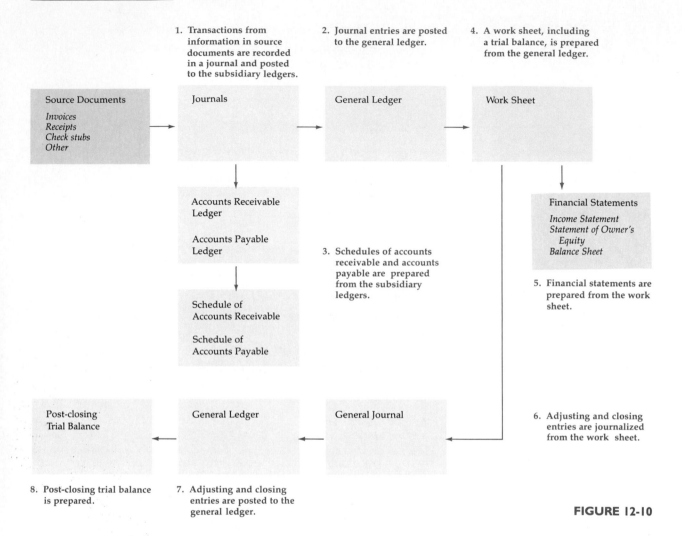

1. Transactions from information in source documents are recorded in a journal and posted to the subsidiary ledgers.

2. Journal entries are posted to the general ledger.

4. A work sheet, including a trial balance, is prepared from the general ledger.

Source Documents

Invoices
Receipts
Check stubs
Other

Journals

General Ledger

Work Sheet

Accounts Receivable Ledger

Accounts Payable Ledger

Financial Statements

Income Statement
Statement of Owner's Equity
Balance Sheet

3. Schedules of accounts receivable and accounts payable are prepared from the subsidiary ledgers.

5. Financial statements are prepared from the work sheet.

Schedule of Accounts Receivable

Schedule of Accounts Payable

Post-closing Trial Balance

General Ledger

General Journal

6. Adjusting and closing entries are journalized from the work sheet.

8. Post-closing trial balance is prepared.

7. Adjusting and closing entries are posted to the general ledger.

FIGURE 12-10

SUBSIDIARY LEDGERS

The place of subsidiary ledgers in the accounting cycle is shown in Figure 12-10. The figure also shows how the schedules of accounts receivable and accounts payable fit into the accounting cycle.

TRANSPORTATION CHARGES ON THE BUYING OF ASSETS OTHER THAN MERCHANDISE

Any freight charges involved in the buying of any other assets, such as supplies or equipment, should be debited to their respective asset accounts. For example, City-Wide Electric Supply bought display cases on account, at a cost of $2,700 plus freight charges of $90. As a convenience, the seller of the display cases prepaid the transportation costs for City-Wide Electric Supply and then added the $90 to the invoice price of the cases. Let's visualize this by means of T accounts.

Store Equipment		Accounts Payable	
+	−	−	+
2,790			2,790

On the other hand, if City-Wide Electric had paid the freight charges separately, the entry for the payment would be a debit to Store Equipment for $90 and a credit to Cash for $90.

INTERNAL CONTROL

We spoke briefly about the efficient management of cash in Chapter 8. We stated that all payments should be made either by check or from the petty cash fund, and all cash received should be deposited in the bank at the end of the day. The handling of cash in this manner is an example of **internal control.** When there is internal control, plans and procedures for the control of operations are made a part of the accounting system. Doing this is necessary when the owner or management must delegate authority. The owner has to take measures to (1) protect assets against fraud and waste, (2) provide for accurate accounting data, (3) promote an efficient operation, and (4) encourage adherence to management policies. We'll be talking about the concept of internal control quite often in the rest of the text.

Internal Control of Purchases

Purchases is one area in which internal control is essential. Efficiency and security require most companies to work out careful procedures for buying and paying for goods. This is understandable, as large sums of money are usually involved. The control aspect generally involves the following measures.

1. Purchases are made only after proper authorization is given. Purchase requisitions and purchase orders are all prenumbered, so that each form can be accounted for.
2. The receiving department carefully checks and counts all goods upon receipt. Later the report of the receiving department is verified against the purchase order and the purchase invoice.
3. The person who authorizes the payment is neither the person doing the ordering nor the person actually writing the check. Payment is authorized only after the verifications have been made.
4. The person who actually writes the check has not been involved in any of the foregoing purchasing procedures.

SUMMARY

In this chapter, we introduced three new accounts: Purchases, which is used to record the cost of merchandise acquired for resale; Freight In, which is used to record freight charges on merchandise shipped FOB shipping point; and Purchases Returns and Allowances, which is used to record deductions from Purchases.

L.O. 1
L.O. 2
The three-column purchases journal handles the purchase of merchandise on account only. Entries from it are posted daily to the accounts payable ledger. At the end of the month, the totals are posted to the general ledger as a debit to the Purchases account, a debit to Freight In, and a credit to the Accounts Payable controlling account.

L.O. 3
When a credit memo is received for the return of merchandise, or as an allowance for damaged merchandise, the buyer credits Purchases Returns and Allowances. If the merchandise was bought on a charge-account basis, the buyer debits Accounts Payable. The transaction is recorded in the general journal. A schedule of accounts payable is prepared from the accounts payable ledger.

L.O. 4

L.O. 5
A multicolumn purchases journal or invoice register handles the buying of anything on account as well as freight charges paid by suppliers on behalf of the buyer. Amounts in the Accounts Payable Credit column are posted daily to the accounts payable ledger. Amounts in the Sundry Accounts Debit column are usually posted daily to the general ledger. Amounts in the special columns are posted as totals at the end of the month.

L.O. 6
As a further shortcut, the firm may post to the accounts of the individual creditors in the accounts payable ledger directly from invoices of purchases of merchandise bought on credit. At the end of the month, the accountant makes a summarizing entry in the general journal, debiting Purchases, Freight In, and assets that were acquired and crediting Accounts Payable for the total of the invoices.

GLOSSARY

Credit memorandum   A business form provided by the seller to a buyer who has either returned a purchase (or part of a purchase) for credit or been granted an allowance for damaged goods.

Crossfooting   Horizontal addition of column totals to prove that the total debits equal the total credits.

FOB destination   The seller pays the freight charges and includes them in the selling price.

FOB shipping point   The buyer pays the freight charges between the point of shipment and the destination. Payment may be made directly to the carrier upon receiving the goods or to the supplier, if the supplier prepaid the freight charges on behalf of the buyer.

Freight In   An expense account used to record the transportation costs of merchandise purchased for resale.

Internal control   Plans and procedures built into the accounting system with the following objectives: (1) to protect assets against fraud and waste, (2) to yield accurate accounting data, (3) to promote an efficient operation, and (4) to encourage adherence to management policies.

Invoice A business form prepared by the seller that lists the items shipped, their cost, terms of the sale, and the mode of shipment. It may also state the freight charges. The buyer considers it a purchase invoice; the seller considers it a sales invoice.

Purchase order A written order from the buyer of goods to the supplier, listing items wanted as well as terms of the transaction.

Purchase requisition A form used to request the Purchasing Department to buy something. This form is intended for internal use within a company.

Purchases discount A cash discount allowed for prompt payment of an invoice; for example, 2 percent if the bill is paid within 10 days.

Purchases journal A special journal used to record the buying of goods on account. It may be used to record the purchase of merchandise only. Or, it may be a multicolumn journal, or invoice register, used to record the buying of anything on account.

Purchases Returns and Allowances The account used by the buyer to record a reduction granted by the supplier either for the return of merchandise or as compensation for damage to the merchandise. The entry in the buyer's account is based on a credit memorandum received from the supplier.

QUESTIONS, EXERCISES, AND PROBLEMS
Discussion Questions

1. Dolliver Hardware purchased the following items: (a) a delivery truck, (b) three dozen hammers, (c) supplies for the office, (d) a broom for the janitor. Which item or items should be debited to the Purchases account?
2. How many copies of a purchase order are usually made, and who receives each copy?
3. What business document authorizes the recording of a purchase transaction?
4. What does a check mark in the Posting Reference column of a purchases journal indicate?
5. How will an error in posting to an individual creditor's account generally be detected?
6. Explain the meaning and importance of the shipping terms *FOB destination* and *FOB shipping point*. Who has title to the goods once they have been shipped?
7. When an owner delegates authority, what measures must be taken to maintain control over the operations?
8. Describe the four procedures that most companies follow to maintain internal control of purchases.

Exercises

L.O. 1,3   **Exercise 12-1** Describe the transactions in the T accounts at the top of the next page.

Cash	Purchases	Purchases Returns and Allowances	Accounts Payable
(c) 770	(a) 840	(b) 70	(b) 70 (a) 840
			(c) 770

L.O. 3   **Exercise 12-2**   Post the following entry to the general ledger and subsidiary ledger accounts:

GENERAL JOURNAL   PAGE ___44___

	DATE	DESCRIPTION	POST. REF.	DEBIT	CREDIT	
1	19–					1
2	June 15	Accounts Payable, C. L. Dreyfus				2
3		Company		3 7 40		3
4		Purchases Returns and Allowances			3 7 40	4
5		Received credit memo no. 1087				5
6		for return of merchandise.				6
7						7

GENERAL LEDGER

ACCOUNT   _Accounts Payable_   ACCOUNT NO. 212

						BALANCE	
DATE	ITEM	POST. REF.	DEBIT	CREDIT		DEBIT	CREDIT
19–							
June 1	Balance	✓					1 6 5 4 20

ACCOUNT   _Purchases Returns and Allowances_   ACCOUNT NO. 512

						BALANCE	
DATE	ITEM	POST. REF.	DEBIT	CREDIT		DEBIT	CREDIT
19–							
June 1	Balance	✓					8 4 20

ACCOUNTS PAYABLE LEDGER

NAME   _C. L. Dreyfus Company_

ADDRESS _____

DATE	ITEM	POST. REF.	DEBIT	CREDIT	BALANCE
19–					
May 27		P94		1 2 8 00	1 2 8 00

L.O. 3   **Exercise 12-3**   Record the following transactions in general journal form:

a. Bought merchandise on account from Smalley Company, invoice no. 9140, $564, net 30 days; FOB shipping point.
b. Paid Goldenwest Freight for shipping charges on Smalley Company purchase, $32.
c. Bought merchandise on account from Randall Company, invoice no. 534, $1,143; net 30 days; freight prepaid and added to invoice; $87 (total $1,230).

L.O. 3   **Exercise 12-4**   Record the following transactions in general journal form:

a. Bought merchandise on account from Bright and Slavich, invoice no. L425, terms 2/10, net 30, FOB destination, $722.
b. Received credit memo no. 219 from Bright and Slavich for merchandise returned, $34.
c. Issued a check to Bright and Slavich in full payment of account.

L.O. 6   **Exercise 12-5**   A business firm that posts directly from its purchase invoices sorts the invoices for the month and finds that the totals are as follows: purchases of merchandise, $8,621; freight charges on merchandise, $162; store supplies, $126; office supplies, $99; office equipment, $142. Record the summarizing entry in the general journal.

L.O. 1   **Exercise 12-6**   The following errors were made in recording transactions in the purchases journal or in posting from it. How will each error come to the attention of the accountant?

a. A credit of $600 to the Baxter and Company account in the accounts payable ledger was posted as $60.
b. The Accounts Payable column total of the purchases journal was understated by $10.
c. An invoice of $240 for merchandise from Thomas Company was recorded as having been received from Thompson Company, another supplier.

L.O. 3   **Exercise 12-7**   Record the following transactions in general journal form:

a. Midtown Supermarket buys four cash registers on account from Standard Equipment Company for $9,600.
b. One of the cash registers purchased for $2,400 is defective and returned to the supplier.

L.O. 3   **Exercise 12-8**   Record entries in general journal form to correct each of the errors described below. Assume that the incorrect entries had been posted and that the corrections are recorded in the same fiscal period in which the errors occurred.

a. The $240 cost of defective store equipment returned to the supplier was recorded as a credit to Purchases Returns and Allowances.
b. Transportation costs of $62 incurred on office equipment bought for use in the business were charged to Freight In.
c. A $46 cash purchase of merchandise from C. L. Stone Company was recorded as a purchase on account.

Problem Set A

L.O. 1,2,4 **Problem 12-1A** The Suburban Bicycle Shop uses a three-column purchases journal. The company is located in Topeka, Kansas. On January 1 of this year, the balances of the ledger accounts are Accounts Payable, $423.08; Purchases, zero; Freight In, zero. In addition to a general ledger, the company also uses an accounts payable ledger. Transactions for January related to the purchase of merchandise are as follows:

Jan. 4 Bought sixty 10-speed bicycles from Nakata Company, $5,980, invoice no. 26145, dated January 3; terms net 60 days; FOB Topeka.

7 Bought tires from Berger Tire Company, $486, invoice no. 9763, dated January 5; terms 2/10, n/30; FOB Topeka.

8 Bought bicycle lights and reflectors from Goddard Products Company, $272, invoice no. 17317, dated January 6; terms net 30 days; FOB Topeka.

11 Bought hand brakes from Brady, Inc., $270, invoice no. 291GE, dated January 9; terms 1/10, n/30; FOB Kansas City, freight prepaid and added to the invoice, $24 (total $294).

19 Bought handle grips from Goddard Products Company, $74.50, invoice no. 17520, dated January 17; terms net 30 days; FOB Topeka.

24 Bought thirty 5-speed bicycles from Nakata Company, $1,396, invoice no. 26942, dated January 23; terms net 60 days; FOB Topeka.

29 Bought knapsacks from Duncan Manufacturing Company, $299.42, invoice no. 762AC, dated January 26; terms 2/10, n/30; FOB Topeka.

31 Bought locks from Lincoln Security, $311.47, invoice no. 27712, dated January 26; terms 2/10, n/30; FOB Dodge City, freight prepaid and added to the invoice, $19 (total $330.47).

Instructions

1. Open the following creditor accounts in the accounts payable ledger and record the January 1 balances, if any, as given: Berger Tire Company, $156; Brady, Inc.; Duncan Manufacturing Company, $82.88; Goddard Products Company; Lincoln Security, $184.20; Nakata Company. For the accounts having balances, write "Balance" in the Item column and place a check mark in the Post. Ref. column.
2. Record the balance of $423.08 in the Accounts Payable controlling account as of January 1. Write "Balance" in the Item column and place a check mark in the Post. Ref. column.
3. Record the transactions in the purchases journal beginning with page 81.
4. Post to the accounts payable ledger daily.
5. Post to the general ledger at the end of the month.
6. Prepare a schedule of accounts payable, and compare the balance of the Accounts Payable controlling account with the total of the schedule of accounts payable.

L.O. 3,4,5 **Problem 12-2A** Bestway Camera is located in Detroit. The company bought the following merchandise and supplies and had the following returns and allowances during April of this year:

Apr.   3 Bought merchandise on account from Dolman Imports, $711, invoice no. C4581, dated April 1; terms 2/10, n/30; FOB Lansing, freight prepaid and added to the invoice, $21 (total $732).

   4 Bought merchandise on account from Neff and Slade, $376, invoice no. 561AM, dated April 2; terms 1/10, n/30; FOB Detroit.

   7 Bought merchandise on account from Rex Photo Supply, $639, invoice no. 65872, dated April 5; terms net 30 days; FOB Detroit.

   11 Bought office supplies on account from Mack and Son, $210, invoice no. 5639, dated April 11; terms net 30 days; FOB Detroit.

   13 Received a credit memo from Neff and Slade for merchandise returned, $33, credit memo no. 617.

   16 Bought merchandise on account from Akers and Company, $605, invoice no. 41832, dated April 15; terms 1/10, n/30; FOB Warren, freight prepaid and added to the invoice, $37 (total $642).

   22 Bought equipment on account from Reece Company, $715, invoice no. L21654, dated April 19; terms net 30 days; FOB Detroit.

   27 Bought merchandise on account from Neff and Slade, $924, invoice no. 598AM, dated April 25; terms 1/10, n/30; FOB Detroit.

   28 Received a credit memo from Rex Photo Supply for merchandise returned, $86, credit memo no. 922.

   29 Bought merchandise on account from Dolman Imports, $1,418, invoice no. C4721, dated April 27; terms 2/10, n/30; FOB Lansing, freight prepaid and added to the invoice, $98 (total $1,516).

   30 Bought store supplies on account from N. D. Ritch, Inc., $71, invoice no. 61875, dated April 29; terms net 30 days; FOB Detroit.

   30 Bought merchandise on account from Akers and Company, $560, invoice no. 42003, dated April 27; terms 1/10, n/30; FOB Warren, freight prepaid and added to the invoice, $32 (total $592).

Instructions

1. Open the following accounts in the general ledger and enter the balances as of April 1.

114 Store Supplies	$ 249.00	511 Purchases	$7,551.19
115 Office Supplies	126.00	512 Purchases Returns	
124 Equipment	9,220.00	and Allowances	216.20
212 Accounts Payable	2,364.19	514 Freight In	422.00

For the accounts having balances, write "Balance" in the Item column and place a check mark in the Post. Ref. column.

2. Open the following accounts in the accounts payable ledger and enter the April 1 balances, if any, as given: Akers and Company, $303.74; Dolman Imports, $880.19; Mack and Son; Neff and Slade; Reece Company; Rex Photo, $1,180.26; N. D. Ritch, Inc. For the accounts having balances, write "Balance" in the Item column and place a check mark in the Post. Ref. column.

3. Record the transactions in either the general journal, starting on page 27, or the purchases journal, on page 6, as appropriate.

4. Post the entries to the creditors' accounts in the accounts payable ledger immediately after you make each journal entry.

5. Post the entries in the Sundry Accounts Debit column of the purchases

journal and in the general journal immediately after you make each of those journal entries.

6. In the space below the purchases journal, show proof that the sum of the debit totals equals the total of the Accounts Payable Credit column.

7. Post the totals of the special columns of the purchases journal at the end of the month.

8. Prepare a schedule of accounts payable, and compare the balance of the Accounts Payable controlling account with the total of the schedule of accounts payable.

L.O. 6 **Problem 12-3A**   Staley Products Company, Pittsburgh, Pennsylvania, records sales of merchandise daily by posting directly from its sales invoices to the accounts receivable ledger. At the end of the month it makes a summarizing entry in the general journal. It records purchases of goods on account the same way, daily, posting directly from the invoices to the accounts payable ledger and making a summarizing entry in the general journal at the end of the month. Sales of merchandise and purchases of goods on account during September of this year were as follows.

Sales of merchandise on account

Sept.   4 Stanley Corp., no. 2818, $2,460.00.
         7 I. D. Keenan, no. 2819, $342.26.
        11 M. R. Brower and Company, no. 2820, $1,726.42.
        15 Thielen and Thomas, no. 2821, $2,549.45.
        21 Francis R. Baldwin, no. 2822, $716.50.
        23 C. R. Polaski, no. 2823, $59.47.
        25 Daniel P. Hall, no. 2824, $435.52.
        26 Braddock and Miner, no. 2825, $1,892.39.
        28 R. A. Harris, no. 2826, $672.55.
        29 Helen C. Becker, no. 2827, $1,884.22.
        30 C. P. Casey, no. 2828, $2,199.75.

Purchases of goods on account

Sept.   3 Fowler Corporation, merchandise, $3,772.40, FOB Pittsburgh.
         7 Lewis and Schiller, merchandise, $2,753.42, FOB Philadelphia, freight prepaid and added to the invoice, $112 (total $2,865.42).
         9 Sitton Manufacturing Company, merchandise, $1,117.50, FOB Pittsburgh.
        17 Hirsch and Wagner, store supplies, $433, FOB Pittsburgh.
        22 Fowler Corporation, merchandise, $236.74, FOB Pittsburgh.
        26 Caldwell Specialty Products, merchandise, $3,212.00, FOB New York, freight prepaid and added to the invoice, $143 (total $3,355.00).
        30 James Office Furnishings, office equipment, $381.20, FOB Pittsburgh.
        30 D. D. Cani, Inc., merchandise, $1,784.52, FOB Pittsburgh.

Instructions

1. Record the summarizing entry for the sales of merchandise on account in the general journal.

2. Record the summarizing entry for the purchase of goods on account in the general journal.

L.O. 1,2,3,4   **Problem 12-4A** The following transactions relate to King Metal Products during April of this year. Terms of sale are 2/10, n/30. The company is located in Los Angeles.

Apr.   1 Sold merchandise on account to Howard Hardware, invoice no. 5522, $584.00.

        4 Bought merchandise on account from Sanger Manufacturing Company, invoice no. C1142, $528, 1/10, n/30; dated April 2; FOB San Diego, freight prepaid and added to the invoice, $33 (total $561).

       9 Sold merchandise on account to Buckley Department Store, invoice no. 5523, $994.

     11 Bought merchandise on account from Beale Products Company, invoice no. 8990, $1,893.65; 2/10, n/30; dated April 11; FOB San Francisco, freight prepaid and added to the invoice, $79 (total $1,972.65).

     16 Sold merchandise on account to B. R. Anders, invoice no. 5524, $856.70.

     19 Issued credit memo no. 32 to Buckley Department Store for merchandise returned, $92.

     24 Bought merchandise on account from Ashford Manufacturing Company, invoice no. P1981, $1,401.50; 2/10, n/30; dated April 22; FOB Santa Rosa, freight prepaid and added to the invoice, $81 (total $1,482.50).

     27 Bought office supplies on account from Chandler and Dunn, invoice no. E621A, dated April 25, $78.40; net 30 days.

     28 Sold merchandise on account to Goddard Specialty Company, invoice no. 5525, $3,852.00.

     29 Issued credit memo no. 33 to B. R. Anders for allowance on damaged merchandise, $86.

     30 Received credit memo no. 356 for merchandise returned to Bonwell, Inc., for $152.22.

Instructions

1. Open the following accounts in the accounts receivable ledger and record the balances as of April 1: B. R. Anders; Buckley Department Store, $352.50; Goddard Specialty Company, $225.50; Howard Hardware, $822.00. For the accounts having balances, write "Balance" in the Item column and place a check mark in the Post. Ref. column.

2. Open the following accounts in the accounts payable ledger and record the balances as of April 1: Ashford Manufacturing Company; Beale Products Company, $122.46; Bonwell, Inc., $255.54; Chandler and Dunn; Sanger Manufacturing Company. For the accounts having balances, write "Balance" in the Item column and place a check mark in the Post. Ref. column.

3. Record the transactions in the sales, purchases, or general journals, as appropriate.

4. Post the entries to the accounts receivable ledger daily.
5. Post the entries to the accounts payable ledger daily.
6. Post the entries in the general journal immediately after you make each journal entry.
7. Post the totals from the special journals at month end.
8. Prepare a schedule of accounts receivable.
9. Prepare a schedule of accounts payable.
10. Compare the totals of the schedules with the balances of the controlling accounts.

Problem Set B

L.O. 1,2,4   **Problem 12-1B**   Minard Appliance uses a three-column purchases journal. The company is located in Fresno, California. On January 1 of this year, the balances of the ledger accounts are Accounts Payable, $559.06; Purchases, zero; Freight In, zero. In addition to a general ledger, Minard Appliance also uses an accounts payable ledger. Transactions for January related to the buying of merchandise are as follows:

Jan.   2 Bought eighty 12-inch, 3-speed Brighton Oscillating Fans from Sweat and Allen, $1,680, invoice no. 268J, dated January 2; terms net 60 days; FOB Fresno.

      4 Bought ten 35-pint-capacity Coster Humidifiers from Shannon Company, $2,100, invoice no. 39426, dated January 2; terms 2/10, n/30; FOB Denver, freight prepaid and added to the invoice, $80 (total $2,180).

      7 Bought ten 16-inch Apex Window Fans from Tedder, Inc., $380, invoice no. 452AD, dated January 6; terms 1/10, n/30; FOB Fresno.

   10 Bought twenty-four 4-blade Tempo Ceiling Fans, Model 2760, from Ulrich Company, $3,648, invoice no. D7742, dated January 7; terms 2/10, n/30; FOB Napa, freight prepaid and added to the invoice, $97 (total $3,745).

   14 Bought four Champion Electric Hedge Trimmers from Fowler Products Company, $164, invoice no. 2542, dated January 13; terms net 30 days; FOB Fresno.

   22 Bought forty Larkin Electric Bug Killers from Sweat and Allen, $2,480, invoice no. 392J, dated January 22; terms net 60 days; FOB Fresno.

   28 Bought ten Champion Electric Blowers from Fowler Products Company, $640, invoice no. 2691, dated January 27; terms net 30 days; FOB Fresno.

   30 Bought ten King Powered Attic Ventilators from Pollard Manufacturing Company, $345, invoice no. 664CC, dated January 27; terms 2/10, n/30; FOB Seattle, freight prepaid and added to the invoice, $45 (total $390).

Instructions

1. Open the following accounts in the accounts payable ledger and record the balances, if any, as given as of January 1: Fowler Products Company; Pollard Manufacturing Company, $163.17; Shannon Company, $167.19;

Sweat and Allen; Tedder, Inc., $228.70; Ulrich Company. For the accounts having balances, write "Balance" in the Item column and place a check mark in the Post. Ref. column.

2. Record the balance of $559.06 in the Accounts Payable controlling account as of January 1. Write "Balance" in the Item column and place a check mark in the Post. Ref. column.

3. Record the transactions in the purchases journal beginning on page 81.

4. Post to the accounts payable ledger daily.

5. Post to the general ledger at the end of the month.

6. Prepare a schedule of accounts payable, and compare the balance of the Accounts Payable controlling account with the total of the schedule of accounts payable.

L.O. 3,4,5

Problem 12-2B Milady Boutique is located in New York City. The company had the following purchases of merchandise and other assets and related returns and allowances during May of this year.

May 4 Bought merchandise on account from Van Dusen, Inc., $737.40, invoice no. 24812, dated May 2; terms 2/10, n/30; FOB New York.

6 Bought merchandise on account from Franklin Brothers, $687.26, invoice no. L213, dated May 4; terms net 30 days; FOB Fort Lee, freight prepaid and added to the invoice, $34 (total $721.26).

9 Bought store supplies on account from Ruiz Company, $441.62, invoice no. B1164, dated May 8; terms net 30 days; FOB New York.

11 Bought office supplies on account from James Office Supply, $244.98, invoice no. 2465, dated May 10; terms net 30 days; FOB New Rochelle, freight prepaid and added to the invoice, $12 (total $256.98). (Record Office Supplies for $256.98.)

14 Received credit memo from Peters Company for merchandise returned, $36, credit memo no. 772.

16 Bought merchandise on account from Van Dusen, Inc., $974.24, invoice no. 26453, dated May 16; terms 1/10, n/30; FOB New York.

21 Bought merchandise on account from Kenton Company, $851, invoice no. H2695, dated May 19; terms net 30 days; FOB Newark, freight prepaid and added to the invoice, $49 (total $900).

26 Bought merchandise on account from Davis and Son, $772.25, invoice no. 52478, dated May 24; terms 1/10, n/30; FOB New York.

29 Received a credit memo from Franklin Brothers for merchandise returned, $87, credit memo no. 344.

30 Bought merchandise on account from Peters Company, $1,248.70, invoice no. B8042, dated May 28; terms 2/10, n/30; FOB Newark, freight prepaid and added to the invoice, $116 (total $1,364.70).

31 Bought merchandise on account from Davis and Son, $256.25, invoice no. 61994, dated May 30; terms net 30 days; FOB New York.

31 Bought merchandise on account from Franklin Brothers, $449.56, invoice no. L285 dated May 29; terms net 30 days; FOB shipping

point, freight prepaid and added to the invoice, $32 (total $481.56).

Instructions

1. Open the following accounts in the general ledger and enter the balances as of May 1.

114 Store Supplies	$ 384.21	511 Purchases	$7,436.70
115 Office Supplies	145.72	512 Purchases Returns	
212 Accounts Payable	3,153.59	and Allowances	287.52
		514 Freight In	586.25

For the accounts having balances, write "Balance" in the Item column and place a check mark in the Post. Ref. column.

2. Open the following accounts in the accounts payable ledger and record the May 1 balances, if any, as given: Davis and Son, $983.76; Franklin Brothers; James Office Supply; Kenton Company; Peters Company, $1,774.21; Ruiz Company; Van Dusen, Inc., $395.62. For the accounts having balances, write "Balance" in the Item column and place a check mark in the Post. Ref. column.

3. Record the transactions in either the general journal, starting on page 27, or page 6 of the purchases journal as appropriate.

4. Post the entries to the creditors' accounts in the accounts payable ledger immediately after you make each journal entry.

5. Post the entries in the general journal and the Sundry Accounts Debit column of the purchases journal immediately after you make each journal entry.

6. In the space below the purchases journal, show proof that the sum of the debit totals equals the total of the Accounts Payable Credit column.

7. Post the totals of the special columns of the purchases journal at the end of the month.

8. Prepare a schedule of accounts payable, and compare the balance of the Accounts Payable controlling account with the total of the schedule of accounts payable.

L.O. 6   **Problem 12-3B**   The Dole Products Company of Dallas, Texas, records sales of merchandise daily by posting directly from its sales invoices to the accounts receivable ledger. At the end of the month, a summarizing entry is made in the general journal. The purchase of goods on account is recorded in a similar manner. Each day's posting is done directly from the invoices to the accounts payable ledger, and a summarizing entry is made in the general journal at the end of the month. Sales of merchandise and purchases of goods on account during May of this year were as follows.

Sales of merchandise on account

May   4 Leland and Fouch, no. 3522, $564.21.
        7 C. L. Fagan, Inc., no. 3523, $642.17.
      11 P. R. Kelsey and Company, no. 3524, $826.48.
      15 Mason and Company, no. 3525, $1,560.05.
      22 C. D. Savale, no. 3526, $952.17.
      24 Lane D. Johnson, no. 3527, $973.14.
      25 Sheila D. Pietre, no. 3528, $1,017.55.

May   28   Miller Corporation, no. 3529, $768.40.
           30   Mason and Company, no. 3530, $466.32.
           31   C. L. Fagan, Inc., no. 3531, $516.24.

Purchases of goods on account

May   3   Moore and Logan, merchandise, $429.42; FOB Dallas.
         9   D and L Manufacturing Company, merchandise, $1,964; FOB Dallas.
       11   Lukens Supply Company, office supplies, $107.22; FOB Dallas.
       19   Dinsdale and Company, merchandise, $225.50; FOB Houston, freight prepaid and added to the invoice, $14 (total $239.50).
       21   Moore and Moore, store supplies, $56.39; FOB Dallas.
       27   Hardy Specialty Products, merchandise, $4,977.53; FOB Dallas.
       31   Atlas Distributing Company, store equipment, $351.16; FOB Dallas.

Instructions

1. Record the summarizing entry for sales of merchandise on account in the general journal.
2. Record the summarizing entry for the purchase of goods on account in the general journal.

L.O. 1,2,3,4   **Problem 12-4B**   The following transactions relate to the Broderick Company of Atlanta during April of this year. Terms of sale are 2/10, n/30.

Apr.   2   Sold merchandise on account to Slocum and Company, invoice no. 1126, $942.
       4   Bought merchandise on account from Padrow Manufacturing Company, invoice no. 16521; $568; 1/10, n/30; dated April 2; FOB Atlanta.
       9   Sold merchandise on account to Pittman and Lowe, invoice no. 1127, $1,376.
     12   Bought merchandise on account from Vinson Company, invoice no. L8552, $2,363; 2/10, n/30; dated April 11; FOB Rome, freight prepaid and added to the invoice, $59 (total $2,422).
     15   Received credit memo no. 79 for merchandise returned to Kreiger and Company, for $118.
     17   Sold merchandise on account to C. N. Howell, Inc., invoice no. 1128, $959.
     19   Issued credit memo no. 34 to Pittman and Lowe for merchandise returned, $86.
     26   Bought merchandise on account from M. R. Pace, Inc., invoice no. 7447, $1,697; 2/10, n/30; dated April 23; FOB Macon, freight prepaid and added to the invoice, $47 (total $1,744).
     29   Bought office supplies on account from Tiffany Stationery Company, invoice no. S336, dated April 29, $134, net 30 days.
     30   Sold merchandise on account to Schmidt and Maki, invoice no. 1129, $2,557.
     30   Issued credit memo no. 35 to Schmidt and Maki for merchandise returned, $162.

Objective 2

Post from a cash
receipts journal to a
general ledger and an
accounts receivable
ledger.

promissory note, instead of Accounts Payable. The Accounts Payable account is reserved for charge accounts with creditors, which are normally paid on a thirty-day basis.

Let us assume that all the month's transactions involving debits to Cash have now been recorded in the cash receipts journal. The cash receipts journal (Figure 13-2) and the T accounts on page 409 illustrate the postings to the general ledger and the accounts receivable ledger.

Individual amounts in the Accounts Receivable Credit column of the cash receipts journal are usually posted daily. Individual amounts in the Sundry Credit column are usually posted daily.

At the end of the month we can post the special column totals in the cash receipts journal to the general ledger accounts. These include Accounts Receivable Credit, Sales Credit, Sales Tax Payable Credit, Credit Card Expense Debit, and Cash Debit.

In the Post. Ref. column, the check marks (√) indicate that the amounts in the Accounts Receivable Credit column have been posted to the individual charge customers' accounts as credits. The account numbers show that the amounts in the Sundry Accounts Credit column have been posted separately to the accounts described in the Account Credited column. A check mark (√) also goes under the total of the Sundry column, where it means "do not post—the figures have already been posted separately."

A check mark in our example thus has two meanings: (1) *the individual account has been posted in the subsidiary ledger*, as in the Accounts Receivable Credit column, and (2) *the total is not to be posted*, as in the Sundry column.

Note the ruling. A single rule is placed above the column totals, and double rules extend through all but the Account Credited column. Also, on the last line, the last day of the month is recorded in the Date column.

Let's say it's the end of the month. Total the columns first. Then begin **crossfooting** the journal by proving that the sum of the debit totals equals the sum of the credit totals. This process must be done before one posts the totals to the general ledger accounts.

Debit Totals		Credit Totals	
Cash	$4,399.52	Sundry Accounts	$3,450.00
Credit Card		Accounts Receivable	296.40
Expense	12.48	Sales	640.00
	$4,412.00	Sales Tax Payable	25.60
			$4,412.00

Post the special column totals to the general ledger, using the letters *CR* as the posting reference. Next, write the general ledger account number in parentheses below the total in the appropriate column.

CASH RECEIPTS JOURNAL

PAGE __41__

	DATE	ACCOUNT CREDITED	POST. REF.	SUNDRY ACCOUNTS CREDIT	ACCOUNTS RECEIVABLE CREDIT	SALES CREDIT	SALES TAX PAYABLE CREDIT	CREDIT CARD EXPENSE DEBIT	CASH DEBIT	
1	19–									1
2	May 3					100 00	4 00		104 00	2
3	4					100 00	4 00	4 16	99 84	3
4	5	J. C. Rowe	✓		208 00				208 00	4
5	7	A. R. Hall,								5
6		Capital	311	3 000 00					3 000 00	6
7	8	Equipment	121	150 00					150 00	7
8	11	Notes								8
9		Payable	211	300 00					300 00	9
10	16		—			200 00	8 00		208 00	10
11	21		—			50 00	2 00	2 08	49 92	11
12	26	Kenneth								12
13		Ralston	✓		62 40				62 40	13
14	28		—			40 00	1 60		41 60	14
15	31		—			150 00	6 00	6 24	149 76	15
16	31	Sylvia								16
17		Harlow	✓		26 00				26 00	17
18	31			3 450 00	296 40	640 00	25 60	12 48	4 399 52	18
19				(✓)	(113)	(411)	(213)	(513)	(111)	19

Accounts Receivable Ledger

Sylvia Harlow

+	–
	May 31 26

Kenneth Ralston

+	–
	May 26 62.40

J. C. Rowe

+	–
	May 5 208

General Ledger

Cash

+	–
May 31 4,399.52	

Accounts Receivable

+	–
	May 31 296.40

Equipment

+	–
	May 8 150

Notes Payable

–	+
	May 11 300

Sales Tax Payable

–	+
	May 31 25.60

A. P. Hall, Capital

–	+
	May 7 3,000

Sales

–	+
	May 31 640

Credit Card Expense

+	–
May 31 12.48	

FIGURE 13-2

Advantages of a Cash Receipts Journal

1. Transactions generally can be recorded on one line.
2. All transactions involving debits to Cash are recorded in one place.
3. It eliminates much repetition in posting when there are numerous transactions involving Cash debits. The Cash Debit side can be posted as one total.
4. Special columns can be used for specialized transactions and posted as one total.

Private Credit Card Companies   In regard to credit card sales, it should be mentioned that many firms also accept credit cards of private companies, such as American Express, Diners Club, and Carte Blanche. Transactions involving this type of credit card are treated as sales on account. For example, total revenue for a hotel for a time period involving credit cards of private companies amounts to $900, plus 8 percent hotel tax. The entry is

Accounts Receivable		Hotel Tax Payable		Hotel Revenue	
+	−	−	+	−	+
972			72		900

Private credit card companies charge a fee or discount for their services. In this case, assume a discount rate of 4 percent ($972 × .04 = $38.88). When $933.12 ($972 − $38.88) is received from the credit card company, the entry is

Cash		Credit Card Expense		Accounts Receivable	
+	−	+	−	+	−
933.12		38.88			972

CREDIT TERMS

The seller always stipulates credit terms: How much credit can a customer be allowed? And how much time should the customer be given to pay the full amount? The **credit period** is the time the seller allows the buyer before full payment has to be made. Retailers generally allow thirty days.

Wholesalers and manufacturers often specify a **cash discount** in their credit terms. A cash discount is the amount a customer can deduct for paying a bill within a short time. The discount is based on the *total amount of the invoice after any returns and allowances and freight charges billed on the invoice have been deducted.* Naturally this discount acts as an incentive for charge customers to pay their bills promptly. Recall that we also discussed cash discounts in Chapter 12.

Let's say that a wholesaler offers customers credit terms of 2/10, n/30. These terms mean that the customer gets a 2 percent discount if the bill is paid within ten days after the invoice date. If the bill is not paid within the ten days, then the entire amount is due within thirty days after the invoice date. Other cash discounts that may be used are the following:

- **1/15, n/60** The seller offers a 1 percent discount if the bill is paid within fifteen days after the invoice date, or the whole bill must be paid within sixty days after the invoice date.
- **2/10, EOM, n/60** The seller offers a 2 percent discount if the bill is paid within ten days after the end of the month, and the whole bill must be paid within sixty days after the last day of the month.

A wholesaler or manufacturer offering a cash discount adopts a single cash discount as a credit policy and makes this available to all its customers. The seller considers cash discounts as **sales discounts;** the buyer, on the other hand, considers cash discounts as purchases discounts. In this section we are concerned with the sales discount. *The Sales Discount account, like Sales Returns and Allowances, is a deduction from Sales.*

To illustrate, we return to City-Wide Electric Supply. We will record the following transactions in T accounts so we can see them at a glance.

Transaction (a) August 1: Sold merchandise on account to L. A. Long Company, invoice no. 320; terms 2/10, n/30; $424.

Transaction (b) August 10: Received check from L. A. Long Company for $415.52 in payment of invoice no. 320, less cash discount ($424.00 − $8.48 = $415.52).

Assets		=	Liabilities		+	Owner's Equity		+	Revenue		−	Expenses	
+	−		−	+		−	+		−	+		+	−
Debit	Credit		Debit	Credit		Debit	Credit		Debit	Credit		Debit	Credit

Accounts Receivable				Sales	
+	−			−	+
(a) 424.00	(b) 424.00				(a) 424.00

Cash				Sales Discount	
+	−			+	−
(b) 415.52				(b) 8.48	

Objective 4

Record transactions for a wholesale merchandising business in a cash receipts journal.

Since City-Wide Electric Supply offers this cash discount to all its customers, and since charge customers often pay their bills within the discount period, City-Wide Electric sets up a Sales Discount Debit column in the cash receipts journal. Note that City-Wide Electric Supply is a wholesaler. Therefore, a column for Sales Tax Payable is not used since few states levy a tax on sales at the wholesale level.

	CASH RECEIPTS JOURNAL							PAGE _18_
DATE	ACCOUNT CREDITED	POST. REF.	SUNDRY ACCOUNTS CREDIT	ACCOUNTS RECEIVABLE CREDIT	SALES CREDIT	SALES DISCOUNT DEBIT	CASH DEBIT	
19–								1
Aug. 10	L. A. Long Co.			4 2 4 00		8 48	4 1 5 52	2

Several other transactions of City-Wide Electric Supply involve increases in cash during August. Remember that the standard credit terms for all charge customers are 2/10, n/30.

Aug. 15 Cash sales for first half of the month, $460.

16 Received check from A. and L. Construction for $92.12 in payment of invoice no. 322, less cash discount ($94.00 − $1.88 = $92.12).

17 Received payment on a promissory note given by John R. Stokes, $300 principal, plus $3 interest. (The amount of the interest is recorded in Interest Income.)

21 Received check from Chavez Hardware for $84.28 in payment of invoice no. 324, less cash discount ($86.00 − $1.72 = $84.28).

23 Sold equipment for cash at cost, $126.

26 R. C. Schmidt, the owner, invested an additional $4,000 cash in the business.

26 Received a check from Home Hardware Company for $210.70 in payment of invoice no. 325 less the cash discount ($215.00 − $4.30 = $210.70).

30 Received check from Harrells Electric for $287.14 in payment of invoice no. 326, less cash discount ($293.00 − $5.86 = $287.14).

31 Cash sales for second half of the month, $620.

31 Received check from Maier, Inc., in payment of invoice no. 321, for $116. (This is longer than the ten-day period, so they missed the cash discount.)

City-Wide Electric records these transactions in its cash receipts journal (Figure 13-3).

CASH RECEIPTS JOURNAL   PAGE __18__

	DATE	ACCOUNT CREDITED	POST. REF.	SUNDRY ACCOUNTS CREDIT	ACCOUNTS RECEIVABLE CREDIT	SALES CREDIT	SALES DISCOUNT DEBIT	CASH DEBIT	
1	19–								1
2	Aug. 10	L. A. Long Company	√		4 2 4 00		8 48	4 1 5 52	2
3	15		—			4 6 0 00		4 6 0 00	3
4	16	A. and L. Construction	√		9 4 00		1 88	9 2 12	4
5	17	Notes Receivable	112	3 0 0 00					5
6		Interest Income	422	3 00				3 0 3 00	6
7	21	Chavez Hardware	√		8 6 00		1 72	8 4 28	7
8	23	Equipment	121	1 2 6 00				1 2 6 00	8
9	26	R. C. Schmidt, Capital	311	4 0 0 0 00				4 0 0 0 00	9
10	26	Home Hardware							10
11		Company	√		2 1 5 00		4 30	2 1 0 70	11
12	30	Harrell's Electric	√		2 9 3 00		5 86	2 8 7 14	12
13	31		—			6 2 0 00		6 2 0 00	13
14	31	Maier, Inc.	√		1 1 6 00			1 1 6 00	14
15	31			4 4 2 9 00	1 2 2 8 00	1 0 8 0 00	2 2 24	6 7 1 4 76	15
16				(√)	(1 1 3)	(4 1 1)	(4 1 3)	(1 1 1)	16
17									17
18									18
19									19
20									20

FIGURE 13-3

Remember

When journalizing a cash receipt involving a sales discount, be sure to credit Accounts Receivable for the total amount of the sales transaction.

After that has been done, the company's accountant proves the equality of debits and credits:

Debit Totals		Credit Totals	
Cash	$6,714.76	Sundry Accounts	$4,429.00
Sales Discount	22.24	Accounts Receivable	1,228.00
	$6,737.00	Sales	1,080.00
			$6,737.00

SALES RETURNS AND ALLOWANCES AND SALES DISCOUNTS ON AN INCOME STATEMENT

In the fundamental accounting equation, to be consistent with the income statement, we placed Sales Returns and Allowances and Sales Discounts under Sales with the plus and minus signs reversed. Both accounts are considered contra revenue accounts and so we subtract their totals from Sales on the income statement. As an example, here is the Revenue from Sales section of the annual income statement of City-Wide Electric Supply taken from the illustration in Chapter 15.

City-Wide Electric Supply
Income Statement
For Year Ended December 31, 19–

Revenue from Sales:			
Sales		$ 186 1 8 0 00	
Less: Sales Returns and Allowances	$ 8 4 0 00		
Sales Discount	1 8 8 0 00	2 7 2 0 00	
Net Sales			$ 183 4 6 0 00

CASH PAYMENTS JOURNAL: SERVICE ENTERPRISE

The cash payments journal, as the name implies, is used to record all transactions in which cash goes out, or decreases. When the cash payments journal is used, all transactions in which cash is credited *must* be recorded in it. This journal may be used for a service as well as a merchandising business.

To get acquainted with the cash payments journal, let's list some typical transactions of a service firm (such as a dry cleaner or a bowling alley) or a professional enterprise that result in a decrease in cash. So that you will see the transactions at a glance, let's record them directly in T accounts.

May   2 Paid C. C. Hardy Company, a creditor, on account, check no. 63, $220.

Accounts Payable		Cash	
−	+	+	−
220			220

May   4 Paid cash for supplies, check no. 64, $90.

Supplies		Cash	
+	−	+	−
90			90

May   5 Paid wages for two weeks, check no. 65, $1,216 (previously recorded in the payroll entry).

Wages Payable		Cash	
−	+	+	−
1,216			1,216

May 6 Paid rent for the month, check no. 66, $350.

Rent Expense		Cash	
+	−	+	−
350			350

The same transactions are now shown in general journal form.

GENERAL JOURNAL   PAGE_____

	DATE		DESCRIPTION	POST. REF.	DEBIT	CREDIT	
1	19–						1
2	May	2	Accounts Payable, C. C. Hardy				2
3			Company		2 2 0 00		3
4			Cash			2 2 0 00	4
5			Paid on account,				5
6			check no. 63.				6
7							7
8		4	Supplies		9 0 00		8
9			Cash			9 0 00	9
10			Paid cash for supplies, check no. 64.				10
11							11
12		5	Wages Payable		1 2 1 6 00		12
13			Cash			1 2 1 6 00	13
14			Paid wages for two weeks, check				14
15			no. 65.				15
16							16
17		6	Rent Expense				17
18			Cash		3 5 0 00		18
19			Paid rent for month, check no. 66.			3 5 0 00	19
20							20
21							21

Now let's appraise these four transactions. The first one would occur very often, as payments to creditors are made several times a month. Of the last three transactions, the debit to Wages Payable might occur twice a month, the debit to Rent Expense once a month, and the debit to Supplies only occasionally.

It is logical to include a Cash Credit column in a cash payments journal, because all transactions recorded in it involve a decrease in cash. Since payments to creditors are made often, there should also be an

Objective 5

Record transactions in a
cash payments journal
for a service enterprise.

Accounts Payable Debit column. One can set up any other column that is
used often enough to warrant it. Otherwise, a Sundry Debit column
takes care of all the other transactions.

Now let's record these same transactions in a cash payments journal
and include a column titled Check Number. If you think a moment, you
will see that this is consistent with good management of cash. All expenditures but Petty Cash expenditures should be paid for by check. First
let's repeat the transactions.

May   2 Paid C. C. Hardy Company, a creditor, on account, check no.
        63, $220.
      4 Paid cash for incidental supplies, check no. 64, $90.
      5 Paid wages for two weeks, check no. 65, $1,216 (previously
        recorded in the payroll entry).
      6 Paid rent for the month, check no. 66, $350.

CASH PAYMENTS JOURNAL   PAGE ___62___

	DATE	CK. NO.	ACCOUNT DEBITED	POST. REF.	SUNDRY ACCOUNTS DEBIT	ACCOUNTS PAYABLE DEBIT	CASH CREDIT	
1	*19–*							1
2	*May* 2	63	*C. C. Hardy Co.*			2 2 0 00	2 2 0 00	2
3	4	64	*Supplies*		9 0 00		9 0 00	3
4	5	65	*Wages Payable*		1 2 1 6 00		1 2 1 6 00	4
5	6	66	*Rent Expense*		3 5 0 00		3 5 0 00	5
6								6

Note that you list all checks in consecutive order, even those checks
that must be voided. In this way, *every* check is accounted for, which is
necessary for internal control.

At the end of the month, post the special columns as totals to the general ledger accounts; do not post the total of the Sundry Accounts Debit
column. A check mark (√) is written below the total of the Sundry Accounts Debit column to indicate that the total amount is not posted. Post
the figures in this column individually, then place the account number in
the Post. Ref. column. Post the amounts in the Accounts Payable Debit
column separately to individual accounts in the accounts payable ledger.
After posting, put a check mark (√) in the Post. Ref. column. The posting
letter designation for the cash payments journal is CP. Other transactions
involving decreases in cash during May are as follows:

May   7 Paid a three-year premium for fire insurance, check no. 67,
        $360.
      9 Paid Treadwell, Inc., a creditor, on account, check no. 68,
        $418.
     11 Issued check no. 69 in payment of delivery expense, $62.

May 14 Paid Johnson and Son, a creditor, on account, check no. 70, $110.

16 Issued check no. 71 to the Melton State Bank, for a Note Payable, $660, $600 on the principal and $60 interest.

19 Voided check no. 72.

19 Bought equipment from Burns Company for $800, paying $200 down. Issued check no. 73. The rest of this entry is recorded in the general journal as explained below.

20 Paid wages for two weeks, check no. 74, $1,340 (previously recorded in the payroll entry).

22 Issued check no. 75 to Peter R. Morton Advertising Agency for advertising, $94.

26 Paid telephone bill, check no. 76, $26.

31 Issued check for freight bill on equipment purchased on May 19, check no. 77, $28.

31 Paid Teller and Noble, a creditor, on account, check no. 78, $160.

These transactions are recorded in the cash payments journal illustrated in Figure 13-4.

FIGURE 13-4

Remember

A check mark may have two meanings: (1) an amount has been posted to the Accounts Receivable or Accounts Payable subsidiary ledger, or (2) "do not post—the amounts have already been posted separately."

CASH PAYMENTS JOURNAL

PAGE 62

	DATE	CK. NO.	ACCOUNT DEBITED	POST. REF.	SUNDRY ACCOUNTS DEBIT	ACCOUNTS PAYABLE DEBIT	CASH CREDIT	
1	19–							1
2	May 2	63	C. C. Hardy Co.	√		2 2 0 00	2 2 0 00	2
3	4	64	Supplies	113	9 0 00		9 0 00	3
4	5	65	Wages Payable	213	1 2 1 6 00		1 2 1 6 00	4
5	6	66	Rent Expense	512	3 5 0 00		3 5 0 00	5
6	7	67	Prepaid Insurance	114	3 6 0 00		3 6 0 00	6
7	9	68	Treadwell, Inc.	√		4 1 8 00	4 1 8 00	7
8	11	69	Delivery Expense	513	6 2 00		6 2 00	8
9	14	70	Johnson and Son	√		1 1 0 00	1 1 0 00	9
10	16	71	Notes Payable	211	6 0 0 00			10
11			Interest Expense	518	6 0 00		6 6 0 00	11
12	19	72	Void					12
13	19	73	Equipment	121	2 0 0 00		2 0 0 00	13
14	20	74	Wages Payable	213	1 3 4 0 00		1 3 4 0 00	14
15	22	75	Advertising					15
16			Expense	515	9 4 00		9 4 00	16
17	26	76	Telephone Expense	516	2 6 00		2 6 00	17
18	31	77	Equipment	121	2 8 00		2 8 00	18
19	31	78	Teller and Noble	√		1 6 0 00	1 6 0 00	19
20	31				4 4 2 6 00	9 0 8 00	5 3 3 4 00	20
21					(√)	(2 1 2)	(1 1 1)	21
22								22

CHECK REGISTER

PAGE _____

	DATE	CK. NO.	PAYEE	ACCOUNT DEBITED	POST. REF.	SUNDRY ACCOUNTS DEBIT	ACCOUNTS PAYABLE DEBIT	PURCHASES DISCOUNT CREDIT	VALLEY BANK CREDIT	
1	19–									1
2	Aug. 8	76	Draper, Inc.	Draper, Inc.	✓		4 2 0 00	7 80	4 1 2 20	2
3	10	77	Payroll	Wages Payable	213	1 6 8 0 00			1 6 8 0 00	3
4	11	78	Adkins	Adkins						4
5			Manufacturing	Manufacturing	✓		6 2 2 00	1 2 44	6 0 9 56	5
6	12	79	Davenport	Supplies	115	7 0 00			7 0 00	6
7	15	80	Sullivan	Sullivan						7
8			Products Co.	Products Co.	✓		1 2 9 00	1 19	1 2 7 81	8
9	16	81	Jones and Son	Purchases	511	2 0 0 00			2 0 0 00	9
10	19	82	Reliable Express							10
11			Co.	Freight In	514	6 0 00			6 0 00	11
12	23	83	Void		✓					12
13	23	84	American Fire	Prepaid						13
14			Ins. Co.	Insurance	116	1 2 0 00			1 2 0 00	14
15	25	85	Payroll	Wages Payable	213	1 7 5 0 00			1 7 5 0 00	15
16	27	86	F. R. Waller	Sales Ret. and						16
17				Allow.	412	4 6 00			4 6 00	17
18	31	87	Reilley and	Reilly and						18
19			Peters Co.	Peters Co.	✓		7 6 0 00		7 6 0 00	19
20	31					3 9 2 6 00	1 9 3 1 00	2 1 43	5 8 3 5 57	20
21						(✓)	(2 1 2)	(5 1 3)	(1 1 1)	21
22										22

FIGURE 13-6

In a small business, the owner or manager usually signs all the checks. However, if the owner delegates the authority to sign checks to some other person, that person should *not* have access to the accounting records. Why? Well, this helps to prevent fraud, because a dishonest employee could conceal a cash disbursement in the accounting records. In other words, for a medium- to large-size business, it's worth a manager's while to keep a separate book, which in this case is the cash payments journal. One person writes the checks; another person records the checks in the cash payments journal. In this way, one person acts as a curb on the other. There would have to be collusion between the two people for embezzlement to take place. Again, this precaution is consistent with a good system of internal control, because it gets as many people into the act as is practical.

TRADE DISCOUNTS

Manufacturers and wholesalers of many lines of products publish annual catalogs listing their products at retail prices. These concerns offer their customers substantial reductions (often as much as 40 percent) from the

Objective 8

Record transactions involving trade discounts.

list or catalog prices. The reductions from the list prices are called **trade discounts.** Remember, firms grant cash discounts for prompt payment of invoices. Trade discounts are *not related* to cash payments. Manufacturers and wholesalers use trade discounts to avoid high costs of reprinting catalogs when selling prices change. To change prices, the manufacturer or wholesaler simply issues a sheet showing a new list of trade discounts to be applied to the catalog prices. Trade discounts can also be used to differentiate between classes of customers. For example, a manufacturer may use one schedule of trade discounts for wholesalers and another schedule for retailers.

Firms may quote trade discounts as a single percentage. Example: A distributor of furnaces grants a single discount of 40 percent off the listed catalog price of $8,000. In this case, the selling price is calculated as follows:

List or catalog price	$8,000
Less trade discount of 40% ($8,000 × .4)	3,200
Selling price	$4,800

Neither the seller nor the buyer records trade discounts in the accounts; they enter only the selling price. By T accounts, the furnace distributor records the sale like this:

Accounts Receivable		Sales	
+	−	−	+
4,800			4,800

The buyer records the purchase as follows:

Purchases		Accounts Payable	
+	−	−	+
4,800			4,800

Firms may also quote trade discounts as a chain, or series, of percentages. For example, a distributor of automobile parts grants discounts of 30 percent, 10 percent, and 10 percent off the listed catalog price of $900. In this case, the selling price is calculated as follows:

List or catalog price	$900.00
Less first trade discount of 30% ($900 × .3)	270.00
Remainder after first discount	$630.00
Less second trade discount of 10% ($630 × .1)	63.00
Remainder after second discount	$567.00
Less third discount of 10% ($567 × .1)	56.70
Selling price	$510.30

By T accounts, the automobile parts distributor records the sale as follows:

The buyer records the purchase as follows:

In the situation involving a chain of discounts, the additional discounts are granted for large-volume transactions, either in dollar amount or in size of shipment, such as carload lots.

Cash discounts could also apply in situations involving trade discounts. Example: Suppose that the credit terms of the above sale include a cash discount of 2/10, n/30, and the buyer pays the invoice within ten days. The seller applies the cash discount to the selling price. By T accounts, the seller records the transaction as

Cash		Sales Discount		Accounts Receivable	
+	−	+	−	+	−
500.09		10.21			510.30

The buyer records the transaction as

Cash		Purchases Discount		Accounts Payable	
+	−	−	+	−	+
	500.09		10.21	510.30	

COMPARISON OF THE FIVE TYPES OF JOURNALS

We have now looked at four special journals and the general journal. It is very important for a business to select and use the journals that will provide the most efficient accounting system possible. Figure 13-7 summarizes the applications of and correct procedures for using the journals we have discussed.

Types of Transactions

Sale of merchandise on account	Purchase of merchandise on account	Receipt of cash	Payment of cash	All other

Evidenced by Source Documents

Sales invoice	Purchase invoice	Credit card receipts Cash Checks	Check stub	Miscellaneous

Types of Journals

Sales journal	Purchases journal	Cash receipts journal	Cash payments journal	General journal

Posting to Ledger Accounts

Individual amounts posted daily to the accounts receivable ledger and the total posted monthly to the general ledger.	*Individual amounts posted daily to the accounts payable ledger and the totals of the special columns posted monthly to the general ledger.*	*Individual amounts in the Accounts Receivable credit column posted daily to the accounts receivable ledger.* *Individual amounts in the Sundry columns posted daily to the general ledger.* *Totals of special columns posted monthly.*	*Individual amounts in the Accounts Payable debit column posted daily to the accounts payable ledger.* *Individual amounts in the Sundry columns posted daily to the general ledger.* *Totals of special columns posted monthly.*	*Entries posted daily to the subsidiary ledgers and the general ledger.*

FIGURE 13-7

Recommended Order of Posting to the Subsidiary Ledgers and the General Ledger

To avoid errors and negative balances in accounts, post from the special journals in this order:

1. Sales Journal
2. Purchases Journal
3. Cash Receipts Journal
4. Cash Payments Journal

Posting general journal entries depends on the specific dates of the transactions.

SUMMARY

L.O. 1,3,4   When a business entity uses a cash receipts journal, it *must* record every transaction which results in a debit to cash in this journal. The person handling the books sets up special columns in the journal to take care of debits or credits to accounts, such as Sales Discount, that are used frequently. In accounting, *Sundry* means miscellaneous, so one records entries in the Sundry column when there is no appropriate special column.

L.O. 2   The accountant posts daily from the Accounts Receivable Credit column to the individual charge customers' accounts in the accounts receivable ledger. After posting, the accountant puts a check mark (√) in the Post. Ref. column. The accountant also posts the amounts in the Sundry Credit column daily. After these entries are posted, the account numbers are recorded in the Post. Ref. column. The special columns are posted as totals at the end of the month. After posting, the accountant writes the account numbers in parentheses under the totals.

L.O. 5,6   When a business entity uses a cash payments journal, it *must* record in this journal every transaction that results in a credit to cash. This enables the accountant to determine quickly the balance of the Cash account. It follows that if all incoming cash is recorded in the cash receipts journal, and if all outgoing cash is recorded in the cash payments journal, then one can readily determine the current balance of cash at any time during the month by adding the receipts to the beginning balance of cash and deducting the outgoing payments.

L.O. 7   Smaller firms often use a check register as a substitute for the cash payments journal. Either book of original entry may be used by service as well as merchandising enterprises. The posting procedure for both a cash payments journal and a check register is similar to the posting procedure for a cash receipts journal.

L.O. 8   In transactions involving trade discounts, one deducts the trade discounts from the list prices to arrive at the selling prices. Both sellers and buyers record the transactions at the selling prices.

GLOSSARY

Bank charge card A bank credit card, like the credit cards used by millions of private citizens. The cardholder pays what she or he owes directly to the issuing bank. The business firm deposits the credit card receipts; the amount of the deposit equals the total of the receipts, less a discount deducted by the bank.

Cash discount The amount a customer can deduct for paying a bill within a specified period of time; used to encourage prompt payment. Not all sellers offer cash discounts.

Cash payments journal A special journal used to record all transactions in which cash goes out, or decreases.

Cash receipts journal A special journal used to record all transactions in which cash comes in, or increases.

Credit period The time the seller allows the buyer before full payment on a charge sale has to be made.

Crossfooting The process of totaling columns in a journal or work sheet to make sure that the sum of the debit totals equals the sum of the credit totals.

Sales discount The cash discount from the seller's point of view; in the buyer's books this is a *purchases discount*.

Trade discounts Substantial reductions from the list or catalog prices of goods, granted by the seller.

QUESTIONS, EXERCISES, AND PROBLEMS

Discussion Questions

1. When a cash receipts journal and a cash payments journal are used, how does one determine the exact balance of cash on a specific date during the month?
2. Describe the meaning of the following: 1/10, n/30; n/30; 1/10 EOM.
3. A firm has two bookkeepers. The new manager decided to assign the general journal to the less experienced bookkeeper. Do you agree? Why?
4. Describe the posting procedure for a cash receipts journal that has a Sundry Accounts Credit column and several other columns, including an Accounts Receivable Credit column.
5. Is the normal balance of Purchases Discount a debit or a credit? Where is it placed on an income statement?
6. In a cash payments journal, both the Accounts Payable Debit column and the Cash Credit column were added incorrectly and are understated by $10. How will this error be discovered?
7. What is the difference between a cash discount and a trade discount?
8. Explain the difference between the handling of delivery costs on merchandise sold and the handling of freight costs on merchandise purchased.

Exercises

L.O. 3 **Exercise 13-1** Record the following transactions in general journal form:

Sept. 4 Sold merchandise on account to L. Halley; 2/10, n/30; $1,200.
        6 Issued credit memo no. 127 to L. Halley for damaged merchandise, $42.
       14 Received a check from L. Halley in full payment of bill.

L.O. 3 **Exercise 13-2** Describe the transaction recorded in the following T accounts:

Cash	Sales Tax Payable	Sales	Credit Card Expense
201.60	10	200	8.40

L.O. 6   **Exercise 13-3**   Label the blanks in the column heads as debit or credit:

CASH PAYMENTS JOURNAL   PAGE_____

	DATE	CK. NO.	ACCOUNT NAME	POST. REF.	SUNDRY ACCOUNTS	ACCOUNTS PAYABLE	PURCHASES DISCOUNT	CASH	
1									1
2									2
3									3
4									4

L.O. 6   **Exercise 13-4**   Record the following transactions in general journal form:

Feb.   7   Bought merchandise on account from Bronstein and Company of Los Angeles; $1,700; terms 2/10, n/30; FOB San Diego, freight prepaid and added to the invoice, $73 (total $1,773).

      15   Received a credit memo no. 127 for $120 for defective goods returned.

      17   Paid Bronstein and Company in full of account.

L.O. 6   **Exercise 13-5**   Describe the transactions recorded in the following T accounts:

Cash	Accounts Payable	Purchases
(c) 2,352	(b) 300 | (a) 2,700	(a) 2,700
	(c) 2,400 |	

Purchases Returns and Allowances	Purchases Discount
(b) 300	(c) 48

L.O. 4   **Exercise 13-6**   Following is a page from a special journal.

     a. What kind of journal is this?
     b. Explain each of the transactions.
     c. Explain the notations in the Post. Ref. column.
     d. Explain the notations below the column totals.

	DATE	ACCOUNT CREDITED	POST. REF.	SUNDRY ACCOUNTS CREDIT	ACCOUNTS RECEIVABLE CREDIT	SALES CREDIT	SALES DISCOUNT DEBIT	CASH DEBIT	
1	19–								1
2	May 2	Della Simpson	√		5 0 0 00		1 0 00	4 9 0 00	2
3	7		—			7 1 0 00		7 1 0 00	3
4	11	Notes Payable	211	2 5 0 0 00				2 5 0 0 00	4
5	21	Harry Walls	√		2 1 0 00			2 1 0 00	5
6	31	L. R. Lee, Capital	311	5 0 0 0 00				5 0 0 0 00	6
7				7 5 0 0 00	7 1 0 00	7 1 0 00	1 0 00	8 9 1 0 00	7
8				(√)	(1 1 3)	(4 1 1)	(4 1 3)	(1 1 1)	8

L.O. 1,2,6   **Exercise 13-7**   Record general journal entries to correct the errors described below. Assume that the incorrect entries had been posted and that the corrections were discovered in the same period in which the errors occurred.

     a. A $240 cash purchase of merchandise from Berne and Lee was recorded as a purchase on account.

     b. A cash sale of $59 to C. R. Gordon was recorded as a sale on account.

     c. A freight cost of $52 incurred on equipment purchased for use in the business was debited to Freight In.

L.O. 3   **Exercise 13-8**   Record the following transactions in general journal form:

Mar.   1 Sold merchandise on account to the Baylor Company; 2/10, n/30; $520.

         9 Purchased merchandise on account from the Dougall Company; 1/10, n/30, FOB shipping point; $640.

      10 Paid freight bill on the merchandise purchased from the Dougall Company, $12.

      12 Received a credit memo from Dougall Company for defective merchandise returned, $90.

      18 Paid the Dougall Company in full within the discount period.

Problem Set A

L.O. 1,2   **Problem 13-1A**   Budget Furniture, a home furnishings store, sells on the bases of (1) cash, (2) charge accounts, and (3) bank credit cards. The following transactions involve cash receipts for the firm for November of this year. The state imposes a 4 percent sales tax on retail sales.

Nov.   7 Total cash sales for the week, $1,700, plus $68 sales tax.

         7 Total sales from bank credit cards for the week, $1,800, plus $72 sales tax. The bank charges 4 percent of the total sales plus tax ($1,872 × .04 = $74.88). (For all sales involving credit cards, record credit card expense at the time of the sale.)

      11 M. R. Vance, the owner, invested an additional $4,728.

      12 Sold office equipment for cash at cost, $366.

      12 Collected cash from T. R. Allison, a charge customer, $53.84.

      14 Total cash sales for the week, $2,593.04, plus $103.72 sales tax.

      14 Total sales for the week on the basis of bank credit cards, $1,440 plus $57.60 sales tax.

      18 Collected cash from N. P. Thorne, a charge customer, $78.52.

      19 Borrowed $5,560 from the bank, receiving the same in cash and giving the bank a promissory note.

      21 Total cash sales for the week, $3,254, plus $130.16 sales tax.

      21 Total sales from bank credit cards for the week, $1,480, plus $59.20 sales tax.

      22 Collected cash from C. E. Barnes, a charge customer, $233.52.

      24 Budget Furniture received cash as a refund for the return of merchandise it purchased, $372.

      27 Collected cash from O. Hauff, a charge customer, $143.12.

Nov.   30 Total sales from bank credit cards for the week, $352.80, plus
            $14.11 sales tax.
        30 Total cash sales for the week, $3,955.68, plus $158.23 sales tax.

Instructions

1. Open the following accounts in the accounts receivable ledger and record
   the November 1 balances as given: T. R. Allison, $193.84; C. E. Barnes,
   $233.52; L. R. Cain, $106.46; L. P. Dunn, $179.52; O. Hauff, $143.12;
   N. P. Thorne, $78.52. Place a check mark in the Post. Ref. column.
2. Record balance of $934.98 in the Accounts Receivable controlling account
   as of November 1.
3. Record the transactions in the cash receipts journal beginning with
   page 16.
4. Post daily to the accounts receivable ledger.
5. Total and rule the cash receipts journal.
6. Prove the equality of debit and credit totals.
7. Post to the Accounts Receivable account in the general ledger.

L.O. 4 **Problem 13-2A**   The C. R. Michaels Company sells candy wholesale,
primarily to vending machine operators. Terms of sales on account are 2/10,
n/30, FOB shipping point. The following transactions involving cash receipts
and sales of merchandise took place in May of this year:

May   2 Received $686 cash from N. Roche in payment of April 23 invoice
           of $700 less cash discount.
        5 Received $990 cash in payment of $900 note receivable and inter-
           est of $90.
        8 Sold merchandise on account to G. Selleck, invoice no. 862, $420.
        9 Received $784 in cash from D. Morton in payment of April 30 in-
           voice of $800, less cash discount.
       15 Received cash from G. Selleck in payment of invoice no. 862, less
           discount.
       16 Cash sales for first half of May, $3,447.
       19 Received $253 in cash from R. O. Huff in payment of April 14 in-
           voice, no discount.
       22 Sold merchandise on account to N. T. Jackson, invoice no. 887,
           $585.
       25 Received $326 cash refund for return of defective equipment
           bought in April for cash.
       28 Sold merchandise on account to M. E. Murray, invoice no. 910,
           $728.
       31 Cash sales for the second half of May, $3,394.

Instructions

1. Journalize the transactions for May in the cash receipts journal and the
   sales journal.
2. Total and rule the journals.
3. Prove the equality of the debit and credit totals.

L.O. 7   Problem 13-3A   Jefferson Company uses a check register to keep track of expenditures. The following transactions occurred during February of this year:

Feb.   1 Issued check no. 4311 to Bennett Company for their invoice no. 3113E recorded previously; $640 less cash discount of $12.80, $627.20.

2 Paid freight bill to Baxter Express Company, $53, for merchandise purchased, issuing check no. 4312.

4 Paid rent for month of February, $345; check no. 4313 to Dixon Realty.

9 Received and paid bill for advertising in *Neighborhood News;* check no. 4314, $48.

10 Paid Dietrich Company $990, check no. 4315, for their invoice no. D642 recorded previously in the amount of $1,000 less 1 percent cash discount.

15 Paid wages for first half of month, $1,538; check no. 4316 (previously recorded).

19 R. Kelly, the owner, withdrew $500 for personal use; check no. 4317.

25 Made payment on bank loan $930; check no. 4318, consisting of $900 on principal and $30 interest, Second National Bank.

27 Issued to Lattimer Company, check no. 4319, $429, for their invoice no. 6317 recorded previously (no discount).

28 Voided check no. 4320.

28 Paid wages recorded previously for the second half of month, $1,538; check no. 4321.

28 Received and paid telephone bill, $56; check no. 4322, payable to Central Telephone Company.

Instructions

1. Record the transactions in the check register.
2. Total and rule the check register.
3. Prove the equality of the debit and credit totals.

L.O. 1,2,3,6   Problem 13-4A   The following transactions were completed by Davis Auto Supply during January, the first month of this fiscal year. Terms of sale are 2/10, n/30.

Jan.   2 Paid rent for the month, $550; check no. 6981.

2 J. Hammonds, the owner, invested an additional $2,240 in the business.

4 Bought merchandise on account from Vaughn and Company, $2,710; their invoice number A694; terms 2/10, n/30; dated January 2.

4 Received check from Vessey Appliance for $980 in payment of invoice for $1,000 less discount.

4 Sold merchandise on account to L. Parker, $650, invoice no. 6483.

Jan.   6 Received check from Peterson, Inc., for $637 in payment of $650 invoice, less discount.

      7 Issued check no. 6982, $588, to Franklin and Son in payment of their invoice no. C127, for $600, less discount.

      7 Bought supplies on account from Duncan Office Supply, $84.80, their invoice no. 190B; terms net 30 days.

      7 Sold merchandise on account to English and Cole, $850, invoice no. 6484.

      9 Issued credit memo no. 43 to L. Parker, $30, for merchandise returned.

   11 Cash sales for January 1 through January 10, $4,442.60.

   11 Paid Vaughn and Company $2,655.80; check no. 6983, in payment of their $2,710 invoice, less discount.

   14 Sold merchandise on account to Vessey Appliance, $1,900, invoice no. 6485.

   14 Received check from L. Parker, $607.60, in payment of $650 invoice, less return of $30 and less discount.

   19 Bought merchandise on account from Crosby Products, $3,600; their invoice no. 7281, dated January 16; terms 2/10, n/60; FOB shipping point, freight prepaid and added to invoice $140 (total $3,740).

   21 Issued check no. 6984, $265, for advertising to Barclay Agency not recorded previously.

   21 Cash sales for January 11 through January 20, $3,565.

   23 Received credit memo no. 163, $96, from Crosby Products for merchandise returned.

   29 Sold merchandise on account to Bryan Supply, $1,864; invoice no. 6486.

   29 Received bill and paid Pacific Freight, check no. 6985, $78, for freight charges on merchandise purchased January 4.

   31 Cash sales for January 21 through January 31, $3,987.

   31 Issued check no. 6986, $45, to M. Pierce for miscellaneous expenses not recorded previously.

   31 Recorded payroll entry from the payroll register: total salaries, $5,800; employees' federal income tax withheld, $812; FICA tax withheld, $440.80.

   31 Recorded the payroll taxes: FICA, $440.80; state unemployment tax, $313.20; federal unemployment tax, $46.40.

   31 Issued check no. 6987, $4,547.20, for salaries for the month.

   31 J. Hammonds, the owner, withdrew $970 for personal use, check no. 6988.

Instructions

1. Record the transactions for January, using a sales journal, page 91; a purchases journal, page 74; a cash receipts journal, page 56; a cash payments journal, page 63; a general journal, page 119. The chart of accounts is shown at the top of the next page.

2. Post daily all entries involving customer accounts to the accounts receivable ledger.

3. Post daily all entries involving creditor accounts to the accounts payable ledger.

111 Cash	411 Sales
113 Accounts Receivable	412 Sales Returns and Allowances
114 Merchandise Inventory	413 Sales Discount
115 Supplies	
116 Prepaid Insurance	511 Purchases
121 Equipment	512 Purchases Returns and Allowances
212 Accounts Payable	513 Purchases Discounts
215 Salaries Payable	514 Freight In
216 Employees' Federal Income Tax Payable	521 Salary Expense
	522 Payroll Tax Expense
217 FICA Tax Payable	527 Rent Expense
218 State Unemployment Tax Payable	531 Miscellaneous Expense
219 Federal Unemployment Tax Payable	
311 J. Hammonds, Capital	
312 J. Hammonds, Drawing	

4. Post daily those entries involving the Sundry columns and the general journal to the general ledger.
5. Add the columns of the special journals, and prove the equality of debit and credit totals on scratch paper.
6. Post the appropriate totals of the special journals to the general ledger.
7. Prepare a trial balance.
8. Prepare a schedule of accounts receivable and a schedule of accounts payable. Do the totals equal the balances of the related controlling accounts?

Problem Set B

L.O. 1,2

Problem 13-1B   Walters and Company, a retail carpet store, sells on the bases of (1) cash, (2) charge accounts, and (3) bank credit cards. The following transactions involved cash receipts for the firm during May of this year. The state imposes a 4 percent sales tax on retail sales.

May   8 Total cash sales for the week, $1,350, plus $54 sales tax.
    8 Total sales for the week paid for by bank credit cards, $1,200, plus $48 sales tax. The bank charges 4 percent on the total of the sales plus tax ($1,248 × .04 = $49.92). (For all sales involving credit cards, record credit card expense at the time of the sale.)
   11 D. C. Walters, the owner, invested an additional $3,000.
   11 Collected cash from N. D. Pryor, a charge customer, $71.70.
   12 Sold store equipment at cost for cash, $240.
   15 Total cash sales for the week, $1,650, plus $66 sales tax.
   15 Total sales for the week paid for by bank credit cards, $900, plus $36 sales tax.
   19 Borrowed $2,400 from the bank, receiving the same in cash and giving the bank a promissory note.

May   21 Collected cash from R. Branch, a charge customer, $78.
       22 Total sales for the week paid for by bank credit cards, $1,050, plus $42 sales tax.
       22 Total cash sales for the week, $2,400, plus $96 sales tax.
       24 Received cash as refund for the return of merchandise purchased, $135.
       26 Collected cash from C. Feller, a charge customer, $156.
       31 Total sales for the week paid for by bank credit cards, $240, plus $9.60 sales tax.
       31 Collected cash from R. D. Thorp, a charge customer, $109.20.
       31 Total cash sales for the week, $2,325, plus $93 sales tax.

Instructions

1. Open the following accounts in the accounts receivable ledger and record the May 1 balances as given: R. Branch, $78; C. Feller, $186; S. R. Pratt, $114.72; N. D. Pryor, $71.70; R. D. Thorp, $176.47; F. N. Weeks, $79.52. Place a check mark in the Post. Ref. column.
2. Record a balance of $706.41 in the Accounts Receivable controlling account as of May 1.
3. Record the transactions in the cash receipts journal beginning with page 62.
4. Post daily to the accounts receivable ledger.
5. Total and rule the cash receipts journal.
6. Prove the equality of debit and credit totals.
7. Post to the Accounts Receivable account in the general ledger.

L.O. 4   **Problem 13-2B**   Peterson Company sells candy wholesale to vending machine operators. Terms of sales on account are 2/10, n/30, FOB shipping point. The following transactions involving cash receipts and sales of merchandise took place in May of this year:

May   1 Received $980 cash from L. Riggan in payment of April 22 invoice of $1,000 less cash discount.
       4 Received $792 cash in payment of $720 note receivable and interest of $72.
       7 Received $686 cash from K. L. Shafer in payment of April 29 invoice of $700, less cash discount.
       8 Sold merchandise on account to D. Perry, invoice no. 272, $486.
       16 Cash sales for first half of May, $3,284.
       17 Received cash from D. Perry in payment of invoice no. 272, less cash discount.
       20 Received $321 cash from L. N. Sharp in payment of April 16 invoice, no discount.
       21 Sold merchandise on account to R. O. Weinstein, invoice no. 285, $836.
       24 Received $318 cash refund for return of defective equipment that was originally bought for cash.
       27 Sold merchandise on account to R. Johnston, invoice no. 292, $540.
       31 Cash sales for second half of May, $3,462.

Instructions

1. Journalize the transactions for May in the cash receipts journal and the sales journal.
2. Total and rule the journals.
3. Prove the equality of debit and credit totals.

L.O. 7 **Problem 13-3B** The Macklin Bookshop uses a check register to keep track of expenditures. The following transactions occurred during February of this year:

Feb.   3 Issued check no. 4312, $705.60, to Kentworth Company for the amount of their invoice no. 68172 recorded previously for $720, less 2 percent cash discount.

4 Paid freight bill to Keller Express Company, $48, for books purchased, issued check no. 4313.

6 Paid rent for the month, $320; check no. 4314, to Moore Land Company.

11 Received and paid bill for advertising in the *Northside News*, $58, check no. 4315.

11 Paid Collins Book Company $930.60, check no. 4316, for their invoice no. A3322 recorded previously for $940 less 1 percent cash discount.

17 Paid wages recorded previously for first half of February, $480; check no. 4317.

21 R. D. Macklin, the owner, withdrew $600 for personal use; check no. 4318.

26 Made payment on bank loan, $550; check no. 4319, consisting of $500 on the principal and $50 interest, Coast National Bank.

27 Paid Garrett Publishing Company $926, check no. 4320, for their invoice no. 7768 recorded previously (no discount).

28 Voided check no. 4321.

28 Paid wages expense recorded previously for second half of February, $480; check no. 4322.

Instructions

1. Record the transactions in the check register.
2. Total and rule the check register.
3. Prove the equality of the debit and credit totals.

L.O. 1,2,3,6 **Problem 13-4B** The following transactions were completed by Davis Auto Supply during January, which is the first month of this fiscal year. Terms of sale are 2/10, n/30.

Jan.   2 Paid rent for the month, $600; check no. 6981.

2 J. Hammonds, the owner, invested an additional $2,200 in the business.

4 Bought merchandise on account from Vaughn and Company, $2,840; their invoice no. A691, dated January 2; terms 2/10, n/30.

Jan. 4 Received check from Vessey Appliance for $980 in payment of $1,000 invoice less discount.

4 Sold merchandise on account to L. Parker, $750, invoice no. 6483.

6 Received check from Peterson, Inc., for $637 in payment of $650 invoice less discount.

7 Issued check no. 6982, $490, to Franklin and Son, in payment of their invoice no. C1272 for $500 less discount.

7 Bought supplies on account from Duncan Office Supply, $98, their invoice no. 1906B; terms net 30 days.

7 Sold merchandise on account to English and Cole, $890, invoice no. 6484.

9 Issued credit memo no. 43 to L. Parker, $50, for merchandise returned.

11 Cash sales for January 1 to January 10, $4,514.

11 Paid Vaughn and Company $2,783.20; check no. 6983, in payment of $2,840 invoice less discount.

14 Sold merchandise on account to Vessey Appliance, $1,950, invoice no. 6485.

18 Bought merchandise on account from Crosby Products, $4,780; their invoice no. 7281D, dated January 16; FOB shipping point, freight prepaid and added to the invoice $150 (total $4,930); terms 2/10, n/60.

21 Issued check no. 6984, $282, in favor of *The Shopper* for advertising not recorded previously.

21 Cash sales for January 11 to January 20, $3,990.

23 Received and paid Ball Fast Freight, check no. 6985, $86, for freight charges on merchandise purchased on January 4.

23 Received credit memo no. 163, $425, from Crosby Products for merchandise returned.

29 Sold merchandise on account to Bryan Supply, $1,940, invoice no. 6486.

31 Cash sales, January 21 to January 31, $4,428.

31 Issued check no. 6986 for $49 payable to M. Dole for miscellaneous expenses.

31 Recorded payroll entry from the payroll register; total salaries, $6,100; employees' federal income tax withheld, $854; FICA tax withheld, $463.60.

31 Recorded the payroll taxes: FICA, $463.60; state unemployment tax, $329.40; federal unemployment tax, $48.80.

31 Issued check no. 6987, $4,782.40, for salaries for the month.

31 J. Hammonds, the owner, withdrew $950 for personal use, check no. 6988.

Instructions

1. Record the transactions for January, using a sales journal, page 73; a purchases journal, page 56; a cash receipts journal, page 38; a cash payments journal, page 45; a general journal, page 100. The chart of accounts is as follows:

111 Cash
113 Accounts Receivable
114 Merchandise Inventory
115 Supplies
116 Prepaid Insurance
121 Equipment

212 Accounts Payable
215 Salaries Payable
216 Employees' Federal Income
      Tax Payable
217 FICA Tax Payable
218 State Unemployment Tax
      Payable
219 Federal Unemployment Tax
      Payable

311 J. Hammonds, Capital
312 J. Hammonds, Drawing

411 Sales
412 Sales Returns and Allowances
413 Sales Discount

511 Purchases
512 Purchases Returns and
      Allowances
513 Purchases Discount
514 Freight In
521 Salary Expense
522 Payroll Tax Expense
527 Rent Expense
531 Miscellaneous Expense

2. Post daily all entries involving customer accounts to the accounts receivable ledger.
3. Post daily all entries involving creditor accounts to the accounts payable ledger.
4. Post daily those entries involving the Sundry columns and the general journal to the general ledger.
5. Add the columns of the special journals, and prove the equality of debit and credit totals on scratch paper.
6. Post the appropriate totals of the special journals to the general ledger.
7. Prepare a trial balance.
8. Prepare a schedule of accounts receivable and a schedule of accounts payable. Do the totals equal the balances of the related controlling accounts?

14 Work Sheet and Adjusting Entries for a Merchandising Business

LEARNING OBJECTIVES

After you have completed this chapter, you will be able to do the following:

1. Make an adjustment for merchandise inventory.
2. Make an adjustment for unearned revenue.
3. Record the adjustment data (including depreciation, expired insurance, supplies used, accrued wages or salaries).
4. Complete the work sheet.
5. Journalize the adjusting entries for a merchandising business.

For quite some time we have been talking about keeping special journals and accounts for a merchandising enterprise. Now let's take another step forward in the accounting cycle for a merchandising business: let's make *adjustments* and prepare *work sheets*.

The column classifications and procedures for completing the work sheet are basically the same as those described in Chapter 5. A merchandising business—like a service business—requires adjustments for supplies used, expired insurance, depreciation, and accrued wages. However, one adjustment applies exclusively to a merchandising enterprise: the adjustment for merchandise inventory. Still another adjustment, which could apply to either a merchandising or a service business, is the adjustment for unearned revenue.

This chapter will also discuss the work sheet with respect to handling the specialized accounts of a merchandising business.

ADJUSTMENT FOR MERCHANDISE INVENTORY

When we introduced the Merchandise Inventory account in Chapter 11, we put it under the heading of assets and said that in our example the balance of the account is changed only after a **physical inventory** (or ac-

Objective 1

Make an adjustment for merchandise inventory.

tual count of the stock of goods on hand) has been taken. This is consistent with a **system of periodic inventories** in which one records the purchase of merchandise as a debit to Purchases for the amount of the cost and the sale of merchandise as a credit to Sales for the amount of the selling price. A company operating with a periodic inventory system takes an inventory count periodically (at least once a year). Next, adjusting entries are made to the Merchandise Inventory account to take off the beginning inventory and add on the ending inventory.

Consider this example: A firm has a Merchandise Inventory balance of $18,000, which represents the cost of the inventory at the beginning of the fiscal period. At the end of the fiscal period, the firm takes an actual count of the stock on hand and determines the cost of the ending inventory to be $22,000. Naturally, in any business, goods are constantly being bought, sold, and replaced. Evidently the reason that the cost of the ending inventory is larger than the cost of the beginning inventory is that the firm bought more than it sold. When we adjust the Merchandise Inventory account, we want to install the new figure of $22,000 in the account. We do this by a two-step process.

Step 1   Eliminate or close the Merchandise Inventory account into Income Summary by the amount of the beginning inventory. Transfer the balance into Income Summary. (Take off the beginning inventory.)

Let's look at this entry in the form of T accounts.

Merchandise Inventory	Income Summary
Bal. 18,000 │ Adj. 18,000	Adj. 18,000 │

We handle this just as we handle the closing of any other account, by balancing off the account, or making the balance equal to zero. We treat the entry as a credit to Merchandise Inventory and then do the opposite to Income Summary, which means we debit this account.

Step 2   Enter the ending Merchandise Inventory, because one must record on the books the cost of the asset remaining on hand. (Add on the ending inventory.)

Let's repeat the T accounts, showing step 1 and adding step 2.

Merchandise Inventory	Income Summary
Bal. 18,000 │ Adj. 18,000	Adj. 18,000 │ Adj. 22,000
Adj. 22,000 │	

In step 2, we debit Merchandise Inventory (recording the asset on the plus side of the account), and we do the opposite to Income Summary.

The reason for adjusting the Merchandise Inventory account in these two steps is that both the beginning and the ending figures appear separately on the income statement (see Figure 15-2), which is prepared directly from the Income Statement columns of the work sheet. This method of adjusting the inventory is considered more meaningful than taking a shortcut and adjusting for the difference between the beginning and the ending inventory values, since the amount of the difference does not appear as a distinct figure on the income statement.

An alternative to the periodic inventory system of handling merchandise inventory is the perpetual inventory system. Under the perpetual system, a company keeps a book record of each item in its inventory of goods on hand. When merchandise is bought, the cost of the merchandise is added to the Merchandise Inventory account directly. When goods are sold, the cost is deducted directly from the Merchandise Inventory account. So, the firm perpetually knows how much stock of goods it has on hand at any one time. Under this system, the Purchases account is eliminated, since the buying of merchandise is debited to the Merchandise Inventory account.

Perpetual inventory systems have been aided greatly by the development of computer programs. To verify the book balance of the inventory, a company makes a physical count. Due to shortages or theft, the amount of the count may be less than the amount recorded in the Merchandise Inventory account. In this event, an adjusting entry is made debiting Cost of Merchandise Sold (like an expense account) and crediting Merchandise Inventory for the amount of the shortage.

ADJUSTMENT FOR UNEARNED REVENUE

Objective 2

Make an adjustment for unearned revenue.

Let's now introduce another adjusting entry: **unearned revenue,** which is revenue received in advance for goods or services to be delivered or performed later. As we said, this entry could pertain to a service as well as to a merchandising business. Frequently, cash is received in advance for services to be performed in the future. For example, a dining hall sells meal tickets in advance, a concert association sells season tickets in advance, a magazine receives subscriptions in advance, and an insurance company receives premiums in advance. If the amounts to be received by each of these organizations will be earned during the present fiscal period, the amounts should be credited to revenue accounts. On the other hand, if the amounts to be received will *not* be earned during the present fiscal period, the amounts should be credited to unearned revenue accounts. **An unearned revenue account is classified as a liability** because an organization is liable for the amount received in advance until it is earned.

To illustrate, assume that Mark Publishing Company receives $60,000 in cash for subscriptions covering two years and records them originally as debits to Cash and credits to Unearned Subscriptions. At the end of the year, Mark finds that $44,000 of the subscriptions have been earned. Accordingly, Mark's accountant makes an adjusting entry, debiting Unearned Subscriptions and crediting Subscriptions Income. In other words, the accountant takes the earned portion out of Unearned Subscriptions and adds it to Subscriptions Income. T accounts show the situation as follows:

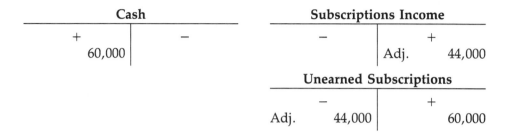

To take another example, suppose that City-Wide Electric offers a course in wiring for home owners and apartment managers. On November 1, City-Wide Electric receives $900 in fees for a three-month course. Because City-Wide Electric's present fiscal period ends on December 31, the three months' worth of fees received in advance will not be earned during this fiscal period. Therefore, City-Wide Electric's accountant records the transaction as a debit to Cash of $900 and a credit to Unearned Course Fees of $900. Unearned Course Fees is a liability account because City-Wide Electric must complete the how-to course or refund a portion of the money it collected. Any account beginning with the word *Unearned* is always a liability.

On December 31, because two months' worth of course fees have now been earned, City-Wide Electric's accountant makes an adjusting entry to transfer $600 ($\frac{2}{3}$ of $900) from Unearned Course Fees to Course Fees Income. By T accounts, the situation looks like this:

Cash			Unearned Course Fees	
+		−	−	+
Nov. 1 900			Dec. 31 Adj. 600	Nov. 1 900
			(2 months)	(3 months)

Course Fees Income	
−	+
	Dec. 31 Adj. 600

City-Wide Electric Supply's chart of accounts is presented on page 445. The account number arrangement will be discussed in Chapter 15.

Assets (100–199)
111 Cash
112 Notes Receivable
113 Accounts Receivable
114 Merchandise Inventory
115 Supplies
116 Prepaid Insurance
121 Land
122 Building
123 Accumulated Depreciation,
    Building
124 Equipment
125 Accumulated Depreciation,
    Equipment

Liabilities (200–299)
211 Notes Payable
212 Accounts Payable
213 Wages Payable
217 Unearned Course Fees
221 Mortgage Payable

Owner's Equity (300–399)
311 R. C. Schmidt, Capital
312 R. C. Schmidt, Drawing
313 Income Summary

Revenue (400–499)
411 Sales
412 Sales Returns
    and Allowances
413 Sales Discount
421 Course Fees Income
422 Interest Income

Expenses (500–599)
511 Purchases
512 Purchases Returns
    and Allowances
513 Purchases Discount
514 Freight In
521 Wages Expense
522 Depreciation Expense,
    Equipment
523 Supplies Expense
531 Depreciation Expense,
    Building
532 Taxes Expense
533 Insurance Expense
534 Interest Expense

Before we demonstrate how to record adjustments, let's first look at the trial balance section of City-Wide Electric Supply's work sheet (Figure 14-1 on page 446). Notice that the adjustments for supplies used, insurance expired, depreciation, and accrued wages are the same type of adjustment we discussed for a service business in Chapter 5.

DATA FOR THE ADJUSTMENTS

Objective 3

Record the adjustment data (including depreciation, expired insurance, supplies used, accrued wages or salaries).

Listing the adjustment data appears to be a relatively minor task. In a business situation, however, one must take actual physical counts of the inventories and match them up with costs. One must check insurance policies to determine the amount of insurance that has expired. Finally, one must systematically write off, or depreciate, the cost of equipment and buildings.

For income tax and accounting purposes, land cannot be depreciated. Even if the building and lot were bought as one package for one price, the buyer must separate the cost of the building from the cost of the land. For real estate taxes, the county assessor appraises the building and

	ACCOUNT NAME	TRIAL BALANCE		ADJUSTMENTS		
		DEBIT	CREDIT	DEBIT	CREDIT	
1	Cash	21 9 2 2 00				1
2	Notes Receivable	4 0 0 0 00				2
3	Accounts Receivable	29 3 6 0 00				3
4	Merchandise Inventory	63 0 0 0 00				4
5	Supplies	1 4 4 0 00				5
6	Prepaid Insurance	9 6 0 00				6
7	Land	12 0 0 0 00				7
8	Building	90 0 0 0 00				8
9	Accumulated Depreciation, Building		32 0 0 0 00			9
10	Equipment	33 6 0 0 00				10
11	Accumulated Depreciation, Equipment		16 4 0 0 00			11
12	Notes Payable		3 0 0 0 00			12
13	Accounts Payable		36 4 0 0 00			13
14	Unearned Course Fees		9 0 0 00			14
15	Mortgage Payable		8 0 0 0 00			15
16	R. C. Schmidt, Capital		136 5 7 4 00			16
17	R. C. Schmidt, Drawing	29 2 0 0 00				17
18	Sales		186 1 8 0 00			18
19	Sales Returns and Allowances	8 4 0 00				19
20	Sales Discount	1 8 8 0 00				20
21	Interest Income		1 2 0 00			21
22	Purchases	83 1 4 0 00				22
23	Purchases Returns and Allowances		8 3 2 00			23
24	Purchases Discount		1 2 4 8 00			24
25	Freight In	2 4 6 0 00				25
26	Wages Expense	45 8 0 0 00				26
27	Taxes Expense	1 9 6 0 00				27
28	Interest Expense	9 2 00				28
29		421 6 5 4 00	421 6 5 4 00			29
30						30

FIGURE 14-1

the land separately. If there is no other qualified appraisal available, one can use the assessor's ratio or percentage as a basis for separating building cost and land cost.

Here are the adjustment data for City-Wide Electric Supply. We will show the adjustments recorded in T accounts.

a–b. Ending merchandise inventory, $58,800

Merchandise Inventory

+		−
Bal. 63,000		(a) Adj. 63,000
(b) Adj. 58,800		

Income Summary

(a) Adj. 63,000	(b) Adj. 58,800

c. Course fees earned, $600

Unearned Course Fees				Course Fees Income			
−		+		−		+	
(c) Adj.	600	Bal.	900			(c) Adj.	600

d. Ending supplies inventory, $412

Supplies				Supplies Expense			
+		−		+		−	
Bal.	1,440	(d) Adj.	1,028	(d) Adj.	1,028		

e. Insurance expired, $320

Prepaid Insurance				Insurance Expense			
+		−		+		−	
Bal.	960	(e) Adj.	320	(e) Adj.	320		

f. Additional year's depreciation of equipment, $4,800

Accumulated Depreciation, Equipment				Depreciation Expense, Equipment			
−		+		+		−	
		Bal.	16,400	(f) Adj.	4,800		
		(f) Adj.	4,800				

g. Additional year's depreciation of building, $4,000

Accumulated Depreciation, Building				Depreciation Expense, Building			
−		+		+		−	
		Bal.	32,000	(g)	4,000		
		(g)	4,000				

h. Wages owed but not paid to employees at end of year, $1,220

Wages Payable				Wages Expense			
−		+		+		−	
		(h)	1,220	Bal.	45,800		
				(h)	1,220		

We now record these in the Adjustments columns of the work sheet, using the same letters to identify the adjustments (see Figure 14-2).

	ACCOUNT NAME	TRIAL BALANCE DEBIT	TRIAL BALANCE CREDIT	ADJUSTMENTS DEBIT	ADJUSTMENTS CREDIT	
1	Cash	21 9 2 2 00				1
2	Notes Receivable	4 0 0 0 00				2
3	Accounts Receivable	29 3 6 0 00				3
4	Merchandise Inventory	63 0 0 0 00		(b) 58 8 0 0 00	(a) 63 0 0 0 00	4
5	Supplies	1 4 4 0 00			(d) 1 0 2 8 00	5
6	Prepaid Insurance	9 6 0 00			(e) 3 2 0 00	6
7	Land	12 0 0 0 00				7
8	Building	90 0 0 0 00				8
9	Accumulated Depreciation, Building		32 0 0 0 00		(g) 4 0 0 0 00	9
10	Equipment	33 6 0 0 00				10
11	Accumulated Depreciation, Equipment		16 4 0 0 00		(f) 4 8 0 0 00	11
12	Notes Payable		3 0 0 0 00			12
13	Accounts Payable		36 4 0 0 00			13
14	Unearned Course Fees		9 0 0 00	(c) 6 0 0 00		14
15	Mortgage Payable		8 0 0 0 00			15
16	R. C. Schmidt, Capital		136 5 7 4 00			16
17	R. C. Schmidt, Drawing	29 2 0 0 00				17
18	Sales		186 1 8 0 00			18
19	Sales Returns and Allowances	8 4 0 00				19
20	Sales Discount	1 8 8 0 00				20
21	Interest Income		1 2 0 00			21
22	Purchases	83 1 4 0 00				22
23	Purchases Returns and Allowances		8 3 2 00			23
24	Purchases Discount		1 2 4 8 00			24
25	Freight In	2 4 6 0 00				25
26	Wages Expense	45 8 0 0 00		(h) 1 2 2 0 00		26
27	Taxes Expense	1 9 6 0 00				27
28	Interest Expense	9 2 00				28
29		421 6 5 4 00	421 6 5 4 00			29
30	Income Summary			(a) 63 0 0 0 00	(b) 58 8 0 0 00	30
31	Course Fees Income				(c) 6 0 0 00	31
32	Supplies Expense			(d) 1 0 2 8 00		32
33	Insurance Expense			(e) 3 2 0 00		33
34	Depreciation Expense, Equipment			(f) 4 8 0 0 00		34
35	Depreciation Expense, Building			(g) 4 0 0 0 00		35
36	Wages Payable				(h) 1 2 2 0 00	36
37				133 7 6 8 00	133 7 6 8 00	37
38						38
39						39
40						40
41						41
42						42
43						43

FIGURE 14-2

COMPLETION OF THE WORK SHEET

Objective 4

Complete the work sheet.

Previously, in introducing work sheets, we included the Adjusted Trial Balance columns as a means of verifying that the accounts were in balance after recording the adjusting entries. At this time, to reduce the number of columns of the work sheet, we will eliminate the Adjusted Trial Balance columns. The account balances after the adjusting entries will be carried directly into the Income Statement and Balance Sheet columns.

The completed work sheet looks like Figure 14-3.

Observe in particular the way we carry forward the figures for Merchandise Inventory and Income Summary. **Income Summary is the only account in which we don't combine the debit and credit figures; instead we carry them into the Income Statement columns in Figure 14-3 as two distinct figures.** As we said, the reason is that both figures appear in the income statement itself. The amount listed as Income Summary in the Income Statement Debit column is the beginning merchandise inventory. The amount listed as Income Summary in the Income Statement Credit column is the ending merchandise inventory. We will talk about this topic in greater detail in Chapter 15.

When developing the work sheet, complete one stage at a time:

1. Record the trial balance, and make sure that the total of the Debit column equals the total of the Credit column.
2. Record the adjustments in the Adjustments columns, and make sure that the totals are equal.
3. Complete the Income Statement and Balance Sheet columns by recording the adjusted balance of each account. Here are the accounts and classifications pertaining to a merchandising business that appear in these columns:

Income Statement		Balance Sheet	
Debit	**Credit**	**Debit**	**Credit**
Expenses + Sales Returns and Allowances + Sales Discount + Purchases + Freight In + Income Summary	Revenues + Purchases Returns and Allowances + Purchases Discount + Income Summary	Assets + Drawing	Liabilities + Capital + Accumulated Depreciation

City-Wide Electric Supply
Work Sheet
For Year Ended December 31, 19–

	ACCOUNT NAME	TRIAL BALANCE DEBIT	TRIAL BALANCE CREDIT
1	Cash	21 9 2 2 00	
2	Notes Receivable	4 0 0 0 00	
3	Accounts Receivable	29 3 6 0 00	
4	Merchandise Inventory	63 0 0 0 00	
5	Supplies	1 4 4 0 00	
6	Prepaid Insurance	9 6 0 00	
7	Land	12 0 0 0 00	
8	Building	90 0 0 0 00	
9	Accumulated Depreciation, Building		32 0 0 0 00
10	Equipment	33 6 0 0 00	
11	Accumulated Depreciation, Equipment		16 4 0 0 00
12	Notes Payable		3 0 0 0 00
13	Accounts Payable		36 4 0 0 00
14	Unearned Course Fees		9 0 0 00
15	Mortgage Payable		8 0 0 0 00
16	R. C. Schmidt, Capital		136 5 7 4 00
17	R. C. Schmidt, Drawing	29 2 0 0 00	
18	Sales		186 1 8 0 00
19	Sales Returns and Allowances	8 4 0 00	
20	Sales Discount	1 8 8 0 00	
21	Interest Income		1 2 0 00
22	Purchases	83 1 4 0 00	
23	Purchases Returns and Allowances		8 3 2 00
24	Purchases Discount		1 2 4 8 00
25	Freight In	2 4 6 0 00	
26	Wages Expense	45 8 0 0 00	
27	Taxes Expense	1 9 6 0 00	
28	Interest Expense	9 2 00	
29		421 6 5 4 00	421 6 5 4 00
30	Income Summary		
31	Course Fees Income		
32	Supplies Expense		
33	Insurance Expense		
34	Depreciation Expense, Equipment		
35	Depreciation Expense, Building		
36	Wages Payable		
37			
38	Net Income		
39			
40			
41			
42			

FIGURE 14-3

	ADJUSTMENTS		INCOME STATEMENT		BALANCE SHEET		
	DEBIT	CREDIT	DEBIT	CREDIT	DEBIT	CREDIT	
					21 922 00		1
					4 000 00		2
					29 360 00		3
	(b) 58 800 00	(a) 63 000 00			58 800 00		4
		(d) 1 028 00			4 12 00		5
		(e) 3 20 00			6 40 00		6
					12 000 00		7
					90 000 00		8
		(g) 4 000 00				36 000 00	9
					33 600 00		10
		(f) 4 800 00				21 200 00	11
						3 000 00	12
						36 400 00	13
	(c) 6 00 00					3 00 00	14
						8 00 00	15
						136 574 00	16
					29 200 00		17
				186 180 00			18
			8 40 00				19
			1 880 00				20
				1 20 00			21
			83 140 00				22
				8 32 00			23
				1 248 00			24
			2 460 00				25
	(h) 1 220 00		47 020 00				26
			1 960 00				27
			9 2 00				28
							29
	(a) 63 000 00	(b) 58 800 00	63 000 00	58 800 00			30
		(c) 6 00 00		6 00 00			31
	(d) 1 028 00		1 028 00				32
	(e) 3 20 00		3 20 00				33
	(f) 4 800 00		4 800 00				34
	(g) 4 000 00		4 000 00				35
		(h) 1 220 00				1 220 00	36
	133 768 00	133 768 00	210 540 00	247 780 00	279 934 00	242 694 00	37
			37 240 00			37 240 00	38
			247 780 00	247 780 00	279 934 00	279 934 00	39
							40
							41
							42

Study the following example, noting especially the way we treat these special accounts for a merchandising business:

Account Name	Location in Work Sheet				
	Income Statement		Balance Sheet		
	Debit	Credit	Debit	Credit	
Merchandise Inventory			58,800 00		
Sales		186,180 00			
Sales Returns and Allowances	840 00				
Sales Discount	1,880 00				
Purchases	83,140 00				
Freight In	2,460 00				
Purchases Returns and Allowances		832 00			
Purchases Discount		1,248 00			
Income Summary	63,000 00	58,800 00			

Objective 5

Journalize the adjusting entries for a merchandising business.

ADJUSTING ENTRIES

Figure 14-4 shows the way the adjusting entries look when they are taken from the Adjustments columns of the work sheet and recorded in the general journal.

SUMMARY

L.O. 1–4 The work sheet is a device accountants use to organize the account balances so that they can prepare the income statement and the balance sheet. Typical adjustments that affect both service and merchandising firms are the recording of supplies used, insurance expired, depreciation of equipment and buildings, accrued wages, and unearned revenue. Merchandising firms have an additional adjustment for Merchandise Inventory. The companion account in this adjusting entry is Income Summary. Adjusting the Merchan-

FIGURE 14-4

	DATE		DESCRIPTION	POST. REF.	DEBIT	CREDIT	
1	19–						1
2			*Adjusting Entries*				2
3	Dec.	31	Income Summary		63 0 0 0 00		3
4			Merchandise Inventory			63 0 0 0 00	4
5							5
6		31	Merchandise Inventory		58 8 0 0 00		6
7			Income Summary			58 8 0 0 00	7
8							8
9		31	Unearned Course Fees		6 0 0 00		9
10			Course Fees Income			6 0 0 00	10
11							11
12		31	Supplies Expense		1 0 2 8 00		12
13			Supplies			1 0 2 8 00	13
14							14
15		31	Insurance Expense		3 2 0 00		15
16			Prepaid Insurance			3 2 0 00	16
17							17
18		31	Depreciation Expense, Equipment		4 8 0 0 00		18
19			Accumulated Depreciation,				19
20			Equipment			4 8 0 0 00	20
21							21
22		31	Depreciation Expense, Building		4 0 0 0 00		22
23			Accumulated Depreciation,				23
24			Building			4 0 0 0 00	24
25							25
26		31	Wages Expense		1 2 2 0 00		26
27			Wages Payable			1 2 2 0 00	27
28							28

GENERAL JOURNAL   PAGE *96*

dise Inventory account is a two-step process. First, eliminate or take off the beginning inventory. Second, restate, or add on, the ending inventory, to record the current balance of the account.

L.O. 5   In the work sheet, carry the Income Summary account as two separate figures from the Adjustments columns into the Income Statement columns.

GLOSSARY

Physical inventory   An actual count of the stock of goods on hand; also referred to as a *periodic inventory*.

Unearned revenue   Revenue received in advance for goods or services to be delivered later; considered to be a liability until the revenue is earned.

QUESTIONS, EXERCISES, AND PROBLEMS
Discussion Questions

1. Name the accounts appearing on a merchandising firm's chart of accounts but not usually listed on a service firm's chart of accounts.
2. Why is it necessary to make adjusting entries?
3. Explain the two-step process for adjusting Merchandise Inventory.
4. For a firm using the periodic inventory system, which inventory (beginning merchandise or ending merchandise) appears in the firm's unadjusted trial balance at the end of the fiscal period?
5. In a company's work sheet, the total of the Income Statement Debit column is $97,000, and the total of the Income Statement Credit column is $86,000. Does the firm have an $11,000 net income or net loss? Why?
6. What is the difference between merchandise inventory and supplies?
7. In which column(s) of the work sheet is Sales Returns and Allowances recorded?
8. When an athletic team received cash for season ticket sales in advance, an entry was made debiting Cash and crediting Unearned Admissions. At the end of the calendar year, a large portion of the home games had been played. What adjusting entry should be made?

Exercises

L.O. 1 **Exercise 14-1** The beginning inventory of a merchandising business was $54,000, and the ending inventory is $62,000. What entries are needed at the end of the fiscal period to adjust Merchandise Inventory?

L.O. 4 **Exercise 14-2** Indicate the column—Income Statement Debit, Income Statement Credit, Balance Sheet Debit, Balance Sheet Credit—in which the balances of the following accounts should appear:

Rent Expense
C. Moore, Drawing
Accumulated Depreciation, Building
Purchases Discount
Merchandise Inventory
Unearned Rent
Income Summary
Sales Discount

L.O. 2 **Exercise 14-3** *Information News* magazine credited Unearned Subscriptions for $72,000 received from subscribers to its new monthly magazine. All subscriptions were for twelve issues. The first issue was mailed September 1 of the present year. Make the adjusting entry on December 31 of this year.

L.O. 5 **Exercise 14-4** From the ledger account for Prepaid Advertising, prepare the complete entries (in the general journal) from which each of the items identified by journal reference was posted.

	ACCOUNT	Prepaid Advertising						ACCOUNT NO. 126		
							BALANCE			
	DATE	ITEM	POST. REF.	DEBIT	CREDIT	DEBIT		CREDIT		
1	19–									1
2	Jan. 1	Balance	√			9 6 0 00				2
3	Apr. 16		CP51	3 2 0 00		1 2 8 0 00				3
4	Sept. 22		CP72	2 1 0 00		1 4 9 0 00				4
5	Dec. 29		CR76		3 0 00	1 4 6 0 00				5
6	31	Adjusting	J121		6 0 0 00	8 6 0 00				6
7										7
8										8

L.O. 3 Exercise 14-5 Determine the amount of expired insurance for the fiscal year, January 1 through December 31, from the following account:

	ACCOUNT	Prepaid Insurance						ACCOUNT NO. 118		
							BALANCE			
	DATE	ITEM	POST. REF.	DEBIT	CREDIT	DEBIT		CREDIT		
1	19–									1
2	Jan. 1	Balance								2
3		(4 months)				4 2 0 00				3
4	May 1	(12 months)	CP59	1 6 8 0 00		2 1 0 0 00				4

L.O. 1 Exercise 14-6 In the Income Statement columns of the work sheet, we record the Income Summary account as $96,000 in the Debit column and $84,000 in the Credit column. Identify the beginning and ending merchandise inventory.

L.O. 5 Exercise 14-7 Prepare the complete entry (in the general journal) from which each of the items identified by number below was posted.

	ACCOUNT	Wages Expense						ACCOUNT NO. 514		
							BALANCE			
	DATE	ITEM	POST. REF.	DEBIT	CREDIT	DEBIT		CREDIT		
1	19–									1
2	Dec. 28	(1)	CP39	2 2 0 0 00		91 7 0 0 00				2
3	31	(2)	J42	6 0 0 00		92 3 0 0 00				3
4	31	(3)	J43		92 3 0 0 00	—		—		4

L.O. 3   **Exercise 14-8**   Because of a sudden illness, Murdock Company's accountant was unable to return to the job by the close of the company's fiscal year. The accountant did not have a chance to discuss what adjusting entries would be necessary at the end of the year, December 31. Fortunately, however, he did jot down a few notes shown below that provided some leads.

a. Two days' salaries will be unpaid at year-end; total weekly (five days) salary is $1,620.
b. Depreciation on equipment for the year is $4,440.
c. Charge off of expired insurance from prepaid account for the year is $782.
d. The latest bill has not been received from the car rental agency for salespeople's cars—should be about $1,560.

Record the adjusting entries.

Problem Set A

L.O. 4   **Problem 14-1A**   The trial balance of Hakala Company as of December 31, the end of its current fiscal year, is as follows:

Hakala Company
Trial Balance
December 31, 19–

ACCOUNT NAME	DEBIT	CREDIT
Cash	9 1 3 6 54	
Merchandise Inventory	62 8 5 4 82	
Store Supplies	1 4 6 6 84	
Prepaid Insurance	1 0 2 0 00	
Store Equipment	37 3 4 0 00	
Accumulated Depreciation, Store Equipment		24 8 3 6 00
Accounts Payable		14 2 8 6 96
Sales Tax Payable		2 4 6 98
R. P. Hakala, Capital		55 0 5 9 84
R. P. Hakala, Drawing	29 0 0 0 00	
Sales		177 9 6 6 34
Sales Returns and Allowances	1 4 9 3 84	
Purchases	78 8 0 0 84	
Purchases Returns and Allowances		1 8 5 7 82
Purchases Discount		1 5 0 3 64
Freight In	2 6 3 7 00	
Salary Expense	36 5 6 8 86	
Rent Expense	14 4 0 0 00	
Miscellaneous Expense	1 0 3 8 84	
	275 7 5 7 58	275 7 5 7 58

Here are the data for the adjustments:

a.–b. Merchandise Inventory at December 31, $65,749.80.
c. Store supplies inventory, $404.32.

    d. Insurance expired, $736.

    e. Salaries accrued, $586.80.

    f. Depreciation of store equipment, $3,920.

Instructions

Complete the work sheet.

L.O. 4,5   **Problem 14-2A**   The balances of the ledger accounts of Balzimer Home Center as of June 30, the end of its fiscal year, are as follows:

Cash	$ 14,775
Accounts Receivable	51,300
Merchandise Inventory	72,900
Supplies	1,470
Prepaid Insurance	1,080
Store Equipment	26,790
Accumulated Depreciation, Store Equipment	16,200
Office Equipment	9,600
Accumulated Depreciation, Office Equipment	4,815
Notes Payable	3,600
Accounts Payable	42,900
Salaries Payable	—
Unearned Rent	2,700
F. C. Balzimer, Capital	95,340
F. C. Balzimer, Drawing	24,000
Income Summary	—
Sales	466,500
Sales Returns and Allowances	3,210
Rent Income	—
Purchases	368,010
Purchases Returns and Allowances	7,170
Purchases Discount	2,280
Freight In	23,490
Salary Expense	44,250
Depreciation Expense, Store Equipment	—
Depreciation Expense, Office Equipment	—
Insurance Expense	—
Supplies Expense	—
Interest Expense	630

Here are the data for the adjustments:

    a.–b. Merchandise Inventory at June 30, $114,600.

    c. Salaries accrued at June 30, $1,440.

    d. Insurance expired during the year, $900.

    e. Supplies inventory at June 30, $285.

    f. Depreciation of store equipment, $3,750.

    g. Depreciation of office equipment, $1,950.

    h. Rent earned, $2,250.

Instructions

1. Complete the work sheet.
2. Journalize the adjusting entries.

L.O. 4,5   **Problem 14-3A** / Here are the accounts in the ledger of Palmer's Jewel Box, with the balances as of December 31, the end of its fiscal year:

Cash	$ 11,280
Accounts Receivable	1,554
Merchandise Inventory	116,100
Store Supplies	1,284
Prepaid Insurance	2,286
Land	15,000
Building	78,000
Accumulated Depreciation, Building	29,340
Store Equipment	77,490
Accumulated Depreciation, Store Equipment	17,160
Accounts Payable	14,070
Sales Tax Payable	2,784
Salaries Payable	—
Mortgage Payable	43,860
L. Palmer, Capital	151,830
L. Palmer, Drawing	46,500
Income Summary	—
Sales	379,254
Sales Returns and Allowances	3,888
Purchases	250,768
Purchases Returns and Allowances	3,261
Purchases Discount	4,410
Freight In	12,200
Salary Expense	23,400
Advertising Expense	1,926
Depreciation Expense, Building	—
Depreciation Expense, Store Equipment	—
Store Supplies Expense	—
Insurance Expense	—
Utilities Expense	1,158
Sales Tax Expense	162
Miscellaneous Expense	813
Interest Expense	2,160

Here are the data for the adjustments.

a.–b. Merchandise Inventory at December 31, $113,070.
c. Insurance expired during the year, $1,254.
d. Depreciation of building, $4,200.
e. Depreciation of store equipment, $8,580.
f. Salaries accrued at December 31, $420.
g. Store supplies inventory at December 31, $318.

Instructions

1. Complete the work sheet.
2. Journalize the adjusting entries.

L.O. 4,5 **Problem 14-4A** Here is a portion of the work sheet of Susan's Flowers for the year ending December 31:

	ACCOUNT NAME	INCOME STATEMENT DEBIT	INCOME STATEMENT CREDIT	BALANCE SHEET DEBIT	BALANCE SHEET CREDIT	
1	Cash			7 7 3 6 00		1
2	Merchandise Inventory			74 2 9 8 00		2
3	Supplies			2 9 8 00		3
4	Prepaid Insurance			2 5 0 00		4
5	Store Equipment			37 9 6 0 00		5
6	Accumulated Depreciation, Store Equipment				29 4 4 0 00	6
7	Accounts Payable				13 7 6 0 00	7
8	S. R. Hale, Capital				75 1 4 2 00	8
9	S. R. Hale, Drawing			30 8 0 0 00		9
10	Sales		171 8 1 6 00			10
11	Sales Returns and Allowances	1 4 3 4 00				11
12	Purchases	85 9 3 4 00				12
13	Purchases Returns and Allowances		9 6 4 00			13
14	Purchases Discount		1 6 3 6 00			14
15	Freight In	2 6 5 8 00				15
16	Salary Expense	37 8 5 2 00				16
17	Rent Expense	14 4 0 0 00				17
18	Income Summary	68 2 2 8 00	74 2 9 8 00			18
19	Depreciation Expense, Store Equipment	4 3 6 0 00				19
20	Insurance Expense	5 5 2 00				20
21	Supplies Expense	8 8 4 00				21
22	Salaries Payable				5 8 8 00	22
23		216 3 0 2 00	248 7 1 4 00	151 3 4 2 00	118 9 3 0 00	23

Instructions

1. Determine the entries that appeared in the Adjustments columns and present them in general journal form.
2. Determine the net income for the year and the amount of the owner's equity at the end of the year.

Problem Set B

L.O. 4 **Problem 14-1B** The trial balance of Swenson Company as of December 31, the end of its current fiscal year, is shown on the next page.

Swenson Company
Trial Balance
December 31, 19–

ACCOUNT NAME	DEBIT	CREDIT
Cash	9 5 6 3 92	
Merchandise Inventory	63 5 2 2 84	
Store Supplies	1 4 4 1 12	
Prepaid Insurance	9 6 0 00	
Store Equipment	37 4 8 0 00	
Accumulated Depreciation, Store Equipment		24 3 2 0 00
Accounts Payable		14 5 7 8 80
Sales Tax Payable		2 4 3 36
D. N. Swenson, Capital		55 6 3 0 00
D. N. Swenson, Drawing	29 4 4 0 00	
Sales		179 0 3 6 74
Sales Returns and Allowances	1 4 4 3 04	
Purchases	76 3 6 8 46	
Purchases Returns and Allowances		1 8 7 8 94
Purchases Discount		1 4 9 7 90
Freight In	4 8 7 5 00	
Salary Expense	36 6 5 8 80	
Rent Expense	14 4 0 0 00	
Miscellaneous Expense	1 0 3 2 56	
	277 1 8 5 74	277 1 8 5 74

Here are the data for the adjustments.

a.–b. Merchandise Inventory at December 31, $66,832.56.
c. Supplies inventory, $396.40.
d. Insurance expired, $360.
e. Salaries accrued, $563.
f. Depreciation of store equipment, $3,880.

Instructions

Complete the work sheet.

L.O. 4,5   **Problem 14-2B** The balances of the ledger accounts of Talbot Furniture as of December 31, the end of its fiscal year, are as follows:

Cash	$ 11,592
Accounts Receivable	42,962
Merchandise Inventory	121,838
Supplies	1,570

Prepaid Insurance	1,628
Store Equipment	$ 36,924
Accumulated Depreciation, Store Equipment	29,420
Office Equipment	9,436
Accumulated Depreciation, Office Equipment	1,720
Notes Payable	4,000
Accounts Payable	30,822
Wages Payable	—
Unearned Rent	3,200
P. Talbot, Capital	120,532
P. Talbot, Drawing	28,000
Income Summary	—
Sales	652,000
Sales Returns and Allowances	9,748
Rent Income	—
Purchases	518,374
Purchases Returns and Allowances	13,440
Purchases Discount	7,634
Freight In	24,724
Wages Expense	55,200
Depreciation Expense, Store Equipment	—
Depreciation Expense, Office Equipment	—
Supplies Expense	—
Insurance Expense	—
Interest Expense	772

Data for the adjustments are as follows.

a.–b. Merchandise Inventory at December 31, $101,676.
c. Wages accrued at December 31, $1,956.
d. Supplies inventory at December 31, $744.
e. Depreciation of store equipment, $5,868.
f. Depreciation of office equipment, $1,732.
g. Insurance expired during the year, $632.
h. Rent earned, $2,400.

Instructions

1. Complete the work sheet.
2. Journalize the adjusting entries.

L.O. 4,5   **Problem 14-3B**   The accounts in the ledger of Monroe Mountain Shop, with the balances as of December 31, the end of its fiscal year, are as follows:

Cash	$ 12,600
Accounts Receivable	2,040
Merchandise Inventory	120,600
Store Supplies	1,620
Prepaid Insurance	2,940

Land	$ 18,000
Building	90,000
Accumulated Depreciation, Building	36,600
Store Equipment	56,100
Accumulated Depreciation, Store Equipment	12,600
Notes Payable	10,800
Accounts Payable	19,260
Sales Tax Payable	5,940
Salaries Payable	—
B. Monroe, Capital	171,000
B. Monroe, Drawing	54,000
Income Summary	—
Sales	468,000
Sales Returns and Allowances	8,700
Purchases	284,820
Purchases Returns and Allowances	6,900
Purchases Discount	4,800
Freight In	18,180
Salary Expense	52,500
Advertising Expense	6,150
Depreciation Expense, Building	—
Depreciation Expense, Store Equipment	—
Store Supplies Expense	—
Insurance Expense	—
Utilities Expense	5,610
Sales Tax Expense	270
Miscellaneous Expense	990
Interest Expense	780

Data for the adjustments are as follows.

a.–b. Merchandise Inventory at December 31, $124,800.
c. Store supplies inventory at December 31, $540.
d. Depreciation of building, $4,200.
e. Depreciation of store equipment, $3,600.
f. Salaries accrued at December 31, $1,650.
g. Insurance expired during the year, $2,280.

Instructions

1. Complete the work sheet.
2. Journalize the adjusting entires.

L.O. 4,5   **Problem 14-4B**   A portion of the work sheet of Hurst Oxygen Company for the year ending December 31 is as follows:

	ACCOUNT NAME	INCOME STATEMENT DEBIT	INCOME STATEMENT CREDIT	BALANCE SHEET DEBIT	BALANCE SHEET CREDIT	
1	Cash			9 3 4 0 00		1
2	Merchandise Inventory			76 9 4 0 00		2
3	Supplies			2 5 6 00		3
4	Prepaid Insurance			2 4 0 00		4
5	Store Equipment			39 2 8 0 00		5
6	Accumulated Depreciation, Store Equipment				26 2 2 0 00	6
7	Accounts Payable				14 6 0 0 00	7
8	P. R. Hurst, Capital				68 9 4 0 00	8
9	P. R. Hurst, Drawing			27 6 0 0 00		9
10	Sales		173 4 2 0 00			10
11	Sales Returns and Allowances	1 5 2 0 00				11
12	Purchases	82 3 1 2 00				12
13	Purchases Returns and Allowances		9 4 0 00			13
14	Purchases Discount		1 6 0 0 00			14
15	Freight In	1 9 4 8 00				15
16	Salary Expense	37 5 6 0 00				16
17	Rent Expense	14 8 0 0 00				17
18	Income Summary	65 6 8 0 00	76 9 4 0 00			18
19	Depreciation Expense, Store Equipment	4 0 4 0 00				19
20	Insurance Expense	7 6 0 00				20
21	Supplies Expense	9 4 4 00				21
22	Salaries Payable				5 6 0 00	22
23		209 5 6 4 00	252 9 0 0 00	153 6 5 6 00	110 3 2 0 00	23

Instructions

1. Determine the entries that appeared in the Adjustments columns and present them in general journal form.
2. Determine the net income for the year and the amount of the owner's equity at the end of the year.

15 Financial Statements and Closing Entries for a Merchandising Firm

LEARNING OBJECTIVES

After you have completed this chapter, you will be able to do the following:

1. Prepare a classified income statement for a merchandising firm.
2. Prepare a classified balance sheet for any type of business.
3. Compute working capital and current ratio.
4. Journalize the closing entries for a merchandising firm.
5. Determine which adjusting entries should be reversed.

Chapters 5 and 7 discussed at length the income statements for a service and a professional enterprise, respectively. Then, in Chapters 11 through 14, we discussed the specialized accounts and journals for merchandising enterprises; in Chapter 14 we also explained the work sheet and the adjusting entries.

This chapter will show you how to formulate financial statements directly from work sheets. We will also explain the functions of closing entries and reversing entries as means of completing the accounting cycle. In Figure 15-1 we will reproduce part of the work sheet for City-Wide Electric Supply that we presented in Chapter 14. First we will look at the financial statements in their entirety, and then we will explain their various subdivisions.

THE INCOME STATEMENT

Objective 1

Prepare a classified income statement for a merchandising firm.

As you know, the work sheet is merely a tool used by accountants to prepare the financial statements. In Figure 15-1, we present the partial work sheet for City-Wide Electric Supply, which includes the Income Statement columns. Of course, **each of the amounts that appear in the Income Statement columns of the work sheet will also be used in the income statement.** Notice that the amounts for the beginning and ending

465

FIGURE 15-1

City-Wide Electric Supply
Work Sheet
For Year Ended December 31, 19–

	ACCOUNT NAME	TRIAL BALANCE		ADJUSTMENTS		INCOME STATEMENT	
		DEBIT	CREDIT	DEBIT	CREDIT	DEBIT	CREDIT
1	Cash	21 9 2 2 00					
2	Notes Receivable	4 0 0 0 00					
3	Accounts Receivable	29 3 6 0 00					
4	Merchandise Inventory	63 0 0 0 00		(b)58 8 0 0 00	(a)63 0 0 0 00		
5	Supplies	1 4 4 0 00			(d) 1 0 2 8 00		
6	Prepaid Insurance	9 6 0 00			(e) 3 2 0 00		
7	Land	12 0 0 0 00					
8	Building	90 0 0 0 00					
9	Accum. Depreciation,						
10	Building		32 0 0 0 00		(g) 4 0 0 0 00		
11	Equipment	33 6 0 0 00					
12	Accum. Depreciation,						
13	Equipment		16 4 0 0 00		(f) 4 8 0 0 00		
14	Notes Payable		3 0 0 0 00				
15	Accounts Payable		36 4 0 0 00				
16	Unearned Course Fees		9 0 0 00	(c) 6 0 0 00			
17	Mortgage Payable		8 0 0 0 00				
18	R. C. Schmidt, Capital		136 5 7 4 00				
19	R. C. Schmidt, Drawing	29 2 0 0 00					
20	Sales		186 1 8 0 00				186 1 8 0 00
21	Sales Returns and						
22	Allowances	8 4 0 00				8 4 0 00	
23	Sales Discount	1 8 8 0 00				1 8 8 0 00	
24	Interest Income		1 2 0 00				1 2 0 00
25	Purchases	83 1 4 0 00				83 1 4 0 00	
26	Purchases Returns and						
27	Allowances		8 3 2 00				8 3 2 00
28	Purchases Discount		1 2 4 8 00				1 2 4 8 00
29	Freight In	2 4 6 0 00				2 4 6 0 00	
30	Wages Expense	45 8 0 0 00		(h) 1 2 2 0 00		47 0 2 0 00	
31	Taxes Expense	1 9 6 0 00				1 9 6 0 00	
32	Interest Expense	9 2 00				9 2 00	
33		421 6 5 4 00	421 6 5 4 00				
34	Income Summary			(a)63 0 0 0 00	(b)58 8 0 0 00	63 0 0 0 00	58 8 0 0 00
35	Course Fees Income				(c) 6 0 0 00		6 0 0 00
36	Supplies Expense			(d) 1 0 2 8 00		1 0 2 8 00	
37	Insurance Expense			(e) 3 2 0 00		3 2 0 00	
38	Depreciation Expense,						
39	Equipment			(f) 4 8 0 0 00		4 8 0 0 00	
40	Depreciation Expense,						
41	Building			(g) 4 0 0 0 00		4 0 0 0 00	
42	Wages Payable				(h) 1 2 2 0 00		
43				133 7 6 8 00	133 7 6 8 00	210 5 4 0 00	247 7 8 0 00
44	Net Income					37 2 4 0 00	
45						247 7 8 0 00	247 7 8 0 00
46							

Merchandise Inventory now appear separately on the Income Summary line. Figure 15-2 shows the entire income statement. Pause for a while and look it over carefully before studying how we will break it down into its components.

The outline of the income statement follows a logical pattern that is much the same for any type of merchandising business. The ability to interpret the income statement and extract parts from it is very useful

FIGURE 15-2

City-Wide Electric Supply
Income Statement
For Year Ended December 31, 19–

Revenue from Sales:				
Sales			$ 186 1 8 0 00	
Less: Sales Returns and Allowances	$ 8 4 0 00			
Sales Discount	1 8 8 0 00		2 7 2 0 00	
Net Sales				$ 183 4 6 0 00
Cost of Merchandise Sold:				
Merchandise Inventory, January 1, 19–			$ 63 0 0 0 00	
Purchases	$83 1 4 0 00			
Less: Purchases Returns and				
Allowances	$ 832.00			
Purchases Discount	1,248.00	2 0 8 0 00		
		$ 81 0 6 0 00		
Add Freight In		2 4 6 0 00		
Net Purchases			83 5 2 0 00	
Merchandise Available for Sale			$ 146 5 2 0 00	
Less Merchandise Inventory, December 31, 19–			58 8 0 0 00	
Cost of Merchandise Sold				87 7 2 0 00
Gross Profit				$ 95 7 4 0 00
Operating Expenses:				
Wages Expense			$ 47 0 2 0 00	
Depreciation Expense, Equipment			4 8 0 0 00	
Supplies Expense			1 0 2 8 00	
Depreciation Expense, Building			4 0 0 0 00	
Taxes Expense			1 9 6 0 00	
Insurance Expense			3 2 0 00	
Total Operating Expenses				59 1 2 8 00
Income from Operations				$ 36 6 1 2 00
Other Income:				
Course Fees Income		$ 6 0 0 00		
Interest Income		1 2 0 00		
Total Other Income		$ 7 2 0 00		
Other Expenses:				
Interest Expense		9 2 00		6 2 8 00
Net Income				$ 37 2 4 0 00

when one is gathering information for decisions. To realize the full value of an income statement, however, you need to know the skeleton outline of an income statement backward and forward; you must be able to visualize it at a moment's notice. So, let's look at the statement piece by piece.

Net Sales	$183,460
− Cost of Merchandise Sold	87,720
Gross Profit	$ 95,740
− Operating Expenses	59,128
Income from Operations	$ 36,612

To put forth the concepts of **gross** and **net,** here is an example of a simple single-sale transaction.

Ann Brighton, a few years back, bought an antique table at a second-hand store for $90. She decided to sell the table for $160. She advertised it in the daily newspaper at a total cost of $6. How much did she make as clear profit?

Sale of Table	$160
Less Cost of Table	90
Gross Profit	$ 70
Less Advertising Expense	6
Net Income or Net Profit (gain on the sale)	$ 64

Gross profit is the profit on the sale of the table before any expense has been deducted, which in this case is $70. **Net income** or net profit is the final or clear profit after all expenses have been deducted. In a single-sale situation such as this, we refer to the final outcome as the net profit. But for a business that has many sales and expenses, most accountants prefer the term *net income*. Regardless of which word one uses, *net* refers to clear profit.

Revenue from Sales

All right, now let's look at the Revenue from Sales section in the income statement of City-Wide Electric Supply.

Revenue from Sales:			
Sales			$ 186 1 8 0 00	
Less: Sales Returns and Allowances	$ 8 4 0 00		
Sales Discount	1 8 8 0 00	2 7 2 0 00	
Net Sales			$ 183 4 6 0 00

When we introduced Sales Returns and Allowances and Sales Discount, we treated them as deductions from Sales. You can see that in the income statement they are deducted from Sales to give us **net sales.** Note that we recorded these items in the same order in which they appear in the ledger.

Cost of Merchandise Sold

The section of the income statement that requires the greatest amount of concentration is the Cost of Merchandise Sold. Let us therefore repeat it in its entirety:

Cost of Merchandise Sold:				
Merchandise Inventory, January 1, 19–			$ 63 0 0 0 00	
Purchases		$83 1 4 0 00		
Less: Purchases Returns and				
Allowances	$ 832.00			
Purchases Discount	1,248.00	2 0 8 0 00		
		$81 0 6 0 00		
Add Freight In		2 4 6 0 00		
Net Purchases			83 5 2 0 00	
Merchandise Available for Sale			$ 146 5 2 0 00	
Less Merchandise Inventory, December 31, 19–			58 8 0 0 00	
Cost of Merchandise Sold				$87 7 2 0 00

First let's look closely at the Purchases section.

Purchases		$83 1 4 0 00		
Less: Purchases Returns and				
Allowances	$ 832.00			
Purchases Discount	1,248.00	2 0 8 0 00		
		$81 0 6 0 00		
Add Freight In		2 4 6 0 00		
Net Purchases			$83 5 2 0 00	

Note the parallel to the Revenue from Sales section. To arrive at Net Purchases, we deduct the sum of Purchases Returns and Allowances and Purchases Discount from Purchases. We must also add Freight In, which does not appear in the Sales section. We list the items in account number order.

Now let's take in the full Cost of Merchandise Sold section. Does this seem like a reasonable summing up of the situation?

Amount we started with (beginning inventory)	$ 63,000
+ Net amount we purchased	83,520
Total amount that could have been sold (available)	$146,520
− Amount left over (ending inventory)	58,800
Cost of the merchandise that was actually sold	$ 87,720

An alternative way of presenting this information is:

Merchandise Inventory, January 1, 19–	$ 63,000
+ Net Purchases	83,520
Merchandise Available for Sale	$146,520
− Merchandise Inventory, December 31, 19–	58,800
Cost of Merchandise Sold	$ 87,720

Remember that **net purchases** means total Purchases less the sum of Purchases Returns and Allowances and Purchases Discount plus Freight In.

Operating Expenses

Operating expenses, as the name implies, are the regular expenses of doing business. As we stated in Chapter 5, we will list the accounts and their respective balances in the order that they appear in the ledger.

Many firms use subclassifications of operating expenses, such as the following:

1. **Selling expenses** Any expenses directly connected with the selling activity, such as

   - Sales Salaries Expense
   - Sales Commissions Expense
   - Advertising Expense
   - Store Supplies Expense
   - Delivery Expense
   - Depreciation Expense, Store Equipment

2. **General expenses** Any expenses related to the office or the administration, or any expense that cannot be directly connected with a selling activity:

   - Office Salaries Expense
   - Taxes Expense
   - Depreciation Expense, Office Equipment
   - Rent Expense
   - Insurance Expense
   - Office Supplies Expense

If the Cash Short and Over account has a debit balance (net shortage), the balance is added to and reported as Miscellaneous General Expense. Conversely, if the Cash Short and Over account has a credit balance (net overage), the balance is added to and reported as Miscellaneous Income, which is classified as Other Income.

In preparing the income statement, classifying expense accounts as selling expenses or general expenses is a matter of judgment. The only reason we're not using this breakdown here is that we're trying to keep the number of accounts to a minimum. In other words, getting bogged down in a large number of accounts could make it more difficult for you to understand the main concepts. We don't want you to lose sight of the forest on account of the trees.

Income from Operations

Now let's repeat the skeleton outline:

> Net Sales
> − Cost of Merchandise Sold
> Gross Profit
> − Operating Expenses
> Income from Operations

If the Operating Expenses are the regular, recurring expenses of doing business, then Income from Operations should be the regular or recurring income from normal business operations. When you are comparing the results of operations over a number of years, the income from operations is the most significant figure to use each year as a basis for comparison.

Other Income

The Other Income classification, as the name implies, records any revenue account other than revenue from Sales. What we are trying to do is to isolate Sales at the top of the income statement as the major revenue account, so that the gross profit figure represents the profit made on the sale of merchandise *only*. Additional accounts that may appear under the heading of Other Income are Rent Income (the firm is subletting part of its premises), Interest Income (the firm holds an interest-bearing note or contract), Gain on Disposal of Plant and Equipment (the firm makes a profit on the sale of plant and equipment), Miscellaneous Income (the firm has an overage recorded in the Cash Short and Over account).

Other Expenses

The classification of Other Expenses records various nonoperating expenses, such as Interest Expense or Loss on Disposal of Plant and Equipment.

FIGURE 15-3

City-Wide Electric Supply
Work Sheet
For Year Ended December 31, 19–

ACCOUNT NAME	TRIAL BALANCE DEBIT	TRIAL BALANCE CREDIT	ADJUSTMENTS DEBIT	ADJUSTMENTS CREDIT	BALANCE SHEET DEBIT	BALANCE SHEET CREDIT
Cash	21 9 2 2 00				21 9 2 2 00	
Notes Receivable	4 0 0 0 00				4 0 0 0 00	
Accounts Receivable	29 3 6 0 00				29 3 6 0 00	
Merchandise Inventory	63 0 0 0 00		(b)58 8 0 0 00	(a)63 0 0 0 00	58 8 0 0 00	
Supplies	1 4 4 0 00			(d)1 0 2 8 00	4 1 2 00	
Prepaid Insurance	9 6 0 00			(e)3 2 0 00	6 4 0 00	
Land	12 0 0 0 00				12 0 0 0 00	
Building	90 0 0 0 00				90 0 0 0 00	
Accum. Depreciation, Building		32 0 0 0 00		(g)4 0 0 0 00		36 0 0 0 00
Equipment	33 6 0 0 00				33 6 0 0 00	
Accum. Depreciation, Equipment		16 4 0 0 00		(f)4 8 0 0 00		21 2 0 0 00
Notes Payable		3 0 0 0 00				3 0 0 0 00
Accounts Payable		36 4 0 0 00				36 4 0 0 00
Unearned Course Fees		9 0 0 00	(c)6 0 0 00			3 0 0 00
Mortgage Payable		8 0 0 0 00				8 0 0 0 00
R. C. Schmidt, Capital		136 5 7 4 00				136 5 7 4 00
R. C. Schmidt, Drawing	29 2 0 0 00				29 2 0 0 00	
Sales		186 1 8 0 00				
Sales Returns and Allowances	8 4 0 00					
Sales Discount	1 8 8 0 00					
Interest Income		1 2 0 00				
Purchases	83 1 4 0 00					
Purchases Returns and Allowances		8 3 2 00				
Purchases Discount		1 2 4 8 00				
Freight In	2 4 6 0 00					
Wages Expense	45 8 0 0 00		(h)1 2 2 0 00			
Taxes Expense	1 9 6 0 00					
Interest Expense	9 2 00					
	421 6 5 4 00	421 6 5 4 00				
Income Summary			(a)63 0 0 0 00	(b)58 8 0 0 00		
Course Fees Income				(c)6 0 0 00		
Supplies Expense			(d)1 0 2 8 00			
Insurance Expense			(e)3 2 0 00			
Depreciation Expense, Equipment			(f)4 8 0 0 00			
Depreciation Expense, Building			(g)4 0 0 0 00			
Wages Payable				(h)1 2 2 0 00		1 2 2 0 00
			133 7 6 8 00	133 7 6 8 00	279 9 3 4 00	242 6 9 4 00
Net Income						37 2 4 0 00
					279 9 3 4 00	279 9 3 4 00

THE STATEMENT OF OWNER'S EQUITY AND THE BALANCE SHEET

Figure 15-3 is a partial work sheet for City-Wide Electric Supply (again, based on the one in Chapter 14). Here again we find that **every figure in the Balance Sheet columns of the work sheet is used in either the statement of owner's equity or the balance sheet.**

The preparation of the financial statements follows the same order that we presented before: first, the income statement; second, the statement of owner's equity; third, the balance sheet. The statement of owner's equity shows why the balance of the Capital account has changed from the beginning of the fiscal period to the end of it. In preparing the statement of owner's equity, one should always look into the ledger for the owner's capital account to find any changes, such as additional investments, made during the year.

In Figure 15-4 we observe the balance of R. C. Schmidt, Capital listed on the work sheet as $136,574. We also note a credit of $8,000 in the ledger account representing an additional investment. Therefore, the beginning balance of R. C. Schmidt, Capital was $128,574 ($136,574 − $8,000).

FIGURE 15-4

City-Wide Electric Supply
Statement of Owner's Equity
For Year Ended December 31, 19–

R. C. Schmidt, Capital, January 1, 19–		$ 128 5 7 4 00
Additional Investment, August 26, 19–		8 0 0 0 00
Total Investment		$ 136 5 7 4 00
Net Income for the Year	$37 2 4 0 00	
Less Withdrawals for the Year	29 2 0 0 00	
Increase in Capital		8 0 4 0 00
R. C. Schmidt, Capital, December 31, 19–		$ 144 6 1 4 00

BALANCE SHEET CLASSIFICATIONS

Objective 2

Prepare a classified balance sheet for any type of business.

Balance sheet classifications are generally uniform for all types of business enterprises. You are strongly urged to take the time to learn the following definitions of the classifications and the order of accounts within them. If you do, you will forever after have a standard routine for compiling a balance sheet, and this routine will save you a lot of grief and time. As you read, refer to Figure 15-5.

City-Wide Electric Supply
Balance Sheet
December 31, 19–

Assets			
Current Assets:			
Cash	$21 9 2 2 00		
Notes Receivable	4 0 0 0 00		
Accounts Receivable	29 3 6 0 00		
Merchandise Inventory	58 8 0 0 00		
Supplies	4 1 2 00		
Prepaid Insurance	6 4 0 00		
Total Current Assets		$ 115 1 3 4 00	
Plant and Equipment:			
Land	$12 0 0 0 00		
Building	$90 0 0 0 00		
Less Accumulated Depreciation	36 0 0 0 00	54 0 0 0 00	
Equipment	$33 6 0 0 00		
Less Accumulated Depreciation	21 2 0 0 00	12 4 0 0 00	
Total Plant and Equipment		78 4 0 0 00	
Total Assets		$ 193 5 3 4 00	
Liabilities			
Current Liabilities:			
Notes Payable	$ 3 0 0 0 00		
Mortgage Payable (current portion)	2 0 0 0 00		
Accounts Payable	36 4 0 0 00		
Wages Payable	1 2 2 0 00		
Unearned Course Fees	3 0 0 00		
Total Current Liabilities		$ 42 9 2 0 00	
Long-Term Liabilities:			
Mortgage Payable		6 0 0 0 00	
Total Liabilities		$ 48 9 2 0 00	
Owner's Equity			
R. C. Schmidt, Capital		144 6 1 4 00	
Total Liabilities and Owner's Equity		$ 193 5 3 4 00	

FIGURE 15-5

Current Assets

Current assets consist of cash and any other assets or resources that are expected to be realized in cash or to be sold or consumed during the normal operating cycle of the business or one year, if the normal operating cycle is less than twelve months.

Accountants list current assets in the order of their convertibility into cash, or, in other words, their **liquidity**. (If you've got an asset such as a car or a diamond and you sell it quickly and turn it into cash, you are said to be turning it into a *liquid* state.) If the first four accounts under Current Assets (see Figure 15-5) are present, always record them in the same order: (1) Cash, (2) Notes Receivable, (3) Accounts Receivable, and (4) Merchandise Inventory.

Notes receivable (current) are short-term promissory notes (promise-to-pay notes) held by the firm. (*Example:* Suppose you own a lumber yard and sell lumber to a builder who does not have enough cash to pay for the lumber but does have a ready buyer for the finished house. The builder therefore gives you a *promissory note,* stating that you will be paid within ninety days.) Notes Receivable is generally placed ahead of Accounts Receivable because promissory notes are considered to be more liquid than Accounts Receivable. (*Reason:* The holder of the note can raise more cash by borrowing from a bank, pledging the notes as security for the loan.) Supplies and Prepaid Insurance are considered prepaid items that will be used up or will expire within the following operating cycle or year. That's why they appear at the bottom of the Current Assets section. There is no particular reason to list Supplies before Prepaid Insurance. Prepaid Insurance could just as easily have preceded Supplies.

Plant and Equipment

Plant and equipment are relatively long-lived assets that are held for use in the production or sale of other assets or services; some accountants refer to them as *fixed assets.* The three types of accounts that usually appear in this category are land, buildings, and equipment (refer to Figure 15-5 again). Note that the Building and Equipment accounts are followed by their respective Accumulated Depreciation accounts. (Remember how we spoke of Accumulated Depreciation accounts as being deductions from assets?) Incidentally, the order of listing of plant and equipment is not uniform in practice. However, in keeping with modern practice, we will list these assets in order of their length of life, with the longest-lived asset being placed first.

Current Liabilities

Current liabilities are debts that will become due within the normal operating cycle of the business, usually within one year; they normally will be paid, when due, from current assets. List current liabilities in the order of their expected payment. Notes Payable (current) is placed ahead of Accounts Payable, just as Notes Receivable is placed ahead of Accounts Receivable. The Mortgage Payable (current portion), which may be placed ahead of Accounts Payable, is the payment one makes to reduce the principal of the mortgage in a given year. Wages Payable and any other accrued liabilities, such as Commissions Payable and the current portion of unearned revenue accounts, usually fall at the bottom of the list of current liabilities.

Long-Term Liabilities

Long-term liabilities are debts that are payable over a comparatively long period, usually more than one year. Ordinarily Mortgage Payable is the only account in this category for a sole-proprietorship (or one-owner) type of business. One single amount in a category can be recorded in the column on the extreme right.

Working Capital and Current Ratio

Both the management and the short-term creditors of a firm are vitally interested in two questions:

1. Does the firm have a sufficient amount of capital to operate?
2. Does the firm have the ability to pay its debts?

Objective 3

Compute working capital and current ratio.

Two measures used to answer these questions are a firm's working capital and its current ratio; the necessary data are taken from a classified balance sheet.

Working capital is determined by subtracting current liabilities from current assets; thus

Working capital = Current assets − Current liabilities

The normal operating cycle for most firms is one year. Because current assets equal cash—or items that can be converted into cash or used up within one year—and current liabilities equal the total amount that the company must pay out within one year, "working capital" is appropriately named. It is the amount of capital the company has available to use or work with. The working capital for City-Wide Electric Supply is as follows:

Working capital = $115,134 − $42,920 = $72,214

Current ratio is useful in revealing a firm's ability to pay its bills. The current ratio is determined by dividing current assets by current liabilities:

$$\text{Current ratio} = \frac{\text{Current assets (amount coming in within one year)}}{\text{Current liabilities (amount going out within one year)}}$$

The current ratio for City-Wide Electric Supply is calculated like this:

$$\text{Current ratio} = \frac{\$115,134}{\$42,920} = 2.68:1 \qquad 42,920 \overline{)115,134.00}^{\,2.68}$$

In the case of City-Wide Electric Supply, $2.68 is available to pay every dollar currently due on December 31.

When banks are considering granting loans to merchandising firms, a minimum current ratio of 2:1 is generally required.

Chart of Accounts

In Chapter 4, when we introduced the chart of accounts and the account number arrangement, we said that the first digit represents the classification of the accounts. A common organization is:

Assets	1--
Liabilities	2--
Owner's Equity	3--
Revenue	4--
Expenses	5--

Since you are now acquainted with classified income statements and balance sheets, we can now introduce the second digit. The second digit stands for the subclassification.

Assets	1--	Revenue	4--
Current Assets	11-	Revenue from Sales	41-
Plant and Equipment	12-	Other Income	42-
Liabilities	2--	Expenses	5--
Current Liabilities	21-	Cost of Merchandise Sold	51-
Long-Term Liabilities	22-	Selling Expenses	52-
		General Expenses	53-
Owner's Equity	3--	Other Expenses	54-
Capital	31-		

The third digit indicates the placement of the account within the subclassification. As an example, account number 411 represents Sales, which is the first account listed under revenue. Account number 312 represents Drawing, which is the second account listed under owner's equity.

CLOSING ENTRIES

In Chapter 6 we discussed closing entries for a service business; now let's look at closing entries for a merchandising business. The same methods apply to both types of business. You follow the same four steps to balance off the revenue, expense, and Drawing accounts.

At the end of a fiscal period, you close the revenue and expense accounts so that you can start the next fiscal period with a clean slate. You also close the Drawing account because it too applies to one fiscal period. As you recall from our discussion in Chapter 6, these accounts are called **temporary-equity** or **nominal accounts**.

ACCOUNT NAME	TRIAL BALANCE DEBIT	TRIAL BALANCE CREDIT	INCOME STATEMENT DEBIT	INCOME STATEMENT CREDIT
Cash	21 9 2 2 00			
Notes Receivable	4 0 0 0 00			
Accounts Receivable	29 3 6 0 00			
Merchandise Inventory	63 0 0 0 00			
Supplies	1 4 4 0 00			
Prepaid Insurance	9 6 0 00			
Land	12 0 0 0 00			
Building	90 0 0 0 00			
Accumulated Depreciation, Building		32 0 0 0 00		
Equipment	33 6 0 0 00			
Accumulated Depreciation, Equipment		16 4 0 0 00		
Notes Payable		3 0 0 0 00		
Accounts Payable		36 4 0 0 00		
Unearned Course Fees		9 0 0 00		
Mortgage Payable		8 0 0 0 00		
R. C. Schmidt, Capital		136 5 7 4 00		
R. C. Schmidt, Drawing	29 2 0 0 00			
Sales		186 1 8 0 00		186 1 8 0 00
Sales Returns and Allowances	8 4 0 00		8 4 0 00	
Sales Discount	1 8 8 0 00		1 8 8 0 00	
Interest Income		1 2 0 00		1 2 0 00
Purchases	83 1 4 0 00		83 1 4 0 00	
Purchases Returns and Allowances		8 3 2 00		8 3 2 00
Purchases Discount		1 2 4 8 00		1 2 4 8 00
Freight In	2 4 6 0 00		2 4 6 0 00	
Wages Expense	45 8 0 0 00		47 0 2 0 00	
Taxes Expense	1 9 6 0 00		1 9 6 0 00	
Interest Expense	9 2 00		9 2 00	
	421 6 5 4 00	421 6 5 4 00		
Income Summary			63 0 0 0 00	58 8 0 0 00
Course Fees Income				6 0 0 00
Supplies Expense			1 0 2 8 00	
Insurance Expense			3 2 0 00	
Depreciation Expense, Equipment			4 8 0 0 00	
Depreciation Expense, Building			4 0 0 0 00	
Wages Payable				
			210 5 4 0 00	247 7 8 0 00
Net Income			37 2 4 0 00	
			247 7 8 0 00	247 7 8 0 00

FIGURE 15-6

You can speed up the preparation of closing entries by balancing off each figure in the Income Statement columns of the work sheet. Figure 15-6 shows the isolated Income Statement columns. After you have looked them over, let's take up the four steps of the closing procedure.

Four Steps in the Closing Procedure

Objective 4

Journalize the closing entries for a merchandising firm.

To repeat, these four steps should be followed when closing:

1. Close the revenue accounts as well as the other accounts appearing in the income statement and having credit balances. **(Debit the figures that are credited in the Income Statement column of the work sheet, except the figure on the Income Summary line.)** This entry is illustrated as follows:

	DATE		DESCRIPTION	POST. REF.	DEBIT	CREDIT	
1	19–						1
2			*Closing Entries*				2
3	Dec.	31	*Sales*		186 1 8 0 00		3
4			*Purchases Returns and Allowances*		8 3 2 00		4
5			*Purchases Discount*		1 2 4 8 00		5
6			*Course Fees Income*		6 0 0 00		6
7			*Interest Income*		1 2 0 00		7
8			*Income Summary*			188 9 8 0 00	8

GENERAL JOURNAL   PAGE 97

2. Close the expense accounts as well as the other accounts appearing in the income statement that have debit balances. **(Credit the figures that are debited in the Income Statement column of the work sheet, except the figure on the Income Summary line.** This entry appears below.)

Note that you close Purchases Discount and Purchases Returns and Allowances in step 1 along with the revenue accounts. Note also that in step 2 you close Sales Discount and Sales Returns and Allowances along with the expense accounts.

	DATE		DESCRIPTION	POST. REF.	DEBIT	CREDIT	
9	Dec.	31	*Income Summary*		147 5 4 0 00		9
10			*Sales Returns and Allowances*			8 4 0 00	10
11			*Sales Discount*			1 8 8 0 00	11
12			*Purchases*			83 1 4 0 00	12
13			*Freight In*			2 4 6 0 00	13
14			*Wages Expense*			47 0 2 0 00	14
15			*Taxes Expense*			1 9 6 0 00	15
16			*Interest Expense*			9 2 00	16
17			*Supplies Expense*			1 0 2 8 00	17
18			*Insurance Expense*			3 2 0 00	18
19			*Depreciation Expense, Equipment*			4 8 0 0 00	19
20			*Depreciation Expense, Building*			4 0 0 0 00	20

3. Close the Income Summary account into R. C. Schmidt, Capital. **(Debit Income Summary by the amount of the net income; credit it by the amount of a net loss.)**

	DATE		DESCRIPTION	POST. REF.	DEBIT	CREDIT	
21	Dec.	31	Income Summary		37 2 4 0 00		21
22			R. C. Schmidt, Capital			37 2 4 0 00	22
23							23
24							24
25							25

Here is what the T accounts look like. Bear in mind that the Income Summary account already contains adjusting entries for merchandise inventory.

Income Summary			
Adjusting (Beginning Merchandise Inventory)	63,000	Adjusting (Ending Merchandise Inventory)	58,800
(Expenses)	147,540	(Revenue)	188,980
Clos. (Net Inc.)	37,240		

R. C. Schmidt, Capital			
−		+	
		Balance	136,574
		(Net Inc.)	37,240

4. Close the Drawing account into the Capital account.

	DATE		DESCRIPTION	POST. REF.	DEBIT	CREDIT	
24	Dec.	31	R. C. Schmidt, Capital		29 2 0 0 00		24
25			R. C. Schmidt, Drawing			29 2 0 0 00	25
26							26
27							27
28							28

Here is what the T accounts would look like:

R. C. Schmidt, Drawing			
+		−	
Balance	29,200	Closing	29,200

R. C. Schmidt, Capital			
−		+	
(Drawing)	29,200	Balance	136,574
		(Net Inc.)	37,240

REVERSING ENTRIES

Reversing entries are general journal entries that are the exact reverse of certain adjusting entries. A reversing entry enables the accountant to record routine transactions in the usual manner, *even though* an adjusting entry affecting one of the accounts involved in the transaction has intervened. We can see this concept best by looking at an example.

Suppose there is an adjusting entry for accrued wages owed to employees at the end of the fiscal year. (We talked about this in Chapter 5.) Assume that the employees of a certain firm are paid altogether $400 per day for a five-day week and that payday occurs every Friday throughout the year. When the employees get their checks at 5:00 P.M. on Friday, the checks include their wages for that day as well as the preceding four days. And say that one year the last day of the fiscal year happens to fall on Wednesday, December 31. A diagram of this situation would look like this:

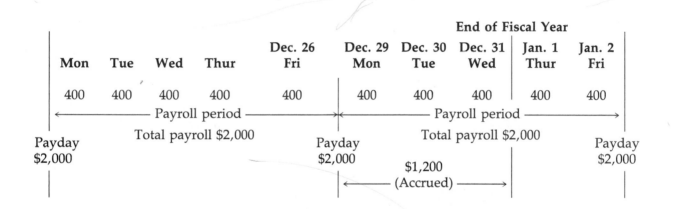

Each Friday during the year, the payroll has been debited to the Wages Expense account and credited to the Cash account. As a result, Wages Expense has a debit balance of $102,800. Here is the adjusting entry in T account form.

Wages Expense				Wages Payable		
+		−		−	+	
Bal.	102,800				Dec. 31 Adj.	1,200
Dec. 31 Adj.	1,200					

Next, along with all the other expense accounts, Wages Expense is closed by crediting it for $104,000. However, Wages Payable continues to have a credit balance of $1,200. In this case, there is only one way out. The $2,000 payroll on January 2 must be split up by debiting Wages Payable $1,200, debiting Wages Expense $800, and crediting Cash $2,000.

The employee who records the payroll not only has to record this particular payroll differently from all other weekly payrolls for the year but also has to refer back to the adjusting entry to determine what portion of the $2,000 is debited to Wages Payable and what portion is debited to Wages Expense. In many companies, however, the employee who records the payroll does not have access to the adjusting entries.

There is a solution to this problem. The need to refer to the earlier entry and divide the debit total between the two accounts is eliminated *if a reversing entry is made on the first day of the following fiscal period*. One makes an entry that is the exact reverse of the adjusting entry, as follows:

	DATE		DESCRIPTION	POST. REF.	DEBIT	CREDIT	
27							27
28			*Reversing Entries*				28
29	Jan.	1	*Wages Payable*		1 2 0 0 00		29
30			*Wages Expense*			1 2 0 0 00	30
31							31

GENERAL JOURNAL — PAGE 118

Let's now bring the T accounts up to date.

Wages Expense			
+		**−**	
Bal.	102,800	Dec. 31 Clos.	104,000
Dec. 31 Adj.	1,200		
		Jan. 1 Rev.	1,200

Wages Payable			
−		**+**	
Jan. 1 Rev.	1,200	Dec. 31 Adj.	1,200

The reversing entry has the effect of transferring the $1,200 liability from Wages Payable to the credit side of Wages Expense. Wages Expense will temporarily have a credit balance until the next payroll is recorded in the routine manner. In our example this occurs on January 2, for $2,000. Here are the T accounts.

Wages Expense			
+		**−**	
Bal.	102,800	Dec. 31 Clos.	104,000
Dec. 31 Adj.	1,200		
Jan. 2	2,000	Jan. 1 Rev.	1,200

Wages Payable			
−		**+**	
Jan. 1 Rev.	1,200	Dec. 31 Adj.	1,200

There is now a *net debit balance* of $800 in Wages Expense, which is the correct amount ($400 for January 1 and $400 for January 2). To see this, look at the following ledger accounts. December 26 was the last payday of one year, and January 2 is the first payday of the next year.

GENERAL LEDGER

ACCOUNT _Wages Expense_   ACCOUNT NO. _514_

	DATE	ITEM	POST. REF.	DEBIT	CREDIT	BALANCE DEBIT	BALANCE CREDIT	
11								11
12	Dec. 26		CP16	2 0 0 0 00		102 8 0 0 00		12
13	31	Adjusting	J116	1 2 0 0 00		104 0 0 0 00		13
14	31	Closing	J117		104 0 0 0	—	—	14
15	19–							15
16	Jan. 1	Reversing	J118		1 2 0 0 00		1 2 0 0 00	16
17	2		CP17	2 0 0 0 00		8 0 0 00		17
18								18
19								19
20								20

ACCOUNT _Wages Payable_   ACCOUNT NO. _213_

	DATE	ITEM	POST. REF.	DEBIT	CREDIT	BALANCE DEBIT	BALANCE CREDIT	
1	19–							1
2	Dec. 31	Adjusting	J116		1 2 0 0 00		1 2 0 0 00	2
3								3
4	19–							4
5	Jan. 1	Reversing	J118	1 2 0 0 00		—	—	5
6								6
7								7
8								8

The reversing entry for accrued salaries or wages applies to service companies as well as to merchandising ones. You can see that a reversing entry simply switches around an adjusting entry. The question is, Which adjusting entries should be reversed? Here's a handy rule of thumb that will help you decide.

Objective 5

Determine which adjusting entries should be reversed.

If an adjusting entry increases an asset account or liability account that does not have a previous balance, then reverse the adjusting entry.

With the exception of the first year of operations, Merchandise Inventory and contra accounts—such as Accumulated Depreciation—always have previous balances. Consequently, adjusting entries involving these accounts should never be reversed.

Let's apply this rule to adjusting entries for City-Wide Electric Supply.

(Do not reverse; Merchandise Inventory is an asset, but it has a previous balance.)

Income Summary		Merchandise Inventory			
		+		–	
Adj. 63,000		Bal. 63,000		Adj.	63,000

(Do not reverse; Merchandise Inventory is an asset, but it has a previous balance.)

Merchandise Inventory		Income Summary	
+	–		
Bal. 63,000	Adj. 63,000	Adj. 63,000	Adj. 58,800
Adj. 58,800			

(Do not reverse; Unearned Course Fees is a liability, but it was decreased. Also, it had a previous balance.)

Course Fees Income		Unearned Course Fees	
–	+	–	+
	Adj. 600	Adj. 600	Bal. 900

(Do not reverse; Supplies is an asset account, but it was decreased. Also, it had a previous balance.)

Supplies Expense		Supplies	
+	–	+	–
Adj. 1,028		Bal. 1,440	Adj. 1,028

(Do not reverse; Prepaid Insurance is an asset account, but it was decreased. Also, it had a previous balance.)

Insurance Expense		Prepaid Insurance	
+	–	+	–
Adj. 320		Bal. 960	Adj. 320

(Do not reverse; Accumulated Depreciation is a contra asset, and it always has a previous balance after the first year.)

Depreciation Expense, Equipment		Accumulated Depreciation, Equipment	
+	–	–	+
Adj. 4,800			Bal. 16,400
			Adj. 4,800

(Do not reverse; Accumulated Depreciation is a contra asset, and it always has a previous balance after the first year.)

Depreciation Expense, Building		Accumulated Depreciation, Building	
+	–	–	+
Adj. 4,000			Bal. 32,000
			Adj. 4,000

(Reverse; Wages Payable is a liability account. It was increased and it had no previous balance.

Wages Expense		Wages Payable	
+	–	–	+
Bal. 45,800			Adj. 1,220
Adj. 1,220			

Whenever we introduce additional adjusting entries, we will make it a point to state whether they should be reversed.

COMPUTERS AT WORK

Integrated Accounting Software

Many small companies can maintain their financial records using only a general ledger accounting software package. However, as it grows, a company must consider expanding its computerized accounting capabilities. As the number of its employees and credit customers expands, the company should explore the options available for software that handles accounts receivable, accounts payable, payroll, and inventory.

A smart company will purchase any computer software with an eye on the future and should therefore choose a general ledger package that can be expanded and integrated with other modules. As these new modules are added, an entry to one will be integrated into the system and posted to the general ledger.

For instance, an accounts receivable module will record a sale to a customer, or a return or payment, on the customer's account, and will automatically update the accounts receivable control account in the general ledger. It can also produce sales and cash receipts journals and aging reports.

Similarly, an accounts payable module will record a purchase on the vendor ledger account, update the general ledger, and even print the check. Besides keeping track of amounts owed to vendors, it can produce purchases and cash payments journals.

Using a payroll module, a company can enter the hours an employee has worked or the salary that employee has earned. The software then consults computer memory for the employee's files and tax tables and updates individual earnings records and the general ledger. It can also produce a payroll register, tax reports, and personnel reports. An inventory module can complete the picture, allowing management to track sales trends and reduce inventory costs. Combined, these integrated modules give a company instantaneous access to virtually all of its accounting information.

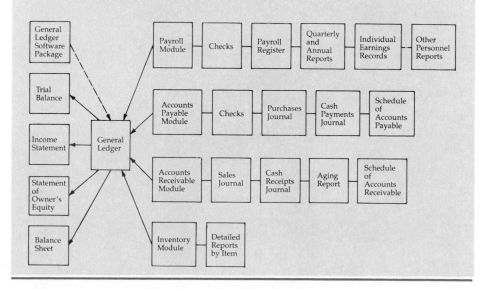

SUMMARY

L.O. 1   Here is the skeleton outline of the income statement:

Net Sales
- Gross Sales
- − Sales Returns and Allowances
- − Sales Discount
- = Net Sales

− Cost of Merchandise Sold
- Beginning Merchandise Inventory
- + Net Purchases
  - Gross Purchases
  - − Purchases Returns and Allowances
  - − Purchases Discount
  - + Freight In
  - = Net Purchases
- = Merchandise Available for Sale
- − Ending Merchandise Inventory
- = Cost of Merchandise Sold

= Gross Profit

− Operating Expenses
- Selling Expenses
- General Expenses

= Income from Operations

+ Other Income
- Interest Income
- Rent Income
- Gain on Disposal of Plant and Equipment

− Other Expenses
- Interest Expense
- Loss of Disposal of Plant and Equipment

= Net Income

L.O. 2   Here is the skeleton outline of the balance sheet:

Assets

Current Assets (Listed in the order of their convertibility into cash.)

1. Cash
2. Notes Receivable

    3. Accounts Receivable
    4. Merchandise Inventory
    5. Prepaid items (Supplies; Prepaid Insurance)

Plant and Equipment (Listed in the order of their length of life; the asset with the longest life is placed first.)

    1. Land
    2. Buildings
    3. Equipment

Liabilities

Current Liabilities (Listed in the order of their urgency of payment, the most pressing obligation is placed first.)

    1. Notes Payable
    2. Mortgage Payable or Contracts Payable (current portion)
    3. Accounts Payable
    4. Accrued liabilities (Wages Payable; Commissions Payable)
    5. Unearned revenue

Long-term Liabilities (Contracts Payable; Mortgage Payable)

Owner's Equity

Capital balance at end of the fiscal year

L.O. 3   **Working Capital and Current Ratio**   These two measures help analysts to determine whether a firm has enough capital to operate and whether it can pay its debts.

Working capital = Current assets − Current liabilities

$$\text{Current ratio} = \frac{\text{Current assets}}{\text{Current liabilities}}$$

L.O. 4   There are four steps in making closing entries for a merchandising business:

Step 1   Close all revenue accounts, Purchases Discount, and Purchases Returns and Allowances into Income Summary.

Step 2   Close all expense accounts, Sales Discount, and Sales Returns and Allowances into Income Summary.

Step 3   Close Income Summary into Capital.

Step 4   Close Drawing into Capital.

L.O. 5   **Reversing Entries**   When you make reversing entries, record them as of the first day of the period following the adjusting entries. Reverse adjusting entries that increase asset and liability accounts that do not have previous balances.

GLOSSARY

Cost of Merchandise Sold   Merchandise Inventory at beginning of fiscal period, plus net purchases, minus Merchandise Inventory at end of fiscal period. Terms often used to describe the same thing are *cost of goods sold* and *cost of sales:*

Merchandise Inventory (beginning)
Plus Net Purchases
_____

Merchandise Available for Sale
Less Merchandise Inventory (ending)
_____

Cost of Merchandise Sold

Current assets   Cash and any other assets or resources that are expected to be realized in cash or to be sold or consumed during the normal operating cycle of the business (or one year if the normal operating cycle is less than twelve months).

Current liabilities   Debts that will become due within the normal operating cycle of a business, usually within one year, and that are normally paid from current assets.

Current ratio   A firm's current assets divided by its current liabilities. Portrays a firm's short-term-debt-paying ability.

General expenses   Expenses incurred in the administration of a business, including office expenses and any expenses that are not wholly classified as Selling Expenses or Other Expenses.

Gross profit   Net Sales minus Cost of Merchandise Sold, or profit before deducting expenses:

Net Sales
Less Cost of Merchandise Sold
_____
Gross Profit

Liquidity   The ability of an asset to be quickly turned into cash, either by selling it or by putting it up as security for a loan.

Long-term liabilities   Debts payable over a comparatively long period, usually more than one year.

Net income   The final figure on an income statement after all expenses have been deducted from revenues. Also called *net profit.*

Net purchases   Total purchases less the sum of Purchases Returns and Allowances and Purchases Discount plus Freight In:

Purchases
Less Purchases Returns and Allowances
Less Purchases Discount
Plus Freight In
_____
Net Purchases

Net sales   Sales, minus Sales Returns and Allowances and minus Sales Discount:

Sales
Less Sales Returns and Allowances
Less Sales Discount
Net Sales

Notes receivable (current) Written promises to pay received from customers and due in a period of less than one year.

Plant and equipment Long-lived assets that are held for use in the production or sale of other assets or services; also called *fixed assets*.

Reversing entries The reverse of certain adjusting entries, recorded as of the first day of the following fiscal period.

Selling expenses Expenses directly connected with the selling activity, such as salaries of sales staff, advertising expenses, and delivery expenses.

Temporary-equity accounts Accounts whose balances apply to one fiscal period only, such as revenues, expenses, and the Drawing account. Temporary-equity accounts are also called *nominal accounts*.

Working capital A firm's current assets less its current liabilities. The amount of capital a firm has available to use or to work with during a normal operating cycle.

QUESTIONS, EXERCISES, AND PROBLEMS
Discussion Questions

1. Name one account in each of the following categories: current assets, plant and equipment, cost of merchandise sold, selling expenses, general expenses, other income, other expenses.
2. Describe how to calculate the cost of merchandise sold.
3. In Chapter 14 and again in this chapter, the Adjusted Trial Balance columns of a work sheet have been omitted. Does this affect the use of the work sheet? Explain.
4. What is the difference between current liabilities and long-term liabilities? Give an example of each type of liability.
5. In the closing procedure, what happens to Sales Discount?
6. How does one determine the current ratio for a firm? What does a current ratio of 2.5:1 mean?
7. What is the correct order for listing accounts in the Current Assets section of the balance sheet?
8. Give an example of a situation in which it is advantageous to make a reversing entry. Explain your answer.

Exercises

L.O. 1 **Exercise 15-1** Organize the following as they appear in the Cost of Merchandise Sold section of an income statement. Determine the cost of merchandise sold.

Purchases Returns and Allowances	$ 8,000
Ending Merchandise Inventory	99,000

Purchases Discount	$ 4,000
Purchases	247,600
Beginning Merchandise Inventory	94,000
Freight In	14,400

L.O. 4 **Exercise 15-2** From the following T accounts, record the closing entries dated June 30:

Sales		Salary Expense		Sales Returns and Allowances	
	202,000	34,000		4,000	

Rent Expense		Purchases		Miscellaneous Expense	
12,000		118,400		6,600	

Purchases Returns and Allowances		N. Faw, Drawing		Purchases Discount	
	2,800	27,000			3,800

N. Faw, Capital		Income Summary		Freight In	
	169,000	44,000	52,000	7,600	

L.O. 2 **Exercise 15-3** Identify each of the following items as (1) a current asset, (2) plant and equipment, (3) a current liability, (4) a long-term liability, or (5) owner's equity:

a. Mortgage Payable (current portion)
b. Cash
c. C. Prater, Capital
d. Building
e. Accounts Receivable
f. Notes Payable (current)
g. Store Equipment
h. Mortgage Payable (due June 30, 1997)
i. Wages Payable
j. Land

L.O. 1 **Exercise 15-4** Calculate the missing items in the following:

Sales	Sales Returns and Allowances	Net Sales	Beginning Inventory	Net Purchases	Merchandise Available	Ending Inventory	Cost of Merchandise Sold	Gross Profit
a. 124,000	3,000	———	74,000	85,000	159,000	68,000	91,000	———
b. 152,000	———	148,000	72,000	130,000	———	98,000	104,000	———
c. ———	6,000	314,000	42,000	———	248,000	46,000	———	112,000

L.O. 3 **Exercise 15-5** On December 31, the following selected accounts and amounts appeared in the balance sheet. Determine the amount of the working capital and the current ratio.

Accounts Payable	$12,000	Wages Payable	$ 6,000
Store Supplies	1,350	Merchandise Inventory	69,000
H. Kolff, Capital	78,000	Notes Payable	15,000
Store Equipment	24,000	Accumulated Depreciation,	
Prepaid Insurance	900	Store Equipment	18,000
Cash	4,500		

L.O. 2 **Exercise 15-6** Arrange the following accounts as they would appear in the Current Assets section of the balance sheet:

Supplies	$ 370	Notes Receivable (current)	$ 2,200
Accounts Receivable	16,000	Prepaid Insurance	420
Prepaid Advertising	2,000	Merchandise Inventory	52,000
Cash	7,400		

L.O. 1 **Exercise 15-7** The Income Statement columns of the December 31 (year-end) work sheet for the Montoys Company appear below. From the information given, prepare an income statement for the company.

ACCOUNT NAME	INCOME STATEMENT	
	DEBIT	CREDIT
Income Summary	13 0 0 0 00	11 0 0 0 00
Sales		142 0 0 0 00
Sales Returns and Allowances	5 5 0 0 00	
Sales Discount	2 1 0 0 00	
Purchases	57 7 5 0 00	
Purchases Returns and Allowances		9 0 0 00
Purchases Discount		1 0 0 0 00
Freight In	3 7 0 0 00	
Selling Expenses	28 5 0 0 00	
General Expenses	24 2 5 0 00	
	134 8 0 0 00	154 9 0 0 00
Net Income	20 1 0 0 00	
	154 9 0 0 00	154 9 0 0 00

L.O. 2 **Exercise 15-8** From the following information, present a statement of owner's equity:

G. R. Fulton, Capital

33,000	Bal.	120,000
		36,000

G. R. Fulton, Drawing

Bal.	33,000	Closing	33,000

Income Summary

Adj.	96,000	Adj.	102,000
	210,000		240,000
Closing	36,000		

Problem Set A

L.O. 1,4   **Problem 15-1A**   A partial work sheet for The Town Shop is presented below. The merchandise inventory at the beginning of the year was $53,200. C. A. Flagel, the owner, withdrew $26,500 during the year.

The Town Shop
Work Sheet
For Year Ended December 31, 19–

ACCOUNT NAME	INCOME STATEMENT DEBIT	INCOME STATEMENT CREDIT
Sales		328 0 0 0 00
Sales Returns and Allowances	4 4 8 0 00	
Sales Discount	3 7 0 7 32	
Interest Income		1 8 4 0 00
Purchases	199 4 9 0 00	
Purchases Returns and Allowances		2 9 8 0 00
Freight In	12 7 5 0 00	
Wages Expense	43 2 0 0 00	
Rent Expense	9 6 0 0 00	
Commissions Expense	10 3 2 0 00	
Interest Expense	9 6 4 22	
Income Summary	53 2 0 0 00	44 3 6 0 00
Supplies Expense	8 3 2 46	
Insurance Expense	1 0 4 0 00	
Depreciation Expense, Equipment	3 6 0 0 00	
Depreciation Expense, Building	4 8 0 0 00	
	347 9 8 4 00	377 1 8 0 00
Net Income	29 1 9 6 00	
	377 1 8 0 00	377 1 8 0 00

Instructions

1. Prepare an income statement.
2. Journalize the closing entries.

L.O. 2,3   **Problem 15-2A**   Here is the partial work sheet for Westhaven Stereo.

Westhaven Stereo
Work Sheet
For Year Ended December 31, 19–

ACCOUNT NAME	BALANCE SHEET	
	DEBIT	CREDIT
Cash	12 9 1 5 00	
Notes Receivable	6 3 0 0 00	
Accounts Receivable	33 2 7 0 00	
Merchandise Inventory	55 3 4 4 00	
Supplies	4 2 0 00	
Prepaid Taxes	6 3 0 00	
Prepaid Insurance	5 4 0 00	
Land	7 8 0 0 00	
Building	60 0 0 0 00	
Accumulated Depreciation, Building		18 9 0 0 00
Store Equipment	4 3 9 2 00	
Accumulated Depreciation, Store Equipment		1 6 7 4 00
Testing Equipment	7 2 3 0 00	
Accumulated Depreciation, Testing Equipment		5 4 2 4 00
Delivery Equipment	5 4 0 0 00	
Accumulated Depreciation, Delivery Equipment		4 4 7 0 00
Notes Payable		4 2 1 5 00
Accounts Payable		28 1 4 0 00
Mortgage Payable (current portion)		1 8 0 0 00
Mortgage Payable		55 2 0 0 00
C. R. Gonzales, Capital		67 3 1 4 00
C. R. Gonzales, Drawing	22 4 4 0 00	
Wages Payable		9 8 4 00
	216 6 8 1 00	188 1 2 1 00
Net Income		28 5 6 0 00
	216 6 8 1 00	216 6 8 1 00

Instructions

1. Prepare a statement of owner's equity (no additional investment).
2. Prepare a balance sheet.
3. Determine the amount of the working capital.
4. Determine the amount of the current ratio (carry to one decimal point).

L.O. 4,5   **Problem 15-3A**   The following partial work sheet covers the affairs of Breski and Company for the year ended June 30.

Breski and Company
Work Sheet
For Year Ended June 30, 19–

ACCOUNT NAME	INCOME STATEMENT DEBIT	INCOME STATEMENT CREDIT	BALANCE SHEET DEBIT	BALANCE SHEET CREDIT
Cash			28 196 61	
Accounts Receivable			92 006 00	
Merchandise Inventory			112 400 00	
Supplies			837 39	
Prepaid Insurance			1 220 00	
Delivery Equipment			12 400 00	
Accumulated Depreciation, Delivery Equipment				5 800 00
Store Equipment			33 400 00	
Accumulated Depreciation, Store Equipment				9 600 00
Accounts Payable				60 200 00
Salaries Payable				1 240 00
L. Breski, Capital				167 820 00
L. Breski, Drawing			28 000 00	
Income Summary	109 200 00	112 400 00		
Sales		520 000 00		
Purchases	380 000 00			
Purchases Returns and Allowances		7 600 00		
Purchases Discount		4 800 00		
Freight In	24 000 00			
Salary Expense	48 000 00			
Truck Expense	8 600 00			
Supplies Expense	2 200 48			
Insurance Expense	1 840 00			
Depreciation Expense, Delivery Equipment	2 400 00			
Depreciation Expense, Store Equipment	2 800 00			
Miscellaneous Expense	1 959 52			
	581 000 00	644 800 00	308 460 00	244 660 00
Net Income	63 800 00			63 800 00
	644 800 00	644 800 00	308 460 00	308 460 00

Instructions

1. Journalize the seven adjusting entries.
2. Journalize the closing entries.
3. Journalize the reversing entry.

L.O. 1,2,4,5   **Problem 15-4A**   The following accounts appear in the ledger of Clark
C•   and Company as of June 30, the end of this fiscal year:

Cash	$ 4,349.76
Accounts Receivable	14,910.00
Merchandise Inventory	51,480.00
Store Supplies	735.52
Prepaid Insurance	975.00
Store Equipment	29,640.00
Accumulated Depreciation, Store Equipment	7,880.00
Accounts Payable	11,085.00
Wages Payable	—
D. E. Clark, Capital	102,195.00
D. E. Clark, Drawing	28,260.00
Income Summary	—
Sales	202,630.00
Sales Returns and Allowances	2,640.00
Purchases	137,050.00
Purchases Returns and Allowances	4,395.00
Purchases Discount	2,565.28
Freight In	9,260.00
Wages Expense	33,100.00
Advertising Expense	8,150.00
Depreciation Expense, Store Equipment	—
Store Supplies Expense	—
Rent Expense	10,200.00
Insurance Expense	—

The data needed for the adjustments on June 30 are as follows:

a.–b. Merchandise inventory, June 30, $48,196
c. Store supplies inventory, June 30, $269.20
d. Insurance expired for the year, $640
e. Depreciation for the year, $6,290
f. Accrued wages on June 30, $472

Instructions

1. Prepare a work sheet for the fiscal year ended June 30.
2. Prepare an income statement.
3. Prepare a statement of owner's equity. No additional investments were
   made during the year.
4. Prepare a balance sheet.
5. Journalize the adjusting entries.
6. Journalize the closing entries.
7. Journalize the reversing entry.

Problem Set B

L.O. 1,4   **Problem 15-1B**   The partial work sheet for the Pope Music Store is presented below. The merchandise inventory at the beginning of the fiscal period was $49,584. F. L. Pope, the owner, withdrew $32,000 during the year.

Pope Music Store
Work Sheet
For Year Ended December 31, 19–

ACCOUNT NAME	INCOME STATEMENT DEBIT	INCOME STATEMENT CREDIT
Sales		326 5 9 2 80
Sales Returns and Allowances	5 2 2 9 20	
Sales Discount	1 9 0 8 00	
Interest Income		3 2 4 98
Purchases	195 1 9 1 00	
Purchases Returns and Allowances		1 6 5 6 00
Freight In	14 2 6 5 00	
Wages Expense	39 5 2 4 00	
Rent Expense	9 3 6 0 00	
Commissions Expense	9 4 4 0 00	
Interest Expense	6 5 6 32	
Income Summary	49 5 8 4 00	43 9 7 2 00
Supplies Expense	6 3 7 20	
Insurance Expense	9 3 6 00	
Depreciation Expense, Equipment	3 3 4 0 00	
Depreciation Expense, Building	4 8 0 0 00	
	334 8 7 0 72	372 5 4 5 78
Net Income	37 6 7 5 06	
	372 5 4 5 78	372 5 4 5 78

Instructions

1. Prepare an income statement.
2. Journalize the closing entries.

L.O. 2,3   **Problem 15-2B**   Here is the partial work sheet for Olsen Mountain Shop.

Olsen Mountain Shop
Work Sheet
For Year Ended December 31, 19–

ACCOUNT NAME	BALANCE SHEET	
	DEBIT	CREDIT
Cash	9 7 2 3 00	
Notes Receivable	3 6 0 0 00	
Accounts Receivable	42 8 7 9 60	
Merchandise Inventory	56 6 9 7 00	
Supplies	4 7 4 00	
Prepaid Taxes	6 1 3 50	
Prepaid Insurance	6 3 0 00	
Land	8 4 0 0 00	
Building	63 0 0 0 00	
Accumulated Depreciation, Building		21 6 0 0 00
Office Equipment	5 4 2 4 00	
Accumulated Depreciation, Office Equipment		4 1 7 0 00
Store Equipment	6 5 7 0 00	
Accumulated Depreciation, Store Equipment		4 9 9 5 00
Delivery Equipment	5 5 6 5 00	
Accumulated Depreciation, Delivery Equipment		4 3 0 5 00
Notes Payable		5 4 3 0 00
Accounts Payable		29 5 9 1 70
Mortgage Payable (current portion)		2 7 0 0 00
Mortgage Payable		55 7 1 3 00
N. Olsen, Capital		65 0 5 8 90
N. Olsen, Drawing	25 1 9 4 00	
Wages Payable		1 2 7 8 00
	228 7 7 0 10	194 8 4 1 60
Net Income		33 9 2 8 50
	228 7 7 0 10	228 7 7 0 10

Instructions

1. Prepare a statement of owner's equity (no additional investment).
2. Prepare a balance sheet.
3. Determine the amount of the working capital.
4. Determine the amount of the current ratio (carry to one decimal point).

L.O. 4,5 **Problem 15-3B** The following partial work sheet covers the affairs of Komo and Company for the year ending June 30:

Komo and Company
Work Sheet
For Year Ended June 30, 19–

ACCOUNT NAME	INCOME STATEMENT DEBIT	INCOME STATEMENT CREDIT	BALANCE SHEET DEBIT	BALANCE SHEET CREDIT
Cash			32 3 8 4 34	
Accounts Receivable			104 6 3 4 54	
Merchandise Inventory			119 4 5 6 00	
Supplies			1 0 3 2 00	
Prepaid Insurance			1 3 2 0 00	
Delivery Equipment			12 9 2 0 00	
Accumulated Depreciation, Delivery Equipment				6 4 8 0 00
Store Equipment			36 5 0 0 00	
Accumulated Depreciation, Store Equipment				10 3 6 0 00
Accounts Payable				67 4 3 7 34
Salaries Payable				8 5 2 00
C. P. Komo, Capital				195 9 2 1 14
C. P. Komo, Drawing			37 4 4 0 00	
Income Summary	115 2 2 6 00	119 4 5 6 00		
Sales		536 3 5 2 40		
Purchases	393 9 3 0 00			
Purchases Returns and Allowances		7 8 2 8 00		
Purchases Discount		5 7 4 6 00		
Freight In	23 3 5 0 00			
Salary Expense	51 4 0 0 00			
Truck Expense	9 3 4 2 00			
Supplies Expense	2 5 6 4 00			
Insurance Expense	1 9 2 0 00			
Depreciation Expense, Delivery Equipment	2 7 0 0 00			
Depreciation Expense, Store Equipment	2 8 9 6 00			
Miscellaneous Expense	1 4 1 8 00			
	604 7 4 6 00	669 3 8 2 40	345 6 8 6 88	281 0 5 0 48
Net Income	64 6 3 6 40			64 6 3 6 40
	669 3 8 2 40	669 3 8 2 40	345 6 8 6 88	345 6 8 6 88

Instructions

1. Journalize the adjusting entries.
2. Journalize the closing entries.
3. Journalize the reversing entry.

L.O. 1,2,4,5   **Problem 15-4B**   The following accounts appear in the ledger of The
Shirer Company on January 31, the end of this fiscal year:

Cash	$ 5,400
Accounts Receivable	14,100
Merchandise Inventory	55,500
Store Supplies	690
Prepaid Insurance	1,080
Store Equipment	27,900
Accumulated Depreciation, Store Equipment	2,700
Accounts Payable	13,800
Wages Payable	—
M. R. Shirer, Capital	113,620
M. R. Shirer, Drawing	36,000
Income Summary	—
Sales	224,000
Sales Returns and Allowances	3,000
Purchases	170,000
Purchases Returns and Allowances	3,450
Purchases Discount	2,400
Freight In	7,000
Wages Expense	27,000
Advertising Expense	3,900
Depreciation Expense, Store Equipment	—
Store Supplies Expense	—
Rent Expense	8,400
Insurance Expense	—

The data needed for adjustments on January 31 are as follows:

a.–b. Merchandise inventory, January 31, $53,400
c. Store supplies inventory, January 31, $390
d. Insurance expired for the year, $615
e. Depreciation for the year, $6,395
f. Accrued wages on January 31, $1,270

Instructions

1. Prepare a work sheet for the fiscal year ended January 31.
2. Prepare an income statement.
3. Prepare a statement of owner's equity. No additional investments were made.
4. Prepare a balance sheet.
5. Journalize the adjusting entries.
6. Journalize the closing entries.
7. Journalize the reversing entry.

REVIEW OF T ACCOUNT PLACEMENT AND REPRESENTATIVE TRANSACTIONS: CHAPTERS 11 THROUGH 15

Review of T Account Placement

The following sums up the placement of T accounts covered in Chapters 11 through 15 in relation to the fundamental accounting equation. Color indicates those accounts that are treated as deductions from the related accounts above them.

Assets		=	Liabilities		+	Owner's Equity		+	Revenue		−	Expenses	
+	−		−	+		−	+		−	+		+	−
Debit	Credit		Debit	Credit		Debit	Credit		Debit	Credit		Debit	Credit

Merchandise Inventory	
+	−

Sales	
−	+

Sales Returns and Allowances	
+	−

Sales Discount	
+	−

Purchases	
+	−

Purchases Returns and Allowances	
−	+

Purchases Discount	
−	+

Freight In	
+	−

Credit Card Expense	
+	−

Review of Representative Transactions

The following table summarizes the recording of transactions covered in Chapters 11 through 15, along with a classification of the accounts involved.

Classifications

Balance Sheet		Income Statement	
CA	Current Assets	S	Revenue from Sales
P & E	Plant and Equipment	CMS	Cost of Merchandise Sold
CL	Current Liabilities	SE	Selling Expenses
LTL	Long-term Liabilities	GE	General Expenses
		OI	Other Income
		OE	Other Expenses

Transaction	Accounts Involved	Class.	Increase or Decrease	Therefore Debit or Credit	Financial Statement
Sold merchandise on account	Accounts Receivable Sales	CA S	I I	Debit Credit	Balance Sheet Income State.
Sold merchandise on account involving sales tax	Accounts Receivable Sales Sales Tax Payable	CA S CL	I I I	Debit Credit Credit	Balance Sheet Income State. Balance Sheet
Issued credit memo to customer for mer-chandise returned	Sales Returns and Allowances 　Accounts Receivable	S CA	I D	Debit Credit	Income State. Balance Sheet
Summarizing en-try for the total of sales invoices for sales on account for the month	Accounts Receivable Sales	CA S	I I	Debit Credit	Balance Sheet Income State.
Bought merchan-dise on account	Purchases 　Accounts Payable	CMS CL	I I	Debit Credit	Income State. Balance Sheet
Bought merchan-dise on account with freight pre-paid as a conve-nience to the buyer	Purchases Freight In 　Accounts Payable	CMS CMS CL	I I I	Debit Debit Credit	Income State. Income State. Balance Sheet
Received credit memo from sup-plier for merchan-dise returned	Accounts Payable Purchases Returns and Allowances	CL CMS	D I	Debit Credit	Balance Sheet Income State.
Summarizing entry for the total of purchases of all types of goods on account	Purchases Store Supplies Office Supplies Store Equipment 　Accounts Payable	CMS CA CA P & E CL	I I I I I	Debit Debit Debit Debit Credit	Income State. Balance Sheet Balance Sheet Balance Sheet Balance Sheet
Paid for trans-portation charges on incoming merchandise	Freight In 　Cash	CMS CA	I D	Debit Credit	Income State. Balance Sheet
Sold merchandise, involving sales tax, for cash	Cash Sales Sales Tax Payable	CA S CL	I I I	Debit Credit Credit	Balance Sheet Income State. Balance Sheet

Transaction	Accounts Involved	Class.	Increase or Decrease	Therefore Debit or Credit	Financial Statement
Sold merchandise involving a sales tax and the customer used a bank charge card	Cash	CA	I	Debit	Balance Sheet
	Credit Card Expense	SE	I	Debit	Income State.
	Sales	S	I	Credit	Income State.
	Sales Tax Payable	CL	I	Credit	Balance Sheet
Charge customer paid bill within the discount period	Cash	CA	I	Debit	Balance Sheet
	Sales Discount	S	I	Debit	Income State.
	Accounts Receivable	CA	D	Credit	Balance Sheet
Paid invoice for the purchase of merchandise within the discount period	Accounts Payable	CL	D	Debit	Balance Sheet
	Cash	CA	D	Credit	Balance Sheet
	Purchases Discount	CMS	I	Credit	Income State.
First adjusting entry for merchandise inventory	Income Summary	—	—	Debit	—
	Merchandise Inventory	CA & CMS	D	Credit	Balance Sheet & Income State.
Second adjusting entry for merchandise inventory	Merchandise Inventory	CA & CMS	I	Debit	Balance Sheet & Income State.
	Income Summary	—	—	Credit	
Adjusting entry for rent earned (Rent Income)	Unearned Rent	CL	D	Debit	Balance Sheet
	Rent Income	OI	I	Credit	Income State.
Reversing entry for adjustment for accrued wages	Wages Payable	CL	D	Debit	Balance Sheet
	Wages Expense	SE or GE	D	Credit	Income State.

APPENDIX C
Financial Statement Analysis

An important function of accounting is to provide tools for interpreting the financial statements or the results of operations. This appendix presents a number of percentages and ratios that are frequently used for analyzing financial statements.

A & L Cycle and Toy will serve as our example (see the following comparative income statement).

A & L Cycle and Toy
Comparative Income Statement
For Years Ended January 31, 19x1 and January 31, 19x0

	19x1 AMOUNT	19x1 PERCENT	19x0 AMOUNT	19x0 PERCENT
Revenue from Sales:				
Sales	$ 453 600 00	106	$ 420 000 00	105
Less Sales Returns and Allowances	25 600 00	6	20 000 00	5
Net Sales	$ 428 000 00	100	$ 400 000 00	100
Cost of Merchandise Sold:				
Merchandise Inventory, February 1	$ 116 000 00	27	$ 64 000 00	16
Purchases (net)	320 000 00	75	300 000 00	75
Merchandise Available for Sale	$ 436 000 00	102	$ 364 000 00	91
Less Merchandise Inventory, January 31	158 000 00	37	116 000 00	29
Cost of Merchandise Sold	$ 278 000 00	65	$ 248 000 00	62
Gross Profit	$ 150 000 00	35	$ 152 000 00	38
Operating Expenses:				
Sales Salary Expense	$ 63 600 00	15	$ 58 000 00	15
Rent Expense	24 000 00	6	24 000 00	6
Advertising Expense	21 400 00	5	16 000 00	4
Depreciation Expense, Equipment	20 000 00	5	18 000 00	5
Insurance Expense	2 000 00	—	2 000 00	—
Store Supplies Expense	1 000 00	—	1 000 00	—
Miscellaneous Expense	1 000 00	—	1 000 00	—
Total Operating Expenses	$ 133 000 00	31	$ 120 000 00	30
Net Income	$ 17 000 00	4	$ 32 000 00	8

For each year, net sales is the base (100 percent). Every other item on the income statement can be expressed as a percentage of net sales for the particular year involved. For example, let's look at the following percentages:

$$\text{Gross profit \% (19x1)} = \frac{\text{Gross profit for 19x1}}{\text{Net sales for 19x1}} = \frac{\$150,000}{\$428,000} = .35 = 35\%$$

$$\text{Gross profit \% (19x0)} = \frac{\text{Gross profit for 19x0}}{\text{Net sales for 19x0}} = \frac{\$152,000}{\$400,000} = .38 = 38\%$$

$$\text{Sales salary expense (19x1)} = \frac{\text{Sales salary expense for 19x1}}{\text{Net sales for 19x1}}$$

$$= \frac{\$63,600}{\$428,000} = .1486 = 15\%$$

$$\text{Sales salary expense (19x0)} = \frac{\text{Sales salary expense for 19x0}}{\text{Net sales for 19x0}}$$

$$= \frac{\$58,000}{\$400,000} = .145 = 15\%$$

Here's how one might interpret a few of the percentages.

19x1

- For every $100 in net sales, gross profit amounted to $35.
- For every $100 in net sales, sales salary expense amounted to $15.
- For every $100 in net sales, net income amounted to $4.

19x0

- For every $100 in net sales, gross profit amounted to $38.
- For every $100 in net sales, sales salary expense amounted to $15.
- For every $100 in net sales, net income amounted to $8.

MERCHANDISE INVENTORY TURNOVER

Merchandise inventory turnover is the number of times a firm's average inventory is sold during a given year.

$$\text{Merchandise inventory turnover} = \frac{\text{Cost of merchandise sold}}{\text{Average merchandise inventory}}$$

Average merchandise inventory
$$= \frac{\text{Beginning merchandise inventory} + \text{Ending merchandise inventory}}{2}$$

19x1

$$\text{Average merchandise inventory} = \frac{\$116,000 + \$158,000}{2}$$

$$= \frac{\$274,000}{2} = \underline{\$137,000}$$

$$\text{Merchandise inventory turnover} = \frac{\$278,000}{\$137,000} = \underline{\underline{2.03}} \text{ times per year}$$

19x0

$$\text{Average merchandise inventory} = \frac{\$64,000 + \$116,000}{2} = \frac{\$180,000}{2} = \underline{\$90,000}$$

$$\text{Merchandise inventory turnover} = \frac{\$248,000}{\$90,000} = \underline{\underline{2.76}} \text{ times per year}$$

With each turnover of merchandise, the company makes a gross profit, so the higher the turnover the better.

ACCOUNTS RECEIVABLE TURNOVER

Accounts receivable turnover is the number of times charge accounts are turned over (paid off) during a given year. A turnover implies a sale on account followed by payment of the debt.

$$\text{Accounts receivable turnover} = \frac{\text{Net sales on account}}{\text{Average accounts receivable}}$$

Average accounts receivable

$$= \frac{\text{Beginning accounts receivable} + \text{Ending accounts receivable}}{2}$$

Going back to A & L Cycle and Toy, let's assume the following information for 19x1 and 19x0:

	19x1	19x0
Net sales on account (from the sales journal)	$330,000	$302,000
Beginning accounts receivable (from Accounts Receivable account)	$39,680	$37,500
Ending accounts receivable (from Accounts Receivable account)	$45,840	$39,680

19x1

$$\text{Average accounts receivable} = \frac{\$39,680 + \$45,840}{2} = \frac{\$85,520}{2} = \underline{\underline{\$42,760}}$$

$$\text{Accounts receivable turnover} = \frac{\$330,000}{\$42,760} = \underline{\underline{7.72}} \text{ times per year}$$

19x0

$$\text{Average accounts receivable} = \frac{\$37,500 + \$39,680}{2} = \frac{\$77,180}{2} = \underline{\underline{\$38,590}}$$

$$\text{Accounts receivable turnover} = \frac{\$302,000}{\$38,590} = \underline{\underline{7.83}} \text{ times per year}$$

A lower turnover rate indicates that a firm is experiencing greater difficulty in collecting charge accounts. In addition, more investment capital is tied up in accounts receivable.

RETURN ON INVESTMENT (YIELD)

Return on investment represents the earning power of the owner's investment in the business.

$$\text{Return on investment} = \frac{\text{Net income for the year}}{\text{Average capital}}$$

$$\text{Average capital} = \frac{\text{Beginning capital} + \text{Ending capital}}{2}$$

Getting back to A & L Cycle and Toy, let's assume the following information for 19x1 and 19x0:

	19x1	19x0
Beginning balance of owner's Capital account	$176,920	$181,440
Ending balance of owner's Capital account	$184,780	$176,920

19x1

$$\text{Average capital} = \frac{\$176,920 + \$184,780}{2} = \frac{\$361,700}{2} = \underline{\underline{\$180,850}}$$

$$\text{Return on investment} = \frac{\$17,000}{\$180,850} = .094 = \underline{\underline{9.4\%}}$$

19x0

$$\text{Average capital} = \frac{\$181,440 + \$176,920}{2} = \frac{\$358,360}{2} = \underline{\underline{\$179,180}}$$

$$\text{Return on investment} = \frac{\$32,000}{\$179,180} = .179 = \underline{\underline{17.9\%}}$$

As a result, we can state the following:

- In 19x1, for an average investment of $100, the business earned $9.40.
- In 19x0, for an average investment of $100, the business earned $17.90.

Problems

Problem C-1   Taber Company's abbreviated comparative income statement for years 19x1 and 19x0 is at the top of the next page.

Instructions

1. For the years 19x1 and 19x0, determine gross profit as a percentage of net sales.
2. For the years 19x1 and 19x0, determine net income as a percentage of net sales.

Taber Company
Comparative Income Statement
For Years Ended December 31, 19x1 and December 31, 19x0

	19x1	19x0
Net Sales	$ 348 0 0 0 00	$ 330 0 0 0 00
Cost of Merchandise Sold	205 3 2 0 00	198 0 0 0 00
Gross Profit	$ 142 6 8 0 00	$ 132 0 0 0 00
Total Operating Expenses	104 4 0 0 00	104 4 0 0 00
Net Income	$ 38 2 8 0 00	$ 27 6 0 0 00

Problem C-2 Taber Company's merchandise inventory figures are:

	19x1	19x0
Beginning merchandise inventory (January 1)	$63,160	$75,788
Ending merchandise inventory (December 31)	$73,720	$63,160

Determine the merchandise inventory turnover for the years 19x1 and 19x0.

Problem C-3 N. E. Taber, Capital account balances are as follows:

January 1, 19x0	$268,336
January 1, 19x1	$352,840
December 31, 19x1	$376,304

Determine the return on investment for the years 19x1 and 19x0.

Index

Note: Boldface indicates a key term and the page where it is defined